Accounting III

Carl S. Warren | James M. Reeve | Jonathan Duchac

CENGAGE
Learning™

Australia • Brazil • Japan • Korea • Mexico • Singapore • Spain • United Kingdom • United States

CENGAGE
Learning™

Accounting III

Carl S. Warren I James M. Reeve
Jonathan Duchac

Executive Editors:
 Maureen Staudt
 Michael Stranz

Senior Project Development Manager:
 Linda DeStefano

Marketing Specialist:
 Sara Mercurio
 Lindsay Shapiro

Senior Production / Manufacturing Manager:
 Donna M. Brown

PreMedia Supervisor:
 Joel Brennecke

Rights & Permissions Specialist:
 Kalina Hintz
 Todd Osborne

Cover Image:
 Getty Images*

* Unless otherwise noted, all cover images used by Custom Solutions, a part of Cengage Learning, have been supplied courtesy of Getty Images with the exception of the Earthview cover image, which has been supplied by the National Aeronautics and Space Administration (NASA).

© 2010 Cengage Learning
Source: ACCOUNTING, WARREN/REEVE/DUCHAC,
ISBN#0324401841, 2006, 2009 South Western Cengage Learning

ALL RIGHTS RESERVED. No part of this work covered by the copyright herein may be reproduced, transmitted, stored or used in any form or by any means graphic, electronic, or mechanical, including but not limited to photocopying, recording, scanning, digitizing, taping, Web distribution, information networks, or information storage and retrieval systems, except as permitted under Section 107 or 108 of the 1976 United States Copyright Act, without the prior written permission of the publisher.

For product information and technology assistance, contact us at
Cengage Learning Customer & Sales Support, 1-800-354-9706

For permission to use material from this text or product,
submit all requests online at **cengage.com/permissions**
Further permissions questions can be emailed to
permissionrequest@cengage.com

ISBN-13: 978-1-111-06562-1

ISBN-10: 1-111-06562-4

Cengage Learning
5191 Natorp Boulevard
Mason, Ohio 45040
USA

Cengage Learning is a leading provider of customized learning solutions with office locations around the globe, including Singapore, the United Kingdom, Australia, Mexico, Brazil, and Japan. Locate your local office at:
international.cengage.com/region

Cengage Learning products are represented in Canada by Nelson Education, Ltd.

For your lifelong learning solutions, visit **www.cengage.com/custom**

Visit our corporate website at **www.cengage.com**

Printed in the United States of America

CUSTOM TABLE OF CONTENTS

Corporations: Organization, Stock Transactions, and Dividends

© MATTHEW CAVANAUGH/ASSOCIATED PRESS

objectives

After studying this chapter, you should be able to:

1   **Describe the nature of the corporate form of organization.**

2   **Describe the two main sources of stockholders' equity.**

3   **Describe and illustrate the characteristics of stock, classes of stock, and entries for issuing stock.**

4   **Journalize the entries for cash dividends and stock dividends.**

5   **Journalize the entries for treasury stock transactions.**

6   **Describe and illustrate the reporting of stockholders' equity.**

7   **Describe the effect of stock splits on corporate financial statements.**

The Yankee Candle Company, Inc.

f you purchased 100 shares of The Yankee Candle Company, Inc., you would own a small interest in the company. Thus, you would own a small amount of the future financial prospects of a company that makes and sells over 80 million candles each year. Yankee's candle products come in hundreds of fragrances, styles, and sizes, including Housewarmer® jar candles, Samplers® votive candles, Tarts® wax potpourri, designer pillars, tapers, and scented tea lights.

How did Yankee Candle begin? Yankee Candle began in 1969 when teenager Mike Kittredge made his first candle with melted crayons in his South Hadley, Massachusetts, family home as a Christmas gift for his mother. A neighbor saw the candle, wanted to buy it, and Yankee Candle was born. Family, friends, and neighbors raved about Mike's candles and kept buying them as fast as he could make them. Mike operated first out of his parent's kitchen, basement, and garage. In 1971, Mike opened his first retail store; in 1974, he moved his candle making to an abandoned mill building; in 1994, Mike moved Yankee Candle to a 294,000-square-foot manufacturing plant in South Deerfield, Massachusetts. In 1998, Mike sold Yankee Candle, which today is traded on the New York Stock Exchange (symbol YCC) with sales of over $550 million and net income of over $82 million.

Before buying your 100 shares of Yankee Candle, you would want to study the financial statements and management's plans for the future. You would want to know whether management planned to issue additional shares of stock that might impact the value of your stock. You would want to know whether Yankee Candle planned to continue paying its semiannual cash dividend of $0.125. You might visit Yankee Candle's Web site (**http://www.yankeecandle.com**). Finally, you would explore other sources of investor information, such as whether financial analysts recommend Yankee Candle stock as a buy or sell.

In this chapter, we describe and illustrate the nature of corporations including the accounting for stock and dividends. This discussion will aid you in making decisions such as whether or not to buy Yankee Candle stock.

Nature of a Corporation

objective 1

Describe the nature of the corporate form of organization.

A corporation was defined in the Dartmouth College case of 1819, in which Chief Justice Marshall of the United States Supreme Court stated: "A corporation is an artificial being, invisible, intangible, and existing only in contemplation of the law."

In the preceding chapters, we used the proprietorship in illustrations. As we mentioned in a previous chapter, more than 70% of all businesses are proprietorships and 10% are partnerships. Most of these businesses are small businesses. The remaining 20% of businesses are corporations. Many corporations are large and, as a result, they generate more than 90% of the total business dollars in the United States.

CHARACTERISTICS OF A CORPORATION

A *corporation* is a legal entity, distinct and separate from the individuals who create and operate it. As a legal entity, a corporation may acquire, own, and dispose of property in its own name. It may also incur liabilities and enter into contracts. Most importantly, it can sell shares of ownership, called **stock**. This characteristic gives corporations the ability to raise large amounts of capital.

The **stockholders** or *shareholders* who own the stock own the corporation. They can buy and sell stock without affecting the corporation's operations or continued existence. Corporations whose shares of stock are traded in public markets are called *public corporations*. Corporations whose shares are not traded publicly are usually owned by a small group of investors and are called *nonpublic* or *private corporations*.

The stockholders of a corporation have *limited liability*. This means that a corporation's creditors usually may not go beyond the assets of the corporation to satisfy

The Coca-Cola Company is a well-known public corporation. Mars, Incorporated, which is owned by family members, is a well-known private corporation.

their claims. Thus, the financial loss that a stockholder may suffer is limited to the amount invested. This feature has contributed to the rapid growth of the corporate form of business.

The stockholders control a corporation by electing a *board of directors*. This board meets periodically to establish corporate policies. It also selects the chief executive officer (CEO) and other major officers to manage the corporation's day-to-day affairs. Exhibit 1 shows the organizational structure of a corporation.

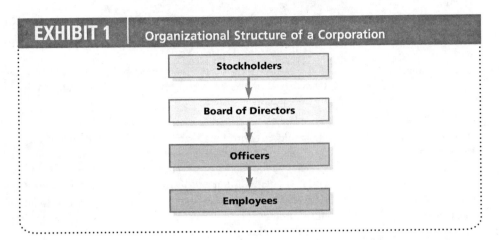

EXHIBIT 1 | **Organizational Structure of a Corporation**

Stockholders → Board of Directors → Officers → Employees

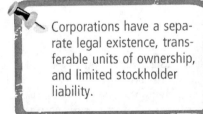

Corporations have a separate legal existence, transferable units of ownership, and limited stockholder liability.

As a separate entity, a corporation is subject to taxes. For example, corporations must pay federal income taxes on their income.[1] Thus, corporate income that is distributed to stockholders in the form of *dividends* has already been taxed. In turn, stockholders must pay income taxes on the dividends they receive. This *double taxation* of corporate earnings is a major disadvantage of the corporate form.[2] The advantages and disadvantages of the corporate form are listed in Exhibit 2.

Integrity, Objectivity, and Ethics in Business

ETHICS

THE RESPONSIBLE BOARD

Recent accounting scandals, such as those involving Enron, WorldCom, and Fannie Mae, have highlighted the roles of boards of directors in executing their responsibilities. For example, eighteen of Enron's former directors and their insurance providers have settled shareholder litigation for $168 million, of which $13 million is to come from the directors' personal assets. Board members are now on notice that their directorship responsibilities are being taken seriously by stockholders.

FORMING A CORPORATION

The first step in forming a corporation is to file an *application of incorporation* with the state. State incorporation laws differ, and corporations often organize in those states with the more favorable laws. For this reason, more than half of the largest companies

---

1 A majority of states also require corporations to pay income taxes.
2 Dividends presently receive a preferential individual tax rate of 15% to reduce the impact of double taxation.

EXHIBIT 2	Advantages and Disadvantages of the Corporate Form

Advantages	Explanation
Separate legal existence	A corporation exists separately from its owners.
Continuous life	A corporation's life is separate from its owners; therefore, it exists indefinitely.
Raising large amounts of capital	The corporate form is suited for raising large amounts of money from shareholders.
Ownership rights are easily transferable	A corporation sells shares of ownership, called *stock*. The stockholders of a public company can transfer their shares of stock to other stockholders through stock markets, such as the New York Stock Exchange.
Limited liability	A corporation's creditors usually may not go beyond the assets of the corporation to satisfy their claims. Thus, the financial loss that a stockholder may suffer is limited to the amount invested.
Disadvantages	
Owner is separate from management	Stockholders control management through a board of directors. The board of directors should represent shareholder interests; however, when the board is not sufficiently independent of management, it is possible that the board of directors and management may not always behave in the best interests of stockholders.
Double taxation of dividends	As a separate legal entity, a corporation is subject to taxation. Thus, net income distributed as dividends will be taxed once at the corporation level, and then again at the individual level.
Regulatory costs	Corporations must satisfy many requirements such as those required by the Sarbanes-Oxley Act of 2002.

A Financial Executives International survey estimated that Sarbanes-Oxley costs the average public company over $3 million per year.

are incorporated in Delaware. Exhibit 3 lists some corporations that you may be familiar with, their states of incorporation, and the location of their headquarters.

After the application of incorporation has been approved, the state grants a *charter* or *articles of incorporation*. The articles of incorporation formally create the corporation.[3] The corporate management and board of directors then prepare a set of *bylaws*, which are the rules and procedures for conducting the corporation's affairs.

EXHIBIT 3	Examples of Corporations and Their States of Incorporation	

Corporation	State of Incorporation	Headquarters
Caterpillar	Delaware	Peoria, Ill.
Delta Air Lines	Delaware	Atlanta, Ga.
The Dow Chemical Company	Delaware	Midland, Mich.
General Electric Company	New York	Fairfield, Conn.
The Home Depot	Delaware	Atlanta, Ga.
Kellogg Company	Delaware	Battle Creek, Mich.
3M	Delaware	St. Paul, Minn.
R.J. Reynolds Tobacco Company	Delaware	Winston-Salem, N.C.
Starbucks Corporation	Washington	Seattle, Wash.
Sun Microsystems, Inc.	Delaware	Palo Alto, Calif.
The Washington Post Company	Delaware	Washington, D.C.
Whirlpool Corporation	Delaware	Benton Harbor, Mich.

3 The articles of incorporation may also restrict a corporation's activities in certain areas, such as owning certain types of real estate, conducting certain types of business activities, or purchasing its own stock.

Costs may be incurred in organizing a corporation. These costs include legal fees, taxes, state incorporation fees, license fees, and promotional costs. Such costs are debited to an expense account entitled *Organizational Expenses*. To illustrate, the recording of a corporation's organizing costs of $8,500 on January 5 is shown below.

Jan.	5	Organizational Expenses	8 5 0 0 00	
		Cash		8 5 0 0 00
		Paid costs of organizing the corporation.		

Integrity, Objectivity, and Ethics in Business

ETHICS

NOT-FOR-PROFIT, OR NOT?

Corporations can be formed for not-for-profit purposes by making a request to the Internal Revenue Service under *Internal Revenue Code* section 501(c)3. Such corporations, such as the Sierra Club and the National Audubon Society, are exempt from federal taxes. Forming businesses inside a 501(c)3 exempt organization that competes with profit-making (and hence, tax-paying) businesses is very controversial. For example, should the local YMCA receive a tax exemption for providing similar services as the local health club business? The IRS is now challenging such businesses and is withholding 501(c)3 status to many organizations due to this issue.

Stockholders' Equity

objective **2**

Describe the two main sources of stockholders' equity.

The owners' equity in a corporation is commonly called **stockholders' equity**, *shareholders' equity*, *shareholders' investment*, or *capital*. In a corporation balance sheet, the Stockholders' Equity section reports the amount of each of the two main sources of stockholders' equity. The first source is capital contributed to the corporation by the stockholders and others, called **paid-in capital** or *contributed capital*. The second source is net income retained in the business, called **retained earnings**.

An example of a Stockholders' Equity section of a corporation balance sheet is shown below.[4]

Stockholders' Equity

Paid-in capital:		
Common stock	$330,000	
Retained earnings	80,000	
Total stockholders' equity		$410,000

The paid-in capital contributed by the stockholders is recorded in separate accounts for each class of stock. If there is only one class of stock, the account is entitled *Common Stock* or *Capital Stock*.

Retained earnings are generated from operations. Net income increases retained earnings, while dividends decrease retained earnings. Thus, retained earnings represents a corporation's accumulated net income that has not been distributed to stockholders as dividends.

The balance of the retained earnings account at the end of the fiscal year is created by closing entries. First, the balance in the income summary account (the net income or net loss) is transferred to Retained Earnings. Second, the balance of the dividends account, which is similar to the drawing account for a proprietorship, is transferred to Retained Earnings.

---

4 The reporting of stockholders' equity is further discussed and illustrated later in this chapter.

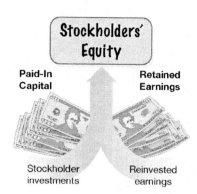

Stockholders' Equity

Paid-In Capital — Retained Earnings

Stockholder investments — Reinvested earnings

Other terms that may be used to identify retained earnings in the financial statements include *earnings retained for use in the business* and *earnings reinvested in the business*. A debit balance in Retained Earnings is called a **deficit**. Such a balance results from accumulated net losses. In the Stockholders' Equity section, a deficit is deducted from paid-in capital in determining total stockholders' equity.

The balance of Retained Earnings should not be interpreted as representing surplus cash or cash left over for dividends. The reason for this is that earnings retained in the business and the related cash generated from these earnings are normally used by management to improve or expand operations. As cash is used to expand or improve operations, its balance decreases. However, the balance of the retained earnings account is unaffected. As a result, over time the balance of the retained earnings account normally becomes less and less related to the balance of the cash account.

Paid-In Capital From Issuing Stock

objective **3**

Describe and illustrate the characteristics of stock, classes of stock, and entries for issuing stock.

As we mentioned in the preceding section, the two main sources of stockholders' equity are paid-in capital (or contributed capital) and retained earnings. The main source of paid-in capital is from issuing stock. In the following paragraphs, we discuss the characteristics of stock, the classes of stock, and entries for recording the issuance of stock.

CHARACTERISTICS OF STOCK

Authorized

Issued

Outstanding

Number of shares authorized, issued, and outstanding

The number of shares of stock that a corporation is *authorized* to issue is stated in its charter. The term *issued* refers to the shares issued to the stockholders. A corporation may, under circumstances we discuss later in this chapter, reacquire some of the stock that it has issued. The stock remaining in the hands of stockholders is then called **outstanding stock**. The relationship between authorized, issued, and outstanding stock is shown in the graphic at the left.

Shares of stock are often assigned a monetary amount, called **par**. Corporations may issue *stock certificates* to stockholders to document their ownership. Printed on a stock certificate is the par value of the stock, the name of the stockholder, and the number of shares owned. Stock may also be issued without par, in which case it is called *no-par stock*. Some states require the board of directors to assign a **stated value** to no-par stock.

Because corporations have limited liability, creditors have no claim against the personal assets of stockholders. However, some state laws require that corporations maintain a minimum stockholder contribution to protect creditors. This minimum amount is called *legal capital*. The amount of required legal capital varies among the states, but it usually includes the amount of par or stated value of the shares of stock issued.

The major rights that accompany ownership of a share of stock are as follows:

1. The right to vote in matters concerning the corporation.
2. The right to share in distributions of earnings.
3. The right to share in assets on liquidation.

As we discuss next, these stock rights normally vary with the class of stock.

Some corporations have stopped issuing stock certificates except on special request. In these cases, the corporation maintains records of ownership.

CLASSES OF STOCK

When only one class of stock is issued, it is called **common stock**. In this case, each share of common stock has equal rights. To appeal to a broader investment market, a

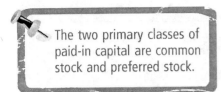

The two primary classes of paid-in capital are common stock and preferred stock.

corporation may issue one or more classes of stock with various preference rights. A common example of such a right is the preference to dividends. Such a stock is generally called a **preferred stock**.

The dividend rights of preferred stock are usually stated in monetary terms or as a percent of par. For example, *$4 preferred stock* has a right to an annual $4 per share dividend. If the par value of the preferred stock were $50, the same right to dividends could be stated as *8% ($4/$50) preferred stock.*[5]

The board of directors of a corporation has the sole authority to distribute dividends to the stockholders. When such action is taken, the directors are said to *declare* a dividend. Since dividends are normally based on earnings, a corporation cannot guarantee dividends even to preferred stockholders. However, because they have first rights to any dividends, the preferred stockholders have a greater chance of receiving regular dividends than do the common stockholders.

To illustrate, assume that a corporation has 1,000 shares of $4 preferred stock and 4,000 shares of common stock outstanding. Also assume that the net income, amount of earnings retained, and the amount of earnings distributed by the board of directors for the first three years of operations are as follows:

	2006	2007	2008
Net income	$20,000	$9,000	$62,000
Amount retained	10,000	6,000	40,000
Amount distributed	$10,000	$3,000	$22,000

Exhibit 4 shows the earnings distributed each year to the preferred stock and the common stock. In this example, the preferred stockholders received dividends of $4, $3, and $4 per share. In contrast, common stockholders received dividends of $1.50 per share in 2006, no dividends in 2007, and $4.50 per share in 2008. You should note that although preferred stockholders have a greater chance of receiving a regular dividend, common stockholders have a greater chance of receiving larger dividends than do the preferred stockholders.[6]

EXHIBIT 4

Dividends to Preferred and Common Stock

	2006	2007	2008
Amount distributed	$10,000	$3,000	$22,000
Preferred dividend (1,000 shares)	4,000	3,000	4,000
Common dividend (4,000 shares)	$ 6,000	$ 0	$18,000
Dividends per share:			
Preferred stock	$ 4.00	$ 3.00	$ 4.00
Common stock	$ 1.50	none	$ 4.50

In addition to dividend preference, preferred stock may be given preferences to assets if the corporation goes out of business and is liquidated. However, claims of creditors must be satisfied first. Preferred stockholders are next in line to receive any remaining assets, followed by the common stockholders.

---

5 In some cases, preferred stock may receive additional dividends if certain conditions are met. Such stock, called *participating preferred stock,* is not often used.

6 In some cases, preferred stock has the right to receive regular dividends that were not paid (not declared) in prior years before any common stock dividends are paid. Such preferred stock, called *cumulative preferred stock,* is described and illustrated in intermediate accounting textbooks.

Example Exercise 13-1

objective **3**

Sandpiper Company has 20,000 shares of 1% preferred stock of $100 par and 100,000 shares of $50 par common stock. The following amounts were distributed as dividends:

Year 1 $10,000
Year 2   25,000
Year 3   80,000

Determine the dividends per share for preferred and common stock for each year.

Follow My Example 13-1

	Year 1	Year 2	Year 3
Amount distributed	$10,000	$25,000	$80,000
Preferred dividend (20,000 shares)	10,000	20,000	20,000
Common dividend (100,000 shares)	$ 0	$ 5,000	$60,000
Dividends per share:			
Preferred stock	$0.50	$1.00	$1.00
Common stock	None	$0.05	$0.60

For Practice: PE 13-1A, PE 13-1B

ISSUING STOCK

A separate account is used for recording the amount of each class of stock issued to investors in a corporation. For example, assume that a corporation is authorized to issue 10,000 shares of $100 par preferred stock and 100,000 shares of $20 par common stock. One-half of each class of authorized shares is issued at par for cash. The corporation's entry to record the stock issue is as follows:[7]

Cash		1,500 0 0 0 00	
Preferred Stock			500 0 0 0 00
Common Stock			1,000 0 0 0 00
Issued preferred stock and common			
stock at par for cash.			

Stock is often issued by a corporation at a price other than its par. This is because the par value of a stock is simply its legal capital. The price at which stock can be sold by a corporation depends on a variety of factors, such as:

1. The financial condition, earnings record, and dividend record of the corporation.
2. Investor expectations of the corporation's potential earning power.
3. General business and economic conditions and prospects.

When stock is issued for a price that is more than its par, the stock has sold at a **premium**. When stock is issued for a price that is less than its par, the stock has sold at a **discount**. Thus, if stock with a par of $50 is issued for a price of $60, the stock has sold at a premium of $10. If the same stock is issued for a price of $45, the stock has sold at a discount of $5. Many states do not permit stock to be issued at a discount. In others, it may be done only under unusual conditions. Since issuing stock at a discount is rare, we will not illustrate it.

---

7 The accounting for investments in stocks from the point of view of the investor is discussed in a later chapter.

The following stock quotation for Wal-Mart is taken from *The Wall Street Journal* from May 12, 2006:

NEW YORK STOCK EXCHANGE

52 Weeks Hi	52 Weeks Lo	Stock	Sym	Div	Yld %	PE	Vol 100s	Close	Net Chg
50.87	42.31	WalMart	WMT	.67	1.4	18	108,765	47.25	–.53

The preceding quotation is interpreted as follows:

Hi	Highest price during the past 52 weeks
Lo	Lowest price during the past 52 weeks
Stock	Name of the company
Sym	Stock exchange symbol (WMT for Wal-Mart)
Div	Dividends paid per share during the past year
Yld %	Annual dividend yield per share based on the closing price (Wal-Mart's 1.4% yield on common stock is computed as $0.67/$47.25)
PE	Price-earnings ratio on common stock (price/earnings per share)
Vol	The volume of stock traded in 100s
Close	Closing price for the day
Net Chg	The net change in price from the previous day

A corporation issuing stock must maintain records of the stockholders in order to issue dividend checks and distribute financial statements and other reports. Large public corporations normally use a financial institution, such as a bank, for this purpose.[8] In such cases, the financial institution is referred to as a *transfer agent* or *registrar*. For example, the transfer agent and registrar for The Coca-Cola Company is First Chicago Trust Company of New York.

PREMIUM ON STOCK

When stock is issued at a premium, Cash or other asset accounts are debited for the amount received. Common Stock or Preferred Stock is then credited for the par amount. The excess of the amount paid over par is a part of the total investment of the stockholders in the corporation. Therefore, such an amount in excess of par should be classified as a part of the paid-in capital. An account entitled *Paid-In Capital in Excess of Par* is usually credited for this amount.

To illustrate, assume that Caldwell Company issues 2,000 shares of $50 par preferred stock for cash at $55. The entry to record this transaction is as follows:

Cash	110 0 0 0 00	
Preferred Stock		100 0 0 0 00
Paid-In Capital in Excess of Par—		
Preferred Stock		10 0 0 0 00
Issued $50 par preferred stock at $55.		

When stock is issued in exchange for assets other than cash, such as land, buildings, and equipment, the assets acquired should be recorded at their fair market value. If this value cannot be objectively determined, the fair market price of the stock issued may be used.

To illustrate, assume that a corporation acquired land for which the fair market value cannot be determined. In exchange, the corporation issued 10,000 shares of its $10 par common. Assuming that the stock has a current market price of $12 per share, this transaction is recorded as follows:

Land	120 0 0 0 00	
Common Stock		100 0 0 0 00
Paid-In Capital in Excess of Par		20 0 0 0 00
Issued $10 par common stock, valued		
at $12 per share, for land.		

---

8 Small corporations may use a subsidiary ledger, called a *stockholders ledger*. In this case, the stock accounts (Preferred Stock and Common Stock) are controlling accounts for the subsidiary ledger.

Business Connections

REAL WORLD

CISCO SYSTEMS, INC.

Cisco Systems, Inc., manufactures and sells networking and communications products worldwide.

The company's technology products include home networking products, which enable users to share Internet access, printers, music, movies, and games. Cisco Systems is incorporated in California and has its headquarters in San Jose, California. Some excerpts from its bylaws are shown below.

© CISCO SYSTEMS, INC.

ARTICLE 2
SHAREHOLDERS' MEETINGS
Section 2.01 Annual Meetings. The annual meeting of the shareholders of the Corporation . . . shall be held each year on the second Thursday in November at 10:00 a.m. . .

ARTICLE 3
BOARD OF DIRECTORS
Section 3.02 Number and Qualification of Directors. The number of authorized directors of this Corporation shall be not less than eight (8) nor more than fifteen (15), the exact number of directors to be (determined) by a . . . resolution of the Board of Directors or shareholders.

Section 3.04 Special Meetings. Special meetings of the Board of Directors may be called at any time by the Chairman of the Board, the President of the Corporation or any two (2) directors.

Section 3.11 Removal. The Board of Directors may declare vacant the office of a director who has been declared of unsound mind by an order of court or who has been convicted of a felony.

ARTICLE 4
OFFICERS
Section 4.01 Number and Term. The officers of the Corporation shall include a President, a Secretary and a Chief Financial Officer, all of which shall be chosen by the Board of Directors. . . .

Section 4.03 Removal and Resignation. Any officer chosen by the Board of Directors may be removed at any time, with or without cause, by the affirmative vote of a majority of all the members of the Board of Directors.

Section 4.05 Chairman of the Board. The Chairman of the Board shall preside at all meetings of the Board of Directors.

Section 4.06 President. The President shall be the general manager and chief executive officer of the Corporation, subject to the control of the Board of Directors, . . . shall preside at all meetings of shareholders, shall have general supervision of the affairs of the Corporation. . . .

Section 4.08 Secretary. The Secretary shall see that notices for all meetings are given in accordance with the provisions of these Bylaws and as required by law, shall keep minutes of all meetings, shall have charge of the seal and the corporate books, and shall have all such other authority . . . as may be delegated or assigned from time to time by the President or by the Board of Directors.

Section 4.10 Treasurer. The Treasurer shall have custody of all moneys and securities of the Corporation and shall keep regular books of account. . . .

Section 4.13 Approval of Loans to Directors and Officers. The Corporation may, upon the approval of the Board of Directors alone, make loans of money or property to, or guarantee the obligations of, any director or officer of the Corporation or its parent or subsidiary, ... provided that (i) the Board of Directors determines that such a loan or guaranty or plan may reasonably be expected to benefit the Corporation . . . and (iii) the approval of the Board of Directors is by a vote sufficient without counting the vote of any interested director or directors.

Section 5.04 Fiscal Year. The fiscal year of the Corporation shall end on the last Saturday of July.

NO-PAR STOCK

In most states, both preferred and common stock may be issued without a par value. When no-par stock is issued, the entire proceeds are credited to the stock account. This is true even though the issue price varies from time to time. For example, assume that a corporation issues 10,000 shares of no-par common stock at $40 a share and at a later date issues 1,000 additional shares at $36. The entries to record the no-par stock are as follows:

Cash			400 0 0 0 00	
Common Stock				400 0 0 0 00
Issued 10,000 shares of no-par				
common at $40.				
Cash			36 0 0 0 00	
Common Stock				36 0 0 0 00
Issued 1,000 shares of no-par				
common at $36.				

Some states require that the entire proceeds from the issue of no-par stock be recorded as legal capital. In this case, the preceding entries would be proper. In other states, no-par stock may be assigned a *stated value per share*. The stated value is recorded like a par value, and the excess of the proceeds over the stated value. To illustrate, assume that in the preceding example the no-par common stock is assigned a stated value of $25. The issuance of the stock would be recorded as follows:

Cash		400 0 0 0 00	
Common Stock			250 0 0 0 00
Paid-In Capital in Excess of Stated Value			150 0 0 0 00
Issued 10,000 shares of no-par common			
at $40; stated value, $25.			
Cash		36 0 0 0 00	
Common Stock			25 0 0 0 00
Paid-In Capital in Excess of Stated Value			11 0 0 0 00
Issued 1,000 shares of no-par common			
at $36; stated value, $25.			

Example Exercise 13-2   objective 3

On March 6, Limerick Corporation issued for cash 15,000 shares of no-par common stock at $30. On April 13, Limerick issued at par 1,000 shares of 4%, $40 par preferred stock for cash. On May 19, Limerick issued for cash 15,000 shares of 4%, $40 par preferred stock at $42.

Journalize the entries to record the March 6, April 13, and May 19 transactions.

Follow My Example 13-2

Mar. 6	Cash	450,000	
	Common Stock		450,000
	(15,000 shares × $30).		
Apr. 13	Cash	40,000	
	Preferred Stock		40,000
	(1,000 shares × $40).		
May 19	Cash	630,000	
	Preferred Stock		600,000
	Paid-In Capital in Excess of Par		30,000
	(15,000 shares × $42)		

For Practice: PE 13-2A, PE 13-2B

Accounting for Dividends

objective **4**

Journalize the entries for cash dividends and stock dividends.

When a board of directors declares a cash dividend, it authorizes the distribution of a portion of the corporation's cash to stockholders. When a board of directors declares a stock dividend, it authorizes the distribution of a portion of its stock. In both cases, the declaration of a dividend reduces the retained earnings of the corporation.[9]

CASH DIVIDENDS

A cash distribution of earnings by a corporation to its shareholders is called a **cash dividend**. Although dividends may be paid in the form of other assets, cash dividends are the most common form.

There are usually three conditions that a corporation must meet to pay a cash dividend:

1. Sufficient retained earnings
2. Sufficient cash
3. Formal action by the board of directors

A large amount of retained earnings does not always mean that a corporation is able to pay dividends. As we indicated earlier in the chapter, the balances of the cash and retained earnings accounts are often unrelated. Thus, a large retained earnings account does not mean that there is cash available to pay dividends.

A corporation's board of directors is not required by law to declare dividends. This is true even if both retained earnings and cash are large enough to justify a dividend. However, many corporations try to maintain a stable dividend record in order to make their stock attractive to investors. Although dividends may be paid once a year or semiannually, most corporations pay dividends quarterly. In years of high profits, a corporation may declare a *special* or *extra* dividend.

You may have seen announcements of dividend declarations in financial newspapers or investor services. An example of such an announcement is shown below.

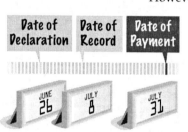

Board of Directors takes action to declare dividends.

ENTRY:
Debit *Cash Dividends*

Credit *Cash Dividends Payable*

Ownership of shares determines who receives dividend (no entry required).

Dividend is paid.

ENTRY:
Debit *Cash Dividends Payable*

Credit *Cash*

> On June 26, the board of directors of The Campbell Soup Company *declared a quarterly cash dividend of $0.225 per common share to stockholders of record as of the close of business on July 8, payable on July 31.*

This announcement includes three important dates: the *date of declaration* (June 26), the *date of record* (July 8), and the *date of payment* (July 31). During the period of time between the record date and the payment date, the stock price is usually quoted as selling *ex-dividends*. This means that since the date of record has passed, a new investor will not receive the dividend.

To illustrate, assume that on *December 1* the board of directors of Hiber Corporation declares the following quarterly cash dividends. The date of record is *December 10*, and the date of payment is *January 2*.

	Dividend per Share	Total Dividends
Preferred stock, $100 par, 5,000 shares outstanding	$2.50	$12,500
Common stock, $10 par, 100,000 shares outstanding	$0.30	30,000
Total		$42,500

9 In rare cases, when a corporation is reducing its operations or going out of business, a dividend may be a distribution of paid-in capital. Such a dividend is called a *liquidating dividend*.

Hiber Corporation records the $42,500 liability for the dividends on December 1, the declaration date, as follows:

Dec.	1	Cash Dividends		42 5 0 0 00	
		Cash Dividends Payable			42 5 0 0 00
		Declared cash dividend.			

No entry is required on the date of record, December 10, since this date merely determines which stockholders will receive the dividend. On the date of payment, January 2, the corporation records the $42,500 payment of the dividends as follows:

Jan.	2	Cash Dividends Payable		42 5 0 0 00	
		Cash			42 5 0 0 00
		Paid cash dividend.			

If Hiber Corporation's fiscal year ends December 31, the balance in Cash Dividends will be transferred to Retained Earnings as a part of the closing process by debiting Retained Earnings and crediting Cash Dividends. Cash Dividends Payable will be listed on the December 31 balance sheet as a current liability.

Example Exercise 13-3 objective 4

The important dates in connection with a cash dividend of $75,000 on a corporation's common stock are February 26, March 30, and April 2. Journalize the entries required on each date.

Follow My Example 13-3

Feb. 26	Cash Dividends	75,000	
	Cash Dividends Payable		75,000
Mar. 30	No entry required.		
Apr. 2	Cash Dividends Payable	75,000	
	Cash		75,000

For Practice: PE 13-3A, PE 13-3B

Integrity, Objectivity, and Ethics in Business

ETHICS

THE PROFESSOR WHO KNEW TOO MUCH

A major Midwestern university released a quarterly "American Customer Satisfaction Index" based upon its research of customers of popular U.S. products and services. Before the release of the index to the public, the professor in charge of the research bought and sold stocks of some of the companies being reported upon. The professor was quoted as saying that he thought it was important to test his theories of customer satisfaction with "real" [his own] money.

Is this proper or ethical? Apparently, the dean of the Business School didn't think so. In a statement to the press,

the dean stated: "I have instructed anyone affiliated with the (index) not to make personal use of information gathered in the course of producing the quarterly index, prior to the index's release to the general public, and they [the researchers] have agreed."

Sources: Jon E. Hilsenrath and Dan Morse, "Researcher Uses Index to Buy, Short Stocks," *The Wall Street Journal*, February 18, 2003; and Jon E. Hilsenrath, "Satisfaction Theory: Mixed Results," *The Wall Street Journal*, February 19, 2003.

STOCK DIVIDENDS

A distribution of shares of stock to stockholders is called a **stock dividend**. Usually, such distributions are in common stock and are issued to holders of common stock. Stock dividends are different from cash dividends in that there is no distribution of cash or other assets to stockholders.

The effect of a stock dividend on the stockholders' equity of the issuing corporation is to transfer retained earnings to paid-in capital. For public corporations, the amount transferred from retained earnings to paid-in capital is normally the *fair value* (market price) of the shares issued in the stock dividend.[10] To illustrate, assume that the stockholders' equity accounts of Hendrix Corporation as of December 15 are as follows:

Common Stock, $20 par (2,000,000 shares issued)	$40,000,000
Paid-In Capital in Excess of Par—Common Stock	9,000,000
Retained Earnings	26,600,000

On December 15, the board of directors declares a stock dividend of 5% or 100,000 shares (2,000,000 shares × 5%) to be issued on January 10 to stockholders of record on December 31. The market price of the stock on the declaration date is $31 a share. The entry to record the declaration is as follows:

Dec.	15	Stock Dividends	3,100 0 0 0 00	
		Stock Dividends Distributable		2,000 0 0 0 00
		Paid-In Capital in Excess of Par—		
		Common Stock		1,100 0 0 0 00
		Declared 5% (100,000 share) stock		
		dividend on $20 par common stock		
		with a market price of $31 per share.		

The $3,100,000 balance in Stock Dividends is closed to Retained Earnings on December 31. The stock dividends distributable account is listed in the Paid-In Capital section of the balance sheet. Thus, the effect of the stock dividend is to transfer $3,100,000 of retained earnings to paid-in capital.

On January 10, the number of shares outstanding is increased by 100,000 by the following entry to record the issue of the stock:

Jan.	10	Stock Dividends Distributable	2,000 0 0 0 00	
		Common Stock		2,000 0 0 0 00
		Issued stock for the stock dividend.		

A stock dividend does not change the assets, liabilities, or total stockholders' equity of the corporation. Likewise, it does not change a stockholder's proportionate interest (equity) in the corporation. For example, if a stockholder owned 1,000 of a corporation's 10,000 shares outstanding, the stockholder owns 10% (1,000/10,000) of the corporation. After declaring a 6% stock dividend, the corporation will issue 600 additional shares (10,000 shares × 6%), and the total shares outstanding will be 10,600. The stockholder of 1,000 shares will receive 60 additional shares and will now own 1,060 shares, which is still a 10% equity interest.

---

10 The use of fair market value is justified as long as the number of shares issued for the stock dividend is small (less than 25% of the shares outstanding).

Example Exercise 13-4 objective 4

Vienna Highlights Corporation has 150,000 shares of $100 par common stock outstanding. On June 14, Vienna Highlights declared a 4% stock dividend to be issued August 15 to stockholders of record on July 1. The market price of the stock was $110 per share on June 14.
Journalize the entries required on June 14, July 1, and August 15.

Follow My Example 13-4

June 14	Stock Dividends (150,000 × 4% × $110)	660,000	
	Stock Dividends Distributable (6,000 × $100)		600,000
	Paid-In Capital in Excess of Par—Common Stock		
	($660,000 − $600,000)		60,000
July 1	No entry required.		
Aug. 15	Stock Dividends Distributable	600,000	
	Common Stock		600,000

For Practice: PE 13-4A, PE 13-4B

Treasury Stock Transactions

objective **5**

Journalize the entries for treasury stock transactions.

The 2005 edition of *Accounting Trends & Techniques* indicated that over 66% of the companies surveyed reported treasury stock.

A corporation may buy its own stock to provide shares for resale to employees, for reissuing as a bonus to employees, or for supporting the market price of the stock. For example, General Motors Corporation bought back its common stock and stated that two primary uses of this stock would be for incentive compensation plans and employee savings plans. Such stock that a corporation has once issued and then reacquires is called **treasury stock**.

A commonly used method of accounting for the purchase and resale of treasury stock is the *cost method*.[11] When the stock is purchased by the corporation, paid-in capital is reduced by debiting *Treasury Stock* for its cost (the price paid for it). The par value and the price at which the stock was originally issued are ignored. In addition, no dividends are paid on stock held as treasury stock. To do so would place the corporation in the position of earning income through dealing with itself.

When the stock is resold, Treasury Stock is credited for its cost, and any difference between the cost and the selling price is normally debited or credited to *Paid-In Capital from Sale of Treasury Stock*.

To illustrate, assume that the paid-in capital of a corporation is as follows:

Common stock, $25 par (20,000 shares authorized and issued)	$500,000	
Excess of issue price over par	150,000	$650,000

The purchase and sale of the treasury stock are recorded as follows:

	Treasury Stock	45 0 0 0 00	
	Cash		45 0 0 0 00
	Purchased 1,000 shares of treasury		
	stock at $45.		

(continued)

---

11 Another method that is infrequently used, called the *par value method*, is discussed in advanced accounting texts.

Cash		12 0 0 0 00	
Treasury Stock			9 0 0 0 00
Paid-In Capital from Sale of Treasury Stock			3 0 0 0 00
Sold 200 shares of treasury stock at $60.			
Cash		8 0 0 0 00	
Paid-In Capital from Sale of Treasury Stock		1 0 0 0 00	
Treasury Stock			9 0 0 0 00
Sold 200 shares of treasury stock at $40.			

As shown above, a sale of treasury stock may result in a decrease in paid-in capital. To the extent that Paid-In Capital from Sale of Treasury Stock has a credit balance, it should be debited for any decrease. Any remaining decrease should then be debited to the retained earnings account.

Example Exercise 13-5   objective 5

On May 3, Buzz Off Corporation reacquired 3,200 shares of its common stock at $42 per share. On July 22, Buzz Off sold 2,000 of the reacquired shares at $47 per share. On August 30, Buzz Off sold the remaining shares at $40 per share.
   Journalize the transactions of May 3, July 22, and August 30.

Follow My Example 13-5

May 3	Treasury Stock (3,200 × $42)	134,400	
	Cash		134,400
July 22	Cash (2,000 × $47)	94,000	
	Treasury Stock (2,000 × $42)		84,000
	Paid-In Capital from Sale of Treasury Stock		
	[2,000 × ($47 − $42)]		10,000
Aug. 30	Cash (1,200 × $40)	48,000	
	Paid-In Capital from Sale of Treasury Stock [1,200 × ($42 − $40)]	2,400	
	Treasury Stock (1,200 × $42)		50,400

For Practice: PE 13-5A, PE 13-5B

Reporting Stockholders' Equity

objective 6

Describe and illustrate the reporting of stockholders' equity.

We illustrated the Stockholders' Equity section of the balance sheet earlier in this chapter. However, as with other sections of the balance sheet, alternative terms and formats may be used in reporting stockholders' equity. In addition, the significant changes in the sources of stockholders' equity—retained earnings and paid-in capital—may be reported in separate statements or notes that support the balance sheet.

STOCKHOLDERS' EQUITY IN THE BALANCE SHEET

Two alternatives for reporting stockholders' equity for the December 31, 2008, balance sheet for Telex Inc. are shown in Exhibit 5. In the first example, each class of stock is listed first, followed by its related paid-in capital accounts. In the second example, the stock accounts are listed first. The other paid-in capital accounts are listed as a single item described as *Additional paid-in capital*. These combined accounts could also be described as *Capital in excess of par (or stated value) of shares* or a similar title.

EXHIBIT 5

Stockholders' Equity
Section of a Balance
Sheet

Telex Inc.
Balance Sheet
December 31, 2008

Stockholders' Equity

Paid-in capital:			
Preferred 10% stock,			
$50 par (2,000 shares			
authorized and issued)	$100,000		
Excess of issue price over par	10,000	$ 110,000	
Common stock, $20 par			
(50,000 shares authorized,			
45,000 shares issued)	$900,000		
Excess of issue price over par	190,000	1,090,000	
From sale of treasury stock		2,000	
Total paid-in capital			$1,202,000
Retained earnings			350,000
Total			$1,552,000
Deduct treasury stock (600 shares at cost)			27,000
Total stockholders' equity			$1,525,000

Telex Inc.
Balance Sheet
December 31, 2008

Stockholders' Equity

Contributed capital:		
Preferred 10% stock,		
$50 par (2,000 shares		
authorized and issued)	$100,000	
Common stock, $20 par		
(50,000 shares authorized,		
45,000 shares issued)	900,000	
Additional paid-in capital	202,000	
Total contributed capital		$1,202,000
Retained earnings		350,000
Total		$1,552,000
Deduct treasury stock (600 shares at cost)		27,000
Total stockholders' equity		$1,525,000

Significant changes in stockholders' equity during a period may be presented either in a *statement of stockholders' equity* or in notes to the financial statements. We illustrate the statement of stockholders' equity later in this section. In addition, relevant rights and privileges of the various classes of stock outstanding must be disclosed.[12] Examples of types of information that must be disclosed include dividend and liquidation preferences, conversion rights, and redemption rights. Such information may be disclosed on the face of the balance sheet or in the accompanying notes.

---

12 *Statement of Financial Accounting Standards No. 129*, "Disclosure Information about Capital Structure" (Financial Accounting Standards Board, Norwalk, CT: 1997).

Example Exercise 13-6

objective 6

Using the following accounts and balances, prepare the Stockholders' Equity section of the balance sheet. Forty thousand shares of common stock are authorized, and 5,000 shares have been reacquired.

Common Stock, $50 par	$1,500,000
Paid-In Capital in Excess of Par	160,000
Paid-In Capital from Sale of Treasury Stock	44,000
Retained Earnings	4,395,000
Treasury Stock	120,000

Follow My Example 13-6

Stockholders' Equity		
Paid-in capital:		
Common stock, $50 par		
(40,000 shares authorized, 30,000 shares issued)	$1,500,000	
Excess of issue price over par	160,000	$1,660,000
From sale of treasury stock		44,000
Total paid-in capital		$1,704,000
Retained earnings		4,395,000
Total		$6,099,000
Deduct treasury stock (5,000 shares at cost)		120,000
Total stockholders' equity		$5,979,000

For Practice: PE 13-6A, PE 13-6B

REAL WORLD

The 2005 edition of *Accounting Trends & Techniques* indicated that 0.8% of the companies surveyed presented a separate statement of retained earnings, 0.5% presented a combined income and retained earnings statement, and 1.3% presented changes in retained earnings in the notes to the financial statements. The other 97% of the companies presented changes in retained earnings in a statement of stockholders' equity.

REPORTING RETAINED EARNINGS

A corporation may report changes in retained earnings by preparing a separate retained earnings statement, a combined income and retained earnings statement, or a statement of stockholders' equity.

When a separate **retained earnings statement** is prepared, the beginning balance of retained earnings is reported. The net income is then added (or net loss is subtracted) and any dividends are subtracted to arrive at the ending retained earnings for the period. An example of a such a statement for Telex Inc. is shown in Exhibit 6.

An alternative format for presenting the retained earnings statement is to combine it with the income statement. An advantage of the combined format is that it emphasizes net income as the connecting link between the income statement and the retained earnings portion of stockholders' equity. Since the combined form is not often used, we do not illustrate it.

Restrictions   The retained earnings available for use as dividends may be limited by action of a corporation's board of directors. These amounts, called **restrictions** or

EXHIBIT 6

Retained Earnings Statement

Telex Inc. Retained Earnings Statement For the Year Ended December 31, 2008			
Retained earnings, January 1, 2008			$245,000
Net income		$180,000	
Less dividends:			
Preferred stock	$10,000		
Common stock	65,000	75,000	
Increase in retained earnings			105,000
Retained earnings, December 31, 2008			$350,000

appropriations, remain part of the retained earnings. However, they must be disclosed, usually in the notes to the financial statements.

Restrictions may be classified as either legal, contractual, or discretionary. The board of directors may be legally required to restrict retained earnings because of state laws. For example, some state laws require that retained earnings be restricted by the amount of treasury stock purchased, so that legal capital will not be used for dividends. The board may also be required to restrict retained earnings because of contractual requirements. For example, the terms of a bank loan may require restrictions, so that money for repaying the loan will not be used for dividends. Finally, the board may restrict retained earnings voluntarily. For example, the board may limit dividend distributions so that more money is available for expanding the business.

Prior Period Adjustments Material errors in a prior period's net income may arise from mathematical mistakes and from mistakes in applying accounting principles. The effect of material errors that are not discovered within the same fiscal period in which they occurred should not be included in determining net income for the current period. Instead, corrections of such errors, called **prior period adjustments**, are reported in the retained earnings statement. These adjustments are reported as an adjustment to the retained earnings balance at the beginning of the period in which the error is discovered and corrected.[13]

Example Exercise 13-7 objective 6

Dry Creek Cameras Inc. reported the following results for the year ending March 31, 2008:

Retained earnings, April 1, 2007	$3,338,500
Net income	461,500
Cash dividends declared	80,000
Stock dividends declared	120,000

Prepare a retained earnings statement for the fiscal year ended March 31, 2008.

Follow My Example 13-7

DRY CREEK CAMERAS INC.
RETAINED EARNINGS STATEMENT
For the Year Ended March 31, 2008

Retained earnings, April 1, 2007		$3,338,500
Net income	$461,500	
Less dividends declared	200,000	
Increase in retained earnings		261,500
Retained earnings, March 31, 2008		$3,600,000

For Practice: PE 13-7A, PE 13-7B

STATEMENT OF STOCKHOLDERS' EQUITY

Significant changes in stockholders' equity should be reported for the period in which they occur. When the only change in stockholders' equity is due to net income or net loss and dividends, a retained earnings statement is sufficient. However, when a corporation also has changes in stock and other paid-in capital accounts, a **statement of stockholders' equity** is normally prepared. This statement is often prepared in a columnar format, where each column represents a major stockholders' equity classification. Changes in each classification are then described in the left-hand column. Exhibit 7 illustrates a statement of stockholders' equity for Telex Inc.

---

13 Prior period adjustments are illustrated in advanced texts.

EXHIBIT 7   Statement of Stockholders' Equity

Telex Inc. Statement of Stockholders' Equity For the Year Ended December 31, 2008						
	Preferred Stock	Common Stock	Additional Paid-In Capital	Retained Earnings	Treasury Stock	Total
Balance, January 1, 2008	$100,000	$850,000	$177,000	$245,000	$(17,000)	$1,355,000
Net income				180,000		180,000
Dividends on preferred stock				(10,000)		(10,000)
Dividends on common stock				(65,000)		(65,000)
Issuance of additional common stock		50,000	25,000			75,000
Purchase of treasury stock					(10,000)	(10,000)
Balance, December 31, 2008	$100,000	$900,000	$202,000	$350,000	$(27,000)	$1,525,000

Stock Splits

objective 7

*Describe the effect
of stock splits on
corporate financial
statements.*

When Nature's Sunshine Products, Inc., declared a 2-for-1 stock split, the company president said:

We believe the split will place our stock price in a range attractive to both individual and institutional investors, broadening the market for the stock.

Corporations sometimes reduce the par or stated value of their common stock and issue a proportionate number of additional shares. When this is done, a corporation is said to have *split* its stock, and the process is called a **stock split**.

When stock is split, the reduction in par or stated value applies to all shares, including the unissued, issued, and treasury shares. A major objective of a stock split is to reduce the market price per share of the stock. This, in turn, should attract more investors to enter the market for the stock and broaden the types and numbers of stockholders.

To illustrate a stock split, assume that Rojek Corporation has 10,000 shares of $100 par common stock outstanding with a current market price of $150 per share. The board of directors declares a 5-for-1 stock split, reduces the par to $20, and increases the number of shares to 50,000. The amount of common stock outstanding is $1,000,000 both before and after the stock split. Only the number of shares and the par per share are changed. Each Rojek Corporation shareholder owns the same total par amount of stock before and after the stock split. For example, a stockholder who owned 4 shares of $100 par stock before the split (total par of $400) would own 20 shares of $20 par stock after the split (total par of $400).

Since there are more shares outstanding after the stock split, we would expect that the market price of the stock would fall. For example, in the preceding example, there would be 5 times as many shares outstanding after the split. Thus, we would expect the market price of the stock to fall from $150 to approximately $30 ($150/5).

Before Stock Split	After 5:1 Stock Split
4 shares, $100 par	20 shares, $20 par
$400 total par value	$400 total par value

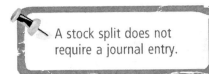

A stock split does not require a journal entry.

Since a stock split changes only the par or stated value and the number of shares outstanding, it is not recorded by a journal entry. Although the accounts are not affected, the details of stock splits are normally disclosed in the notes to the financial statements.

Financial Analysis and Interpretation

The **dividend yield** indicates the rate of return to stockholders in terms of cash dividend distributions. Although the dividend yield can be computed for both preferred and common stock, it is most often computed for common stock. This is because most preferred stock has a stated dividend rate or amount. In contrast, the amount of common stock dividends normally varies with the profitability of the corporation.

The dividend yield is computed by dividing the annual dividends paid per share of common stock by the market price per share at a specific date, as shown below.

$$\text{Dividend Yield} = \frac{\text{Dividends per Share of Common Stock}}{\text{Market Price per Share of Common Stock}}$$

To illustrate, the market price of Mattel, Inc., common stock was $18.89 as of the close of business, January 10, 2005. During the past year, Mattel had paid dividends of $0.45 per share. Thus, the dividend yield of Mattel's common stock is 2.38% ($0.45/$18.89). Because the market price of a corporation's stock will vary from day to day, its dividend yield will also vary from day to day. Fortunately, the dividend yield is provided with newspaper listings of market prices and most Internet quotation services, such as from Yahoo's Finance Web site.

The recent dividend yields for some selected companies are as follows:

Company	Dividend Yield (%)
AT&T Corporation	5.06
Duke Energy Corporation	4.46
General Motors Corporation	8.10
Hewlett-Packard Development Company, LP	1.05
The Home Depot	0.82
Oracle	None
The Coca-Cola Company	1.00

As can be seen, the dividend yield varies widely across firms. Growth companies often do not pay dividends, but instead, reinvest their earnings in research and development, such as with Oracle.

At a Glance

1. Describe the nature of the corporate form of organization.

Key Points	Key Learning Outcomes	Example Exercises	Practice Exercises
Corporations have a separate legal existence, transferable units of stock, unlimited life, and limited stockholders' liability. The advantages and disadvantages of the corporate form are summarized in Exhibit 2. Costs incurred in organizing a corporation are debited to Organizational Expense.	• Describe the characteristics of corporations. • List the advantages and disadvantages of the corporate form. • Prepare a journal entry for the costs of organizing a corporation.		

2. Describe the two main sources of stockholders' equity.

Key Points	Key Learning Outcomes	Example Exercises	Practice Exercises
The two main sources of stockholders' equity are (1) capital contributed by the stockholders and others, called *paid-in capital*, and (2) net income retained in the business, called *retained earnings*. Stockholders' equity is reported in a corporation balance sheet according to these two sources.	• Describe what is meant by paid-in capital. • Describe what is meant by net income retained in the business. • Prepare a simple Stockholders' Equity section of the balance sheet.		

3. Describe and illustrate the characteristics of stock, classes of stock, and entries for issuing stock.

Key Points	Key Learning Outcomes	Example Exercises	Practice Exercises
The main source of paid-in capital is from issuing common and preferred stock. Stock issued at par is recorded by debiting Cash and crediting the class of stock issued for its par amount. Stock issued for more than par is recorded by debiting Cash and crediting Paid-In Capital in Excess of Par for the difference between the cash received and the par value of the stock. When stock is issued in exchange for assets other than cash, the assets acquired are recorded at their fair market value. When no-par stock is issued, the entire proceeds are credited to the stock account. No-par stock may be assigned a stated value per share, and the excess of the proceeds over the stated value may be credited to Paid-In Capital in Excess of Stated Value.	• Describe the characteristics of common and preferred stock including rights to dividends. • Journalize the entry for common and preferred stock issued at par. • Journalize the entry for common and preferred stock issued at more than par. • Journalize the entry for issuing no-par stock.	13-1 13-2 13-2 13-2	13-1A, 13-1B 13-2A, 13-2B 13-2A, 13-2B 13-2A, 13-2B

4. Journalize the entries for cash dividends and stock dividends.

Key Points	Key Learning Outcomes	Example Exercises	Practice Exercises
The entry to record a declaration of cash dividends debits Dividends and credits Dividends Payable. When a stock dividend is declared, Stock Dividends is debited for the fair value of the stock to be issued. Stock Dividends Distributable is credited for the par or stated value of the common stock to be issued. The difference between the fair value of the stock and its par or stated value is credited to Paid-In Capital in Excess of Par—Common Stock. When the stock is issued on the date of payment, Stock Dividends Distributable is debited and Common Stock is credited for the par or stated value of the stock issued.	• Journalize the entries for the declaration and payment of cash dividends. • Journalize the entries for the declaration and payment of stock dividends.	13-3 13-4	13-3A, 13-3B 13-4A, 13-4B

5. Journalize the entries for treasury stock transactions.

Key Points	Key Learning Outcomes	Example Exercises	Practice Exercises
When a corporation buys its own stock, the cost method of accounting is normally used. Treasury Stock is debited for its cost, and Cash is credited. If the stock is resold, Treasury Stock is credited for its cost and any difference between the cost and the selling price is normally debited or credited to Paid-In Capital from Sale of Treasury Stock.	• Define *treasury stock*. • Describe the accounting for treasury stock. • Journalize entries for the purchase and sale of treasury stock.	13-5	13-5A, 13-5B

6. Describe and illustrate the reporting of stockholders' equity.

Key Points	Key Learning Outcomes	Example Exercises	Practice Exercises
Two alternatives for reporting stockholders' equity are shown in Exhibit 5. Changes in retained earnings are reported in a retained earnings statement, as shown in Exhibit 6. Restrictions to retained earnings should be disclosed. Any prior period adjustments are reported in the retained earnings statement. Changes in stockholders' equity may be reported on a statement of stockholders' equity, as shown in Exhibit 7.	• Prepare the Stockholders' Equity section of the balance sheet. • Prepare a retained earnings statement. • Describe retained earnings restrictions and prior period adjustments. • Prepare a statement of stockholders' equity.	13-6 13-7	13-6A, 13-6B 13-7A, 13-7B

7. Describe the effect of stock splits on corporate financial statements.

Key Points	Key Learning Outcomes	Example Exercises	Practice Exercises
When a corporation reduces the par or stated value of its common stock and issues a proportionate number of additional shares, a stock split has occurred. There are no changes in the balances of any accounts, and no entry is required for a stock split.	• Define and give an example of a stock split. • Describe the accounting for and effects of a stock split on the financial statements.		

Key Terms

cash dividend (578)
common stock (572)
deficit (572)
discount (574)
dividend yield (587)
outstanding stock (572)
paid-in capital (571)
par (572)
preferred stock (573)

premium (574)
prior period adjustments (585)
restrictions (584)
retained earnings (571)
retained earnings statement (584)
stated value (572)
statement of stockholders' equity (585)
stock (568)

stock dividend (580)
stock split (586)
stockholders (568)
stockholders' equity (571)
treasury stock (581)

Illustrative Problem

Altenburg Inc. is a lighting fixture wholesaler located in Arizona. During its current fiscal year, ended December 31, 2008, Altenburg Inc. completed the following selected transactions:

Feb. 3. Purchased 2,500 shares of its own common stock at $26, recording the stock at cost. (Prior to the purchase, there were 40,000 shares of $20 par common stock outstanding.)

May 1. Declared a semiannual dividend of $1 on the 10,000 shares of preferred stock and a 30¢ dividend on the common stock to stockholders of record on May 31, payable on June 15.

June 15. Paid the cash dividends.

Sept. 23. Sold 1,000 shares of treasury stock at $28, receiving cash.

Nov. 1. Declared semiannual dividends of $1 on the preferred stock and 30¢ on the common stock. In addition, a 5% common stock dividend was declared on the common stock outstanding, to be capitalized at the fair market value of the common stock, which is estimated at $30.

Dec. 1. Paid the cash dividends and issued the certificates for the common stock dividend.

Instructions
Journalize the entries to record the transactions for Altenburg Inc.

Solution

2008				
Feb.	3	Treasury Stock	65 0 0 0 00	
		Cash		65 0 0 0 00
May	1	Cash Dividends	21 2 5 0 00	
		Cash Dividends Payable		21 2 5 0 00
		(10,000 × $1) + [(40,000 − 2,500)		
		× $0.30].		
June	15	Cash Dividends Payable	21 2 5 0 00	
		Cash		21 2 5 0 00
Sept.	23	Cash	28 0 0 0 00	
		Treasury Stock		26 0 0 0 00
		Paid-In Capital from Sale of Treasury Stock		2 0 0 0 00
Nov.	1	Cash Dividends	21 5 5 0 00	
		Cash Dividends Payable		21 5 5 0 00
		(10,000 × $1) + [(40,000 − 1,500)		
		× $0.30].		
	1	Stock Dividends	57 7 5 0 00 *	
		Stock Dividends Distributable		38 5 0 0 00
		Paid-In Capital in Excess of		
		Par—Common Stock		19 2 5 0 00
		*(40,000 − 1,500) × 5% × $30.		
Dec.	1	Cash Dividends Payable	21 5 5 0 00	
		Stock Dividends Distributable	38 5 0 0 00	
		Cash		21 5 5 0 00
		Common Stock		38 5 0 0 00

Self-Examination Questions

(Answers at End of Chapter)

1. Which of the following is a disadvantage of the corporate form of organization?
   A. Limited liability
   B. Continuous life
   C. Owner is separate from management
   D. Ability to raise capital

2. Paid-in capital for a corporation may arise from which of the following sources?
   A. Issuing preferred stock
   B. Issuing common stock
   C. Selling the corporation's treasury stock
   D. All of the above

3. The Stockholders' Equity section of the balance sheet may include:
   A. Common Stock.
   B. Stock Dividends Distributable.
   C. Preferred Stock.
   D. All of the above.

4. If a corporation reacquires its own stock, the stock is listed on the balance sheet in the:
   A. Current Assets section.
   B. Long-Term Liabilities section.
   C. Stockholders' Equity section.
   D. Investments section.

5. A corporation has issued 25,000 shares of $100 par common stock and holds 3,000 of these shares as treasury stock. If the corporation declares a $2 per share cash dividend, what amount will be recorded as cash dividends?
   A. $22,000   C. $44,000
   B. $25,000   D. $50,000

Eye Openers

1. Describe the stockholders' liability to creditors of a corporation.
2. Why are most large businesses organized as corporations?
3. Of two corporations organized at approximately the same time and engaged in competing businesses, one issued $150 par common stock, and the other issued $1 par common stock. Do the par designations provide any indication as to which stock is preferable as an investment? Explain.
4. A stockbroker advises a client to "buy preferred stock. . . . With that type of stock, . . . [you] will never have to worry about losing the dividends." Is the broker right?
5. What are some of the factors that influence the market price of a corporation's stock?
6. When a corporation issues stock at a premium, is the premium income? Explain.
7. (a) What are the three conditions for the declaration and the payment of a cash dividend? (b) The dates in connection with the declaration of a cash dividend are February 6, March 9, and April 5. Identify each date.
8. A corporation with both preferred stock and common stock outstanding has a substantial credit balance in its retained earnings account at the beginning of the current fiscal year. Although net income for the current year is sufficient to pay the preferred dividend of $250,000 each quarter and a common dividend of $610,000 each quarter, the board of directors declares dividends only on the preferred stock. Suggest possible reasons for passing the dividends on the common stock.
9. An owner of 200 shares of Felt Company common stock receives a stock dividend of 4 shares. (a) What is the effect of the stock dividend on the stockholder's proportionate interest (equity) in the corporation? (b) How does the total equity of 204 shares compare with the total equity of 200 shares before the stock dividend?
10. a. Where should a declared but unpaid cash dividend be reported on the balance sheet?
    b. Where should a declared but unissued stock dividend be reported on the balance sheet?
11. a. In what respect does treasury stock differ from unissued stock?
    b. How should treasury stock be presented on the balance sheet?
12. A corporation reacquires 8,000 shares of its own $10 par common stock for $120,000, recording it at cost. (a) What effect does this transaction have on revenue or expense of the period? (b) What effect does it have on stockholders' equity?

13. The treasury stock in Eye Opener 12 is resold for $158,000. (a) What is the effect on the corporation's revenue of the period? (b) What is the effect on stockholders' equity?
14. What is the primary advantage of combining the retained earnings statement with the income statement?
15. What are the three classifications of restrictions of retained earnings, and how are such restrictions normally reported in the financial statements?
16. Indicate how prior period adjustments would be reported on the financial statements presented only for the current period.
17. When is a statement of stockholders' equity normally prepared?
18. What is the primary purpose of a stock split?

Practice Exercises

PE 13-1A
Dividends per share
obj. 3

Golf-Easy Company has 10,000 shares of 3% preferred stock of $50 par and 25,000 shares of $100 par common stock. The following amounts were distributed as dividends:

Year 1	$ 40,000
Year 2	10,000
Year 3	120,000

Determine the dividends per share for preferred and common stock for each year.

PE 13-1B
Dividends per share
obj. 3

Marsala Company has 5,000 shares of 2% preferred stock of $75 par and 10,000 shares of $150 par common stock. The following amounts were distributed as dividends:

Year 1	$20,000
Year 2	4,000
Year 3	40,000

Determine the dividends per share for preferred and common stock for each year.

PE 13-2A
Entries for issuing stock
obj. 3

On August 3, Waterways Corporation issued for cash 45,000 shares of no-par common stock (with a stated value of $100) at $128. On September 22, Waterways issued at par 2,000 shares of 1%, $75 par preferred stock for cash. On November 4, Waterways issued for cash 3,000 shares of 1%, $75 par preferred stock at $80.
  Journalize the entries to record the August 3, September 22, and November 4 transactions.

PE 13-2B
Entries for issuing stock
obj. 3

On July 6, Istanbul Artifacts Corporation issued for cash 800,000 shares of no-par common stock at $1.20. On August 30, Istanbul Artifacts issued at par 10,000 shares of 2%, $50 par preferred stock for cash. On October 14, Istanbul Artifacts issued for cash 7,500 shares of 2%, $50 par preferred stock at $54.
  Journalize the entries to record the July 6, August 30, and October 14 transactions.

PE 13-3A
Entries for cash dividends
obj. 4

The important dates in connection with a cash dividend of $48,000 on a corporation's common stock are July 16, August 15, and September 30. Journalize the entries required on each date.

PE 13-3B
Entries for cash dividends
obj. 4

The important dates in connection with a cash dividend of $90,000 on a corporation's common stock are October 1, November 1, and December 24. Journalize the entries required on each date.

PE 13-4A
Entries for stock dividends
obj. 4

Stonehenge Corporation has 300,000 shares of $40 par common stock outstanding. On February 13, Stonehenge Corporation declared a 3% stock dividend to be issued April 30 to stockholders of record on March 14. The market price of the stock was $63 per share on February 13.

Journalize the entries required on February 13, March 14, and April 30.

PE 13-4B
Entries for stock dividends
obj. 4

Big Ben Corporation has 250,000 shares of $50 par common stock outstanding. On May 10, Big Ben Corporation declared a 2% stock dividend to be issued August 1 to stockholders of record on June 9. The market price of the stock was $60 per share on May 10.

Journalize the entries required on May 10, June 9, and August 1.

PE 13-5A
Entries for treasury stock
obj. 5

On January 24, Thunderstorm Inc. reacquired 6,000 shares of its common stock at $18 per share. On March 15, Thunderstorm sold 4,500 of the reacquired shares at $21 per share. On June 2, Thunderstorm sold the remaining shares at $17 per share.

Journalize the transactions of January 24, March 15, and June 2.

PE 13-5B
Entries for treasury stock
obj. 5

On October 2, Baja Clothing Inc. reacquired 12,000 shares of its common stock at $6 per share. On November 15, Baja Clothing sold 8,400 of the reacquired shares at $9 per share. On December 22, Baja Clothing sold the remaining shares at $5 per share.

Journalize the transactions of October 2, November 15, and December 22.

PE 13-6A
Stockholders' Equity section of balance sheet
obj. 6

Using the following accounts and balances, prepare the Stockholders' Equity section of the balance sheet. Thirty thousand shares of common stock are authorized, and 2,000 shares have been reacquired.

Common Stock, $80 par	$2,000,000
Paid-In Capital in Excess of Par	315,000
Paid-In Capital from Sale of Treasury Stock	33,000
Retained Earnings	1,112,000
Treasury Stock	180,000

PE 13-6B
Stockholders' Equity section of balance sheet
obj. 6

Using the following accounts and balances, prepare the Stockholders' Equity section of the balance sheet. Fifty thousand shares of common stock are authorized, and 5,000 shares have been reacquired.

Common Stock, $75 par	$3,375,000
Paid-In Capital in Excess of Par	485,000
Paid-In Capital from Sale of Treasury Stock	18,000
Retained Earnings	1,452,000
Treasury Stock	420,000

PE 13-7A
Retained earnings statement
obj. 6

Dynamic Leaders Inc. reported the following results for the year ending July 31, 2008:

Retained earnings, August 1, 2007	$988,500
Net income	325,000
Cash dividends declared	35,000
Stock dividends declared	90,000

Prepare a retained earnings statement for the fiscal year ended July 31, 2008.

PE 13-7B
Retained earnings statement
obj. 6

Maxima Retractors Inc. reported the following results for the year ending October 31, 2008:

Retained earnings, November 1, 2007	$2,906,000
Net income	553,000
Cash dividends declared	100,000
Stock dividends declared	200,000

Prepare a retained earnings statement for the fiscal year ended October 31, 2008.

Exercises

EX 13-1
Dividends per share
obj. 3

✓ *Preferred stock, 1st year: $0.80*

Electro-Rad Inc., a developer of radiology equipment, has stock outstanding as follows: 50,000 shares of 2%, preferred stock of $50 par, and 100,000 shares of $25 par common. During its first four years of operations, the following amounts were distributed as dividends: first year, $40,000; second year, $98,000; third year, $120,000; fourth year, $195,000. Calculate the dividends per share on each class of stock for each of the four years.

EX 13-2
Dividends per share
obj. 3

✓ *Preferred stock, 1st year: $0.15*

CompuLead Inc., a software development firm, has stock outstanding as follows: 40,000 shares of 1%, preferred stock of $25 par, and 50,000 shares of $75 par common. During its first four years of operations, the following amounts were distributed as dividends: first year, $6,000; second year, $26,000; third year, $4,000; fourth year, $60,000. Calculate the dividends per share on each class of stock for each of the four years.

EX 13-3
Entries for issuing par stock
obj. 3

On February 4, Cinderella Rocks Inc., a marble contractor, issued for cash 30,000 shares of $20 par common stock at $64, and on March 31, it issued for cash 18,000 shares of $75 par preferred stock at $90.

a. Journalize the entries for February 4 and March 31.
b. What is the total amount invested (total paid-in capital) by all stockholders as of March 31?

EX 13-4
Entries for issuing no-par stock
obj. 3

On July 17, America Carpet Inc., a carpet wholesaler, issued for cash 150,000 shares of no-par common stock (with a stated value of $5) at $36, and on September 20, it issued for cash 10,000 shares of $50 par preferred stock at $80.

a. Journalize the entries for July 17 and September 20, assuming that the common stock is to be credited with the stated value.
b. What is the total amount invested (total paid-in capital) by all stockholders as of September 20?

EX 13-5
Issuing stock for assets other than cash
obj. 3

On November 10, Craddock's Corporation, a wholesaler of hydraulic lifts, acquired land in exchange for 15,000 shares of $8 par common stock with a current market price of $32. Journalize the entry to record the transaction.

EX 13-6
Selected stock transactions
obj. 3

Country Sounds Corp., an electric guitar retailer, was organized by Julie Arnold, Joe Harris, and Scott Pickens. The charter authorized 500,000 shares of common stock with a par of $12. The following transactions affecting stockholders' equity were completed during the first year of operations:

a. Issued 20,000 shares of stock at par to Julie Arnold for cash.
b. Issued 500 shares of stock at par to Scott Pickens for promotional services provided in connection with the organization of the corporation, and issued 18,000 shares of stock at par to Scott Pickens for cash.
c. Purchased land and a building from Joe Harris. The building is mortgaged for $200,000 for 25 years at 7%, and there is accrued interest of $2,200 on the mortgage note at the time of the purchase. It is agreed that the land is to be priced at $75,000 and the building at $240,000, and that Joe Harris's equity will be exchanged for stock at par. The corporation agreed to assume responsibility for paying the mortgage note and the accrued interest.

Journalize the entries to record the transactions.

EX 13-7
Issuing stock
obj. 3

Angel Creek Nursey, with an authorization of 40,000 shares of preferred stock and 150,000 shares of common stock, completed several transactions involving its stock on August 15, the first day of operations. The trial balance at the close of the day follows:

Cash	450,000	
Land	100,000	
Buildings	80,000	
Preferred 2% Stock, $80 par		160,000
Paid-In Capital in Excess of Par—Preferred Stock		20,000
Common Stock, $50 par		400,000
Paid-In Capital in Excess of Par—Common Stock		50,000
	630,000	630,000

All shares within each class of stock were sold at the same price. The preferred stock was issued in exchange for the land and buildings.

Journalize the two entries to record the transactions summarized in the trial balance.

EX 13-8
Issuing stock
obj. 3

Heritage Products Inc., a wholesaler of office products, was organized on February 19 of the current year, with an authorization of 60,000 shares of 3% preferred stock, $40 par and 300,000 shares of $75 par common stock. The following selected transactions were completed during the first year of operations:

Feb. 19. Issued 20,000 shares of common stock at par for cash.
    27. Issued 100 shares of common stock at par to an attorney in payment of legal fees for organizing the corporation.
Mar. 13. Issued 6,000 shares of common stock in exchange for land, buildings, and equipment with fair market prices of $80,000, $350,000, and $45,000, respectively.
May 6. Issued 5,000 shares of preferred stock at $46 for cash.

Journalize the transactions.

EX 13-9
Entries for cash dividends
obj. 4

The dates of importance in connection with a cash dividend of $275,000 on a corporation's common stock are July 2, August 1, and September 1. Journalize the entries required on each date.

EX 13-10
Entries for stock dividends
obj. 4

✓ b. (1) $34,500,000
(3) $85,100,000

Earthworks Health Co. is an HMO for 12 businesses in the St. Louis area. The following account balances appear on the balance sheet of Earthworks Health Co.: Common stock (400,000 shares authorized), $100 par, $30,000,000; Paid-in capital in excess of par—common stock, $4,500,000; and Retained earnings, $50,600,000. The board of directors declared a 2% stock dividend when the market price of the stock was $120 a share. Earthworks Health Co. reported no income or loss for the current year.

a. Journalize the entries to record (1) the declaration of the dividend, capitalizing an amount equal to market value, and (2) the issuance of the stock certificates.
b. Determine the following amounts before the stock dividend was declared: (1) total paid-in capital, (2) total retained earnings, and (3) total stockholders' equity.
c. Determine the following amounts after the stock dividend was declared and closing entries were recorded at the end of the year: (1) total paid-in capital, (2) total retained earnings, and (3) total stockholders' equity.

EX 13-11
Treasury stock transactions
obj. 5

✓ b. $9,000 credit

Mountain Springs Inc. bottles and distributes spring water. On May 2 of the current year, Mountain Springs reacquired 3,000 shares of its common stock at $72 per share. On August 14, Mountain Springs sold 2,500 of the reacquired shares at $76 per share. The remaining 500 shares were sold at $70 per share on November 7.

a. Journalize the transactions of May 2, August 14, and November 7.
b. What is the balance in Paid-In Capital from Sale of Treasury Stock on December 31 of the current year?
c. ▬▬▬► For what reasons might Mountain Springs have purchased the treasury stock?

EX 13-12
Treasury stock transactions
objs. 5, 6
✓ b. $36,900 credit

Azalea Gardens Inc. develops and produces spraying equipment for lawn maintenance and industrial uses. On September 9 of the current year, Azalea Gardens Inc. reacquired 12,000 shares of its common stock at $89 per share. On October 31, 10,500 of the reacquired shares were sold at $92 per share, and on December 4, 900 of the reacquired shares were sold at $95.

a. Journalize the transactions of September 9, October 31, and December 4.
b. What is the balance in Paid-In Capital from Sale of Treasury Stock on December 31 of the current year?
c. What is the balance in Treasury Stock on December 31 of the current year?
d. How will the balance in Treasury Stock be reported on the balance sheet?

EX 13-13
Treasury stock transactions
objs. 5, 6
✓ b. $12,000 credit

Tacoma Inc. bottles and distributes spring water. On June 12 of the current year, Tacoma Inc. reacquired 15,000 shares of its common stock at $48 per share. On August 10, Tacoma Inc. sold 9,000 of the reacquired shares at $50 per share. The remaining 6,000 shares were sold at $47 per share on December 20.

a. Journalize the transactions of June 12, August 10, and December 20.
b. What is the balance in Paid-In Capital from Sale of Treasury Stock on December 31 of the current year?
c. Where will the balance in Paid-In Capital from Sale of Treasury Stock be reported on the balance sheet?
d. ▬▬▶ For what reasons might Tacoma Inc. have purchased the treasury stock?

EX 13-14
Reporting paid-in capital
obj. 6
✓ Total paid-in capital, $2,494,500

The following accounts and their balances were selected from the unadjusted trial balance of Sailors Inc., a freight forwarder, at August 31, the end of the current fiscal year:

Preferred 3% Stock, $100 par	$1,500,000
Paid-In Capital in Excess of Par—Preferred Stock	180,000
Common Stock, no par, $10 stated value	675,000
Paid-In Capital in Excess of Stated Value—Common Stock	125,000
Paid-In Capital from Sale of Treasury Stock	14,500
Retained Earnings	2,106,500

Prepare the Paid-In Capital portion of the Stockholders' Equity section of the balance sheet. There are 500,000 shares of common stock authorized and 50,000 shares of preferred stock authorized.

EX 13-15
Stockholders' Equity section of balance sheet
obj. 6
✓ Total stockholders' equity, $4,020,000

The following accounts and their balances appear in the ledger of Heart and Saul Inc. on April 30 of the current year:

Common Stock, $50 par	$ 900,000
Paid-In Capital in Excess of Par	110,000
Paid-In Capital from Sale of Treasury Stock	42,000
Retained Earnings	3,178,000
Treasury Stock	210,000

Prepare the Stockholders' Equity section of the balance sheet as of April 30. Twenty-five thousand shares of common stock are authorized, and 3,500 shares have been reacquired.

EX 13-16
Stockholders' Equity section of balance sheet
obj. 6
✓ Total stockholders' equity, $4,726,500

Sports Car Inc. retails racing products for BMWs, Porsches, and Ferraris. The following accounts and their balances appear in the ledger of Sports Car Inc. on November 30, the end of the current year:

Common Stock, $5 par	$ 875,000
Paid-In Capital in Excess of Par—Common Stock	700,000
Paid-In Capital in Excess of Par—Preferred Stock	25,000
Paid-In Capital from Sale of Treasury Stock—Common	16,000
Preferred 3% Stock, $75 par	937,500
Retained Earnings	2,338,000
Treasury Stock—Common	165,000

Twenty thousand shares of preferred and 400,000 shares of common stock are authorized. There are 22,000 shares of common stock held as treasury stock.

Prepare the Stockholders' Equity section of the balance sheet as of November 30, the end of the current year.

EX 13-17
Retained earnings statement

obj. 6

✓ *Retained earnings, August 31, $1,950,000*

Stillwater Corporation, a manufacturer of industrial pumps, reports the following results for the year ending August 31, 2008:

Retained earnings, September 1, 2007	$1,752,000
Net income	378,000
Cash dividends declared	80,000
Stock dividends declared	100,000

Prepare a retained earnings statement for the fiscal year ended August 31, 2008.

EX 13-18
Stockholders' Equity section of balance sheet

obj. 6

✓ *Corrected total stockholders' equity, $5,439,000*

List the errors in the following Stockholders' Equity section of the balance sheet prepared as of the end of the current year.

Stockholders' Equity

Paid-in capital:		
Preferred 1% stock, $75 par		
(8,000 shares authorized and issued)	$ 600,000	
Excess of issue price over par	56,000	$ 656,000
Retained earnings		1,278,000
Treasury stock (4,000 shares at cost)		320,000
Dividends payable		18,000
Total paid-in capital		$2,272,000
Common stock, $50 par (100,000 shares		
authorized, 60,000 shares issued)		3,900,000
Organizing costs		75,000
Total stockholders' equity		$6,247,000

EX 13-19
Statement of stockholders' equity

obj. 6

✓ *Total stockholders' equity, Dec. 31, $3,529,000*

The stockholders' equity T accounts of Family Greeting Cards Inc. for the current fiscal year ended December 31, 2008, are as follows. Prepare a statement of stockholders' equity for the fiscal year ended December 31, 2008.

COMMON STOCK

	Jan.	1	Balance	600,000
	Apr.	9	Issued	
			50,000 shares	150,000
	Dec. 31		Balance	750,000

PAID-IN CAPITAL IN EXCESS OF PAR

	Jan.	1	Balance	350,000
	Apr.	9	Issued	
			50,000 shares	100,000
	Dec. 31		Balance	450,000

TREASURY STOCK

Aug. 7	Purchased	
	6,000 shares	24,000

RETAINED EARNINGS

June 30	Dividend	40,000	Jan.	1	Balance	2,108,000
Dec. 30	Dividend	40,000	Dec. 31		Closing	
					(net income)	325,000
		___	Dec. 31		Balance	2,353,000

EX 13-20
Effect of stock split
obj. 7

Rolling Pin Corporation wholesales ovens and ranges to restaurants throughout the Midwest. Rolling Pin Corporation, which had 50,000 shares of common stock outstanding, declared a 3-for-1 stock split (2 additional shares for each share issued).

a. What will be the number of shares outstanding after the split?
b. If the common stock had a market price of $180 per share before the stock split, what would be an approximate market price per share after the split?

EX 13-21
Effect of cash dividend and stock split
objs. 4, 7

Indicate whether the following actions would (+) increase, (−) decrease, or (0) not affect Indigo Inc.'s total assets, liabilities, and stockholders' equity:

		Assets	Liabilities	Stockholders' Equity
(1)	Declaring a cash dividend	_____	_____	_____
(2)	Paying the cash dividend declared in (1)	_____	_____	_____
(3)	Authorizing and issuing stock certificates in a stock split	_____	_____	_____
(4)	Declaring a stock dividend	_____	_____	_____
(5)	Issuing stock certificates for the stock dividend declared in (4)	_____	_____	_____

EX 13-22
Selected dividend transactions, stock split
objs. 4, 7

Selected transactions completed by NuCraft Boating Supply Corporation during the current fiscal year are as follows:

Mar. 5. Split the common stock 4 for 1 and reduced the par from $100 to $25 per share. After the split, there were 800,000 common shares outstanding.
May 15. Declared semiannual dividends of $2 on 15,000 shares of preferred stock and $0.12 on the common stock to stockholders of record on June 14, payable on July 14.
July 14. Paid the cash dividends.
Nov. 15. Declared semiannual dividends of $2 on the preferred stock and $0.14 on the common stock (before the stock dividend). In addition, a 1% common stock dividend was declared on the common stock outstanding. The fair market value of the common stock is estimated at $30.
Dec. 15. Paid the cash dividends and issued the certificates for the common stock dividend.

Journalize the transactions.

EX 13-23
Dividend yield

At the market close on May 12, 2006, Bank of America Corporation had a closing stock price of $49.69. In addition, Bank of America had earnings per share of $4.05 and dividend per share was $1.95. Determine Bank of America's dividend yield. Round to one decimal place.

EX 13-24
Dividend yield

General Electric Company had earnings per share of $1.72 for 2005 and $1.56 for 2004. In addition, the dividends per share were $0.91 for 2005 and $0.82 for 2004. The market price of GE's stock closed at $35.05 and $36.50 on December 31, 2005 and 2004, respectively.

a. Determine the dividend yield for General Electric on December 31, 2005 and 2004. Round percentages to two decimal places.
b. ━━━ Interpret these measures.

EX 13-25
Dividend yield

eBay Inc. developed a Web-based marketplace at **http://www.ebay.com**, in which individuals can buy and sell a variety of items. eBay also acquired PayPal, an online payments system that allows businesses and individuals to send and receive online payments securely. In a recent annual report, eBay published the following dividend policy:

We have never paid cash dividends on our stock, and currently anticipate that we will continue to retain any future earnings to finance the growth of our business.

Given eBay's dividend policy, why would an investor be attracted to its stock?

Problems Series A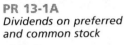

PR 13-1A
Dividends on preferred and common stock

obj. 3

✓ *1. Common dividends in 2004: $20,000*

Olympic Theatre Inc. owns and operates movie theaters throughout Texas and California. Olympic Theatre has declared the following annual dividends over a six-year period: 2003, $21,000; 2004, $50,000; 2005, $15,000; 2006, $80,000; 2007, $90,000; and 2008, $140,000. During the entire period, the outstanding stock of the company was composed of 10,000 shares of 4% preferred stock, $75 par, and 100,000 shares of common stock, $10 par.

Instructions
1. Calculate the total dividends and the per-share dividends declared on each class of stock for each of the six years. Summarize the data in tabular form, using the following column headings:

Year	Total Dividends	Preferred Dividends		Common Dividends	
		Total	Per Share	Total	Per Share
2003	$ 21,000				
2004	50,000				
2005	15,000				
2006	80,000				
2007	90,000				
2008	140,000				

2. Calculate the average annual dividend per share for each class of stock for the six-year period.
3. Assuming that the preferred stock was sold at $80 and common stock was sold at par at the beginning of the six-year period, calculate the average annual percentage return on initial shareholders' investment, based on the average annual dividend per share (a) for preferred stock and (b) for common stock.

PR 13-2A
Stock transactions for corporate expansion

obj. 3

On January 31 of the current year, the following accounts and their balances appear in the ledger of Gargantuan Corp., a meat processor:

Preferred 3% Stock, $25 par (50,000 shares authorized, 30,000 shares issued)	$ 750,000
Paid-In Capital in Excess of Par—Preferred Stock	90,000
Common Stock, $30 par (400,000 shares authorized, 120,000 shares issued)	3,600,000
Paid-In Capital in Excess of Par—Common Stock	300,000
Retained Earnings	5,794,000

At the annual stockholders' meeting on April 2, the board of directors presented a plan for modernizing and expanding plant operations at a cost of approximately $2,550,000. The plan provided (a) that a building, valued at $1,200,000, and the land on which it is located, valued at $300,000, be acquired in accordance with preliminary negotiations by the issuance of 45,000 shares of common stock, (b) that 15,000 shares of the unissued preferred stock be issued through an underwriter, and (c) that the corporation borrow $500,000. The plan was approved by the stockholders and accomplished by the following transactions:

June 6. Issued 45,000 shares of common stock in exchange for land and a building, according to the plan.
14. Issued 15,000 shares of preferred stock, receiving $36 per share in cash.
30. Borrowed $500,000 from Mt. Baker National Bank, giving a 7% mortgage note.

No other transactions occurred during June.

Instructions

Journalize the entries to record the foregoing transactions.

PR 13-3A
Selected stock transactions

objs. 3, 4, 5

f. Cash dividends, $86,500

The following selected accounts appear in the ledger of Clear Skies Environmental Corporation on July 1, 2008, the beginning of the current fiscal year:

Preferred 2% Stock, $100 par (25,000 shares authorized, 18,000 shares issued)	$1,800,000
Paid-In Capital in Excess of Par—Preferred Stock	216,000
Common Stock, $40 par (100,000 shares authorized, 70,000 shares issued)	2,800,000
Paid-In Capital in Excess of Par—Common Stock	700,000
Retained Earnings	3,200,000

During the year, the corporation completed a number of transactions affecting the stockholders' equity. They are summarized as follows:

a. Issued 12,000 shares of common stock at $62, receiving cash.
b. Sold 5,000 shares of preferred 2% stock at $124.
c. Purchased 10,000 shares of treasury common for $580,000.
d. Sold 7,500 shares of treasury common for $457,500.
e. Sold 1,500 shares of treasury common for $82,500.
f. Declared cash dividends of $2 per share on preferred stock and $0.50 per share on common stock.
g. Paid the cash dividends.

Instructions

Journalize the entries to record the transactions. Identify each entry by letter.

PR 13-4A
Entries for selected corporate transactions

objs. 3, 4, 5, 6

✓ *4. Total stockholders' equity, $9,869,000*

Eureka Enterprises Inc. manufactures bathroom fixtures. The stockholders' equity accounts of Eureka Enterprises Inc., with balances on January 1, 2008, are as follows:

Common Stock, $10 stated value (500,000 shares authorized, 380,000 shares issued)	$3,800,000
Paid-In Capital in Excess of Stated Value	760,000
Retained Earnings	4,390,000
Treasury Stock (25,000 shares, at cost)	500,000

The following selected transactions occurred during the year:

Jan. 10. Paid cash dividends of $0.20 per share on the common stock. The dividend had been properly recorded when declared on December 30 of the preceding fiscal year for $71,000.

Mar. 3. Issued 20,000 shares of common stock for $460,000.

May 21. Sold all of the treasury stock for $650,000.

July 1. Declared a 3% stock dividend on common stock, to be capitalized at the market price of the stock, which is $30 per share.

Aug. 15. Issued the certificates for the dividend declared on July 1.

Sept. 30. Purchased 10,000 shares of treasury stock for $230,000.

Dec. 27. Declared a $0.25-per-share dividend on common stock.

31. Closed the credit balance of the income summary account, $639,500.

31. Closed the two dividends accounts to Retained Earnings.

Instructions

1. Enter the January 1 balances in T accounts for the stockholders' equity accounts listed. Also prepare T accounts for the following: Paid-In Capital from Sale of Treasury Stock; Stock Dividends Distributable; Stock Dividends; Cash Dividends.
2. Journalize the entries to record the transactions, and post to the eight selected accounts.
3. Prepare a retained earnings statement for the year ended December 31, 2008.
4. Prepare the Stockholders' Equity section of the December 31, 2008, balance sheet.

PR 13-5A
Entries for selected corporate transactions

objs. 3, 4, 5, 7

✓ *Nov. 15, cash dividends, $82,800*

Selected transactions completed by Oceano Boating Corporation during the current fiscal year are as follows:

Jan. 3. Split the common stock 2 for 1 and reduced the par from $50 to $25 per share. After the split, there were 400,000 common shares outstanding.

Feb. 20. Purchased 50,000 shares of the corporation's own common stock at $32, recording the stock at cost.

May 1. Declared semiannual dividends of $0.80 on 30,000 shares of preferred stock and $0.14 on the common stock to stockholders of record on May 15, payable on June 1.

June 1. Paid the cash dividends.

Aug. 5. Sold 42,000 shares of treasury stock at $39, receiving cash.

Nov. 15. Declared semiannual dividends of $0.80 on the preferred stock and $0.15 on the common stock (before the stock dividend). In addition, a 2% common stock dividend was declared on the common stock outstanding. The fair market value of the common stock is estimated at $40.

Dec. 31. Paid the cash dividends and issued the certificates for the common stock dividend.

Instructions
Journalize the transactions.

Problems Series B

PR 13-1B
Dividends on preferred and common stock

obj. 3

✓ *1. Common dividends in 2003: $40,000*

Rainer Bike Corp. manufactures mountain bikes and distributes them through retail outlets in Oregon and Washington. Rainer Bike Corp. has declared the following annual dividends over a six-year period: 2003, $60,000; 2004, $8,000; 2005, $30,000; 2006, $40,000; 2007, $80,000; and 2008, $115,000. During the entire period, the outstanding stock of the company was composed of 40,000 shares of 2% preferred stock, $25 par, and 50,000 shares of common stock, $1 par.

Instructions

1. Determine the total dividends and the per-share dividends declared on each class of stock for each of the six years. Summarize the data in tabular form, using the following column headings:

Year	Total Dividends	Preferred Dividends		Common Dividends	
		Total	Per Share	Total	Per Share
2003	$ 60,000				
2004	8,000				
2005	30,000				
2006	40,000				
2007	80,000				
2008	115,000				

2. Determine the average annual dividend per share for each class of stock for the six-year period.

3. Assuming that the preferred stock was sold at par and common stock was sold at $18.75 at the beginning of the six-year period, calculate the average annual percentage return on initial shareholders' investment, based on the average annual dividend per share (a) for preferred stock and (b) for common stock.

PR 13-2B
Stock transaction for corporate expansion

obj. 3

I-Can-See Optics produces medical lasers for use in hospitals. The accounts and their balances appear in the ledger of I-Can-See Optics on November 30 of the current year at the top of the following page.

Preferred 2% Stock, $80 par (40,000 shares authorized,	
25,000 shares issued)	$ 2,000,000
Paid-In Capital in Excess of Par—Preferred Stock	120,000
Common Stock, $100 par (500,000 shares authorized,	
50,000 shares issued)	5,000,000
Paid-In Capital in Excess of Par—Common Stock	300,000
Retained Earnings	12,794,000

At the annual stockholders' meeting on December 10, the board of directors presented a plan for modernizing and expanding plant operations at a cost of approximately $3,800,000. The plan provided (a) that the corporation borrow $900,000, (b) that 10,000 shares of the unissued preferred stock be issued through an underwriter, and (c) that a building, valued at $1,675,000, and the land on which it is located, valued at $250,000, be acquired in accordance with preliminary negotiations by the issuance of 16,000 shares of common stock. The plan was approved by the stockholders and accomplished by the following transactions:

Jan.   6. Borrowed $900,000 from City National Bank, giving a 6% mortgage note.
      15. Issued 10,000 shares of preferred stock, receiving $95 per share in cash.
      31. Issued 16,000 shares of common stock in exchange for land and a building, according to the plan.

No other transactions occurred during January.

Instructions
Journalize the entries to record the foregoing transactions.

PR 13-3B
Selected stock transactions
objs. 3, 4, 5

✓ f. Cash dividends, $123,900

Buellton Welding Corporation sells and services pipe welding equipment in California. The following selected accounts appear in the ledger of Buellton Welding Corporation on January 1, 2008, the beginning of the current fiscal year:

Preferred 2% Stock, $50 par (100,000 shares authorized,	
50,000 shares issued)	$ 2,500,000
Paid-In Capital in Excess of Par—Preferred Stock	180,000
Common Stock, $15 par (900,000 shares authorized,	
600,000 shares issued)	9,000,000
Paid-In Capital in Excess of Par—Common Stock	1,500,000
Retained Earnings	13,100,000

During the year, the corporation completed a number of transactions affecting the stockholders' equity. They are summarized as follows:

a. Purchased 25,000 shares of treasury common for $650,000.
b. Sold 18,000 shares of treasury common for $576,000.
c. Sold 10,000 shares of preferred 2% stock at $80.
d. Issued 40,000 shares of common stock at $30, receiving cash.
e. Sold 6,000 shares of treasury common for $150,000.
f. Declared cash dividends of $1 per share on preferred stock and $0.10 per share on common stock.
g. Paid the cash dividends.

Instructions
Journalize the entries to record the transactions. Identify each entry by letter.

PR 13-4B
Entries for selected corporate transactions
objs. 3, 4, 5, 6

✓ 4. Total stockholders' equity, $11,160,300

GPS Enterprises Inc. produces aeronautical navigation equipment. The stockholders' equity accounts of GPS Enterprises Inc., with balances on January 1, 2008, are as follows:

Common Stock, $20 stated value (250,000 shares authorized,	
150,000 shares issued)	$3,000,000
Paid-In Capital in Excess of Stated Value	600,000
Retained Earnings	6,175,000
Treasury Stock (10,000 shares, at cost)	280,000

The following selected transactions occurred during the year:

Jan. 12. Paid cash dividends of $0.25 per share on the common stock. The dividend had been properly recorded when declared on December 28 of the preceding fiscal year for $35,000.

Feb. 19. Sold all of the treasury stock for $360,000.

Apr. 3. Issued 40,000 shares of common stock for $1,600,000.

July 30. Declared a 2% stock dividend on common stock, to be capitalized at the market price of the stock, which is $45 per share.

Aug. 30. Issued the certificates for the dividend declared on July 30.

Nov. 7. Purchased 15,000 shares of treasury stock for $600,000.

Dec. 30. Declared a $0.25-per-share dividend on common stock.

31. Closed the credit balance of the income summary account, $350,000.

31. Closed the two dividends accounts to Retained Earnings.

Instructions

1. Enter the January 1 balances in T accounts for the stockholders' equity accounts listed. Also prepare T accounts for the following: Paid-In Capital from Sale of Treasury Stock; Stock Dividends Distributable; Stock Dividends; Cash Dividends.

2. Journalize the entries to record the transactions, and post to the eight selected accounts.

3. Prepare a retained earnings statement for the year ended December 31, 2008.

4. Prepare the Stockholders' Equity section of the December 31, 2008, balance sheet.

PR 13-5B
Entries for selected corporate transactions

objs. 3, 4, 5, 7

✓ *Sept. 1, Cash dividends, $169,100*

Moro Bay Corporation manufactures and distributes leisure clothing. Selected transactions completed by Moro Bay during the current fiscal year are as follows:

Jan. 10. Split the common stock 4 for 1 and reduced the par from $20 to $5 per share. After the split, there were 500,000 common shares outstanding.

Mar. 1. Declared semiannual dividends of $1 on 125,000 shares of preferred stock and $0.12 on the 500,000 shares of $5 par common stock to stockholders of record on March 31, payable on April 30.

Apr. 30. Paid the cash dividends.

July 9. Purchased 40,000 shares of the corporation's own common stock at $16, recording the stock at cost.

Aug. 29. Sold 30,000 shares of treasury stock at $21, receiving cash.

Sept. 1. Declared semiannual dividends of $1 on the preferred stock and $0.09 on the common stock (before the stock dividend). In addition, a 1% common stock dividend was declared on the common stock outstanding, to be capitalized at the fair market value of the common stock, which is estimated at $22.

Oct. 31. Paid the cash dividends and issued the certificates for the common stock dividend.

Instructions

Journalize the transactions.

Special Activities

SA 13-1
Board of directors' actions

Bernie Ebbers, the CEO of WorldCom, a major telecommunications company, was having personal financial troubles. Ebbers pledged a large stake of his WorldCom stock as security for some personal loans. As the price of WorldCom stock sank, Ebbers' bankers threatened to sell his stock in order to protect their loans. To avoid having his stock sold, Ebbers asked the board of directors of WorldCom to loan him nearly $400 million of corporate assets at 2.5% interest to pay off his bankers. The board agreed to lend him the money.

Comment on the decision of the board of directors in this situation.

SA 13-2
Ethics and professional conduct in business

ETHICS

Gigi Liken and Ron Bobo are organizing Gold Unlimited Inc. to undertake a high-risk gold-mining venture in Canada. Gigi and Ron tentatively plan to request authorization for 75,000,000 shares of common stock to be sold to the general public. Gigi and Ron have decided to establish par of $1 per share in order to appeal to a wide variety of potential investors. Gigi and Ron feel that investors would be more willing to invest in the company if they received a large quantity of shares for what might appear to be a "bargain" price.

➡ Discuss whether Gigi and Ron are behaving in a professional manner.

SA 13-3
Issuing stock

Las Animas Inc. began operations on January 2, 2008, with the issuance of 100,000 shares of $50 par common stock. The sole stockholders of Las Animas Inc. are Cindy Stern and Dr. Kassay Heyen, who organized Las Animas Inc. with the objective of developing a new flu vaccine. Dr. Heyen claims that the flu vaccine, which is nearing the final development stage, will protect individuals against 80% of the flu types that have been medically identified. To complete the project, Las Animas Inc. needs $5,000,000 of additional funds. The local banks have been unwilling to loan the funds because of the lack of sufficient collateral and the riskiness of the business.

The following is a conversation between Cindy Stern, the chief executive officer of Las Animas Inc., and Dr. Kassay Heyen, the leading researcher.

Stern: What are we going to do? The banks won't loan us any more money, and we've got to have $5 million to complete the project. We are so close! It would be a disaster to quit now. The only thing I can think of is to issue additional stock. Do you have any suggestions?

Heyen: I guess you're right. But if the banks won't loan us any more money, how do you think we can find any investors to buy stock?

Stern: I've been thinking about that. What if we promise the investors that we will pay them 2% of net sales until they have received an amount equal to what they paid for the stock?

Heyen: What happens when we pay back the $5 million? Do the investors get to keep the stock? If they do, it'll dilute our ownership.

Stern: How about, if after we pay back the $5 million, we make them turn in their stock for $100 per share? That's twice what they paid for it, plus they would have already gotten all their money back. That's a $100 profit per share for the investors.

Heyen: It could work. We get our money, but don't have to pay any interest, dividends, or the $50 until we start generating net sales. At the same time, the investors could get their money back plus $50 per share.

Stern: We'll need current financial statements for the new investors. I'll get our accountant working on them and contact our attorney to draw up a legally binding contract for the new investors. Yes, this could work.

In late 2008, the attorney and the various regulatory authorities approved the new stock offering, and 100,000 shares of common stock were privately sold to new investors at the stock's par of $50.

In preparing financial statements for 2008, Cindy Stern and Debra Allen, the controller for Las Animas Inc., have the following conversation.

Allen: Cindy, I've got a problem.

Stern: What's that, Debra?

Allen: Issuing common stock to raise that additional $5 million was a great idea. But . . .

Stern: But what?

Allen: I've got to prepare the 2008 annual financial statements, and I am not sure how to classify the common stock.

Stern: What do you mean? It's common stock.

Allen: I'm not so sure. I called the auditor and explained how we are contractually obligated to pay the new stockholders 2% of net sales until $50 per share is paid. Then, we may be obligated to pay them $100 per share.

Stern: So . . .

Allen: So the auditor thinks that we should classify the additional issuance of $5 million as debt, not stock! And, if we put the $5 million on the balance sheet as debt, we will violate our other loan agreements with the banks. And, if these agreements are violated, the banks may call in all our debt immediately. If they do that, we are in deep trouble. We'll probably have to file for bankruptcy. We just don't have the cash to pay off the banks.

1. ▭▭▶ Discuss the arguments for and against classifying the issuance of the $5 million of stock as debt.
2. ▭▭▶ What do you think might be a practical solution to this classification problem?

SA 13-4
Interpret stock exchange listing

The Wall Street Journal reported the following stock exchange information for General Electric Company (GE) on May 12, 2006:

52 Weeks		Stock	Sym	Div	Yld%	PE	Vol 100s	LAST	Net Chg
Hi	Lo								
37^{34}	32^{21}	GenElec	GE	1.00	2.9	22	227,456	34^{51}	−.19

a. If you owned 500 shares of GE, what amount would you receive as a quarterly dividend?
b. Calculate and prove the dividend yield. Round to two decimal places.
c. What is GE's percentage change in market price from the May 10, 2006, close? Round to one decimal place.
d. If you bought 500 shares of GE at the close price on May 11, 2006, how much would it cost, and who gets the money?

SA 13-5
Dividends

Sentinel Inc. has paid quarterly cash dividends since 1995. These dividends have steadily increased from $0.05 per share to the latest dividend declaration of $0.40 per share. The board of directors would like to continue this trend and is hesitant to suspend or decrease the amount of quarterly dividends. Unfortunately, sales dropped sharply in the fourth quarter of 2008 because of worsening economic conditions and increased competition. As a result, the board is uncertain as to whether it should declare a dividend for the last quarter of 2008.

On November 1, 2008, Sentinel Inc. borrowed $800,000 from American National Bank to use in modernizing its retail stores and to expand its product line in reaction to its competition. The terms of the 10-year, 6% loan require Sentinel Inc. to:

a. Pay monthly interest on the last day of the month.
b. Pay $80,000 of the principal each November 1, beginning in 2009.
c. Maintain a current ratio (current assets/current liabilities) of 2.
d. Maintain a minimum balance (a compensating balance) of $40,000 in its American National Bank account.

On December 31, 2008, $200,000 of the $800,000 loan had been disbursed in modernization of the retail stores and in expansion of the product line. Sentinel Inc.'s balance sheet as of December 31, 2008, is shown at the top of the following page.

The board of directors is scheduled to meet January 6, 2009, to discuss the results of operations for 2008 and to consider the declaration of dividends for the fourth quarter of 2008. The chairman of the board has asked for your advice on the declaration of dividends.

1. ▭▭▶ What factors should the board consider in deciding whether to declare a cash dividend?
2. ▭▭▶ The board is considering the declaration of a stock dividend instead of a cash dividend. Discuss the issuance of a stock dividend from the point of view of (a) a stockholder and (b) the board of directors.

(continued)

Sentinel Inc.
Balance Sheet
December 31, 2008

Assets

Current assets:

Cash		$ 64,000
Marketable securities		600,000
Accounts receivable	$ 146,400	
Less allowance for doubtful accounts	10,400	136,000
Merchandise inventory		200,000
Prepaid expenses		7,200
Total current assets			$1,007,200

Property, plant, and equipment:

Land		$ 240,000	
Buildings	$1,520,000		
Less accumulated depreciation	344,000	1,176,000	
Equipment	$ 736,000		
Less accumulated depreciation	176,000	560,000	
Total property, plant, and equipment			1,976,000
Total assets			$2,983,200

Liabilities

Current liabilities:

Accounts payable	$ 114,880	
Notes payable (American National Bank)	80,000	
Salaries payable	5,120	
Total current liabilities		$ 200,000

Long-term liabilities:

Notes payable (American National Bank)	720,000	
Total liabilities		$ 920,000

Stockholders' Equity

Paid-in capital:

Common stock, $20 par (50,000 shares authorized, 40,000 shares issued)	$ 800,000	
Excess of issue price over par	64,000	
Total paid-in capital		$ 864,000
Retained earnings		1,199,200
Total stockholders' equity		2,063,200
Total liabilities and stockholders' equity		$2,983,200

SA 13-6
Profiling a corporation

Group Project

Internet Project

Select a public corporation you are familiar with or which interests you. Using the Internet, your school library, and other sources, develop a short (1 to 2 pages) profile of the corporation. Include in your profile the following information:

1. Name of the corporation.
2. State of incorporation.
3. Nature of its operations.
4. Total assets for the most recent balance sheet.
5. Total revenues for the most recent income statement.
6. Net income for the most recent income statement.
7. Classes of stock outstanding.
8. Market price of the stock outstanding.
9. High and low price of the stock for the past year.
10. Dividends paid for each share of stock during the past year.

In groups of three or four, discuss each corporate profile. Select one of the corporations, assuming that your group has $100,000 to invest in its stock. Summarize why your group selected the corporation it did and how financial accounting information may have affected your decision. Keep track of the performance of your corporation's stock for the remainder of the term.

Note: Most major corporations maintain "home pages" on the Internet. This home page provides a variety of information on the corporation and often includes the corporation's financial statements. In addition, the New York Stock Exchange Web site (**http://www.nyse .com**) includes links to the home pages of many listed companies. Financial statements can also be accessed using EDGAR, the electronic archives of financial statements filed with the Securities and Exchange Commission (SEC).

SEC documents can also be retrieved using the EdgarScan™ service from Pricewater- houseCoopers at **http://edgarscan.pwcglobal.com**. To obtain annual report information, key in a company name in the appropriate space. EdgarScan will list the reports available to you for the company you've selected. Select the most recent annual report filing, identified as a 10-K or 10-K405. EdgarScan provides an outline of the report, including the separate financial statements, which can also be selected in an Excel® spreadsheet.

Answers to Self-Examination Questions

1. **C** The separation of the owner from management (answer C) is a disadvantage of the corporate form of organization. This is because management may not always behave in the best interests of the owners. Limited liability (answer A), continuous life (answer B), and the ability to raise capital (answer D) are all advantages of the corporate form of organization.

2. **D** Paid-in capital is one of the two major subdivisions of the stockholders' equity of a corporation. It may result from many sources, including the issuance of preferred stock (answer A), issuing common stock (answer B), or the sale of a corporation's treasury stock (answer C).

3. **D** The Stockholders' Equity section of corporate balance sheets is divided into two principal subsections: (1) investments contributed by the stockholders and others and (2) net income retained in the business.

Included as part of the investments by stockholders and others is the par of common stock (answer A), stock dividends distributable (answer B), and the par of preferred stock (answer C).

4. **C** Reacquired stock, known as *treasury stock*, should be listed in the Stockholders' Equity section (answer C) of the balance sheet. The price paid for the treasury stock is deducted from the total of all the stockholders' equity accounts.

5. **C** If a corporation that holds treasury stock declares a cash dividend, the dividends are not paid on the treasury shares. To do so would place the corporation in the position of earning income through dealing with itself. Thus, the corporation will record $44,000 (answer C) as cash dividends [(25,000 shares issued less 3,000 shares held as treasury stock) × $2 per share dividend].

chapter 14

Income Taxes, Unusual Income Items, and Investments in Stocks

© NEIL BRAKE/ASSOCIATED PRESS

objectives

After studying this chapter, you should be able to:

1 *Journalize the entries for corporate income taxes, including deferred income taxes.*

2 *Describe and illustrate the reporting of unusual items on the income statement.*

3 *Prepare an income statement reporting earnings per share data.*

4 *Describe the concept and the reporting of comprehensive income.*

5 *Describe the accounting for investments in stocks.*

Gaylord Entertainment Co.

I f you apply for a bank loan, you will be required to list your assets and liabilities on a loan application. In addition, you will be asked to indicate your monthly income. Assume that the day you fill out the application, you win $4,000 in the state lottery. The $4,000 lottery winnings increase your assets by $4,000. Should you also show your lottery winnings as part of your monthly income?

The answer, of course, is no. Winning the lottery is an unusual event and, for most of us, a nonrecurring event. In determining whether to grant the loan, the bank is interested in your ability to make monthly loan payments. Such payments depend upon your recurring monthly income.

Businesses also experience unusual and nonrecurring events that affect their financial statements. Such events should be clearly disclosed in the financial statements so that stakeholders in the business will not misinterpret the financial effects of the events.

Gaylord Entertainment Co. is an example of such a company. Gaylord has pioneered the self-contained "all-in-one-place" hotel and resort concept, with the Gaylord Opryland, Gaylord Texan, and Gaylord Palms resorts. In addition, Gaylord owns ResortQuest and Ryman Auditorim (the original Grand Ole Opry) in Nashville, Tennessee. While Gaylord's operating income is positive, it has continued to report net losses over a number of recent years, due to losses from discontinued operations. Such unusual items are identified on Gaylord's income statement to alert users of the nonrecurring nature of some of its activities.

In this chapter, we discuss unusual items that affect income statements, such as those for Gaylord Entertainment, and illustrate how such items should be reported. We also discuss other specialized accounting and reporting topics, including accounting for income taxes, comprehensive income, and investments.

Corporate Income Taxes

objective 1

Journalize the entries for corporate income taxes, including deferred income taxes.

Under the U.S. tax code, corporations are taxable entities that must pay federal income taxes.[1] Depending upon where it is located, a corporation may also be required to pay state and local income taxes. Although we limit our discussion to federal income taxes, the basic concepts also apply to other income taxes.

PAYMENT OF INCOME TAXES

Most corporations are required to pay estimated federal income taxes in four installments throughout the year. For example, assume that a corporation with a calendar-year accounting period estimates its income tax expense for the year as $84,000. The entry to record the first of the four estimated tax payments of $21,000 (1/4 of $84,000) is as follows:

Individuals pay quarterly estimated taxes if the amount of tax withholding is not sufficient to pay their taxes at the end of the year. This usually occurs when a significant portion of an individual's income is from self-employment, rent, dividends, or interest.

Apr.	15	Income Tax Expense	21 0 0 0 00	
		Cash		21 0 0 0 00

---

1 Limited liability companies (LLCs) are not separate taxable entities and thus are not subject to federal (and most state) income taxes. For this reason, the material in this section would not generally apply to an LLC.

At year-end, the actual taxable income and the related tax are determined.[2] If additional taxes are owed, the additional liability is recorded. If the total estimated tax payments are greater than the tax liability based on actual taxable income, the overpayment should be debited to a receivable account and credited to *Income Tax Expense*.[3]

Income taxes are normally disclosed as a deduction at the bottom of the income statement in determining net income, as shown below, in an excerpt from an income statement for Procter & Gamble.

Year Ended June 30, 2005	(Amounts in Millions)
Net Sales	$56,741
Cost of products sold	27,804
Marketing, research, and administrative expenses	18,010
Income from Operations	$10,927
Interest expense	(834)
Other income, net	346
Earnings Before Income Taxes	$10,439
Income taxes	3,182
Net Earnings	$ 7,257

The ratio of reported income tax expense to earnings before taxes is shown for selected industries, as follows:

Industry	Percent of Reported Income Tax Expense to Earnings before Taxes
Automobiles	33%
Banking	35
Computers	23
Food	35
Integrated oil	39
Pharmaceuticals	30
Retail	39
Telecommunication	37
Transportation	38

As you can see, the reported income tax expense is normally between 30%–40% of earnings before tax. Therefore, taxes are a significant expense for most companies and must be considered when analyzing a company. Differences in tax rates between industries can be due to tax regulations unique to certain industries.

ALLOCATING INCOME TAXES

The **taxable income** of a corporation is determined according to the tax laws and is reported to taxing authorities on the corporation's tax return.[4] It is often different from the income before income taxes reported in the income statement according to

---

2 A corporation's income tax returns and supporting records are subject to audits by taxing authorities, who may assess additional taxes. Because of this possibility, the liability for income taxes is sometimes described in the balance sheet as *Estimated income tax payable*.

3 Another common term used for income taxes on the income statement and note disclosures is *Provision for income taxes*.

4 Accounting for deferred income taxes is a complex topic that is treated in greater detail in advanced accounting texts. The treatment here provides a general overview and conceptual understanding of the topic.

generally accepted accounting principles. As a result, the *income tax based on taxable income* usually differs from the *income tax based on income before taxes*. This difference may need to be allocated between various financial statement periods, depending on the nature of the items causing the differences.

Some differences between taxable income and income before income taxes are created because items are recognized in one period for tax purposes and in another period for income statement purposes. Such differences, called **temporary differences**, reverse or turn around in later years. Some examples of items that create temporary differences are listed below.

1. *Revenues or gains are taxed **after** they are reported in the income statement.* Example: In some cases, companies that make sales under an installment plan recognize revenue for financial reporting purposes when a sale is made but defer recognizing revenue for tax purposes until cash is collected.
2. *Expenses or losses are deducted in determining taxable income **after** they are reported in the income statement.* Example: Product warranty expense estimated and reported in the year of the sale for financial statement reporting is deducted for tax reporting when paid.
3. *Revenues or gains are taxed **before** they are reported in the income statement.* Example: Cash received in advance for magazine subscriptions is included in taxable income when received but included in the income statement only when earned in a future period.
4. *Expenses or losses are deducted in determining taxable income **before** they are reported in the income statement.* Example: MACRS depreciation is used for tax purposes, and the straight-line method is used for financial reporting purposes.

Since temporary differences reverse in later years, they do not change or reduce the total amount of taxable income over the life of a business. Exhibit 1 illustrates the reversing nature of temporary differences in which a business uses MACRS depreciation for tax purposes and straight-line depreciation for financial statement purposes. Exhibit 1 assumes that MACRS recognizes more depreciation in the early years and less depreciation in the later years. The total depreciation expense is the same for both methods over the life of the asset.

As Exhibit 1 illustrates, temporary differences affect only the timing of when revenues and expenses are recognized for tax purposes. As a result, the total amount of taxes paid does not change. Only the timing of the payment of taxes is affected. As shown in Exhibit 1, most managers use tax-planning techniques so that temporary differences delay or defer the payment of taxes to later years. As a result, at the end of

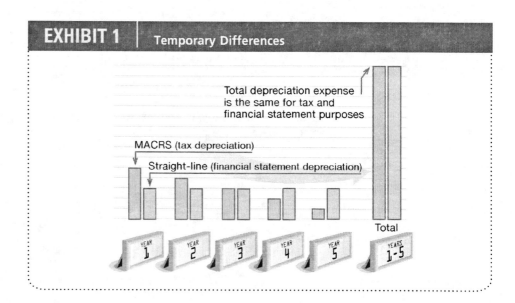

EXHIBIT 1 | **Temporary Differences**

each year the amount of the current tax liability and the postponed (deferred) liability must be recorded.

To illustrate, assume that at the end of the first year of operations a corporation reports $300,000 income before income taxes on its income statement. If we assume an income tax rate of 40%, the income tax expense reported on the income statement is $120,000 ($300,000 × 40%).[5] However, to reduce the amount owed for current income taxes, the corporation uses tax planning to reduce the taxable income to $100,000. Thus, the income tax actually due for the year is only $40,000 ($100,000 × 40%). The $80,000 ($120,000 − $40,000) difference between the two tax amounts is created by temporary differences in recognizing revenue. This amount is deferred to future years. The example is summarized below.

Income tax expense based on $300,000 reported income at 40%	$120,000
Income tax payable based on $100,000 taxable income at 40%	40,000
Income tax deferred to future years	$ 80,000

To match the current year's expenses (including income tax) against the current year's revenue on the income statement, income tax is allocated between periods, using the following journal entry:

Income Tax Expense		120 0 0 0 00	
Income Tax Payable			40 0 0 0 00
Deferred Income Tax Payable			80 0 0 0 00

The income tax expense reported on the income statement is the total tax, $120,000, expected to be paid on the income for the year. In future years, the $80,000 in *Deferred Income Tax Payable* will be transferred to *Income Tax Payable* as the temporary differences reverse and the taxes become due. For example, if $48,000 of the deferred tax reverses and becomes due in the second year, the following journal entry would be made in the second year:

Deferred Income Tax Payable		48 0 0 0 00	
Income Tax Payable			48 0 0 0 00

REPORTING AND ANALYZING TAXES

The balance of *Deferred Income Tax Payable* at the end of a year is reported as a liability.[6] The amount due within one year is classified as a current liability. The remainder is classified as a long-term liability or reported in a Deferred Credits section following the Long-Term Liabilities section.[7]

Differences between taxable income and income (before taxes) reported on the income statement may also arise because certain revenues are exempt from tax and certain expenses are not deductible in determining taxable income. Such differences, which will not reverse with the passage of time, are sometimes called **permanent differences**. For example, interest income on municipal bonds may be exempt from taxation. Such differences create no special financial reporting problems, since the amount of income tax determined according to the tax laws is the *same* amount reported on the income statement.

Interest from investments in municipal bonds is also tax exempt for individual taxpayers.

---

5 For purposes of illustration, the 40% rate is assumed to include all federal, state, and local income taxes.
6 In some cases, a deferred tax asset may arise for tax benefits to be received in the future. Such deferred tax assets are reported as either current or long-term assets, depending on when the benefits are expected to be realized.
7 Additional note disclosures for deferred income taxes are also required. These are discussed in advanced accounting texts.

Example Exercise 14-1   objective **1**

A corporation has $200,000 of income before income taxes, a 40% tax rate, and $130,000 of taxable income. Provide the journal entry for the current year's taxes.

Follow My Example 14-1

Income Tax Expense 80,000
   Income Tax Payable   52,000
   Deferred Income Tax Payable   28,000

Income tax expense based on $200,000 reported income at 40% $80,000
Income tax payable based on $130,000 taxable income at 40%   52,000
Income tax deferred to future years $28,000

For Practice: PE 14-1A, PE 14-1B

Reporting Unusual Items on the Income Statement

objective **2**

Describe and illustrate the reporting of unusual items on the income statement.

Generally accepted accounting principles require that certain unusual items be reported separately on the current or prior period's income statement. These items can be classified into items affecting the current period income statement and those affecting prior period income statements as shown below.

> Unusual Items Affecting the Current Period's Income Statement
> > Fixed asset impairments
> > Restructuring charges
> > Discontinued operations
> > Extraordinary item
>
> Unusual Items Affecting the Prior Period's Income Statement
> > Errors
> > Change in accounting principles

The first category of unusual items affects the current period's income statement. However, the location of the disclosure on the income statement is different between these items. Fixed asset impairment and restructuring charges are reported above income from continuing operations as shown in item 1 of Exhibit 2. That is, fixed asset impairment and restructuring charges are subtracted in arriving at income from continuing operations. Although discontinued operations and extraordinary items affect net income, they are reported below income from continuing operations as shown in item 2 of Exhibit 2.

In the following paragraphs, we first describe and illustrate unusual items affecting the current period's income statement. We then discuss unusual items affecting prior period income statements as shown in item 3 of Exhibit 2.

UNUSUAL ITEMS AFFECTING THE CURRENT PERIOD'S INCOME STATEMENT

Unusual items affecting the current period's income statement include fixed asset impairments, restructuring charges, discontinued operations, and extraordinary items. Fixed asset impairments and restructuring charges, sometimes termed *special charges* when combined, will be discussed first. Following these, we will discuss discontinued operations and extraordinary items.

EXHIBIT 2   Reporting of Unusual Items on the Income Statement

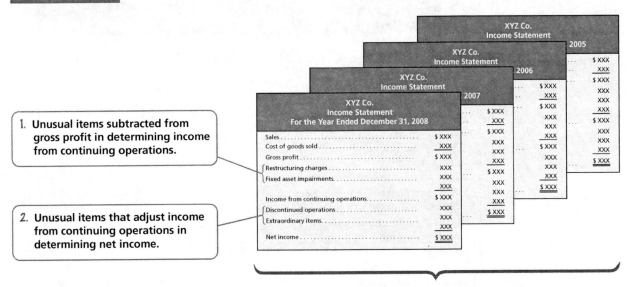

1. Unusual items subtracted from gross profit in determining income from continuing operations.

2. Unusual items that adjust income from continuing operations in determining net income.

3. Unusual items affecting prior period income statements.

Fixed Asset Impairments   A **fixed asset impairment** occurs when the fair value of a fixed asset falls below its book value (cost less accumulated depreciation) and is not expected to recover.[8] Examples of events that might cause an asset impairment are (1) decreases in the market price of fixed assets, (2) significant changes in the business or regulations related to fixed assets, (3) adverse conditions affecting the use of fixed assets, or (4) expected cash flow losses from using fixed assets.[9] For example, on March 1, assume that Jones Corporation consolidates operations by closing a factory. As a result of the closing, plant and equipment is impaired by $750,000. The journal entry to record the impairment is as follows:

Mar.	1	Loss on Fixed Asset Impairment	750 0 0 0 00	
		Equipment		750 0 0 0 00

The loss on fixed asset impairment is reported as a separate expense item deducted from gross profit in determining income from continuing operations, as illustrated for Jones Corporation in Exhibit 3. In addition, note disclosure should describe the nature of the asset impaired and the cause of the impairment.

The loss reduces the book value of the fixed asset and thus reduces the depreciation expense for future periods. If the asset is later sold, the gain or loss on the sale would be based on the lower book value. Thus, asset impairment accounting recognizes the loss when it is first identified, rather than when the asset is later sold.

---

8 Fixed assets that are discontinued components, such as an operating segment, subsidiary, or asset group, should be treated as discontinued items, as discussed in a later section.
9 *Statement of Financial Accounting Standards No. 144,* "Accounting for the Impairment or Disposal of Long-Lived Assets" (Norwalk, CT: Financial Accounting Standards Board, 2001).

EXHIBIT 3

Unusual Items in the
Income Statement

Jones Corporation
Income Statement
For the Year Ended December 31, 2008

Net sales		$12,350,000
Cost of merchandise sold		5,800,000
Gross profit		$ 6,550,000
Selling and administrative expenses	$3,490,000	
Loss from asset impairment	750,000	
Restructuring charge	1,000,000	5,240,000
Income from continuing operations before income tax		$ 1,310,000
Income tax expense		620,000
Income from continuing operations		$ 690,000
Loss on discontinued operations (net of applicable income tax benefit of $50,000)		100,000
Income before extraordinary items		$ 590,000
Extraordinary item:		
Gain on condemnation of land (net of applicable income tax of $65,000)		150,000
Net income		$ 740,000

Integrity, Objectivity, and Ethics in Business

ETHICS

WHEN IS AN ASSET IMPAIRED?

The asset impairment principle is designed to reduce the subjectivity of timing asset write-downs. That is, write-downs should occur when the impairment is deemed permanent. In practice, however, judgment is still needed in determining when such impairment has occurred. Ethical managers will recognize asset write-downs when they occur, not when it is most convenient. For example, the SEC investigated Avon Products, Inc., for delaying the write-off of a computer software project. In settling the formal investigation, Avon had to restate its earnings to reflect the earlier write-off date.

Restructuring Charges   **Restructuring charges** are costs incurred with actions such as canceling contracts, laying off or relocating employees, and combining operations. Often, these events incur initial one-time costs in order to obtain long-term savings. For example, terminated employees often receive a one-time termination or severance benefit at the time of their dismissal. Employee termination benefits are normally the most significant restructuring charges; thus, they will be the focus of this section.

Employee termination benefits arise when a plan specifying the number of terminated employees, the benefit, and the benefit timing has been authorized by senior management and communicated to the employees.[10] To illustrate, assume that the management of Jones Corporation communicates a plan to terminate 200 employees from the closed manufacturing plant on March 1. The plan calls for a termination benefit of $5,000 per employee. Once the plan is communicated to employees, they have the legal right to work for 60 days but may elect to leave the firm earlier. That is, employees may be paid severance at the end of 60 days or at any time in between.

---

10 *Statement of Financial Accounting Standards No. 146*, "Accounting for Costs Associated with Exit or Disposal Activities" (Norwalk, CT: Financial Accounting Standards Board, 2002).

The expense and liability to provide employee benefits should be recognized at fair value on the plan communication date.[11] The fair value of this plan would be $1,000,000 (200 employees × $5,000), which is the aggregate expected cost of terminating the employees. Thus, the $1,000,000 restructuring charge would be recorded as follows:

Mar.	1	Restructuring Charge	1000 0 0 0 00	
		Employee Termination Obligation		1000 0 0 0 00

The restructuring charge is reported as a separate expense deducted from gross profit in determining income from continuing operations, as shown in Exhibit 3. The employee termination obligation would be shown as a current liability. If the plan called for expected severance payments beyond one year, then a long-term liability would be recognized. In addition, a note should disclose the nature and cause of the restructuring event and the costs associated with the type of restructuring event.

The actual benefits paid to terminated employees should be debited to the liability as employees leave the firm. For example, assume that 25 employees find other employment and leave the company on March 25. The entry to record the severance payment to these employees would be as follows:

Mar.	25	Employee Termination Obligation	125 0 0 0 00	
		Cash		125 0 0 0 00

Example Exercise 14-2 objective 2

On December 20 of the current year, Torre Corporation determined that equipment had been impaired so that the book value of the equipment was reduced by $180,000. In addition, the senior management of the company communicated an employee severance plan whereby 80 employees could receive a termination benefit of $7,000 per employee. Provide the journal entry for the asset impairment and the restructuring charge.

Follow My Example 14-2

Dec. 20	Loss on Fixed Asset Impairment	180,000	
	Equipment		180,000
	Restructuring Charge	560,000*	
	Employee Termination Obligation		560,000

*80 employees × $7,000

For Practice: PE 14-2A, PE 14-2B

Discontinued Operations A gain or loss from disposing of a business segment or component of an entity is reported on the income statement as a gain or loss from **discontinued operations**. The term *business segment* refers to a major line of business for a company, such as a division, department, or certain class of customer. A *component* of an entity is the lowest level at which the operations and cash flows can be clearly distinguished, operationally and for financial reporting purposes, from the rest of the

---

11 For long-term severance agreements, present value concepts may be required to determine fair value. We will assume short-term agreements where the time value of money is assumed to be immaterial. Present value concepts are discussed in Chapter 15.

entity.[12] Examples would be a store for a retailer, a territory for a sales organization, or a product category for a consumer products company.

To illustrate the disclosure, assume that Jones Corporation has separate divisions that produce electrical products, hardware supplies, and lawn equipment. Jones sells its electrical products division at a loss. As shown in Exhibit 3 on page 616, this loss is deducted from Jones's income from continuing operations (income from its hardware and lawn equipment divisions). In addition, a note should disclose the identity of the segment sold, the disposal date, a description of the segment's assets and liabilities, and the manner of disposal.

Extraordinary Items   An **extraordinary item** results from events and transactions that (1) are significantly different (unusual) from the typical or the normal operating activities of the business *and* (2) occur infrequently. The gains and losses resulting from natural disasters that occur infrequently, such as floods, earthquakes, and fires, are extraordinary items. Gains or losses from condemning land or buildings for public use are also extraordinary. Such gains and losses, other than those from disposing of a business segment, should be reported in the income statement as extraordinary items, as shown in Exhibit 3.

Sometimes, extraordinary items result in unusual financial results. For example, Delta Air Lines once reported an extraordinary gain of over $5.5 million as the result of the crash of one of its 727s. The plane that crashed was insured for $6.5 million, but its book value in Delta's accounting records was $962,000. Gains and losses on the disposal of fixed assets are *not* extraordinary items. This is because (1) they are not unusual and (2) they recur from time to time in the normal operations of a business. Likewise, gains and losses from the sale of investments are usual and recurring for most businesses.

UNUSUAL ITEMS AFFECTING THE PRIOR PERIOD'S INCOME STATEMENT

In addition to unusual items impacting the income statement, there are two major items that require a retroactive restatement of prior period earnings. These two items are:

1. Errors in the recognition, measurement, presentation, or disclosure of financial statements, and
2. Changes from one generally accepted accounting principle to another generally accepted accounting principle.[13]

A retroactive restatement requires previously issued financial statements to be adjusted for the impact of errors and changes in accounting principle. If an error is discovered that impacts a prior period financial statement, the prior period statement, and all following statements, should be restated to reflect the correction. If there is a change from one generally accepted accounting principle to another generally accepted accounting principle, then the change is applied to prior period financial statements. That is, the prior period financial statements are restated as if the new accounting principle had always been used.[14] Thus, in both cases, these changes do *not* impact current period earnings, but will impact the earnings reported in past periods. As a result, the present Retained Earnings and other balance sheet accounts will be restated to reflect these prior period changes. Illustrations of these types of adjustments are provided in advanced accounting courses.

---

12 *Statement of Financial Accounting Standards No. 144*, op. cit., par. 41.
13 *Statement of Financial Accounting Standards No. 154*, "Accounting Changes and Error Corrections" (Norwalk, CT: Financial Accounting Standards Board, 2005).
14 Changes from one acceptable depreciation method to another acceptable depreciation method are an exception to this general rule and are to be treated prospectively as a change in estimate, as discussed in Chapter 10.

Earnings per Common Share

objective **3**

Prepare an income statement reporting earnings per share data.

The amount of net income is often used by investors and creditors in evaluating a company's profitability. However, net income by itself is difficult to use in comparing companies of different sizes. Also, trends in net income may be difficult to evaluate, using only net income, if there have been significant changes in a company's stockholders' equity. Thus, the profitability of companies is often expressed as earnings per share. **Earnings per common share (EPS)**, sometimes called *basic earnings per share*, is the net income per share of common stock outstanding during a period.

Because of its importance, earnings per share is reported in the financial press and by various investor services, such as Moody's and Standard & Poor's. Changes in earnings per share can lead to significant changes in the price of a corporation's stock in the marketplace. For example, the stock of eBay Inc. fell by over 19% to $83 per share after the company announced earnings per share of 33¢ as compared to Wall Street analysts' estimate of 34¢ per share.

Corporations whose stock is traded in a public market must report earnings per common share on their income statements.[15] If no preferred stock is outstanding, the earnings per common share is calculated as follows:

$$\text{Earnings per Common Share} = \frac{\text{Net Income}}{\text{Number of Common Shares Outstanding}}$$

When the number of common shares outstanding has changed during the period, a weighted average number of shares outstanding is used. If a company has preferred stock outstanding, the net income must be reduced by the amount of any preferred dividends, as shown below.

$$\text{Earnings per Common Share} = \frac{\text{Net Income} - \text{Preferred Stock Dividends}}{\text{Number of Common Shares Outstanding}}$$

Comparing the earnings per share of two or more years, based on only the net incomes of those years, could be misleading. For example, assume that Jones Corporation, whose partial income statement was presented in Exhibit 3, reported $700,000 net income for 2007. Also assume that no extraordinary or other unusual items were reported in 2007. Jones has no preferred stock outstanding and has 200,000 common shares outstanding in 2007 and 2008. The earnings per common share is $3.50 ($700,000/200,000 shares) for 2007 and $3.70 ($740,000/200,000 shares) for 2008. Comparing the two earnings per share amounts suggests that operations have improved. However, the 2008 earnings per share comparable to the $3.50 is $3.45, which is the income from continuing operations of $690,000 divided by 200,000 shares. The latter amount indicates a slight downturn in normal earnings.

When unusual items reported *below* income from continuing operations exist, earnings per common share should be reported for those items. To illustrate, a partial income statement for Jones Corporation, showing earnings per common share, is shown in Exhibit 4. In this income statement, Jones reports all the earnings per common share amounts on the face of the income statement. However, only earnings per share amounts for income from continuing operations and net income are required to be presented on the face of the statement. The other per share amounts may be presented in the notes to the financial statements.[16]

In the preceding paragraphs, we have assumed a simple capital structure with only common stock or common stock and preferred stock outstanding. Often, however, corporations have complex capital structures with various types of securities outstanding, such as convertible preferred stock, options, warrants, and contingently

---

15 *Statement of Financial Accounting Standards No. 128,* "Earnings per Share" (Norwalk, CT: Financial Accounting Standards Board, 1997).
16 Ibid., pars. 36 and 37.

EXHIBIT 4

Income Statement
with Earnings
per Share

Jones Corporation
Income Statement
For the Year Ended December 31, 2008

Earnings per common share:	
Income from continuing operations..	$ 3.45
Loss on discontinued operations, net of $50,000 tax benefit.................	0.50
Income before extraordinary items......................................	$ 2.95
Extraordinary item:	
Gain on condemnation of land, net of applicable income	
tax of $65,000..	0.75
Net income..	$ 3.70

issuable shares. In such cases, the possible effects of converting such securities to common stock must be calculated and reported as *earnings per common share assuming dilution* or *diluted earnings per share*.[17] This topic is discussed further in advanced accounting texts.

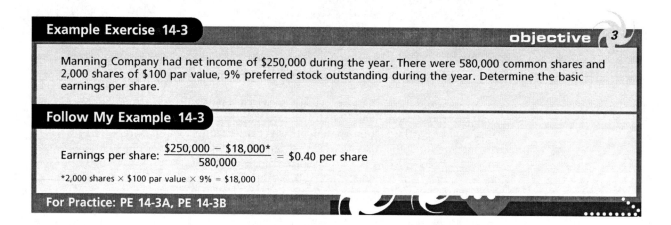

Example Exercise 14-3   objective 3

Manning Company had net income of $250,000 during the year. There were 580,000 common shares and 2,000 shares of $100 par value, 9% preferred stock outstanding during the year. Determine the basic earnings per share.

Follow My Example 14-3

Earnings per share: $\dfrac{\$250{,}000 - \$18{,}000^*}{580{,}000} = \$0.40$ per share

*2,000 shares × $100 par value × 9% = $18,000

For Practice: PE 14-3A, PE 14-3B

Comprehensive Income

objective 4

Describe the concept and the reporting of comprehensive income.

Comprehensive income is defined as all changes in stockholders' equity during a period, except those resulting from dividends and stockholders' investments. Companies must report traditional net income plus or minus other comprehensive income items to arrive at comprehensive income.

Other comprehensive income items include foreign currency items, pension liability adjustments, and unrealized gains and losses on investments. Generally accepted accounting principles (GAAP) require these items to be disclosed separately from earnings. To the extent that other comprehensive income items give rise to tax effects, the taxes should be allocated to these items similar to that illustrated in Exhibit 4 for extraordinary items. The cumulative effects of other comprehensive income items must be reported separately from retained earnings and paid-in capital, on the balance sheet, as **accumulated other comprehensive income**. When other comprehen-

---

17 Ibid., pars. 11–39.

In the 2005 edition of *Accounting Trends & Techniques*, over 95% of the surveyed companies reported other comprehensive income, and the majority of these companies disclosed it in the statement of stockholders' equity.

sive income items are not present, the income statement and balance sheet formats are similar to those we have illustrated in this and preceding chapters.

Companies may report comprehensive income on the income statement, in a separate statement of comprehensive income, or in the statement of stockholders' equity. In addition, companies may use terms other than comprehensive income, such as "total nonowner changes in equity."

To illustrate reporting for comprehensive income, assume that Triple-A Enterprises Inc. reported comprehensive income on a separate statement, called the *statement of comprehensive income*, as follows:

Triple-A Enterprises Inc. Statement of Comprehensive Income For the Year Ended December 31, 2008	
Net income	$8 5 0 0 00
Other comprehensive income, net of tax	9 0 00
Total comprehensive income	$8 5 9 0 00

The Stockholders' Equity section of the balance sheet for Triple-A Enterprises is as follows:

Triple-A Enterprises Inc. Stockholders' Equity December 31, 2008 and 2007	2008	2007
Stockholders' equity:		
Common stock	$ 20 0 0 0 00	$ 20 0 0 0 00
Paid-in capital in excess of par	36 0 0 0 00	36 0 0 0 00
Retained earnings	165 5 0 0 00	157 0 0 0 00
Accumulated other comprehensive income	1 2 9 0 00	1 2 0 0 00
Total stockholders' equity	$222 7 9 0 00	$214 2 0 0 00

Accumulated other comprehensive income is the cumulative effect of other comprehensive income items. Thus, the additional other comprehensive income of $90 for 2008 is added to the accumulated other comprehensive income on December 31, 2007, to yield the December 31, 2008, balance of $1,290.

You should note that comprehensive income does not affect net income or retained earnings. In the next section, we will illustrate the determination of other comprehensive income, using unrealized gains and losses on investments.

Example Exercise 14-4

objective 4

Myers Company had a net income of $74,000 and other comprehensive income of $12,500 for 2008. On January 1, 2008, the Retained Earnings balance was $425,000, and the Accumulated Other Comprehensive Income balance was $57,000. Determine the (a) comprehensive income for 2008, (b) Retained Earnings balance on December 31, 2008, and (c) Accumulated Other Comprehensive Income balance on December 31, 2008.

(continued)

Follow My Example 14-4

 a. $86,500 = $74,000 + $12,500
 b. $499,000 = $425,000 + $74,000
 c. $69,500 = $57,000 + $12,500

For Practice: PE 14-4A, PE 14-4B

Accounting for Investments in Stocks

objective   5

Describe the accounting for investments in stocks.

Corporations not only issue stock, but they also purchase stocks of other companies for investment purposes. Like individuals, businesses have a variety of reasons for investing in stocks, called **equity securities**. A business may purchase stocks as a means of earning a return (income) on excess cash that it does not need for its normal operations. Such investments are usually for a short period of time. In other cases, a business may purchase the stock of another company as a long-term investment. Such investments can be as a means of developing or maintaining business relationships with another company. Sometimes, a business will purchase most, if not all, of the common stock of another company for purposes of owning and controlling another entity. This is termed a *business combination*. In this section, we will discuss short-term investments in equity securities, long-term investments in equity securities, sales of investments, and business combinations. First, however, we will introduce two major equity security classifications according to generally accepted accounting principles.

The equity securities in which a business invests may be classified as trading securities or available-for-sale securities. **Trading securities** are securities that management intends to actively trade for profit. Businesses holding trading securities are those whose normal operations involve buying and selling securities. Examples of such businesses include banks and insurance companies. **Available-for-sale securities** are securities that management expects to sell in the future but which are not actively traded for profit. For example, Warren Buffett, one of the wealthiest men in the world, invests through a public company called Berkshire Hathaway Inc. In a recent annual report, Berkshire Hathaway reported over $35 billion of equity investment holdings listed on its balance sheet as available-for-sale securities. Some of these investments include The Coca-Cola Company, McDonald's, and American Express Company. In this section, we describe and illustrate the accounting for available-for-sale equity securities. The accounting for trading securities is described and illustrated in advanced accounting texts.

SHORT-TERM INVESTMENTS IN STOCKS

Rather than allow excess cash to be idle until it is needed, a business may invest in available-for-sale securities. These investments are classified as **temporary investments** or *marketable securities*. Although such investments may be retained for several years,

Integrity, Objectivity, and Ethics in Business

WHAT DOES IT TAKE TO SUCCEED IN LIFE?

The answer to this question, according to Warren Buffett, the noted investment authority, is three magic ingredients: intelligence, energy, and integrity. According to Buffett, "If you lack the third ingredient, the other two will kill you." In other words, without integrity, your intelligence and energy may very well misguide you.

Source: Eric Clifford, *University of Tennessee Torchbearer,* Summer 2002.

they continue to be classified as temporary, provided they meet two conditions. First, the securities are readily marketable and can be sold for cash at any time. Second, management intends to sell the securities when the business needs cash for operations.

Temporary investments in available-for-sale securities are recorded in a current asset account, *Marketable Securities*, at their cost. This cost includes all amounts spent to acquire the securities, such as broker's commissions. Any dividends received on the investment are recorded as a debit to *Cash* and a credit to *Dividend Revenue*.[18]

To illustrate, assume that on June 1 Crabtree Co. purchased 2,000 shares of Inis Corporation common stock at $89.75 per share plus a brokerage fee of $500. On October 1, Inis declared a $0.90 per share cash dividend payable on November 30. Crabtree's entries to record the stock purchase and the receipt of the dividend are as follows:

June	1	Marketable Securities	180 0 0 0 00	
		Cash		180 0 0 0 00
		Purchased 2,000 shares of Inis Corporation		
		common stock [($89.75 × 2,000 shares) +		
		$500].		
Nov.	30	Cash	1 8 0 0 00	
		Dividend Revenue		1 8 0 0 00
		Received dividend on Inis Corporation		
		common stock (2,000 shares × $0.90).		

On the balance sheet, temporary investments are reported at their fair market value. Market values are normally available from stock quotations in financial newspapers, such as *The Wall Street Journal*. Any difference between the fair market values of the securities and their cost is an **unrealized holding gain or loss**. This gain or loss is termed "unrealized" because a transaction (the sale of the securities) is necessary before a gain or loss becomes real (realized).

To illustrate, assume that Crabtree Co.'s portfolio of temporary investments was purchased during 2008 and has the following fair market values and unrealized gains and losses on December 31, 2008:

Common Stock	Cost	Market	Unrealized Gain (Loss)
Edwards Inc.	$150,000	$190,000	$ 40,000
SWS Corp.	200,000	200,000	—
Inis Corporation	180,000	210,000	30,000
Bass Co.	160,000	150,000	(10,000)
Total	$690,000	$750,000	$ 60,000

If income taxes of $18,000 are allocated to the unrealized gain, Crabtree's temporary investments should be reported at their total cost of $690,000, plus the unrealized gain (net of applicable income tax) of $42,000 ($60,000 − $18,000), as shown in Exhibit 5.

The unrealized gain (net of applicable taxes) of $42,000 should also be reported as an *other comprehensive income item*, as we mentioned in the preceding section. For example, assume that Crabtree Co. has net income of $720,000 for the year ended December 31, 2008. Crabtree elects to report comprehensive income in the *statement of comprehensive income*, as shown in Exhibit 6. In addition, the accumulated other comprehensive income on the balance sheet would also be $42,000, representing the beginning balance of zero plus other comprehensive income of $42,000, as shown in Exhibit 5.

---

18 Stock dividends received on an investment are not journalized, since they have no effect on the investor's assets and revenues.

EXHIBIT 5

Temporary
Investments on the
Balance Sheet

Crabtree Co.
Balance Sheet (selected items)
December 31, 2008

Assets

Current assets:

Cash		$119,500
Temporary investments in marketable		
securities at cost	$690,000	
Unrealized gain (net of applicable		
income tax of $18,000)	42,000	732,000

Stockholders' Equity

Accumulated other comprehensive income	$ 42,000

EXHIBIT 6

Statement of
Comprehensive
Income

Crabtree Co.
Statement of Comprehensive Income
For the Year Ended December 31, 2008

Net income	$720,000
Other comprehensive income:	
Unrealized gain on temporary investments in marketable	
securities (net of applicable income tax of $18,000)	42,000
Comprehensive income	$762,000

Unrealized losses are reported in a similar manner. Unrealized gains and losses are reported as other comprehensive income items until the related securities are sold. When temporary securities are sold, the unrealized gains or losses become realized and are included in determining net income.

Example Exercise 14-5   objective **5**

Drew Company began operations on January 1, 2008, and purchased temporary investments in marketable securities during the year at a cost of $75,000. The end-of-period market value for these investments was $110,000. Net income was $180,000 for 2008. Determine (a) the reported amount of marketable securities on the December 31, 2008, balance sheet and (b) the comprehensive income for 2008. Assume a tax rate of 40%.

Follow My Example 14-5

a.	Initial cost		$ 75,000
	Unrealized gain ($110,000 − $75,000)	$35,000	
	Less: Tax on unrealized gain ($35,000 × 40%)	14,000	
	Unrealized gain, net of tax		21,000
	Reported amount of marketable securities		$ 96,000
b.	Net income		$180,000
	Unrealized gain ($110,000 − $75,000)	$35,000	
	Less: Tax on unrealized gain ($35,000 × 40%)	14,000	
	Other comprehensive income, net of tax		21,000
	Comprehensive income		$201,000

For Practice: PE 14-5A, PE 14-5B

LONG-TERM INVESTMENTS IN STOCKS

Long-term investments in stocks are not intended as a source of cash in the normal operations of the business. Rather, such investments are often held for their income, long-term gain potential, or influence over another business entity. They are reported in the balance sheet under the caption **Investments**, which usually follows the Current Assets section.

Long-term investments in stock are treated as available-for-sale securities, as we illustrated previously for short-term available-for-sale securities. Thus, a long-term investment treated as an available-for-sale security is recorded at cost and reported at fair market value net of any applicable income tax effects. In addition, any unrealized gains and losses are reported as part of the comprehensive income.[19] For example, Delta Air Lines disclosed investments in Priceline.com preferred stock as a noncurrent investment at the appraised fair market value.

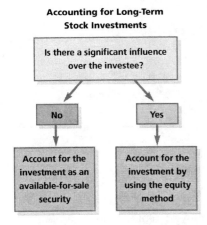

Accounting for Long-Term Stock Investments

However, if the investor (the buyer of the stock) has significant influence over the operating and financing activities of the investee (company whose stock is owned), the **equity method** is used. When the equity method is used, a stock purchase is recorded at cost, as shown previously. Evidence of significant influence includes the percentage of ownership, the existence of intercompany transactions, and the interchange of managerial personnel. Generally, if the investor owns 20% or more of the voting stock of the investee, it is assumed that the investor has significant influence over the investee.

Under the equity method, the investment is *not* subsequently adjusted to fair value. Rather, the book value of the investment is adjusted as follows:

1. The investor's share of the periodic net income of the investee is recorded as an *increase in the investment account* and as *income for the period*. Likewise, the investor's share of an investee's net loss is recorded as a *decrease in the investment account* and as a *loss for the period*.
2. The investor's share of cash dividends from the investee is recorded as an *increase in the cash account* and a *decrease in the investment account*.

To illustrate, assume that on January 2, Hally Inc. pays cash of $350,000 for 40% of the common stock and net assets of Brock Corporation. Assume also that, for the year ending December 31, Brock Corporation reports net income of $105,000 and declares and pays $45,000 in dividends. Using the equity method, Hally Inc. (the investor) records these transactions as follows:

REAL WORLD

The 2005 edition of *Accounting Trends & Techniques* indicated that over 50% of the companies surveyed used the equity method to account for investments.

Jan.	2	Investment in Brock Corporation Stock	350 000 00	
		Cash		350 000 00
		Purchased 40% of Brock Corporation stock.		
Dec.	31	Investment in Brock Corporation Stock	42 000 00	
		Income of Brock Corporation		42 000 00
		Recorded 40% share of Brock Corporation net income of $105,000.		
Dec.	31	Cash	18 000 00	
		Investment in Brock Corporation Stock		18 000 00
		Recorded 40% share of Brock Corporation dividends.		

---

19 An exception to reporting unrealized gains and losses as part of comprehensive income is made if the decrease in the market value for a stock is considered permanent. In this case, the cost of the individual stock is written down (decreased), and the amount of the write-down is included in net income.

The combined effect of recording 40% of Brock Corporation's net income and dividends is to increase Hally's interest in the net assets of Brock by $24,000 ($42,000 − $18,000), as shown below.

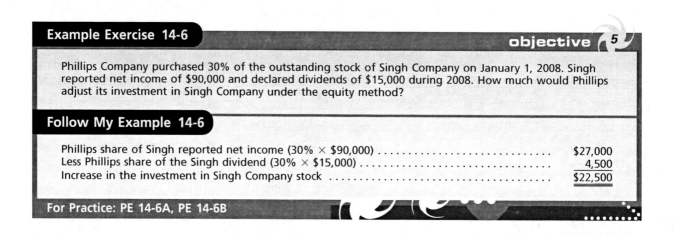

Investment and Dividends

The equity method causes the investment account to mirror the proportional changes in the book value of the investee. Thus, Brock Corporation's book value increased by $60,000 ($105,000 − $45,000), while the investment in Brock Corporation stock account increased by Hally's proportional share of that increase, or $24,000 ($60,000 × 40%). Thus, both the book value of Brock Corporation and Hally's investment in Brock increased at the same rate from the original cost.

Example Exercise 14-6   objective 5

Phillips Company purchased 30% of the outstanding stock of Singh Company on January 1, 2008. Singh reported net income of $90,000 and declared dividends of $15,000 during 2008. How much would Phillips adjust its investment in Singh Company under the equity method?

Follow My Example 14-6

Phillips share of Singh reported net income (30% × $90,000)	$27,000
Less Phillips share of the Singh dividend (30% × $15,000)	4,500
Increase in the investment in Singh Company stock	$22,500

For Practice: PE 14-6A, PE 14-6B

SALE OF INVESTMENTS IN STOCKS

Accounting for the sale of stock is the same for both short- and long-term investments. When shares of stock are sold, the investment account is credited for the carrying amount (book value) of the shares sold. The cash or receivables account is debited for the proceeds (sales price less commission and other selling costs). Any difference between the proceeds and the carrying amount is recorded as a gain or loss on the sale and is included in determining net income.

To illustrate, assume that an investment in Drey Inc. stock has a carrying amount of $15,700 when it is sold on March 1. If the proceeds from the sale of the stock are $17,500, the entry to record the transaction is as follows:

Mar.	1	Cash	17 5 0 0 00	
		Investment in Drey Inc. Stock		15 7 0 0 00
		Gain on Sale of Investments		1 8 0 0 00

BUSINESS COMBINATIONS

A business may make an investment in another business by acquiring a controlling share, often greater than 50%, of the outstanding voting stock of another corporation by paying cash or exchanging stock. This is termed a **business combination**. Businesses may combine in order to produce more efficiently, diversify product lines, expand geographically, or acquire know-how.

A corporation owning all or a majority of the voting stock of another corporation is called a **parent company**. The corporation that is controlled is called the **subsidiary company**. For example, PayPal became a subsidiary of eBay Inc. when eBay exchanged eBay common stock for all the outstanding common stock of PayPal. Although parent and subsidiary corporations may operate as a single economic unit, they continue to maintain separate accounting records and prepare their own periodic financial statements.

At the end of the year, the financial statements of the parent and subsidiary are combined and reported as a single company.[20] These combined financial statements are called **consolidated financial statements**. Such statements are usually identified by adding "and subsidiary(ies)" to the name of the parent corporation or by adding "consolidated" to the statement title. For example, eBay's income statement is titled, "Consolidated Statement of Income." To the stockholders of the parent company, consolidated financial statements are more meaningful than separate statements for each corporation. This is because the parent company, in substance, controls the subsidiaries, even though the parent and its subsidiaries are separate entities. Accounting for business combinations and preparing consolidated financial statements are discussed in greater detail in advanced accounting courses.

Business Connections

1 + 1 = 3

Companies merge in order to create synergy, which occurs when the value of the companies as a single unit is greater than their value as separate companies. How do mergers create synergy? The four basic strategies for creating value in a merger are explained below.

1. *Reduce costs:* When two companies combine, they may be able to eliminate duplicate administrative expenses. For example, the combined company does not need two CEOs or two CFOs, or the company can run on a single computer system or distribution network. Hewlett-Packard Company, identified cost savings such as these in justifying its acquisition of Compaq Computer Corporation.
2. *Replace management:* If the target company has been suffering from mismanagement, the acquirer can purchase the target for a low price and replace the target company's management.

3. *Horizontal integration:* The acquirer may purchase the target company because it has a complementary product line, territory, or customer base to its own. The new combined entity is able to serve customers with a broader reach than were two separate entities. For example, The Walt Disney Company purchased Pixar in order to reestablish its presence as the premier animation movie studio in the era of digital animation.
4. *Vertical integration:* A vertical integration occurs when a business acquires a supplier or customer. Acquiring a supplier may provide a more stable source of supply of a strategic resource and reduce coordination costs. For example, Delta Air Lines acquired Comair Holdings Inc., a regional jet carrier, to supply passengers from smaller cities into its large city hub system.

---

20 When a parent company owns less than 100% of the subsidiary stock, the amount owned by the outsiders is often termed a minority interest and is reported immediately following the consolidated total liabilities. Accounting for the minority interest is covered in advanced accounting texts.

Financial Analysis and Interpretation

A firm's growth potential and future earnings prospects are indicated by how much the market is willing to pay per dollar of a company's earnings. This ratio, called the **price-earnings ratio**, or *P/E ratio*, is commonly included in stock market quotations reported by the financial press. A high P/E ratio indicates that the market expects high growth and earnings in the future. Likewise, a low P/E ratio indicates lower growth and earnings expectations.

The price-earnings ratio on common stock is computed by dividing the stock's market price per share at a specific date by the company's annual earnings per share, as shown below.

$$\text{Price-Earnings Ratio} = \frac{\text{Market Price per Share of Common Stock}}{\text{Earnings per Share of Common Stock}}$$

Investors that invest in high price-earnings ratio companies are often referred to as *growth* investors. Growth investors pay a high price for shares because they expect the company to grow and provide a superior return. That is, high price-earnings ratios can be related to investor optimism. Examples of growth companies are Google (P/E 87), eBay Inc. (P/E 54), and Genentech, Inc. (P/E 72). Growth companies are considered risky because high growth expectations are already reflected in the market price. Thus, if the company's high growth expectations are not realized, the stock price will likely fall.

In contrast, investors in low price-earnings ratio companies are often referred to as *value* investors. Value investors invest in companies with stable and predictable earnings. The value investor believes that the low price-earnings ratio investment is safer than a high price-earnings investment, since the stock is priced at a "bargain" level. Value investing is generally considered the "tortoise" strategy to the growth investor's "hare" strategy. Examples of value stocks are Bank of America Corporation (P/E 11), H.J. Heinz Company (P/E 16), and Ford Motor Company (P/E 9).

To illustrate the calculation of the price-earnings ratio, assume that Harper Inc. reported earnings per share of $1.64 in 2008 and $1.35 in 2007. The market prices per common share are $24.60 at the end of 2008 and $16.20 at the end of 2007. The price-earnings ratio on this stock is computed as follows:

Price-Earnings Ratio

Year 2008	15 ($24.60/$1.64)
Year 2007	12 ($16.20/$1.35)

The price-earnings ratio indicates that a share of Harper Inc.'s common stock was selling for 12 times the amount of earnings per share at the end of 2007. At the end of 2008, the common stock was selling for 15 times the amount of earnings per share. These results would indicate a generally improving expectation of growth and earnings for Harper Inc. However, a prospective investor should also consider the price-earnings ratios for competing firms in the same industry.

At a Glance

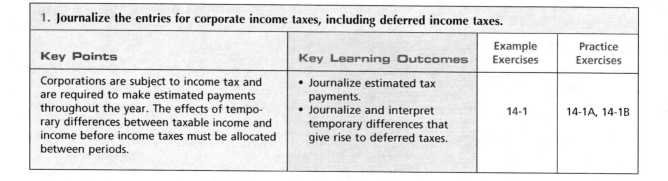

1. Journalize the entries for corporate income taxes, including deferred income taxes.

Key Points	Key Learning Outcomes	Example Exercises	Practice Exercises
Corporations are subject to income tax and are required to make estimated payments throughout the year. The effects of temporary differences between taxable income and income before income taxes must be allocated between periods.	• Journalize estimated tax payments. • Journalize and interpret temporary differences that give rise to deferred taxes.	14-1	14-1A, 14-1B

2. Describe and illustrate the reporting of unusual items on the income statement.

Key Points	Key Learning Outcomes	Example Exercises	Practice Exercises
Fixed asset impairments and restructuring charges are separately disclosed and deducted as part of operating expenses in determining income from continuing operations. The gain or loss from disposal of a business and gains and losses from unusual and infrequent (extra-ordinary) events are disclosed separately below income from continuing operations. Errors and changes from one generally accepted accounting method to another are treated as restatements of prior period financial statements.	• Identify, journalize, and report fixed asset impairments and restructuring charges. • Identify and report gains and losses from discontinued operations and extraordinary items. • Describe unusual items affecting prior period financial statements.	14-2	14-2A, 14-2B

3. Prepare an income statement reporting earnings per share data.

Key Points	Key Learning Outcomes	Example Exercises	Practice Exercises
Earnings per share is a required disclosure. Basic earnings per share removes preferred dividends in the numerator of the calculation. Earnings per share should be separately disclosed for discontinued operations and extraordinary items.	• Calculate basic earnings per share. • Prepare earnings per share disclosures for discontinued operations and extraordinary items.	14-3	14-3A, 14-3B

4. Describe the concept and the reporting of comprehensive income.

Key Points	Key Learning Outcomes	Example Exercises	Practice Exercises
Comprehensive income is all the changes in stockholders' equity during a period except those resulting from dividends and stockholders' investments. Total comprehensive income includes other comprehensive income, which consists of items excluded from net income, such as unrealized gains and losses on certain investments in debt or equity securities. Accumulated other comprehensive income is separately reported in the Stockholders' Equity section of the balance sheet.	• Prepare a statement of comprehensive income. • Determine and report accumulated other comprehensive income.	14-4 14-4	14-4A, 14-4B 14-4A, 14-4B

5. Describe the accounting for investments in stocks.

Key Points	Key Learning Outcomes	Example Exercises	Practice Exercises
Short- and long-term investments in marketable securities may be accounted for as available-for-sale securities. Available-for-sale securities are recognized at fair value on the balance sheet, with changes in fair value being recognized as other comprehensive income. Long-term investments in equity securities in which there is a significant influence are accounted for under the equity method. Investments as the result of a business combination are accounted for as consolidations.	• Identify, journalize, and report changes in market value for available-for-sale securities. • Identify, journalize, and report investments under the equity method. • Define and describe the accounting for a business combination.	14-5 14-6	14-5A, 14-5B 14-6A, 14-6B

Key Terms

accumulated other comprehensive income (620)
available-for-sale securities (622)
business combinations (627)
comprehensive income (620)
consolidated financial statements (627)
discontinued operations (617)
earnings per common share (EPS) (619)

equity method (625)
equity securities (622)
extraordinary item (618)
fixed asset impairment (615)
investments (625)
other comprehensive income items (620)
parent company (627)
permanent differences (613)
price-earnings ratio (628)

restructuring charges (616)
subsidiary company (627)
taxable income (611)
temporary differences (612)
temporary investments (622)
trading securities (622)
unrealized holding gain or loss (623)

Illustrative Problem

The following data were selected from the records of Botanica Greenhouses Inc. for the current fiscal year ended August 31:

Administrative expenses	$ 82,200
Cost of merchandise sold	750,000
Fixed asset impairment	115,000
Gain on condemnation of land	25,000
Income tax:	
Applicable to continuing operations	27,200
Applicable to gain on condemnation of land	10,000
Applicable to loss on discontinued operations (reduction)	24,000
Interest expense	15,200
Loss on discontinued operations	60,200
Restructuring charge	40,000
Sales	1,252,500
Selling expenses	182,100

Instructions

Prepare a multiple-step income statement, concluding with a section for earnings per share in the form illustrated in this chapter. There were 10,000 shares of common stock (no preferred) outstanding throughout the year. Assume that the gain on condemnation of land is an extraordinary item.

Solution

Botanica Greenhouses Inc. Income Statement For the Year Ended August 31, 2008		
Sales		$1,252,500
Cost of merchandise sold.		750,000
Gross profit.		$ 502,500
Operating expenses:		
Selling expenses	$182,100	
Administrative expenses	82,200	
Fixed asset impairment.	115,000	
Restructuring charge	40,000	
Total operating expenses.		419,300
Income from operations		$ 83,200
Other expense:		
Interest expense		15,200
Income from continuing operations before		
income tax		$ 68,000
Income tax expense.		27,200
Income from continuing operations		$ 40,800
Loss on discontinued operations	$ 60,200	
Less applicable income tax	24,000	36,200
Income before extraordinary item.		$ 4,600
Extraordinary item:		
Gain on condemnation of land	$ 25,000	
Less applicable income tax	10,000	15,000
Net income		$ 19,600
Earnings per share:		
Income from continuing operations		$4.08
Loss on discontinued operations		3.62
Income before extraordinary item		$0.46
Extraordinary item		1.50
Net income		$1.96

Self-Examination Questions  (Answers at End of Chapter)

1. During its first year of operations, a corporation elected to use the straight-line method of depreciation for financial reporting purposes and MACRS in determining taxable income. If the income tax rate is 40% and the amount of depreciation expense is $60,000 under the straight-line method and $100,000 under MACRS, what is the amount of income tax deferred to future years?
   A. $16,000   C. $40,000
   B. $24,000   D. $60,000

2. A material gain resulting from condemning land for public use would be reported on the income statement as a(n):
   A. extraordinary item.
   B. other income item.
   C. restructuring charge.
   D. fixed asset impairment.

3. Gwinnett Corporation's temporary investments cost $100,000 and have a market value of $120,000 at the end of the accounting period. Assuming a tax rate of

40%, the difference between the cost and market value would be reported as a:
A. $12,000 realized gain.
B. $12,000 unrealized gain.
C. $20,000 realized gain.
D. $20,000 unrealized gain.

4. Cisneros Corporation owns 75% of Harrell Inc. During the current year, Harrell Inc. reported net income of $150,000 and declared dividends of $40,000. How much would Cisneros Corporation increase Investment in Harrell Inc. Stock for the current year?

A. $0   C. $82,500
B. $30,000   D. $112,500

5. Harkin Company has a market price of $60 per share on December 31. The total stockholders' equity is $2,400,000, and the net income is $800,000. There are 200,000 shares outstanding. Preferred dividends are $50,000. The price-earnings ratio would be:
A. 3.
B. 15.
C. 16.
D. 20.

Eye Openers

1. How would the amount of deferred income tax payable be reported in the balance sheet if (a) it is payable within one year and (b) it is payable beyond one year?
2. Darnell Company owns plant and equipment that has a book value of $120 million. Due to a permanent decline in consumer demand for the products produced by this plant, the market value of the plant and equipment is appraised at $20 million. Describe the accounting treatment for this impairment.
3. How should the severance costs of terminated employees be accounted for?
4. During the current year, 40 acres of land that cost $200,000 were condemned for construction of an interstate highway. Assuming that an award of $320,000 in cash was received and that the applicable income tax on this transaction is 40%, how would this information be presented in the income statement?
5. Mann Corporation realized a material gain when its facilities at a designated floodway were acquired by the urban renewal agency. How should the gain be reported in the income statement?
6. An annual report of Ford Motor Company disclosed the sale of its ownership interest in Visteon Corporation, a major automotive components manufacturer. The estimated after-tax loss on disposal of these operations was $2.3 billion. Indicate how the loss from discontinued operations should be reported by Ford on its income statement.
7. How is the change from one acceptable accounting principle to another acceptable accounting principle shown on the income statement?
8. A corporation reports earnings per share of $1.38 for the most recent year and $1.10 for the preceding year. The $1.38 includes a $0.40-per-share gain from insurance proceeds related to a fully depreciated asset that was destroyed by fire.
   a. Should the composition of the $1.38 be disclosed in the financial reports?
   b. On the basis of the limited information presented, would you conclude that operations had improved or declined?
9. a. List some examples of other comprehensive income items.
   b. Does the reporting of other comprehensive income affect the determination of net income and retained earnings?
10. Why might a business invest in another company's stock?
11. How are temporary investments in marketable securities reported on the balance sheet?
12. How are unrealized gains and losses on temporary investments in marketable securities reported on the statement of comprehensive income?
13. a. What method of accounting is used for long-term investments in stock in which there is significant influence over the investee?
    b. Under what caption are long-term investments in stock reported on the balance sheet?
14. Glover Inc. received a $0.20-per-share cash dividend on 50,000 shares of Gestalt Corporation common stock, which Glover Inc. carries as a long-term investment. Assuming that Glover Inc. uses the equity method of accounting for its investment in Gestalt Corporation, what account would be credited for the receipt of the $10,000 dividend?

15. An annual report of The Campbell Soup Company reported on its income statement $2.4 million as "equity in earnings of affiliates." Journalize the entry that Campbell would have made to record this equity in earnings of affiliates.
16. How is an investment as the result of a business combination reported?

Practice Exercises

PE 14-1A
Deferred tax entries
obj. 1

A corporation has $540,000 of income before income taxes, a 35% tax rate, and $480,000 of taxable income. Provide the journal entry for the current year's taxes.

PE 14-1B
Deferred tax entries
obj. 1

Bismark Corp. has $90,000 of income before income taxes, a 40% tax rate, and $76,000 of taxable income. Provide the journal entry for the current year's taxes.

PE 14-2A
Journalize fixed asset impairment and restructuring charge
obj. 2

On December 15 of the current year, Adams Corporation determined that equipment had been impaired so that the book value of the equipment was reduced by $46,000. In addition, the senior management of the company communicated an employee severance plan whereby 15 employees could receive a termination benefit of $4,000 per employee. Provide the journal entry for the asset impairment and the restructuring charge.

PE 14-2B
Journalize fixed asset impairment and restructuring charge
obj. 2

On December 23 of the current year, Dallas Corporation determined that land had been impaired so that the book value of the land was reduced by $320,000. In addition, the senior management of the company communicated an employee severance plan whereby 45 employees could receive a termination benefit of $9,000 per employee. Provide the journal entry for the asset impairment and the restructuring charge.

PE 14-3A
Calculate earnings per share
obj. 3

Wyoming Company had net income of $2,430,000 during the year. There were 240,000 common shares and 30,000 shares of $100 par value, 9% preferred stock outstanding during the year. Determine the basic earnings per share.

PE 14-3B
Calculate earnings per share
obj. 3

Broad Plain Inc. had net income of $350,000 during the year. There were 420,000 common shares and 5,000 shares of $100 par value, 7% preferred stock outstanding during the year. Determine the basic earnings per share.

PE 14-4A
Comprehensive income
obj. 4

Zorba Company had a net income of $104,000 and other comprehensive income of $13,400 for 2008. On January 1, 2008, the Retained Earnings balance was $565,000, and the Accumulated Other Comprehensive Income balance was $71,000. Determine the (a) comprehensive income for 2008, (b) Retained Earnings balance on December 31, 2008, and (c) Accumulated Other Comprehensive Income balance on December 31, 2008.

PE 14-4B
Comprehensive income
obj. 4

Manitoba Company had a net income of $856,000 and other comprehensive income of $123,500 for 2008. On January 1, 2008, the Retained Earnings balance was $3,460,000, and the Accumulated Other Comprehensive Income balance was $624,000. Determine the (a) comprehensive income for 2008, (b) Retained Earnings balance on December 31, 2008, and (c) Accumulated Other Comprehensive Income balance on December 31, 2008.

PE 14-5A
Temporary investments
obj. 5

Mansfield Company began operations on January 1, 2008, and purchased temporary investments in marketable securities during the year at a cost of $123,000. The end-of-period market value for these investments was $137,000. Net income was $151,000 for 2008. Determine (a) the reported amount of marketable securities on the December 31, 2008, balance sheet and (b) the comprehensive income for 2008. Assume a tax rate of 40%.

PE 14-5B
Temporary investments
obj. 5

Aaron Company began operations on January 1, 2008, and purchased temporary investments in marketable securities during the year at a cost of $56,000. The end-of-period market value for these investments was $49,700. Net income was $97,500 for 2008. Determine (a) the reported amount of marketable securities on the December 31, 2008, balance sheet and (b) the comprehensive income for 2008. Assume a tax rate of 35%.

PE 14-6A
Equity method
obj. 5

Gilliam Company purchased 35% of the outstanding stock of Forrester Company on January 1, 2008. Forrester reported net income of $675,000 and declared dividends of $155,000 during 2008. How much would Gilliam adjust its investment in Forrester Company under the equity method?

PE 14-6B
Equity method
obj. 5

Miranda Company purchased 25% of the outstanding stock of Orson Company on January 1, 2008. Orson reported a net loss of $300,000 and declared dividends of $40,000 during 2008. How much would Miranda adjust its investment in Orson Company under the equity method?

Exercises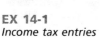

EX 14-1
Income tax entries
obj. 1

Journalize the entries to record the following selected transactions of Lone Star Leather Co.:

Apr. 15. Paid the first installment of the estimated income tax for the current fiscal year ending December 31, $90,000. No entry had been made to record the liability.
June 15. Paid the second installment of $90,000.
Sept. 15. Paid the third installment of $90,000.
Dec. 31. Recorded the estimated income tax liability for the year just ended and the deferred income tax liability, based on the transactions above and the following data:

Income tax rate	40%
Income before income tax	$950,000
Taxable income according to tax return	$800,000

Jan. 15. Paid the fourth installment of $50,000.

EX 14-2
Deferred income taxes
obj. 1

Storage Systems Inc. recognized service revenue of $420,000 on its financial statements in 2007. Assume, however, that the Tax Code requires this amount to be recognized for tax purposes in 2008. The taxable income for 2007 and 2008 is $2,600,000 and $3,000,000, respectively. Assume a tax rate of 40%.

   Prepare the journal entries to record the tax expense, deferred taxes, and taxes payable for 2007 and 2008, respectively.

EX 14-3
Deferred income taxes
obj. 1

Eason Company began operations on January 1, 2007, and reported net income of $260,000 during the year. Eason had a taxable income of $350,000 for 2007. The difference between the reported net income and taxable income will reverse in 2008. The reported net income for 2008 was $405,000. There were no other temporary differences. The tax rate is 35% for both years. Prepare the journal entries to record the tax expense, deferred taxes, and taxes payable for 2007 and 2008, respectively.

EX 14-4
Fixed asset impairment
obj. 2

✓ *a. $74,000,000*

Laser Pulse Communications Inc. spent $90 million expanding its fiber optic communication network between Chicago and Los Angeles during 2006. The fiber optic network was assumed to have a 10-year life, with a $10 million salvage value, when it was put into service on January 1, 2007. The network is depreciated using the straight-line method. At the end of 2008, the expected traffic volume on the fiber optic network was only 60% of what was originally expected. The reduced traffic volume caused the fair market value of the asset to be estimated at $50 million on December 31, 2008. The loss is not expected to be recoverable.

a. Determine the book value of the network on December 31, 2008, prior to the impairment adjustment.
b. Provide the journal entry to record the fixed asset impairment on December 31, 2008.
c. Provide the balance sheet disclosure for fixed assets on December 31, 2008.

EX 14-5
Fixed asset impairment
obj. 2

Harmony Resorts Inc. owns and manages resort properties. On January 15, 2008, one of its properties was found to be adjacent to a toxic chemical disposal site. As a result of the negative publicity, this property's bookings dropped 40% during 2008. On December 31, 2008, the accounts of the company showed the following details regarding the impaired property:

Land	$ 30,000,000
Buildings and improvements (net)	120,000,000
Equipment (net)	25,000,000
Total	$175,000,000

Management decides that closing the resort is the only option. As a result, it is estimated that the buildings and improvements will be written off completely. The land can be sold for other uses for $17 million, while the equipment can be disposed of for $6 million, net of disposal costs.

a. Provide the journal entry to record the asset impairment on December 31, 2008.
b. ⬛▷ Provide the note disclosure for the impairment.

EX 14-6
Restructuring charge
obj. 2

✓ *a. Restructuring charge,*
$4,680,000

Morton Company's board of directors approved and communicated an employee severance plan in response to a decline in demand for the company's products. The plan called for the elimination of 180 headquarters positions by providing a severance equal to 5% of the annual salary multiplied by the number of years of service. The average annual salary of the eliminated positions is $65,000. The average tenure of terminated employees is eight years. The plan was communicated to employees on November 1, 2008. Actual termination notices will be distributed over the period between December 1, 2008, and April 1, 2009. On December 21, 2008, 50 employees received a lay-off notice and were terminated with severance.

a. Provide the appropriate journal entry for the restructuring charge.
b. Provide the journal entry to record the severance payment on December 21, 2008, assuming that the actual tenure and salary of terminated employees were consistent with the overall average.
c. Provide the balance sheet and note disclosures on December 31, 2008.

EX 14-7
Restructuring charge
obj. 2

✓ *a. Restructuring charge,*
$3,774,000

Kiwi Juice Company has been suffering a downturn in its juice business due to adverse publicity regarding the caffeine content of its drink products. As a result, the company has been required to restructure operations. The board of directors approved and communicated a plan on July 1, 2008, calling for the following actions:

1. Close a juice plant on October 15, 2008. Closing, equipment relocation, and employee relocation costs are expected to be $600,000 during October.
2. Eliminate 300 plant positions. A severance will be paid to the terminated employees equal to 400% of their estimated monthly earnings payable in four quarterly installments on October 15, 2008; January 15, 2009; April 15, 2009; and July 15, 2009.

3. Terminate a juice supply contract, activating a $150,000 cancellation penalty, payable upon notice of termination. The notice will be formally delivered to the supplier on August 15, 2008.

The 300 employees earn an average of $14 per hour. The average employee works 180 hours per month.

a. Determine the total restructuring charge for 2008.
b. Provide the journal entry for the restructuring charge on July 1, 2008. (*Note:* Use Restructuring Obligation as the liability account, since the charges involve more than just employee terminations.)
c. Provide the journal entry for the October 15, 2008, employee severance payment.
d. Provide the balance sheet disclosure for December 31, 2008.
e. ▭▭➤ Provide a note disclosure for December 31, 2008.

EX 14-8
Restructuring charges and asset impairments
obj. 2

✓ *a. Severance restructuring charge, $780,000*

TransCo Inc. has suffered losses due to increased competition in its service market from low-cost independent truckers. As a result, on December 31, 2008, the board of directors of the company approved and communicated a restructuring plan that calls for selling 50 tractor-trailers out of a fleet of 400. In addition, the plan calls for the elimination of 50 driver positions and 15 staff support positions. The market price for used tractor-trailers is depressed due to general overcapacity in the transportation industry. As a result, the market value of tractor-trailers is estimated to be only 60% of the book value of these assets. It is not believed that the impairment in fixed assets is recoverable. The cost and accumulated depreciation of the total tractor-trailer fleet on December 31 are $48 million and $14 million, respectively. The restructuring plan will provide a severance to the drivers and staff totaling $12,000 per employee, payable on March 14, 2009, which is the expected employee termination date.

a. Provide the journal entries on December 31, 2008, for the fixed asset impairment and the employee severance costs.
b. ▭▭➤ Provide the balance sheet and note disclosure on December 31, 2008.
c. Provide the journal entry for March 14, 2009.

EX 14-9
Extraordinary item
obj. 2

A company received life insurance proceeds on the death of its president before the end of its fiscal year. It intends to report the amount in its income statement as an extraordinary item.

▭▭➤ Would this reporting be in conformity with generally accepted accounting principles? Discuss.

EX 14-10
Extraordinary item
obj. 2

For the year ended December 31, 2002, Delta Air Lines, provided the following note to its financial statements:

> On September 22, 2001, the Air Transportation Safety and System Stabilization Act (Stabilization Act) became effective. The Stabilization Act is intended to preserve the viability of the U.S. air transportation system following the terrorist attacks on September 11, 2001 by, among other things, (1) providing for payments from the U.S. Government totaling $5 billion to compensate U.S. air carriers for losses incurred from September 11, 2001, through December 31, 2001, as a result of the September 11 terrorist attacks and (2) permitting the Secretary of Transportation to sell insurance to U.S. air carriers.
>
> Our allocated portion of compensation under the Stabilization Act was $668 million. Due to uncertainties regarding the U.S. government's calculation of compensation, we recognized $634 million of this amount in our 2001 Consolidated Statement of Operations. We recognized the remaining $34 million of compensation in our 2002 Consolidated Statement of Operations. We received $112 million and $556 million in cash for the years ended December 31, 2002 and 2001, respectively, under the Stabilization Act.

▭▭➤ Do you believe that the income related to the Stabilization Act should be reported as an extraordinary item on the income statement of Delta Air Lines?

EX 14-11
Extraordinary items
obj. 2

Below are three separate historical incidents giving rise to losses for three different companies.

a. In 1980, Weyerhaeuser, a major wood products company, lost $36 million in timber, logs, and building equipment as a result of the volcanic eruption of Mount St. Helens in the state of Washington.
b. In 2001, Dow Jones & Company, Inc., the publisher of *The Wall Street Journal*, suffered $1.7 million in losses due to damage in its headquarters building as a result of the 9/11 terrorist incident.
c. In 2005, Northrop Grumman Corporation, a major defense contractor, reported significant losses in its shipbuilding yards along the Gulf Coast as a result of Hurricane Katrina. The losses were sufficient to cut its projected earnings in half for the year.

In each case, identify whether the loss should be reported as extraordinary.

EX 14-12
Identifying extraordinary items
obj. 2

Assume that the amount of each of the following items is material to the financial statements. Classify each item as either normally recurring (NR) or extraordinary (E).

a. Restructuring charge related to employee termination benefits.
b. Loss on sale of fixed assets.
c. Uninsured flood loss. (Flood insurance is unavailable because of periodic flooding in the area.)
d. Interest revenue on notes receivable.
e. Loss on disposal of equipment considered to be obsolete because of development of new technology.
f. Uninsured loss on building due to hurricane damage. The firm was organized in 1920 and had not previously incurred hurricane damage.
g. Uncollectible accounts expense.
h. Gain on sale of land condemned for public use.

EX 14-13
Income statement
objs. 2, 3

✓ *Net income, $126,600*

Wind Surfer Inc. produces and distributes equipment for sailboats. On the basis of the following data for the current fiscal year ended June 30, 2008, prepare a multiple-step income statement for Wind Surfer, including an analysis of earnings per share in the form illustrated in this chapter. There were 20,000 shares of $150 par common stock outstanding throughout the year.

Administrative expenses	$ 104,000
Cost of merchandise sold	467,500
Gain on condemnation of land (extraordinary item)	58,000
Income tax applicable to gain on condemnation of land	23,200
Income tax reduction applicable to loss from discontinued operations	32,000
Income tax applicable to income from continuing operations	93,200
Loss on discontinued operations	80,000
Loss from fixed asset impairment	120,000
Restructuring charge	50,000
Sales	1,100,000
Selling expenses	125,500

EX 14-14
Income statement
objs. 2, 3

✓ *Correct EPS for net income, $0.47*

Audio Affection Inc. sells automotive and home stereo equipment. It has 50,000 shares of $100 par common stock outstanding and 10,000 shares of $2, $100 par cumulative preferred stock outstanding as of December 31, 2008. List the errors you find in the following income statement for the year ended December 31, 2008.

(continued)

Audio Affection Inc.
Income Statement
For the Year Ended December 31, 2008

Net sales		$967,000
Cost of merchandise sold		578,000
Gross profit		$389,000
Operating expenses:		
Selling expenses	$127,000	
Administrative expenses	142,000	269,000
Income from continuing operations before income tax		$120,000
Income tax expense		48,000
Income from continuing operations		$ 72,000
Fixed asset impairment		(24,000)
Income before condemnation of land, restructuring charge, and discontinued operations		$ 48,000
Extraordinary items:		
Gain on condemnation of land, net of applicable income tax of $20,000		30,000
Restructuring charge, net of applicable income tax of $8,000		(12,000)
Loss on discontinued operations (net of applicable income tax of $15,000)		(22,500)
Net income		$ 43,500
Earnings per common share:		
Income from continuing operations		$ 1.44
Fixed asset impairment		(0.48)
Income before extraordinary item and discontinued operations		$ 0.96
Extraordinary items:		
Gain on condemnation of land		0.60
Restructuring charge		(0.24)
Loss on discontinued operations		(0.45)
Net income		$ 0.87

EX 14-15
Earnings per share with preferred stock

obj. **3**

FirstLight Lighting Company had earnings for 2008 of $150,600. The company had 90,000 shares of common stock outstanding during the year. In addition, the company issued 2,000 shares of $100 par value preferred stock on January 5, 2008. The preferred stock has a dividend of $6 per share. There were no transactions in either common or preferred stock during 2008.

Determine the basic earnings per share for FirstLight.

EX 14-16
Comprehensive income

obj. **4**

a. $1,693,000

The statement of comprehensive income for Lancaster Company was as follows:

Lancaster Company
Statement of Comprehensive Income
For the Year Ended December 31, 2008

Net income	$460,000
Other comprehensive income:	
Unrealized loss on temporary investments in marketable equity securities (net of $25,000 tax benefit)	(45,000)
Total comprehensive income	$415,000

The balance sheet dated December 31, 2007, showed a Retained Earnings balance of $1,483,000 and an Accumulated Other Comprehensive Income balance of $171,000. The company paid $250,000 in dividends during 2008.

a. Determine the December 31, 2008, Retained Earnings balance.
b. Determine the December 31, 2008, Accumulated Other Comprehensive Income (Loss) balance.

EX 14-17
*Comprehensive income
and temporary
investments*

objs. **4, 5**

✓c. $84,000

The statement of comprehensive income for the years ended December 31, 2008 and 2009, plus selected items from comparative balance sheets of Johnson Wholesalers Inc. are as follows:

Johnson Wholesalers Inc.
Statement of Comprehensive Income
For the Years Ended December 31, 2008 and 2009

	2008	2009
Net income	a.	$100,000
Other comprehensive income (loss), net of tax	b.	4,000
Total comprehensive income	c.	e.

Johnson Wholesalers Inc.
Selected Balance Sheet Items
December 31, 2007, 2008, and 2009

	Dec. 31, 2007	Dec. 31, 2008	Dec. 31, 2009
Temporary investments in marketable securities at fair market value, net of taxes on unrealized gains or losses	$ 32,000	d.	f.
Retained earnings	175,000	$250,000	g.
Accumulated other comprehensive income or (loss)	(8,000)	1,000	h.

There were no dividends or purchases or sales of temporary investments. Other comprehensive items included only after-tax unrealized gains and losses on investments. Determine the missing lettered items.

EX 14-18
*Comprehensive income
and temporary
investments*

objs. **4, 5**

✓a. Total comprehensive income, $205,000

During 2008, Mango Corporation held a portfolio of available-for-sale securities having a cost of $260,000. There were no purchases or sales of investments during the year. The market values after adjusting for the impact of taxes, at the beginning and end of the year, were $215,000 and $270,000, respectively. The net income for 2008 was $150,000, and no dividends were paid during the year. The Stockholders' Equity section of the balance sheet was as follows on December 31, 2007:

Mango Corporation
Stockholders' Equity
December 31, 2007

Common stock	$ 35,000
Paid-in capital in excess of par value	350,000
Retained earnings	435,000
Accumulated other comprehensive loss	(45,000)
Total	$775,000

a. Prepare a statement of comprehensive income for 2008.
b. Prepare the stockholders' equity section of the balance sheet for December 31, 2008.

EX 14-19
*Temporary investments
and other comprehensive
income*

objs. **4, 5**

✓a. 2009 unrealized gain, $54,000

The temporary investments of Catalyst Inc. only include 10,000 shares of Bristol Inc. common stock purchased on January 10, 2008, for $20 per share. As of the December 31, 2008, balance sheet date, assume that the share price declined to $16 per share. As of the December 31, 2009, balance sheet date, assume that the share price rose to $25 per share. The investment was held through December 31, 2009. Assume a tax rate of 40%.

a. Determine the net after-tax unrealized gain or loss from holding the Bristol common stock for 2008 and 2009.
b. What is the balance of Accumulated Other Comprehensive Income or Loss for December 31, 2008, and December 31, 2009?
c. Where is Accumulated Other Comprehensive Income or Deficit disclosed on the financial statements?

EX 14-20
Temporary investments in marketable securities
obj. 5

During 2008, its first year of operations, Geo-Metrics Corporation purchased the following securities as a temporary investment:

Security	Shares Purchased	Cost	Cash Dividends Received
M-Labs Inc.	1,000	$19,000	$ 750
Spectrum Corp.	2,500	38,000	1,400

a. Record the purchase of the temporary investments for cash.
b. Record the receipt of the dividends.

EX 14-21
Financial statement reporting of temporary investments
objs. 4, 5

✓*b. Comprehensive income, $101,800*

Using the data for Geo-Metrics Corporation in Exercise 14-20, assume that as of December 31, 2008, the M-Labs Inc. stock had a market value of $25 per share and the Spectrum Corp. stock had a market value of $14 per share. For the year ending December 31, 2008, Geo-Metrics Corporation had net income of $100,000. Its tax rate is 40%.

a. Prepare the balance sheet presentation for the temporary investments.
b. Prepare a statement of comprehensive income presentation for the temporary investments.

EX 14-22
Entries for investment in stock, receipt of dividends, and sale of shares
obj. 5

On February 27, Ball Corporation acquired 4,000 shares of the 50,000 outstanding shares of Bat Co. common stock at 40.75 plus commission charges of $200. On July 8, a cash dividend of $1.75 per share and a 2% stock dividend were received. On December 7, 1,000 shares were sold at 53, less commission charges of $65. Record the entries to record (a) the purchase of the stock, (b) the receipt of dividends, and (c) the sale of the 1,000 shares.

EX 14-23
Entries using equity method for stock investment
obj. 5

At a total cost of $1,960,000, Turner Corporation acquired 70,000 shares of May Corp. common stock as a long-term investment. Turner Corporation uses the equity method of accounting for this investment. May Corp. has 280,000 shares of common stock outstanding, including the shares acquired by Turner Corporation. Journalize the entries by Turner Corporation to record the following information:

a. May Corp. reports net income of $3,000,000 for the current period.
b. A cash dividend of $3.80 per common share is paid by May Corp. during the current period.

EX 14-24
Equity method for stock investment
obj. 5

Sweet Company's balance sheet disclosed its long-term investment in Sour Company for comparative years as follows:

	Dec. 31, 2008	Dec. 31, 2007
Investment in Sour Company stock (in millions)	$146	$135

In addition, the 2008 Sweet Company income statement disclosed equity earnings in the Sour Company investment as $15 million. Sweet Company neither purchased nor sold Sour Company stock during 2008. The market value of Sour Company stock on December 31, 2008, was $154.

▶ Explain the change in the Investment in Sour Company Stock from December 31, 2007, to December 31, 2008.

EX 14-25
Price-earnings ratio

Goodman Company had a net income of $672,000 for 2008. Goodman Company's balance sheet disclosed the stockholders' equity on December 31, 2008, as follows:

Preferred stock, 8,000 shares of $100 par value, 6% stock	$ 800,000
Common stock, 120,000 shares of $1 par value stock issued and outstanding	120,000
Paid-in capital in excess of par value	2,400,000
Total stockholders' equity	$3,320,000

The price of Goodman common stock was $72.80 per share on December 31, 2008. Determine the price-earnings ratio for Goodman Company.

EX 14-26
Price-earnings ratio calculations

✓ *a. 2005: 9.7*

ExxonMobil Corporation is one of the largest companies in the world. The company explores, develops, refines, and markets petroleum products. The basic earnings per share for three comparative years were as follows:

	Years Ended Dec. 31,		
	2005	**2004**	**2003**
Basic earnings per share	$5.76	$3.91	$3.24

The market prices at the end of each year were $56, $51, and $41 for December 31, 2005, 2004, and 2003, respectively.

a. Determine the price-earnings ratio for 2005, 2004, and 2003, using end-of-year prices. Round to one decimal place.
b. Interpret your results over the three years.

Problems Series A

PR 14-1A
Income tax allocation

obj. 1

✓ *1. Year-end balance, 3rd year, $12,000*

Differences between the accounting methods applied to accounts and financial reports and those used in determining taxable income yielded the following amounts for the first four years of a corporation's operations:

	First Year	**Second Year**	**Third Year**	**Fourth Year**
Income before income taxes	$250,000	$300,000	$500,000	$400,000
Taxable income	200,000	280,000	540,000	430,000

The income tax rate for each of the four years was 40% of taxable income, and each year's taxes were promptly paid.

Instructions

1. Determine for each year the amounts described by the following captions, presenting the information in the form indicated:

Year	Income Tax Deducted on Income Statement	Income Tax Payments for the Year	Deferred Income Tax Payable	
			Year's Addition (Deduction)	Year-End Balance

2. Total the first three amount columns.

PR 14-2A
Income tax; income statement

objs. 2, 3, 4

✓ *Net income, $34,300*

The following data were selected from the records of Xtreme World Inc. for the current fiscal year ended June 30, 2008:

Advertising expense	$ 57,000
Cost of merchandise sold	345,000
Depreciation expense—office equipment	16,000
Depreciation expense—store equipment	45,000
Gain on discontinued operations	38,000
Income tax:	
Applicable to continuing operations	10,500
Applicable to gain on disposal of business segment	11,400
Applicable to loss on condemnation of land (reduction)	7,200
Insurance expense	9,000
Interest expense	18,000
Loss from condemnation of land	24,000

(continued)

Loss from fixed asset impairment	$ 40,000
Miscellaneous administrative expense	11,000
Miscellaneous selling expense	14,000
Office salaries expense	70,000
Rent expense	25,000
Restructuring charge	50,000
Sales	865,000
Sales commissions expense	130,000
Unrealized gain on temporary investments	35,000

Instructions
Prepare a multiple-step income statement, concluding with a section for earnings per share in the form illustrated in this chapter. There were 5,000 shares of common stock (no preferred) outstanding throughout the year. Assume that the loss on the condemnation of land is an extraordinary item.

PR 14-3A
*Income statement;
retained earnings
statement; balance sheet*
objs. 1, 2, 3, 4

✓ *Net income, $67,200*

The following data were taken from the records of Amana Bread Corporation for the year ended October 31, 2008:

Income statement data:

Administrative expenses	$ 80,000
Cost of merchandise sold	458,000
Gain on condemnation of land	80,000
Income tax:	
Applicable to continuing operations	36,800
Applicable to loss from discontinued business segment	24,000
Applicable to gain on condemnation of land	32,000
Interest expense	5,000
Interest revenue	4,000
Loss from discontinued operations	60,000
Loss from fixed asset impairment	35,000
Restructuring charge	65,000
Sales	955,000
Selling expenses	224,000

Retained earnings and balance sheet data:

Accounts payable	$ 47,800
Accounts receivable	185,000
Accumulated depreciation	465,000
Accumulated other comprehensive loss	28,000
Allowance for doubtful accounts	5,400
Cash	165,300
Common stock, $1 par (100,000 shares authorized; 82,000 shares issued)	82,000
Deferred income taxes payable (current portion, $5,400)	28,300
Dividends:	
Cash dividends for common stock	35,000
Cash dividends for preferred stock	16,000
Stock dividends for common stock	12,000
Dividends payable	12,750
Employee termination obligation (current)	45,000
Equipment	1,958,000
Income tax payable	11,200
Interest receivable	2,500
Merchandise inventory (October 31, 2008), at lower of cost (FIFO) or market	122,000
Notes receivable	42,500
Paid-in capital from sale of treasury stock	16,000
Paid-in capital in excess of par—common stock	451,000
Paid-in capital in excess of par—preferred stock	8,000
Patents	14,000
Preferred 8% stock, $100 par (10,000 shares authorized; 2,000 shares issued)	200,000
Prepaid expenses	2,600
Retained earnings, November 1, 2007	1,277,250
Temporary investment in marketable equity securities	122,000
Treasury stock (2,000 shares of common stock at cost of $20 per share)	40,000
Unrealized loss on temporary equity securities (net of taxes)	28,000

Instructions
1. Prepare a multiple-step income statement for the year ended October 31, 2008, concluding with earnings per share. In computing earnings per share, assume that the average number of common shares outstanding was 80,000 and preferred dividends were $16,000. Assume that the gain on condemnation of land is an extraordinary item.
2. Prepare a retained earnings statement for the year ended October 31, 2008.
3. Prepare a balance sheet in report form as of October 31, 2008.

PR 14-4A
Entries for investments in stock
obj. 5

Samson Company is a wholesaler of men's hair products. The following transactions relate to certain securities acquired by Samson Company, which has a fiscal year ending on December 31:

2006
Jan. 3. Purchased 4,000 shares of the 100,000 outstanding common shares of Nichols Corporation at 55 plus commission and other costs of $480.
July 2. Received the regular cash dividend of $1.25 a share on Nichols Corporation stock.
Dec. 5. Received the regular cash dividend of $1.25 a share plus an extra dividend of $0.10 a share on Nichols Corporation stock.

   (Assume that all intervening transactions have been recorded properly and that the number of shares of stock owned have not changed from December 31, 2006, to December 31, 2008.)

2009
Jan. 2. Purchased controlling interest in Telico Inc. for $540,000 by purchasing 32,000 shares directly from the estate of the founder of Telico. There are 128,000 shares of Telico Inc. stock outstanding.
July 6. Received the regular cash dividend of $1.25 a share and a 4% stock dividend on the Nichols Corporation stock.
Oct. 23. Sold 800 shares of Nichols Corporation stock at 68. The broker deducted commission and other costs of $140, remitting the balance.
Dec. 10. Received a cash dividend at the new rate of $1.50 a share on the Nichols Corporation stock.
    31. Received $38,000 of cash dividends on Telico Inc. stock. Telico Inc. reported net income of $260,000 in 2009. Samson uses the equity method of accounting for its investment in Telico Inc.

Instructions
Record the entries for the preceding transactions.

Problems Series B

PR 14-1B
Income tax allocation
obj. 1

✓ 1. Year-end balance, 3rd year, $4,200

Differences between the accounting methods applied to accounts and financial reports and those used in determining taxable income yielded the following amounts for the first four years of a corporation's operations:

	First Year	Second Year	Third Year	Fourth Year
Income before income taxes	$50,000	$65,000	$90,000	$100,000
Taxable income	35,000	60,000	98,000	112,000

The income tax rate for each of the four years was 35% of taxable income, and each year's taxes were promptly paid.

Instructions
1. Determine for each year the amounts described by the following captions, presenting the information in the form indicated:

(continued)

Year	Income Tax Deducted on Income Statement	Income Tax Payments for the Year	Deferred Income Tax Payable	
			Year's Addition (Deduction)	Year-End Balance

2. Total the first three amount columns.

PR 14-2B
Income tax; income statement

objs. 2, 3, 4

✓ *Net income, $203,000*

ATV Inc. sells off-road motorcycles and vehicles. The following data were selected from the records of ATV Inc. for the current fiscal year ended March 31, 2008:

Advertising expense	$ 36,000
Cost of merchandise sold	1,640,000
Depreciation expense—office equipment	32,000
Depreciation expense—store equipment	145,000
Gain on condemnation of land	54,000
Income tax:	
Applicable to continuing operations	94,200
Applicable to loss from discontinued operations (reduction)	23,400
Applicable to gain on condemnation of land	16,200
Interest revenue	25,000
Loss from disposal of business segment	78,000
Loss from fixed asset impairment	32,000
Miscellaneous administrative expense	41,000
Miscellaneous selling expense	25,000
Office salaries expense	230,000
Rent expense	100,000
Restructuring charge	70,000
Sales	2,800,000
Sales salaries expense	160,000
Unrealized loss on temporary investments	40,000

Instructions

Prepare a multiple-step income statement, concluding with a section for earnings per share in the form illustrated in this chapter. There were 20,000 shares of common stock (no preferred) outstanding throughout the year. Assume that the gain on the condemnation of land is an extraordinary item.

PR 14-3B
Income statement; retained earnings statement; balance sheet

objs. 1, 2, 3, 4

✓ *Net income, $128,700*

The following data were taken from the records of Disk N' Dat Corporation for the year ended August 31, 2008.

Income statement data:

Administrative expenses	$ 23,000
Cost of merchandise sold	232,000
Gain on condemnation of land	75,000
Income tax:	
Applicable to continuing operations	70,200
Applicable to loss from discontinued operation	14,400
Applicable to gain on condemnation of land	30,000
Interest expense	3,000
Interest revenue	2,500
Loss from disposal of discontinued operation	36,000
Loss from fixed asset impairment	14,000
Restructuring charge	45,000
Sales	550,000
Selling expenses	60,000

Retained earnings and balance sheet data:

Accounts payable	$ 12,000
Accounts receivable	28,000
Accumulated depreciation	145,000

Accumulated other comprehensive income	$ 9,000
Allowance for doubtful accounts	2,500
Cash	87,500
Common stock, $1 par (100,000 shares authorized; 46,000 shares issued)	46,000
Deferred income taxes payable (current portion, $4,700)	12,800
Dividends:	
Cash dividends for common stock	21,000
Cash dividends for preferred stock	9,000
Stock dividends for common stock	5,000
Dividends payable	7,500
Employee termination obligation (current)	30,000
Equipment	1,350,000
Income tax payable	21,450
Interest receivable	500
Merchandise inventory (August 31, 2008), at lower of cost (FIFO) or market	87,000
Paid-in capital from sale of treasury stock	5,000
Paid-in capital in excess of par—common stock	820,000
Paid-in capital in excess of par—preferred stock	20,000
Patents	40,000
Preferred 6% stock, $100 par (30,000 shares authorized; 1,500 shares issued)	150,000
Prepaid expenses	15,900
Retained earnings, September 1, 2007	397,950
Temporary investments in marketable equity securities (at cost)	125,000
Treasury stock (1,000 shares of common stock at cost of $30 per share)	30,000
Unrealized gain on marketable equity securities	9,000

Instructions

1. Prepare a multiple-step income statement for the year ended August 31, 2008, concluding with earnings per share. In computing earnings per share, assume that the average number of common shares outstanding was 45,000 and preferred dividends were $9,000. Assume that the gain on the condemnation of land is an extraordinary item.
2. Prepare a retained earnings statement for the year ended August 31, 2008.
3. Prepare a balance sheet in report form as of August 31, 2008.

PR 14-4B
Entries for investments in stock

obj. 5

Encore Design Inc. produces and sells theater set designs and costumes. The following transactions relate to certain securities acquired by Encore Design Inc., which has a fiscal year ending on December 31:

2006
Feb. 10. Purchased 8,000 shares of the 150,000 outstanding common shares of Mode Corporation at 36 plus commission and other costs of $864.
July 15. Received the regular cash dividend of $1.10 a share on Mode Corporation stock.
Dec. 15. Received the regular cash dividend of $1.10 a share plus an extra dividend of $0.05 a share on Mode Corporation stock.

> (Assume that all intervening transactions have been recorded properly and that the number of shares of stock owned have not changed from December 31, 2006, to December 31, 2008.)

2009
Jan. 3. Purchased controlling interest in Applause Inc. for $675,000 by purchasing 30,000 shares directly from the estate of the founder of Applause. There are 100,000 shares of Applause Inc. stock outstanding.
Apr. 14. Received the regular cash dividend of $1.10 a share and a 2% stock dividend on the Mode Corporation stock.
July 26. Sold 1,000 shares of Mode Corporation stock at 32. The broker deducted commission and other costs of $125, remitting the balance.
Dec. 15. Received a cash dividend at the new rate of $1.20 a share on the Mode Corporation stock.
   31. Received $12,500 of cash dividends on Applause Inc. stock. Applause Inc. reported net income of $325,000 in 2009. Encore Design uses the equity method of accounting for its investment in Applause Inc.

Instructions
Journalize the entries for the preceding transactions.

Special Activities

SA 14-1
Equity method disclosure

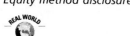

The following note to the consolidated financial statements for Goodyear Tire & Rubber Company relates to the principles of consolidation used in preparing the financial statements:

> *The Company's investments in 20% to 50% owned companies in which it has the ability to exercise significant influence over operating and financial policies are accounted for by the equity method. Accordingly, the Company's share of the earnings of these companies is included in consolidated net income.*

Is it a requirement that Goodyear use the equity method in this situation? Explain.

SA 14-2
Special charges analysis

The two-year comparative income statements and a note disclosure for Mercury Shoes Inc. were as follows:

Income Statement
Mercury Shoes Inc.
For the Years Ended December 31, 2008 and 2007

	2008	2007
Sales	$510,000	$430,000
Cost of merchandise sold	224,400	193,500
Gross profit	$285,600	$236,500
Selling and administrative expenses	122,400	107,500
Loss on fixed asset impairment	127,500	—
Income from operations	$ 35,700	$129,000
Income tax expense	14,280	51,600
Net income	$ 21,420	$ 77,400

Note: A fixed asset impairment of $127,500 was recognized in 2008 as the result of abandoning an order management software system. The system project was started in early 2007 and ran into significant delays and performance problems throughout 2008. It was determined that there was no incremental benefit from completing the system. Thus, the accumulated costs associated with the system were written off.

1. Divide each amount in the 2008 and 2007 income statements by total sales for the given year.
2. Interpret the performance of the company in 2008.

SA 14-3
Comprehensive income

The Stockholders' Equity section of Yum! Brands, Inc., the operator of Pizza Hut, KFC, and Taco Bell restaurants, for two recent comparative dates was as follows:

Yum! Brands, Inc.
Stockholders' Equity (selected items)
December 31, 2005 and December 31, 2004
(in millions)

	Dec. 31, 2005	Dec. 31, 2004
Common stock, no par value	$ 0	$ 659
Retained earnings	1,619	1,067
Accumulated other comprehensive income (loss)	(170)	(131)
Total stockholders' equity	$1,449	$1,595

1. What is the "other" comprehensive income or loss for the year ended December 31, 2005?
2. Explain the concept of other comprehensive income.

SA 14-4
*Ethics and professional
conduct in business*

ETHICS

Dillon Osborn is the president and chief operating officer of Dollars N' Sense Corporation, a developer of personal financial planning software. During the past year, Dollars N' Sense Corporation was forced to sell 10 acres of land to the city of Houston for expansion of a freeway exit. The corporation fought the sale; but after condemnation hearings, a judge ordered it to sell the land. Because of the land's location and the fact that Dollars N' Sense Corporation had purchased the land over 15 years ago, the corporation recorded a $0.20-per-share gain on the sale. Always looking to turn a negative into a positive, Dillon has decided to announce the corporation's earnings per share of $1.05, without identifying the $0.20 impact of selling the land. Although he will retain majority ownership, Dillon plans on selling 20,000 of his shares in the corporation sometime within the next month.

Are Dillon's plans to announce earnings per share of $1.05 without mentioning the $0.20 impact of selling the land ethical and professional?

SA 14-5
*Reporting extraordinary
item*

Sunshine Fruit Co. is in the process of preparing its annual financial statements. Sunshine Fruit is a large citrus grower located in central Florida. The following is a discussion between Curtis Kirk, the controller, and Liz Gwinn, the chief executive officer and president of Sunshine Fruit Co.

Liz: Curtis, I've got a question about your rough draft of this year's income statement.
Curtis: Sure, Liz. What's your question?
Liz: Well, your draft shows a net loss of $750,000.
Curtis: That's right. We'd have had a profit, except for this year's frost damage. I figured that the frost destroyed over 30% of our crop. We had a good year otherwise.
Liz: That's my concern. I estimated that if we eliminate the frost damage, we'd show a profit of . . . let's see . . . about $250,000.
Curtis: That sounds about right.
Liz: This income statement seems misleading. Why can't we show the loss on the frost damage separately? That way the bank and our outside investors will be able to see that this year's loss is just temporary. I'd hate to get them upset over nothing.
Curtis: Maybe we can do something. I recall from my accounting courses something about showing unusual items separately. Let's see . . . yes, I remember. They're called extraordinary items.
Liz: Well, we haven't had any frost damage in over five years. This year's damage is certainly extraordinary. Let's do it!

Discuss the appropriateness of revising Sunshine Fruit's income statement to report the frost damage separately as an extraordinary item.

SA 14-6
*Extraordinary items and
discontinued operations*

REAL WORLD

Group Project

Internet Project

In groups of three or four, search company annual reports, news releases, or the Internet for extraordinary items and announcements of discontinued operations. Identify the most unusual extraordinary item in your group. Also, select a discontinued operation of a well-known company that might be familiar to other students or might interest them.

Prepare a brief analysis of the earnings per share impact of both the extraordinary item and the discontinued operation. Estimate the *potential* impact on the company's market price by multiplying the current price-earnings ratio by the earnings per share amount of each item.

One Internet site that has annual reports is EDGAR (Electronic Data Gathering, Analysis, and Retrieval), the electronic archives of financial statements filed with the Securities and Exchange Commission. SEC documents can be retrieved using the EdgarScan service from PricewaterhouseCoopers at **http://edgarscan.pwcglobal.com**.

To obtain annual report information, type in a company name in the appropriate space. EdgarScan will list the reports available to you for the company you've selected. Select the most recent annual report filing, identified as a 10-K or 10-K405. EdgarScan provides an outline of the report, including the separate financial statements. You can double click the income statement and balance sheet for the selected company into an Excel™ spreadsheet for further analysis.

Answers to Self-Examination Questions

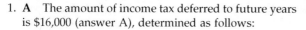

1. **A** The amount of income tax deferred to future years is $16,000 (answer A), determined as follows:

Depreciation expense, MACRS	$100,000
Depreciation expense, straight-line method	60,000
Excess expense in determining taxable income	$ 40,000
Income tax rate	× 40%
Income tax deferred to future years	$ 16,000

2. **A** Events and transactions that are distinguished by their unusual nature and by the infrequency of their occurrence, such as a gain on condemning land for public use, are reported in the income statement as extraordinary items (answer A). A restructuring charge (answer C) and fixed asset impairment (answer D) are unusual items that are related to different accounting events than land condemnation.

3. **B** The difference between the cost of temporary investments held as available-for-sale securities and their market value is reported as an unrealized gain, net of applicable income taxes, as shown below.

Market value of investments	$120,000
Cost of investments	100,000
	$ 20,000
Applicable taxes (40%)	8,000
Unrealized gain, net of taxes	$ 12,000

The unrealized gain of $12,000 (answer B) is reported on the balance sheet as an addition to the cost of the investments and as part of other comprehensive income.

4. **C** Under the equity method of accounting for investments in stocks, Cisneros Corporation records its share of both net income and dividends of Harrell Inc. in Investment in Harrell Inc. Stock. Thus, Investment in Harrell Inc. Stock would increase by $82,500 [($150,000 × 75%) − ($40,000 × 75%)] for the current year. $30,000 (answer B) is only Cisneros Corporation's share of Harrell's dividends for the current year. $112,500 (answer D) is only Cisneros Corporation's share of Harrell's net income for the year.

5. **C** Price-Earnings Ratio =

$$\frac{\text{Market Price per Common Share}}{\text{Earnings per Share}}, \text{ or}$$

$$\frac{\$60}{(\$800,000 - \$50,000)/200,000} = 16$$

Bonds Payable and Investments in Bonds

© UNDER ARMOUR®/PRNEWSFOTO (AP TOPIC GALLERY)

objectives

After studying this chapter, you should be able to:

1 Compute the potential impact of long-term borrowing on earnings per share.

2 Describe the characteristics, terminology, and pricing of bonds payable.

3 Journalize entries for bonds payable.

4 Describe and illustrate the payment and redemption of bonds payable.

5 Journalize entries for the purchase, interest, discount and premium amortization, and sale of bond investments.

6 Prepare a corporation balance sheet.

Under Armour®

Most of us don't have enough money in our bank accounts to buy a house or a car by simply writing a check. Just imagine if you had to save the complete purchase price of a house before you could buy it! To help us make these types of purchases, banks will typically lend us the money, as long as we agree to repay the loan along with interest in smaller payments in the future. Loans such as this, or long-term debt, allow us to purchase assets such as houses and cars today, which benefit us over the long term.

The use of debt can also help a business reach its objectives. Most businesses have to borrow money in order to acquire assets that they will use to generate income. For example, Under Armour®, a maker of performance athletic clothing, uses debt to acquire assets that it needs to manufacture and sell its prod-

ucts. Since it began in 1995, the company has used long-term debt to transform itself from a small business to a leading athletic wear company. The company now sells products in over 8,000 retail stores across the world. In addition, Under Armour® products are used by a number of teams in the National Football League, Major League Baseball, the National Hockey League, and in Olympic sports.

While debt can help companies like Under Armour® grow to achieve financial success, too much debt can be a financial burden that may even lead to bankruptcy. Just like individuals, businesses must manage debt wisely. In this chapter, we will discuss the nature of, accounting for, analysis of, and investments in long-term debt.

Financing Corporations

objective **1**

Compute the potential impact of long-term borrowing on earnings per share.

Bonds of major corporations are actively traded on bond exchanges. You can purchase bonds through a financial services firm, such as Merrill Lynch & Co. Inc., A. G. Edwards & Sons, Inc., or Edward Jones.

As discussed above, both individuals and corporations use debt to purchase assets or resources today that they might otherwise be unable to afford. Corporations often finance their operations by purchasing on credit and issuing notes or bonds. We have discussed accounts payable and notes payable in earlier chapters. A **bond** is simply a form of an interest-bearing note. Like a note, a bond requires periodic interest payments, and the face amount must be repaid at the maturity date. Bondholders are creditors of the issuing corporation, and their claims on the assets of the corporation rank ahead of stockholders.

One of the many factors that influence the decision to issue debt or equity is the effect of each alternative on earnings per share. To illustrate the possible effects, assume that a corporation's board of directors is considering the following alternative plans for financing a $4,000,000 company:

	Plan 1	Plan 2	Plan 3
Issue 12% bonds	—	—	$2,000,000
Issue 9% preferred stock, $50 par value	—	$2,000,000	1,000,000
Issue common stock, $10 par value	$4,000,000	2,000,000	1,000,000
	$4,000,000	$4,000,000	$4,000,000

In each case, we assume that the stocks or bonds are issued at their par or face amount. The corporation is expecting to earn $800,000 annually, before deducting interest on the bonds and income taxes estimated at 40% of income. Exhibit 1 shows the effect of the three plans on the income of the corporation and the earnings per share on common stock.

EXHIBIT 1

Effect of Alternative
Financing Plans—
$800,000 Earnings

	Plan 1	Plan 2	Plan 3
12% bonds	—	—	$2,000,000
Preferred 9% stock, $50 par	—	$2,000,000	1,000,000
Common stock, $10 par	$4,000,000	2,000,000	1,000,000
Total	$4,000,000	$4,000,000	$4,000,000
Earnings before interest and income tax ...	$ 800,000	$ 800,000	$ 800,000
Deduct interest on bonds	—	—	240,000
Income before income tax	$ 800,000	$ 800,000	$ 560,000
Deduct income tax	320,000	320,000	224,000
Net income	$ 480,000	$ 480,000	$ 336,000
Dividends on preferred stock	—	180,000	90,000
Available for dividends on common stock ..	$ 480,000	$ 300,000	$ 246,000
Shares of common stock outstanding	÷ 400,000	÷ 200,000	÷ 100,000
Earnings per share on common stock	$ 1.20	$ 1.50	$ 2.46

When interest rates are low,
corporations usually finance
their operations with debt. For
example, as interest rates fell
in recent years, corporations
issued large amounts of new
debt.

Exhibit 1 indicates that Plan 3 yields the highest earnings per share on common stock and is thus the most attractive for common stockholders. If the estimated earnings are more than $800,000, the difference between the earnings per share to common stockholders under Plan 1 and Plan 3 is even greater.[1] However, if smaller earnings occur, Plans 2 and 3 become less attractive to common stockholders. To illustrate, the effect of earnings of $440,000 rather than $800,000 is shown in Exhibit 2.

In addition to the effect on earnings per share, the board of directors should consider other factors in deciding whether to issue debt or equity. For example, once bonds are issued, periodic interest payments and repayment of the face value of the bonds are beyond the control of the corporation. That is, if these payments are not made, the bondholders could seek court action and force the company into bankruptcy. In contrast, a corporation is not legally obligated to pay dividends.

EXHIBIT 2

Effect of Alternative
Financing Plans—
$440,000 Earnings

	Plan 1	Plan 2	Plan 3
12% bonds	—	—	$2,000,000
Preferred 9% stock, $50 par	—	$2,000,000	1,000,000
Common stock, $10 par	$4,000,000	2,000,000	1,000,000
Total	$4,000,000	$4,000,000	$4,000,000
Earnings before interest and income tax ...	$ 440,000	$ 440,000	$ 440,000
Deduct interest on bonds	—	—	240,000
Income before income tax	$ 440,000	$ 440,000	$ 200,000
Deduct income tax	176,000	176,000	80,000
Net income	$ 264,000	$ 264,000	$ 120,000
Dividends on preferred stock	—	180,000	90,000
Available for dividends on common stock ..	$ 264,000	$ 84,000	$ 30,000
Shares of common stock outstanding	÷ 400,000	÷ 200,000	÷ 100,000
Earnings per share on common stock	$ 0.66	$ 0.42	$ 0.30

---

1 The higher earnings per share under Plan 3 is due to a finance concept known as *leverage*. This concept is discussed further in a later chapter.

Example Exercise 15-1

objective **1**

Gonzales Co. is considering the following alternative plans for financing its company:

	Plan 1	Plan 2
Issue 10% bonds (at face value)	—	$2,000,000
Issue common stock, $10 par	$3,000,000	1,000,000

Income tax is estimated at 40% of income.

Determine the earnings per share of common stock under the two alternative financing plans, assuming income before bond interest and income tax is $750,000.

Follow My Example 15-1

	Plan 1	Plan 2
Earnings before bond interest and income tax	$750,000	$750,000
Bond interest	0	200,000[2]
Balance	$750,000	$550,000
Income tax	300,000[1]	220,000[3]
Net income	$450,000	$330,000
Dividends on preferred stock	0	0
Earnings available for common stock	$450,000	$330,000
Number of common shares	/300,000	/100,000
Earnings per share on common stock	$ 1.50	$ 3.30

[1]$750,000 × 40%   [2]$2,000,000 × 10%   [3]$550,000 × 40%

For Practice: PE 15-1A, PE 15-1B

Characteristics, Terminology, and Pricing of Bonds Payable

objective **2**

Describe the characteristics, terminology, and pricing of bonds payable.

In addition to their face values, interest rates, interest payment dates, and maturity dates, bonds may differ in a variety of ways. In this section, we describe the common characteristics of bonds and how bonds may differ from one another. In doing so, we introduce common terms used to describe types of bonds. In addition, we describe and illustrate how the price investors are willing to pay for a bond is determined.

BOND CHARACTERISTICS AND TERMINOLOGY

A corporation that issues bonds enters into a contract, called a **bond indenture** or *trust indenture*, with the bondholders. A bond issue is normally divided into a number of individual bonds. Usually, the face value of each bond, called the *principal*, is $1,000 or a multiple of $1,000. The interest on bonds may be payable annually, semiannually, or quarterly. Most bonds pay interest semiannually.

The prices of bonds are quoted as a percentage of the bonds' face value. Thus, investors could purchase or sell Wal-Mart bonds quoted at 113.84 for $1,138.40. Likewise, bonds quoted at 109 could be purchased or sold for $1,090.

When all bonds of an issue mature at the same time, they are called *term bonds*. If the maturities are spread over several dates, they are called *serial bonds*. For example, one-tenth of an issue of $1,000,000 bonds, or $100,000, may mature 16 years from the issue date, another $100,000 in the 17th year, and so on, until the final $100,000 matures in the 25th year.

Bonds that may be exchanged for other securities, such as common stock, are called *convertible bonds*. Bonds that a corporation reserves the right to redeem before their maturity are called *callable bonds*. Bonds issued on the basis of the general credit of the corporation are called *debenture bonds*.

REAL WORLD

Time Inc. 7.625% bonds maturing in 2031 were listed as selling for 112.1081 on January 24, 2006.

PRICING OF BONDS PAYABLE

When a corporation issues bonds, the price that buyers are willing to pay for the bonds depends upon the following three factors:

1. The face amount of the bonds, which is the amount due at the maturity date.
2. The periodic interest to be paid on the bonds.
3. The market rate of interest.

Market = Contract Rate

Selling price of bond = $1,000

$1,000 BOND

Market Rate > Contract Rate

Selling price of bond < $1,000

$1,000 BOND — Discount

Market Rate < Contract Rate

Selling price of bond > $1,000

$1,000 BOND + Premium

The face amount and the periodic interest to be paid on the bonds are identified in the bond indenture. The periodic interest is expressed as a percentage of the face amount of the bond. This percentage or rate of interest is called the **contract rate** or *coupon rate*.

The *market* or **effective rate of interest** is determined by transactions between buyers and sellers of similar bonds. The market rate of interest is affected by a variety of factors, including investors' assessment of current economic conditions as well as future expectations.

If the contract rate of interest equals the market rate of interest, the bonds will sell at their face amount. If the market rate is higher than the contract rate, the bonds will sell at a **discount**, or less than their face amount. Why is this the case? Buyers are not willing to pay the face amount for bonds whose contract rate is lower than the market rate. The discount, in effect, represents the amount necessary to make up for the difference in the market and the contract interest rates. In contrast, if the market rate is lower than the contract rate, the bonds will sell at a **premium**, or more than their face amount. In this case, buyers are willing to pay more than the face amount for bonds whose contract rate is higher than the market rate.

The face amount of the bonds and the periodic interest on the bonds represent cash to be received by the buyer in the future. The buyer determines how much to pay for the bonds by computing the present value of these future cash receipts, using the market rate of interest. The concept of present value is based on the time value of money.

The time value of money concept recognizes that an amount of cash to be received today is worth more than the same amount of cash to be received in the future. For example, what would you rather have: $100 today or $100 one year from now? You would rather have the $100 today because it could be invested to earn income. For example, if the $100 could be invested to earn 10% per year, the $100 will accumulate to $110 ($100 plus $10 earnings) in one year. In this sense, you can think of the $100 in hand today as the **present value** of $110 to be received a year from today. This present value is illustrated in the following time line:

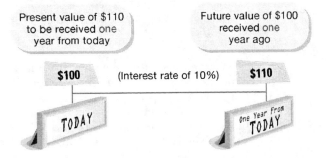

Present value of $110 to be received one year from today

Future value of $100 received one year ago

$100 — (Interest rate of 10%) — $110

TODAY

One Year From TODAY

A related concept to present value is **future value**. In the preceding illustration, the $110 to be received a year from today is the future value of $100 today, assuming an interest rate of 10%.

Present Value of the Face Amount of Bonds The present value of the face amount of bonds is the value today of the amount to be received at a future maturity date. For

Integrity, Objectivity, and Ethics in Business

CREDIT QUALITY

The market rate of interest for a corporate bond is influenced by a number of factors, including the credit quality of the issuer. In June 2002, WorldCom disclosed a massive accounting fraud within the company, prompting credit rating agencies and bond investors to drastically lower their assessment of the company's credit quality. As a result, the price of WorldCom's $30 billion in bond debt dropped to 15 cents on the dollar, or $4.5 billion in a few short weeks.

example, assume that you are to receive the face value of a $1,000 bond in one year. If the market rate of interest is 10%, the present value of the face value of the $1,000 bond is $909.09 ($1,000/1.10). This present value is illustrated in the following time line:

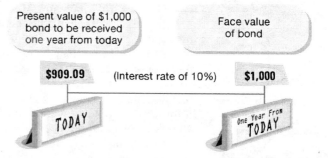

If you are to receive the face value of a $1,000 bond in two years, with interest of 10% compounded at the end of the first year, the present value is $826.45 ($909.09/1.10).[2] We illustrate this present value in the following time line:

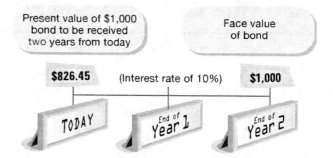

Spreadsheet software with built-in present value functions can be used to calculate present values.

You can determine the present value of the face amount of bonds to be received in the future by a time line and a series of divisions. In practice, however, it is easier to use a table of present values. The *present value of $1 table* can be used to find the present value factor for $1 to be received after a number of periods in the future. The face amount of the bonds is then multiplied by this factor to determine its present value. Exhibit 3 is a partial table of the present value of $1.[3]

---

2 Note that the future value of $826.45 in two years, at an interest rate of 10% compounded annually, is $1,000.

3 To simplify the illustrations and homework assignments, the tables presented in this chapter are limited to 10 periods for a small number of interest rates, and the amounts are carried to only five decimal places. Computer programs are available for determining present value factors for any number of interest rates, decimal places, or periods. More complete interest tables are presented in Appendix A.

EXHIBIT 3 — Present Value of $1 at Compound Interest

Periods	5%	5½%	6%	6½%	7%	10%	11%	12%	13%	14%
1	0.95238	0.94787	0.94340	0.93897	0.93458	0.90909	0.90090	0.89286	0.88496	0.87719
2	0.90703	0.89845	0.89000	0.88166	0.87344	0.82645	0.81162	0.79719	0.78315	0.76947
3	0.86384	0.85161	0.83962	0.82785	0.81630	0.75132	0.73119	0.71178	0.69305	0.67497
4	0.82270	0.80722	0.79209	0.77732	0.76290	0.68301	0.65873	0.63552	0.61332	0.59208
5	0.78353	0.76513	0.74726	0.72988	0.71299	0.62092	0.59345	0.56743	0.54276	0.51937
6	0.74622	0.72525	0.70496	0.68533	0.66634	0.56447	0.53464	0.50663	0.48032	0.45559
7	0.71068	0.68744	0.66506	0.64351	0.62275	0.51316	0.48166	0.45235	0.42506	0.39964
8	0.67684	0.65160	0.62741	0.60423	0.58201	0.46651	0.43393	0.40388	0.37616	0.35056
9	0.64461	0.61763	0.59190	0.56735	0.54393	0.42410	0.39092	0.36061	0.33288	0.30751
10	0.61391	0.58543	0.55840	0.53273	0.50835	0.38554	0.35218	0.32197	0.29459	0.26974

Exhibit 3 indicates that the present value of $1 to be received in two years with a market rate of interest of 10% a year is 0.82645. Multiplying the $1,000 face amount of the bond in the preceding example by 0.82645 yields $826.45.

In Exhibit 3, the Periods column represents the number of compounding periods, and the percentage columns represent the compound interest rate per period. For example, 10% for two years compounded *annually*, as in the preceding example, is 10% for two periods. Likewise, 10% for two years compounded *semiannually* would be 5% (10% per year/2 semiannual periods) for four periods (2 years × 2 semiannual periods). Similarly, 10% for three years compounded semiannually would be 5% (10%/2) for six periods (3 years × 2 semiannual periods).

Example Exercise 15-2 — objective 2

Using Exhibit 3, what is the present value of $4,000 to be received in five years, if the market rate of interest is 10% compounded annually?

Follow My Example 15-2

$2,483.68. [$4,000 × 0.62092 (Present value of $1 for 5 periods at 10%)]

For Practice: PE 15-2A, PE 15-2B

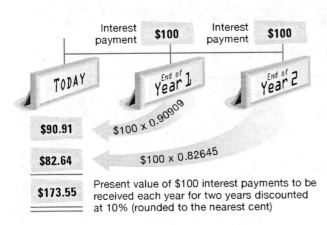

Present value of $100 interest payments to be received each year for two years discounted at 10% (rounded to the nearest cent)

Present Value of the Periodic Bond Interest Payments The present value of the periodic bond interest payments is the value today of the amount of interest to be received at the end of each interest period. Such a series of equal cash payments at fixed intervals is called an **annuity**.

The **present value of an annuity** is the sum of the present values of each cash flow. To illustrate, assume that the $1,000 bond in the preceding example pays interest of 10% annually and that the market rate of interest is also 10%. In addition, assume that the bond matures at the end of two years. The present value of the two interest payments of $100 ($1,000 × 10%) is $173.55, as shown in the time line to the left. It can be determined by using the present value table shown in Exhibit 3.

Instead of using present value of amount tables, such as Exhibit 3, separate present value tables are normally used for annuities. Exhibit 4 is a partial table of the *present value of an annuity of $1* at compound interest. It shows the present value of $1 to be received at the end of each period for various compound rates of interest. For example, the present value of $100 to be received at the end of each of the next two years at 10% compound interest per period is $173.55 ($100 × 1.73554). This amount is the same amount that we computed previously.

EXHIBIT 4   Present Value of Annuity of $1 at Compound Interest

Periods	5%	5½%	6%	6½%	7%	10%	11%	12%	13%	14%
1	0.95238	0.94787	0.94340	0.93897	0.93458	0.90909	0.90090	0.89286	0.88496	0.87719
2	1.85941	1.84632	1.83339	1.82063	1.80802	1.73554	1.71252	1.69005	1.66810	1.64666
3	2.72325	2.69793	2.67301	2.64848	2.62432	2.48685	2.44371	2.40183	2.36115	2.32163
4	3.54595	3.50515	3.46511	3.42580	3.38721	3.16987	3.10245	3.03735	2.97447	2.91371
5	4.32948	4.27028	4.21236	4.15568	4.10020	3.79079	3.69590	3.60478	3.51723	3.43308
6	5.07569	4.99553	4.91732	4.84101	4.76654	4.35526	4.23054	4.11141	3.99755	3.88867
7	5.78637	5.68297	5.58238	5.48452	5.38929	4.86842	4.71220	4.56376	4.42261	4.28830
8	6.46321	6.33457	6.20979	6.08875	5.97130	5.33493	5.14612	4.96764	4.79677	4.63886
9	7.10782	6.95220	6.80169	6.65610	6.51523	5.75902	5.53705	5.32825	5.13166	4.94637
10	7.72174	7.53763	7.36009	7.18883	7.02358	6.14457	5.88923	5.65022	5.42624	5.21612

As we stated earlier, the amount buyers are willing to pay for a bond is the sum of the present value of the face value and the periodic interest payments, calculated by using the market rate of interest. In our example, this calculation is as follows:

Present value of face value of $1,000 due in 2 years, at 10% compounded annually: $1,000 × 0.82645 (present value factor of $1 for 2 periods at 10%)	$ 826.45
Present value of 2 annual interest payments of $100, at 10% compounded annually: $100 × 1.73554 (present value of annuity of $1 for 2 periods at 10%)	173.55
Total present value of bonds	$1,000.00

In this example, the market rate and the contract rate of interest are the same. Thus, the present value is the same as the face value.

Example Exercise 15-3
objective 2

Calculate the present value of a $20,000, 5%, five-year bond that pays $1,000 ($20,000 × 5%) interest annually, if the market rate of interest is 5%. Use Exhibits 3 and 4 for computing present values.

Follow My Example 15-3

Present value of face amount of $20,000 due in 5 years, at 5% compounded annually: $20,000 × 0.78353 (present value factor of $1 for 5 periods at 5%)	$15,671*
Present value of 5 annual interest payments of $1,000, at 5% interest compounded annually: $1,000 × 4.32948 (present value of annuity of $1 for 5 periods at 5%)	4,329*
Total present value of bonds	$20,000

*Rounded to the nearest dollar.

For Practice: PE 15-3A, PE 15-3B

Accounting for Bonds Payable

objective **3**

Journalize entries for bonds payable.

In the preceding section, we described and illustrated how present value concepts are used in determining how much buyers are willing to pay for bonds. In this section, we describe and illustrate how corporations record the issuance of bonds and the payment of bond interest.

BONDS ISSUED AT FACE AMOUNT

To illustrate the journal entries for issuing bonds, assume that on January 1, 2007, a corporation issues for cash $100,000 of 12%, five-year bonds, with interest of $6,000 payable *semiannually*. The market rate of interest at the time the bonds are issued is 12%. Since the contract rate and the market rate of interest are the same, the bonds will sell at their face amount. This amount is the sum of (1) the present value of the face amount of $100,000 to be repaid in five years and (2) the present value of 10 *semi-annual* interest payments of $6,000 each. This computation and a time line are shown below.

Present value of face amount of $100,000 due in 5 years, at 12% compounded semiannually: $100,000 × 0.55840 (present value of $1 for 10 periods at 6%)	$ 55,840
Present value of 10 semiannual interest payments of $6,000, at 12% compounded semiannually: $6,000 × 7.36009 (present value of annuity of $1 for 10 periods at 6%)	44,160*
Total present value of bonds	$100,000

*Because the present value tables are rounded to five decimal places, minor rounding differences may appear in the illustrations.

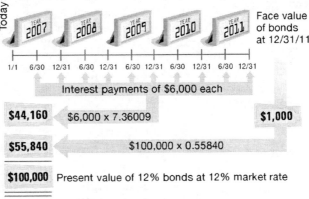

The following entry records the issuing of the $100,000 bonds at their face amount:

2007 Jan.	1	Cash		100 0 0 0 00	
		Bonds Payable			100 0 0 0 00
		Issued $100,000 bonds payable at			
		face amount.			

Every six months after the bonds have been issued, interest payments of $6,000 are made. The first interest payment is recorded as shown at the top of the following page.

June 30	Interest Expense	6 0 0 0 00	
	Cash		6 0 0 0 00
	Paid six months' interest on bonds.		

At the maturity date, the payment of the principal of $100,000 is recorded as follows:

2011 Dec. 31	Bonds Payable	100 0 0 0 00	
	Cash		100 0 0 0 00
	Paid bond principal at maturity date.		

BONDS ISSUED AT A DISCOUNT

What if the market rate of interest is higher than the contract rate of interest? If the market rate of interest is 13% and the contract rate is 12% on the five-year, $100,000 bonds, the bonds will sell at a discount. The present value of these bonds is calculated as follows:

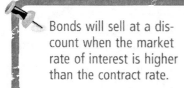

Bonds will sell at a discount when the market rate of interest is higher than the contract rate.

Present value of face amount of $100,000 due in 5 years,
  at 13% compounded semiannually: $100,000 × 0.53273
  (present value of $1 for 10 periods at 6½%) $53,273
Present value of 10 semiannual interest payments of $6,000,
  at 13% compounded semiannually: $6,000 × 7.18883
  (present value of an annuity of $1 for 10 periods at 6½%) 43,133
Total present value of bonds $96,406

The two present values that make up the total are both less than the related amounts in the preceding example. This is because the market rate of interest was 12% in the first example, while the market rate of interest is 13% in this example. The present value of a future amount becomes less and less as the interest rate used to compute the present value increases.

The entry to record the issuing of the $100,000 bonds at a discount is shown below.

2007 Jan. 1	Cash	96 4 0 6 00	
	Discount on Bonds Payable	3 5 9 4 00	
	Bonds Payable		100 0 0 0 00
	Issued $100,000 bonds at discount.		

The $3,594 discount may be viewed as the amount that is needed to entice investors to accept a contract rate of interest that is below the market rate. You may think of the discount as the market's way of adjusting a bond's contract rate of interest to the higher market rate of interest. Using this logic, generally accepted accounting principles require that bond discounts be amortized as interest expense over the life of the bond.

Example Exercise 15-4   **objective** ⟨3⟩

On the first day of the fiscal year, a company issues a $1,000,000, 6%, five-year bond that pays semiannual interest of $30,000 ($1,000,000 × 6% × ½), receiving cash of $845,562. Journalize the entry to record the issuance of the bonds.

(continued)

Follow My Example 15-4

Cash	845,562	
Discount on Bonds Payable	154,438	
Bonds Payable		1,000,000

For Practice: PE 15-4A, PE 15-4B

AMORTIZING A BOND DISCOUNT

There are two methods of amortizing a bond discount: (1) the *straight-line method* and (2) the **effective interest rate method**, often called the *interest method*. Both methods amortize the same total amount of discount over the life of the bonds. The interest method is required by generally accepted accounting principles. However, the straight-line method is acceptable if the results obtained do not materially differ from the results that would be obtained by using the interest method. Because the straight-line method illustrates the basic concept of amortizing discounts and is simpler, we will use it in this chapter. We illustrate the interest method in an appendix to this chapter.

The straight-line method of amortizing a bond discount provides for amortization in equal periodic amounts. Applying this method to the preceding example yields amortization of $\frac{1}{10}$ of $3,594, or $359.40, each half year. The amount of the interest expense on the bonds is the same, $6,359.40 ($6,000 + $359.40), for each half year. The entry to record the first interest payment and the amortization of the related discount follows.

2007 June	30	Interest Expense	6 3 5 9 40		
		Discount on Bonds Payable		3 5 9 40	
		Cash		6 0 0 0 00	
		Paid semiannual interest and			
		amortized ¹⁄₁₀ of bond discount.			

Example Exercise 15-5   objective 3

Using the bond from Example Exercise 15-4, journalize the first interest payment and the amortization of the related bond discount.

Follow My Example 15-5

Interest Expense	45,444	
Discount on Bonds Payable		15,444
Cash		30,000
Paid interest and amortized the bond discount ($154,438/10).		

For Practice: PE 15-5A, PE 15-5B

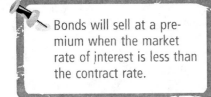

Bonds will sell at a premium when the market rate of interest is less than the contract rate.

BONDS ISSUED AT A PREMIUM

If the market rate of interest is 11% and the contract rate is 12% on the five-year, $100,000 bonds, the bonds will sell at a premium. The present value of these bonds is computed as shown at the top of the following page.

Present value of face amount of $100,000 due in 5 years,
  at 11% compounded semiannually: $100,000 × 0.58543
  (present value of $1 for 10 periods at 5½%) . . . . $ 58,543
Present value of 10 semiannual interest payments of $6,000,
  at 11% compounded semiannually: $6,000 × 7.53763
  (present value of an annuity of $1 for 10 periods at 5½%)   45,226
Total present value of bonds $103,769

The entry to record the issuing of the bonds is as follows:

2007 Jan.	1	Cash	103 7 6 9 00	
		Bonds Payable		100 0 0 0 00
		Premium on Bonds Payable		3 7 6 9 00
		Issued $100,000 bonds at a premium.		

Example Exercise 15-6   **objective** 3

A company issues a $2,000,000, 12%, five-year bond that pays semiannual interest of $120,000
($2,000,000 × 12% × ½), receiving cash of $2,154,435. Journalize the bond issuance.

Follow My Example 15-6

Cash   2,154,435
    Premium on Bonds Payable   154,435
    Bonds Payable   2,000,000

For Practice: PE 15-6A, PE 15-6B

AMORTIZING A BOND PREMIUM

The amortization of bond premiums is basically the same as that for bond discounts,
except that interest expense is decreased. In the above example, the straight-line method
yields amortization of $\frac{1}{10}$ of $3,769, or $376.90, each half year. The entry to record the
first interest payment and the amortization of the related premium is as follows:

2007 June	30	Interest Expense	5 6 2 3 10	
		Premium on Bonds Payable	3 7 6 90	
		Cash		6 0 0 0 00
		Paid semiannual interest and		
		amortized $\frac{1}{10}$ of bond premium.		

Example Exercise 15-7   **objective** 3

Using the bond from Example Exercise 15-6, journalize the first interest payment and the amortization of
the related bond premium.

Follow My Example 15-7

Interest Expense   104,556
Premium on Bonds Payable   15,444
    Cash   120,000
    Paid interest and amortized the bond premium ($154,435/10).

For Practice: PE 15-7A, PE 15-7B

ZERO-COUPON BONDS

Some corporations issue bonds that provide for only the payment of the face amount at the maturity date. Such bonds are called *zero-coupon bonds*. Because they do not provide for interest payments, these bonds sell at a large discount. For example, Merrill Lynch & Co. Inc.'s zero-coupon bonds maturing in 2028 were selling for 21.50.

The issuing price of zero-coupon bonds is the present value of their face amount. To illustrate, if the market rate of interest is 13%, the present value of $100,000 zero-coupon, five-year bonds is calculated as follows:

REAL WORLD

Some bonds with high contract rates, as well as some zero-coupon bonds, are issued by weak companies. Because such bonds are high-risk bonds, they are called **junk bonds**.

Present value of $100,000 due in 5 years, at 13%
compounded semiannually: $100,000 × 0.53273
(present value of $1 for 10 periods at 6½%) $53,273

The accounting for zero-coupon bonds is similar to that for interest-bearing bonds that have been sold at a discount. The discount is amortized as interest expense over the life of the bonds. The entry to record the issuing of the bonds is as follows:

2007					
Jan.	1	Cash		53 2 7 3 00	
		Discount on Bonds Payable		46 7 2 7 00	
		Bonds Payable			100 0 0 0 00
		Issued $100,000 zero-coupon			
		bonds			

Business Connections

REAL WORLD

CH-CH-CH-CHANGES IN BOND TRENDS

How would you like to tune into some of the royalties from your favorite rock star or song? In the past decade, several well-known rock stars have offered bonds backed by future royalties from their hit songs and albums. These include rock icons like James Brown, Rod Stewart, and Iron Maiden.

The trend toward linking music royalties to bonds began when rock star David Bowie packaged royalties from his 25-album catalog of over 300 songs as a $55 million bond issue. These "Bowie Bonds" had an average maturity of 10 years and paid 7.9% annual interest. On the issue date, Moody's Investors Service gave the bonds its highest rating, AAA. Potential investors were confident in the bonds, knowing that Bowie never sold fewer than

a million albums a year prior to the bond issuance. In addition, Bowie reportedly had a steady cash flow of $1 million per year from his existing music catalog. However, in recent years, investor confidence in these bonds has eroded. In May 2004, Moody's Investors Service downgraded the bonds to Baa3. This rating indicates that Moody's is skeptical of the catalog's ability to satisfy bond interest and principal payments.

While Bowie Bonds have fallen on hard times in recent years, they did give rise to a variety of similar bonds that were backed by the future earnings of intellectual property. These include intangibles like copyrights from music and films, patents from prescription drugs and technology, trade secrets, and Internet Web site names.

© TIM AYLEN/ATLANTIS PARADISE ISLAND/PRNEWSFOTO (AP TOPIC GALLERY)

Payment and Redemption of Bonds Payable

objective 4

Describe and illustrate the payment and redemption of bonds payable.

The face value of bonds payable should be paid at the maturity date of the bonds. The entry to record the payment of bonds at their maturity date is a debit to Bonds Payable and a credit to Cash.

The bond indenture may require that funds for the payment of the face value of the bonds at maturity be set aside over the life of the bond issue. A bond indenture may restrict dividend payments to stockholders as a means of increasing the likelihood that the bonds will be paid at maturity. Finally, the bond indenture may allow for the early payment or redemption of the bond issue.

BOND SINKING FUNDS

Since the payment of bonds normally involves a large amount of cash, a bond indenture may require that cash be periodically transferred into a special cash fund over the life of the bond issue. Doing so ensures that an adequate amount of cash will be available at the maturity date for the payment of the face amount of the bonds. This special type of cash fund is called a **sinking fund**.

When cash is transferred to the sinking fund, it is recorded in an account called *Sinking Fund Cash*. When investments are purchased with the sinking fund cash, they are recorded in an account called *Sinking Fund Investments*. As income (interest or dividends) is received, it is recorded in an account called *Sinking Fund Revenue*.

Sinking fund revenue represents earnings of the corporation and is reported in the income statement as other income. The cash and the securities making up the sinking fund are reported in the balance sheet as investments, immediately below the Current Assets section.

A bond indenture may restrict dividend payments to stockholders as a means of increasing the likelihood that the bonds will be paid at maturity. In addition to or instead of this restriction, the bond indenture may require that funds for the payment of the face value of the bonds at maturity be set aside over the life of the bond issue. The amounts set aside are kept separate from other assets in the sinking fund.

BOND REDEMPTION

Pacific Bell issued 7.5% bonds, maturing in 2033 but callable in 2023.

A corporation may call or redeem bonds before they mature. This is often done if the market rate of interest declines significantly after the bonds have been issued. In this situation, the corporation may sell new bonds at a lower interest rate and use the funds to redeem the original bond issue. The corporation can thus save on future interest expenses.

A corporation often issues callable bonds to protect itself against significant declines in future interest rates. However, callable bonds are more risky for investors, who may not be able to replace the called bonds with investments paying an equal amount of interest.

Callable bonds can be redeemed by the issuing corporation within the period of time and at the price stated in the bond indenture. Normally, the call price is above the face value. A corporation may also redeem its bonds by purchasing them on the open market.

A corporation usually redeems its bonds at a price different from that of the carrying amount (or book value) of the bonds. The **carrying amount** of bonds payable is the balance of the bonds payable account (face amount of the bonds) less any unamortized discount or plus any unamortized premium. If the price paid for redemption is below the bond carrying amount, the difference in these two amounts is recorded as a gain. If the price paid for the redemption is above the carrying amount, a loss is recorded. Gains and losses on the redemption of bonds are reported in the Other Income and Expense section of the income statement.

To illustrate, assume that on June 30 a corporation has a bond issue of $100,000 outstanding, on which there is an unamortized premium of $4,000. Assuming that the corporation purchases one-fourth ($25,000) of the bonds for $24,000 on June 30, the entry to record the redemption is as follows:

2007 June	30	Bonds Payable		25 0 0 0 00	
		Premium on Bonds Payable		1 0 0 0 00	
		Cash			24 0 0 0 00
		Gain on Redemption of Bonds			2 0 0 0 00
		Redeemed $25,000 bonds for $24,000.			

In the preceding entry, only a portion of the premium relating to the redeemed bonds is written off. The difference between the carrying amount of the bonds purchased, $26,000 ($25,000 + $1,000), and the price paid for the redemption, $24,000, is recorded as a gain.

If the corporation calls the entire bond issue for $105,000 on June 30, the entry to record the redemption is as follows:

2007 June	30	Bonds Payable		100 0 0 0 00	
		Premium on Bonds Payable		4 0 0 0 00	
		Loss on Redemption of Bonds		1 0 0 0 00	
		Cash			105 0 0 0 00
		Redeemed $100,000 bonds for $105,000.			

Example Exercise 15-8   objective 4

A $500,000 bond issue on which there is an unamortized discount of $40,000 is redeemed for $475,000. Journalize the redemption of the bonds.

Follow My Example 15-8

Bonds Payable	500,000	
Loss on Redemption of Bonds	15,000	
Discount on Bonds Payable		40,000
Cash		475,000

For Practice: PE 15-8A, PE 15-8B

Investments in Bonds

objective 5

Journalize entries for the purchase, interest, discount and premium amortization, and sale of bond investments.

REAL WORLD

The Walt Disney Company's 5.875% bonds maturing in 2017 were listed as selling for 103.375 on January 20, 2006.

Throughout this chapter, we have discussed bonds and the related transactions of the issuing corporation (the debtor). However, these transactions also affect investors. In this section, we discuss the accounting for bonds from the point of view of investors, and assume that the investor uses the cost principle to account for these investments.

ACCOUNTING FOR BOND INVESTMENTS—PURCHASE, INTEREST, AND AMORTIZATION

Bonds may be purchased either directly from the issuing corporation or through an organized bond exchange. Bond exchanges publish daily bond quotations. These quotations normally include the bond interest rate, maturity date, volume of sales, and the high, low, and closing prices for each corporation's bonds traded during the day. Prices for bonds are quoted as a percentage of the face amount. Thus, the price of a $1,000 bond quoted at 99.5 would be $995, while the price of a bond quoted at 104.25 would be $1,042.50.

As with other assets, the cost of a bond investment includes all costs related to the purchase. For example, for bonds purchased through an exchange, the amount paid as a broker's commission should be included as part of the cost of the investment.

When bonds are purchased between interest dates, the buyer normally pays the seller the interest accrued from the last interest payment date to the date of purchase. The amount of the interest paid is normally debited to *Interest Revenue*, since it is an offset against the amount that will be received at the next interest date.

To illustrate, assume that an investor purchases a $1,000 bond at 102 plus a brokerage fee of $5.30 and accrued interest of $10.20. The investor records the transaction as shown at the top of the following page.

2007 Apr.	2	Investment in Lewis Co. Bonds	1 0 2 5 30	
		Interest Revenue	1 0 20	
		Cash		1 0 3 5 50

The cost of the bond is recorded in a single investment account. The face amount of the bond and the premium (or discount) are normally not recorded in separate accounts. This is different from the accounting for bonds payable. Separate premium and discount accounts are usually not used by investors, because they usually do not hold bond investments until the bonds mature.

When bonds held as long-term investments are purchased at a price other than the face amount, the premium or discount should be amortized over the remaining life of the bonds. The amortization of premiums and discounts affects the investment and interest accounts as shown below.

> A premium or discount on a bond investment is recorded in the investment account and is amortized over the remaining life of the bonds.

Premium Amortization:				Discount Amortization:		
Interest Revenue	XXX			Investment in Bonds	XXX	
Investment in Bonds		XXX		Interest Revenue		XXX

The amount of the amortization can be determined by using either the straight-line or interest methods. Unlike bonds payable, the amortization of premiums and discounts on bond investments is usually recorded at the end of the period, rather than when interest is received.

To illustrate the accounting for bond investments, assume that on July 1, 2007, Crenshaw Inc. purchases $50,000 of 8% bonds of Deitz Corporation, due in $8\frac{3}{4}$ years. Crenshaw Inc. purchases the bonds directly from Deitz Corporation to yield an effective interest rate of 11%. The purchase price is $41,706 plus interest of $1,000 ($50,000 × 8% × $\frac{3}{12}$) accrued from April 1, 2007, the date of the last semiannual interest payment. Entries in the accounts of Crenshaw Inc. at the time of purchase and for the remainder of the fiscal period ending December 31, 2007, are as follows:

Calculations:

Cost of $50,000 of Deitz
   Corporation bonds $41,706
Interest accrued
   ($50,000 × 8% × $\frac{3}{12}$)   1,000
Total $42,706

$50,000 × 8% × $\frac{6}{12}$ = $2,000

$50,000 × 8% × $\frac{3}{12}$ = $1,000

Face value of bonds $50,000
Cost of bond invest.   41,706
Discount on bond
   investment $ 8,294

Number of months
  to maturity
  ($8\frac{3}{4}$ years × 12)   105 months
Monthly amortization
  ($8,294/105 months,
  rounded to nearest
  dollar) $79 per mo.
Amortization for
  6 months ($79 × 6) $474

2007 July	1	Investment in Deitz Corporation Bonds	41 7 0 6 00	
		Interest Revenue	1 0 0 0 00	
		Cash		42 7 0 6 00
		Purchased investment in bonds, plus		
		accrued interest.		
Oct.	1	Cash	2 0 0 0 00	
		Interest Revenue		2 0 0 0 00
		Received semiannual interest for		
		April 1 to October 1.		
Dec.	31	Interest Receivable	1 0 0 0 00	
		Interest Revenue		1 0 0 0 00
		Accrued interest from October 1		
		to December 31.		
	31	Investment in Deitz Corporation Bonds	4 7 4 00	
		Interest Revenue		4 7 4 00
		Amortization of discount from July 1		
		to December 31.		

The effect of these entries on the interest revenue account is shown below.

Interest Revenue

July 1	1,000	Oct. 1	2,000	
		Dec. 31 Adj.	1,000	
		31 Adj.	474	
		Adj. Bal.	2,474	

ACCOUNTING FOR BOND INVESTMENTS—SALE

Many long-term investments in bonds are sold before their maturity date. When this occurs, the seller receives the sales price (less commissions and other selling costs) plus any accrued interest since the last interest payment date. Before recording the cash proceeds, the seller should amortize any discount or premium for the current period up to the date of sale. Any gain or loss on the sale is then recorded when the cash proceeds are recorded. Such gains and losses are normally reported in the Other Income and Expense section of the income statement.

To illustrate, assume that the Deitz Corporation bonds in the preceding example are sold for $47,350 plus accrued interest on June 30, 2014. The *carrying amount* of the bonds (cost plus amortized discount) as of January 1, 2014 (78 months after their purchase) is $47,868 [$41,706 + ($79 per month × 78 months)]. The entries to amortize the discount for the current year and to record the sale of the bonds are as follows:

Calculations:

$79 × 6 months

2014 June	30	Investment in Deitz Corporation Bonds		4 7 4 00	
		Interest Revenue			4 7 4 00
		Amortized discount for current year.			
	30	Cash		48 3 5 0 00	
		Loss on Sale of Investments		9 9 2 00	
		Interest Revenue			1 0 0 0 00
		Investment in Deitz Corporation Bonds			48 3 4 2 00
		Received interest and proceeds			
		from sale of bonds.			
		Interest for April 1 to June 30 =			
		$50,000 × 8% × 3/12 = $1,000			

Carrying amount of
bonds on
Jan. 1, 2014 $47,868
Discount amortized,
Jan. 1 to
June 30, 2014   474
Carrying amount of
bonds on
June 30, 2014 $48,342
Proceeds of sale   47,350
Loss on sale $ 992

Example Exercise 15-9   **objective** 5

On October 1, 2008, Viewtec Corporation purchases $10,000 of 6% bonds of Watson Corporation, due in 9¼ years. The bonds were purchased at a price of $8,341 plus interest of $150 ($10,000 × 6% × 3/12) accrued from July 1, 2008, the date of the last semiannual interest payment.

a. Journalize the purchase of the bonds plus accrued interest.
b. Journalize the entry to record the amortization of the discount on December 31. (Round to the nearest dollar.)

Follow My Example 15-9

a. 2008
    Oct. 1   Investment in Watson Corporation Bonds   8,341
                Interest Revenue   150
                    Cash   8,491

b. 2008   Investment in Watson Corporation Bonds 45*
    Dec. 1   Interest Revenue   45
    *[($10,000 − $8,341)/111 months] × 3 months

For Practice: PE 15-9A, PE 15-9B

Corporation Balance Sheet

objective   **6**

Prepare a corporation balance sheet.

In previous chapters, we illustrated the income statement and retained earnings statement for a corporation. The consolidated balance sheet in Exhibit 5 illustrates the presentation of many of the items discussed in this and preceding chapters. These items include bond sinking funds, investments in bonds, goodwill, deferred income taxes, and bonds payable and unamortized discount.

BALANCE SHEET PRESENTATION OF BONDS PAYABLE

In Exhibit 5, Escoe Corporation's bonds payable are reported as long-term liabilities. If there were two or more bond issues, the details of each would be reported on the balance sheet or in a supporting schedule or note. Separate accounts are normally maintained for each bond issue.

When the balance sheet date is within one year of the maturity date of the bonds, the bonds may be classified as a current liability. This would be the case if the bonds are to be paid out of current assets. If the bonds are to be paid from a sinking fund or if they are to be refinanced with another bond issue, they should remain in the noncurrent category. In this case, the details of the retirement of the bonds are normally disclosed in a note to the financial statements.

The balance in Escoe's discount on bonds payable account is reported as a *deduction* from the bonds payable. Conversely, the balance in a bond premium account would be reported as an *addition* to the related bonds payable. Either on the face of the financial statements or in accompanying notes, a description of the bonds (terms, due date, and effective interest rate) and other relevant information such as sinking fund requirements should be disclosed.[4] Finally, the market (fair) value of the bonds payable should also be disclosed.

BALANCE SHEET PRESENTATION OF BOND INVESTMENTS

Investments in bonds or other debt securities that management intends to hold to their maturity are called **held-to-maturity securities**. Such securities are classified as long-term investments under the caption Investments. These investments are reported at their cost less any amortized premium or plus any amortized discount. In addition, the market (fair) value of the bond investments should be disclosed, either on the face of the balance sheet or in an accompanying note.

4 *Statement of Financial Accounting Standards No. 129,* "Disclosure Information About Capital Structure," Financial Accounting Standards Board (Norwalk, Connecticut: 1997).

EXHIBIT 5   Balance Sheet of a Corporation

Escoe Corporation and Subsidiaries
Consolidated Balance Sheet
December 31, 2008

Assets

Current assets:

Cash and cash equivalents			$ 407,500
Accounts and notes receivable		$ 722,000	
Less allowance for doubtful receivables		37,000	685,000
Inventories, at lower of cost (first-in, first-out) or market			917,500
Prepaid expenses			70,000
Total current assets			$2,080,000

Investments:

Bond sinking fund (market value, $473,000)		$ 422,500
Investment in bonds of Dalton (market value, $231,000)		240,000
Total investments		662,500

	Cost	Accumulated Depreciation	Book Value	
Property, plant, and equipment (depreciated by the straight-line method):				
Land	$ 250,000	—	$ 250,000	
Buildings	920,000	$ 379,955	540,045	
Machinery and equipment	2,764,400	766,200	1,998,200	
Total property, plant, and equipment	$3,934,400	$1,146,155		2,788,245

Intangible assets:	
Goodwill	350,000
Total assets	$5,880,745

Liabilities

Current liabilities:

Accounts payable	$ 623,810
Income tax payable	120,500
Dividends payable	94,000
Accrued liabilities	81,400
Deferred income tax payable	10,000
Total current liabilities	$ 929,710

Long-term liabilities:

Debenture 8% bonds payable, due December 31, 2026		
(market value, $950,000)		$1,000,000
Less unamortized discount		60,000
Total long-term liabilities		940,000

Deferred credits:

Deferred income tax payable	85,500
Total liabilities	$1,955,210

Stockholders' Equity

Paid-in capital:

Common stock, $20 par (250,000 shares authorized, 100,000 shares issued)	$2,000,000	
Excess of issue price over par	320,000	
Total paid-in capital	$2,320,000	
Retained earnings	1,605,535	
Total stockholders' equity		3,925,535
Total liabilities and stockholders' equity		$5,880,745

Financial Analysis and Interpretation

Analysts often assess the relative risk of the bondholders in terms of the **number of times interest charges are earned** during the year. The higher the ratio, the greater the chance that interest payments will continue to be made if earnings decrease.

The amount available to make interest payments is not affected by taxes on income. This is because interest is deductible in determining taxable income. To illustrate, the following data were taken from the 2005 annual report of Briggs & Stratton Corporation:

Interest expense	$36,883,000
Income before income tax	$174,315,000

The number of times interest charges are earned, 5.73, is calculated below.

$$\frac{\text{Number of Times}}{\text{Interest Charges Are Earned}} = \frac{\text{Income Before Income Tax + Interest Expense}}{\text{Interest Expense}}$$

$$\frac{\text{Number of Times}}{\text{Interest Charges Are Earned}} = \frac{\$174,315,000 + \$36,883,000}{\$36,883,000} = 5.73$$

The number of times interest charges are earned indicates that the debtholders of Briggs & Stratton Corporation have adequate protection against a potential drop in earnings jeopardizing their receipt of interest payments. However, a final assessment should include a review of trends of past years and a comparison with industry averages.

Appendix

Effective Interest Rate Method of Amortization

The effective interest rate method of amortizing discounts and premiums provides for a constant rate of interest on the carrying amount of the bonds at the beginning of each period. This is in contrast to the straight-line method, which provides for a constant amount of interest expense.

The interest rate used in the interest method of amortization is the market rate on the date the bonds are issued. The carrying amount of the bonds to which the interest rate is applied is the face amount of the bonds minus any unamortized discount or plus any unamortized premium. Under the interest method, the interest expense to be reported on the income statement is computed by multiplying the effective interest rate by the carrying amount of the bonds. The difference between the interest expense computed in this way and the periodic interest payment is the amount of discount or premium to be amortized for the period.

AMORTIZATION OF DISCOUNT BY THE INTEREST METHOD

To illustrate the interest method for amortizing bond discounts, we assume the following data from the chapter illustration of issuing $100,000 bonds at a discount:

Face value of 12%, 5-year bonds, interest compounded semiannually	$100,000
Present value of bonds at effective (market) rate of interest of 13%	96,406
Discount on bonds payable	$ 3,594

Applying the interest method to these data yields the amortization table in Exhibit 6. You should note the following items in this table:

1. The interest paid (Column A) remains constant at 6% of $100,000, the face amount of the bonds.
2. The interest expense (Column B) is computed at $6\frac{1}{2}$% of the bond carrying amount at the beginning of each period. This results in an increasing interest expense each period.
3. The excess of the interest expense over the interest payment of $6,000 is the amount of discount to be amortized (Column C).
4. The unamortized discount (Column D) decreases from the initial balance, $3,594, to a zero balance at the maturity date of the bonds.
5. The carrying amount (Column E) increases from $96,406, the amount received for the bonds, to $100,000 at maturity.

EXHIBIT 6   Amortization of Discount on Bonds Payable

Interest Payment	A Interest Paid (6% of Face Amount)	B Interest Expense ($6\frac{1}{2}$% of Bond Carrying Amount)	C Discount Amortization (B – A)	D Unamortized Discount (D – C)	E Bond Carrying Amount ($100,000 – D)
				$3,594	$ 96,406
1	$6,000	$6,266 ($6\frac{1}{2}$% of $96,406)	$266	3,328	96,672
2	6,000	6,284 ($6\frac{1}{2}$% of $96,672)	284	3,044	96,956
3	6,000	6,302 ($6\frac{1}{2}$% of $96,956)	302	2,742	97,258
4	6,000	6,322 ($6\frac{1}{2}$% of $97,258)	322	2,420	97,580
5	6,000	6,343 ($6\frac{1}{2}$% of $97,580)	343	2,077	97,923
6	6,000	6,365 ($6\frac{1}{2}$% of $97,923)	365	1,712	98,288
7	6,000	6,389 ($6\frac{1}{2}$% of $98,288)	389	1,323	98,677
8	6,000	6,414 ($6\frac{1}{2}$% of $98,677)	414	909	99,091
9	6,000	6,441 ($6\frac{1}{2}$% of $99,091)	441	468	99,532
10	6,000	6,470 ($6\frac{1}{2}$% of $99,532)	468*	—	100,000

*Cannot exceed unamortized discount.

The entry to record the first interest payment on June 30, 2007, and the related discount amortization is as follows:

2007 June	30	Interest Expense		6 2 6 6 00	
		Discount on Bonds Payable			2 6 6 00
		Cash			6 0 0 0 00
		Paid semiannual interest and amortized			
		bond discount for $\frac{1}{2}$ year.			

If the amortization is recorded only at the end of the year, the amount of the discount amortized on December 31 would be $550. This is the sum of the first two semiannual amortization amounts ($266 and $284) from Exhibit 6.

AMORTIZATION OF PREMIUM BY THE INTEREST METHOD

To illustrate the interest method for amortizing bond premiums, we assume the following data from the chapter illustration of issuing $100,000 bonds at a premium:

Present value of bonds at effective (market) rate of interest of 11% $103,769
Face value of 12%, 5-year bonds, interest compounded semiannually 100,000
Premium on bonds payable $ 3,769

Using the interest method to amortize the above premium yields the amortization table in Exhibit 7. You should note the following items in this table:

1. The interest paid (Column A) remains constant at 6% of $100,000, the face amount of the bonds.
2. The interest expense (Column B) is computed at 5½% of the bond carrying amount at the beginning of each period. This results in a decreasing interest expense each period.
3. The excess of the periodic interest payment of $6,000 over the interest expense is the amount of premium to be amortized (Column C).
4. The unamortized premium (Column D) decreases from the initial balance, $3,769, to a zero balance at the maturity date of the bonds.
5. The carrying amount (Column E) decreases from $103,769, the amount received for the bonds, to $100,000 at maturity.

EXHIBIT 7 Amortization of Premium on Bonds Payable

Interest Payment	A Interest Paid (6% of Face Amount)	B Interest Expense (5½% of Bond Carrying Amount)	C Premium Amortization (A − B)	D Unamortized Premium (D − C)	E Bond Carrying Amount ($100,000 + D)
				$3,769	$103,769
1	$6,000	$5,707 (5½% of $103,769)	$293	3,476	103,476
2	6,000	5,691 (5½% of $103,476)	309	3,167	103,167
3	6,000	5,674 (5½% of $103,167)	326	2,841	102,841
4	6,000	5,656 (5½% of $102,841)	344	2,497	102,497
5	6,000	5,637 (5½% of $102,497)	363	2,134	102,134
6	6,000	5,617 (5½% of $102,134)	383	1,751	101,751
7	6,000	5,596 (5½% of $101,751)	404	1,347	101,347
8	6,000	5,574 (5½% of $101,347)	426	921	100,921
9	6,000	5,551 (5½% of $100,921)	449	472	100,472
10	6,000	5,526 (5½% of $100,472)	472*	—	100,000

*Cannot exceed unamortized premium.

The entry to record the first interest payment on June 30, 2007, and the related premium amortization is as follows:

2007 June	30	Interest Expense	5 7 0 7 00	
		Premium on Bonds Payable	2 9 3 00	
		Cash		6 0 0 0 00
		Paid semiannual interest and amortized		
		bond premium for ½ year.		

If the amortization is recorded only at the end of the year, the amount of the premium amortized on December 31, 2007, would be $602. This is the sum of the first two semiannual amortization amounts ($293 and $309) from Exhibit 7.

At a Glance ↘

1. Compute the potential impact of long-term borrowing on earnings per share.

Key Points	Key Learning Outcomes	Example Exercises	Practice Exercises
Corporations can finance their operations by issuing bonds or additional equity. A bond is simply a form of an interest-bearing note. One of the many factors that influence a corporation's decision on whether it should issue debt or equity is the effect each alternative has on earnings per share.	• Define the concept of a bond. • Calculate and compare the effect of alternative financing plans on earnings per share.	15-1	15-1A, 15-1B

2. Describe the characteristics, terminology, and pricing of bonds payable.

Key Points	Key Learning Outcomes	Example Exercises	Practice Exercises
A corporation that issues bonds enters into a contract, or bond indenture. The characteristics of a bond depend on the type of bonds issued by a corporation. When a corporation issues bonds, the price that buyers are willing to pay for the bonds depends upon (1) the face amount of the bonds, (2) the periodic interest to be paid on the bonds, and (3) the market rate of interest. The price that a buyer is willing to pay for a bond is the sum of (1) the present value of the face amount and (2) the present value of the periodic interest payments.	• Define the characteristics of a bond. • Describe the various types of bonds. • Describe the factors that determine the price of a bond. • Define a bond discount or premium. • Calculate the present value of the face amount of a bond. • Calculate the present value of the periodic bond interest payments.	15-2 15-3	15-2A, 15-2B 15-3A, 15-3B

3. Journalize entries for bonds payable.

Key Points	Key Learning Outcomes	Example Exercises	Practice Exercises
The journal entry for issuing bonds payable debits Cash for the proceeds received and credits Bonds Payable for the face amount of the bonds. Any difference between the face amount of the bonds and the proceeds is debited to Discount on Bonds Payable or credited to Premium on Bonds Payable. A discount or premium on bonds payable is amortized to interest expense over the life of the bonds.	• Calculate the price of a bond. • Journalize the issuance of bonds at face value and the payment of periodic interest. • Journalize the issuance of bonds at a discount. • Journalize the amortization of a bond discount or premium. • Journalize the issuance of bonds at a premium. • Journalize the amortization of a bond premium.	15-4 15-5 15-6 15-7	15-4A, 15-4B 15-5A, 15-5B 15-6A, 15-6B 15-7A, 15-7B

(continued)

4. Describe and illustrate the payment and redemption of bonds payable.

Key Points	Key Learning Outcomes	Example Exercises	Practice Exercises
At the maturity date, the entry to record the payment at face value of a bond is a debit to Bonds Payable and a credit to Cash. Since the payment of bonds normally involves a large amount of cash, a bond indenture may require that cash be periodically transferred into a sinking fund. When a corporation redeems bonds, bonds payable is debited for the face amount of the bonds, the premium (discount) on bonds payable account is debited (credited) for its balance, Cash is credited, and any gain or loss on the redemption is recorded.	• Explain bond redemptions. • Journalize the redemption of bonds payable.	15-8	15-8A, 15-8B

5. Journalize entries for the purchase, interest, discount and premium amortization, and sale of bond investments.

Key Points	Key Learning Outcomes	Example Exercises	Practice Exercises
A long-term investment in bonds is recorded by debiting Investments in Bonds. When bonds are purchased between interest dates, the amount of interest paid should be debited to Interest Revenue. Any discount or premium on bond investments should be amortized, using the straight-line or effective interest rate methods. When bonds held as long-term investments are sold, any discount or premium for the current period should first be amortized.	• Journalize the purchase of bond investments. • Prepare the journal entry to record the receipt of periodic interest from bond investments. • Prepare the adjusting journal entry to accrue interest on bond investments and amortization of discounts and premiums on bond investments. • Journalize the sale of bond investments.	15-9	15-9A, 15-9B

6. Prepare a corporation balance sheet.

Key Points	Key Learning Outcomes	Example Exercises	Practice Exercises
Bonds payable are usually reported as long-term liabilities. A discount on bonds should be reported as deduction from the related bonds payable. A premium on bonds should be reported as an addition to related bonds payable. Investments in bonds that are held-to-maturity securities are reported as investments at cost less any amortized premium or plus any amortized discount.	• Illustrate the balance sheet presentation of bond investments and bonds payable.		

Key Terms

annuity (655)
bond (650)
bond indenture (652)
carrying amount (662)
contract rate (653)
discount (653)

effective interest rate method (659)
effective rate of interest (653)
future value (653)
held-to-maturity securities (666)
number of times interest charges
  are earned (668)

premium (653)
present value (653)
present value of an annuity (655)
sinking fund (662)

Illustrative Problem

The fiscal year of Russell Inc., a manufacturer of acoustical supplies, ends December 31. Selected transactions for the period 2007 through 2014, involving bonds payable issued by Russell Inc., are as follows:

2007
June 30. Issued $2,000,000 of 25-year, 7% callable bonds dated June 30, 2007, for cash of $1,920,000. Interest is payable semiannually on June 30 and December 31.
Dec. 31. Paid the semiannual interest on the bonds.
    31. Recorded straight-line amortization of $1,600 of discount on the bonds.
    31. Closed the interest expense account.

2008
June 30. Paid the semiannual interest on the bonds.
Dec. 31. Paid the semiannual interest on the bonds.
    31. Recorded straight-line amortization of $3,200 of discount on the bonds.
    31. Closed the interest expense account.

2014
June 30. Recorded the redemption of the bonds, which were called at 101.5. The balance in the bond discount account is $57,600 after the payment of interest and amortization of discount have been recorded. (Record the redemption only.)

Instructions

1. Journalize entries to record the preceding transactions.
2. Determine the amount of interest expense for 2007 and 2008.
3. Determine the carrying amount of the bonds as of December 31, 2008.

Solution

1.

2007				
June	30	Cash	1,920 000 00	
		Discount on Bonds Payable	80 000 00	
		Bonds Payable		2,000 000 00
Dec.	31	Interest Expense	70 000 00	
		Cash		70 000 00
Dec.	31	Interest Expense	1 600 00	
		Discount on Bonds Payable		1 600 00
		Amortization of discount from July 1		
		to December 31.		
	31	Income Summary	71 600 00	
		Interest Expense		71 600 00

(continued)

2008					
June	30	Interest Expense		70 00 0 00	
		Cash			70 0 0 0 00
Dec.	31	Interest Expense		70 0 0 0 00	
		Cash			70 0 0 0 00
	31	Interest Expense		3 2 0 0 00	
		Discount on Bonds Payable			3 2 0 0 00
		Amortization of discount from			
		January 1 to December 31.			
	31	Income Summary		143 2 0 0 00	
		Interest Expense			143 2 0 0 00
2014					
June	30	Bonds Payable		2,000 0 0 0 00	
		Loss on Redemption of Bonds Payable		87 6 0 0 00	
		Discount on Bonds Payable			57 6 0 0 00
		Cash			2,030 0 0 0 00

2. a. 2007—$71,600
   b. 2008—$143,200

3. Initial carrying amount of bonds $1,920,000
   Discount amortized on December 31, 2007   1,600
   Discount amortized on December 31, 2008   3,200
   Carrying amount of bonds, December 31, 2008 $1,924,800

Self-Examination Questions   (Answers at End of Chapter)

1. If a corporation plans to issue $1,000,000 of 12% bonds at a time when the market rate for similar bonds is 10%, the bonds can be expected to sell at:
   A. their face amount.
   B. a premium.
   C. a discount.
   D. a price below their face amount.

2. If the bonds payable account has a balance of $900,000 and the discount on bonds payable account has a balance of $72,000, what is the carrying amount of the bonds?
   A. $828,000   C. $972,000
   B. $900,000   D. $580,000

3. The cash and securities that make up the sinking fund established for the payment of bonds at maturity are classified on the balance sheet as:

   A. current assets.   C. long-term liabilities.
   B. investments.   D. current liabilities.

4. If a firm purchases $150,000 of bonds of X Company at 101 plus accrued interest of $2,000 and pays broker's commissions of $50, the amount debited to Investment in X Company Bonds would be:
   A. $150,000.   C. $153,500.
   B. $151,550.   D. $153,550.

5. The balance in the discount on bonds payable account would usually be reported in the balance sheet in the:
   A. Current Assets section.
   B. Current Liabilities section.
   C. Long-Term Liabilities section.
   D. Investments section.

Eye Openers

1. Describe the two distinct obligations incurred by a corporation when issuing bonds.
2. Explain the meaning of each of the following terms as they relate to a bond issue: (a) convertible, (b) callable, and (c) debenture.

3. What is meant by the phrase "time value of money"?

4. What has the higher present value: (a) $18,000 to be received at the end of two years, or (b) $9,000 to be received at the end of each of the next two years?

5. If you asked your broker to purchase for you a 9% bond when the market interest rate for such bonds was 10%, would you expect to pay more or less than the face amount for the bond? Explain.

6. A corporation issues $5,000,000 of 7% bonds to yield interest at the rate of 5%. (a) Was the amount of cash received from the sale of the bonds greater or less than $5,000,000? (b) Identify the following terms related to the bond issue: (1) face amount, (2) market or effective rate of interest, (3) contract rate of interest, and (4) maturity amount.

7. If bonds issued by a corporation are sold at a premium, is the market rate of interest greater or less than the contract rate?

8. The following data relate to a $2,000,000, 8% bond issue for a selected semiannual interest period:

Bond carrying amount at beginning of period	$2,125,000
Interest paid during period	160,000
Interest expense allocable to the period	148,750

(a) Were the bonds issued at a discount or at a premium? (b) What is the unamortized amount of the discount or premium account at the beginning of the period? (c) What account was debited to amortize the discount or premium?

9. Assume that Smith Co. amortizes premiums and discounts on bonds payable at the end of the year rather than when interest is paid. What accounts would be debited and credited to record (a) the amortization of a discount on bonds payable and (b) the amortization of a premium on bonds payable?

10. Would a zero-coupon bond ever sell for its face amount?

11. What is the purpose of a bond sinking fund?

12. Assume that two 30-year, 10% bond issues are identical, except that one bond issue is callable at its face amount at the end of five years. Which of the two bond issues do you think will sell for a lower value?

13. Bonds Payable has a balance of $500,000, and Discount on Bonds Payable has a balance of $22,000. If the issuing corporation redeems the bonds at 97, is there a gain or loss on the bond redemption?

14. Where are investments in bonds that are classified as held-to-maturity securities reported on the balance sheet?

15. At what amount are held-to-maturity investments in bonds reported on the balance sheet?

Practice Exercises

PE 15-1A
Determining the effect of alternative financing plans on earnings per share

obj. 1

Wilkinson Co. is considering the following alternative financing plans.

	Plan 1	Plan 2
Issue 12% bonds (at face value)	$1,000,000	$500,000
Issue preferred $2 stock, $10 per share	—	700,000
Issue common stock, $10 par	1,000,000	800,000

Income tax is estimated at 40% of income.

Determine the earnings per share of common stock, assuming income before bond interest and income tax is $400,000.

PE 15-1B
Determining the effect of alternative financing plans on earnings per share

obj. 1

Knight Co. is considering the following alternative financing plans.

	Plan 1	Plan 2
Issue 9% bonds (at face value)	$3,000,000	$2,400,000
Issue preferred $2.50 stock, $25 per share	—	1,200,000
Issue common stock, $20 par	3,000,000	2,400,000

Income tax is estimated at 40% of income.

Determine the earnings per share of common stock, assuming income before bond interest and income tax is $500,000.

PE 15-2A
Determine the present value of a future amount
obj. 2

Using Exhibit 3, what is the present value of $7,000 to be received in 10 years, if the market rate of interest is 7% compounded annually?

PE 15-2B
Determine the present value of a future amount
obj. 2

Using Exhibit 3, what is the present value of $3,000 to be received in seven years, if the market rate of interest is 12% compounded annually?

PE 15-3A
Determine the present value of a bond
obj. 2

Calculate the present value of a $150,000, 7%, 10-year bond that pays $10,500 ($150,000 × 7%) interest annually, if the market rate of interest is 7%. Use Exhibits 3 and 4 for computing present values.

PE 15-3B
Determine the present value of a bond
obj. 2

Calculate the present value of an $80,000, 10%, five-year bond that pays $8,000 ($80,000 × 10%) interest annually, if the market rate of interest is 10%. Use Exhibits 3 and 4 for computing present values.

PE 15-4A
Record the issuance of bonds payable
obj. 3

On the first day of the fiscal year, a company issues a $500,0000, 10%, 10-year bond that pays semiannual interest of $25,000 ($500,000 × 10% × ½), receiving cash of $463,202. Journalize the bond issuance.

PE 15-4B
Record the issuance of bonds payable
obj. 3

On the first day of the fiscal year, a company issues a $1,500,000, 8%, five-year bond that pays semiannual interest of $60,000 ($1,500,000 × 8% × ½), receiving cash of $1,330,403. Journalize the bond issuance.

PE 15-5A
Record the interest for bonds payable
obj. 3

Using the bond from Practice Exercise 15-4A, journalize the first interest payment and the amortization of the related bond discount.

PE 15-5B
Record the interest for bonds payable
obj. 3

Using the bond from Practice Exercise 15-4B, journalize the first interest payment and the amortization of the related bond discount.

PE 15-6A
Record the issuance of bonds payable
obj. 3

A company issues a $2,000,000, 12%, five-year bond that pays semiannual interest of $120,000 ($2,000,000 × 12% × ½), receiving cash of $2,154,429. Journalize the bond issuance.

PE 15-6B
Record the issuance of bonds payable
obj. 3

A company issues a $1,000,000, 10%, ten-year bond that pays semiannual interest of $50,000 ($1,000,000 × 10% × ½), receiving cash of $1,065,040. Journalize the bond issuance.

PE 15-7A
Record the interest for bonds payable
obj. 3

Using the bond from Practice Exercise 15-6A, journalize the first interest payment and the amortization of the related bond premium.

PE 15-7B
Record the interest for bonds payable
obj. 3

Using the bond from Practice Exercise 15-6B, journalize the first interest payment and the amortization of the related bond premium.

PE 15-8A
Record the redemption of bonds payable
obj. 4

A $700,000 bond issue on which there is an unamortized discount of $60,000 is redeemed for $685,000. Journalize the redemption of the bonds.

PE 15-8B
Record the redemption of bonds payable
obj. 4

A $250,000 bond issue on which there is an unamortized premium of $20,000 is redeemed for $245,000. Journalize the redemption of the bonds.

PE 15-9A
Record the purchase of a bond investment
obj. 5

On September 1, 2008, Wilkerson Corporation purchases $70,000 of 8% bonds of Maxtech Corporation, due in $9\frac{1}{4}$ years. The bonds were purchased at a price of $56,000 plus interest of $1,400 ($70,000 × 8% × $\frac{3}{12}$) accrued from June 1, 2008, the date of the last semiannual interest payment. (a) Journalize the purchase of the bonds plus accrued interest. (b) Journalize the entry to record the amortization of the discount on December 31.

PE 15-9B
Record the purchase of a bond investment
obj. 5

On March 1, 2008, Gordon Corporation purchases $50,000 of 10% bonds of PUA-Tech Corporation, due in $9\frac{1}{4}$ years. The bonds were purchased at a price of $40,000 plus interest of $1,250 ($50,000 × 10% × $\frac{3}{12}$) accrued from December 1, 2007, the date of the last semiannual interest payment. (a) Journalize the purchase of the bonds plus accrued interest. (b) Journalize the entry to record the amortization of the discount on December 31.

Exercises

EX 15-1
Effect of financing on earnings per share
obj. 1
✓ a. $0.68

Bliss Co., which produces and sells skiing equipment, is financed as follows:

Bonds payable, 6% (issued at face amount)	$4,000,000
Preferred $2 stock (nonparticipating), $25 par	4,000,000
Common stock, $20 par	4,000,000

Income tax is estimated at 40% of income.

Determine the earnings per share of common stock, assuming that the income before bond interest and income tax is (a) $1,000,000, (b) $1,800,000, and (c) $3,200,000.

EX 15-2
Evaluate alternative financing plans
obj. 1

Based upon the data in Exercise 15-1, discuss factors other than earnings per share that should be considered in evaluating such financing plans.

EX 15-3
Corporate financing
obj. 1

The financial statements for Williams-Sonoma, Inc., are presented in Appendix D at the end of the text. What is the major source of financing for Williams-Sonoma?

EX 15-4
Present value of amounts due
obj. 2

Determine the present value of $200,000 to be received in three years, using an interest rate of 7%, compounded annually, as follows:

a. By successive divisions. (Round to the nearest dollar.)
b. By using the present value table in Exhibit 3.

EX 15-5
Present value of an annuity
obj. 2

Determine the present value of $75,000 to be received at the end of each of four years, using an interest rate of 5%, compounded annually, as follows:

a. By successive computations, using the present value table in Exhibit 3.
b. By using the present value table in Exhibit 4.

EX 15-6
Present value of an annuity
obj. 2
✓ $24,924,420

On January 1, 2008, you win $40,000,000 in the state lottery. The $40,000,000 prize will be paid in equal installments of $2,000,000 over 20 years. The payments will be made on December 31 of each year, beginning on December 31, 2008. If the current interest rate is 5%, determine the present value of your winnings. Use the present value tables in Appendix A.

EX 15-7
Present value of an annuity
obj. 2

Assume the same data as in Exercise 15-6, except that the current interest rate is 10%.
➤ Will the present value of your winnings using an interest rate of 10% be one-half the present value of your winnings using an interest rate of 5%? Why or why not?

EX 15-8
Present value of bonds payable; discount
objs. 2, 3

Caps Co. produces and sells bottle capping equipment for soft drink and spring water bottlers. To finance its operations, Caps Co. issued $20,000,000 of five-year, 9% bonds with interest payable semiannually at an effective interest rate of 10%. Determine the present value of the bonds payable, using the present value tables in Exhibits 3 and 4. Round to the nearest dollar.

EX 15-9
Present value of bonds payable; premium
objs. 2, 3
✓ $15,565,317

Clowney Co. issued $15,000,000 of five-year, 12% bonds with interest payable semiannually, at an effective interest rate of 11%. Determine the present value of the bonds payable, using the present value tables in Exhibits 3 and 4. Round to the nearest dollar.

EX 15-10
Bond price
objs. 2, 3

McDonald's 6.375% bonds due in 2028 were reported as selling for 108.89.
➤ Were the bonds selling at a premium or at a discount? Explain.

EX 15-11
Entries for issuing bonds
obj. 3

Wolfe Co. produces and distributes fiber optic cable for use by telecommunications companies. Wolfe Co. issued $12,000,000 of 10-year, 8% bonds on May 1 of the current year, with interest payable on May 1 and November 1. The fiscal year of the company is the calendar year. Journalize the entries to record the following selected transactions for the current year:

May   1. Issued the bonds for cash at their face amount.
Nov. 1. Paid the interest on the bonds.
Dec. 31. Recorded accrued interest for two months.

EX 15-12
Entries for issuing bonds and amortizing discount by straight-line method
obj. 3

On the first day of its fiscal year, Ellis Company issued $12,000,000 of five-year, 10% bonds to finance its operations of producing and selling home improvement products. Interest is payable semiannually. The bonds were issued at an effective interest rate of 12%, resulting in Ellis Company receiving cash of $11,116,854.

✓ *b. $1,376,629*

a. Journalize the entries to record the following:
   1. Sale of the bonds.
   2. First semiannual interest payment. (Amortization of discount is to be recorded annually.)
   3. Second semiannual interest payment.
   4. Amortization of discount at the end of the first year, using the straight-line method. (Round to the nearest dollar.)
b. Determine the amount of the bond interest expense for the first year.

EX 15-13
Computing bond proceeds, entries for issuing bonds and amortizing premium by straight-line method
objs. 2, 3

Hemby Corporation wholesales oil and grease products to equipment manufacturers. On March 1, 2008, Hemby Corporation issued $4,000,000 of five-year, 13% bonds at an effective interest rate of 11%. Interest is payable semiannually on March 1 and September 1. Journalize the entries to record the following:

a. Sale of bonds on March 1, 2008. (Use the tables of present values in Exhibits 3 and 4 to determine the bond proceeds. Round to the nearest dollar.)
b. First interest payment on September 1, 2008, and amortization of bond premium for six months, using the straight-line method. (Round to the nearest dollar.)

EX 15-14
Entries for issuing and calling bonds; loss
objs. 3, 4

Farrar Corp., a wholesaler of office furniture, issued $7,000,000 of 20-year, 9% callable bonds on April 1, 2008, with interest payable on April 1 and October 1. The fiscal year of the company is the calendar year. Journalize the entries to record the following selected transactions:

2008
Apr. 1. Issued the bonds for cash at their face amount.
Oct. 1. Paid the interest on the bonds.

2012
Oct. 1. Called the bond issue at 103, the rate provided in the bond indenture. (Omit entry for payment of interest.)

EX 15-15
Entries for issuing and calling bonds; gain
objs. 3, 4

Rolfes Corp. produces and sells designer clothing. To finance its operations, Rolfes Corp. issued $4,000,000 of 30-year, 7% callable bonds on January 1, 2008, with interest payable on January 1 and July 1. The fiscal year of the company is the calendar year. Journalize the entries to record the following selected transactions:

2008
Jan. 1. Issued the bonds for cash at their face amount.
July 1. Paid the interest on the bonds.

2014
July 1. Called the bond issue at 96, the rate provided in the bond indenture. (Omit entry for payment of interest.)

EX 15-16
Reporting bonds
objs. 4, 6

At the beginning of the current year, two bond issues (X and Y) were outstanding. During the year, bond issue X was redeemed and a significant loss on the redemption of bonds was reported as an extraordinary item on the income statement. At the end of the year, bond issue Y was reported as a current liability because its maturity date was early in the following year. A sinking fund of cash and securities sufficient to pay the series Y bonds was reported in the balance sheet as *Investments*.
⟶ Identify the flaws in the reporting practices related to the two bond issues.

EX 15-17
Amortizing discount on bond investment
obj. 5

A company purchased a $5,000, 25-year zero-coupon bond for $820 to yield 8.5% to maturity. How is the interest revenue computed?

EX 15-18
Entries for purchase and sale of investment in bonds; loss
obj. 5

Nanotech Innovations Co. sells orthopedic supplies to hospitals. Journalize the entries to record the following selected transactions of Nanotech Innovations Co.:

a. Purchased for cash $600,000 of Sanhueza Co. 7% bonds at 102 plus accrued interest of $10,500.
b. Received first semiannual interest.
c. At the end of the first year, amortized $960 of the bond premium.
d. Sold the bonds at 98 plus accrued interest of $3,500. The bonds were carried at $606,720 at the time of the sale.

EX 15-19
Entries for purchase and sale of investment in bonds; gain
obj. 5

Burtard Company develops and sells graphics software for use by architects. Journalize the entries to record the following selected transactions of Burtard Company:

a. Purchased for cash $450,000 of Blaga Co. 8% bonds at 97 plus accrued interest of $9,000.
b. Received first semiannual interest.
c. Amortized $1,080 of the bond investment at the end of the first year.
d. Sold the bonds at 101 plus accrued interest of $3,000. The bonds were carried at $442,440 at the time of the sale.

EX 15-20
Number of times interest charges earned

The following data were taken from recent annual reports of Southwest Airlines, which operates a low-fare airline service to over 50 cities in the United States.

	Current Year	Preceding Year
Interest expense	$ 88,000,000	$ 91,000,000
Income before income tax	489,000,000	708,000,000

a. Determine the number of times interest charges were earned for the current and preceding years. Round to one decimal place.
b. ➝ What conclusions can you draw?

APPENDIX EX 15-21
Amortize discount by interest method
✓ b. $1,179,806

On the first day of its fiscal year, Pedro Dynamite Company issued $11,000,000 of five-year, 9% bonds to finance its operations of producing and selling home electronics equipment. Interest is payable semiannually. The bonds were issued at an effective interest rate of 12%, resulting in Pedro Dynamite Company receiving cash of $9,785,645.

a. Journalize the entries to record the following:
1. Sale of the bonds.
2. First semiannual interest payment. (Amortization of discount is to be recorded annually.)
3. Second semiannual interest payment.
4. Amortization of discount at the end of the first year, using the interest method. (Round to the nearest dollar.)
b. Compute the amount of the bond interest expense for the first year.

APPENDIX EX 15-22
Amortize premium by interest method
✓ b. $294,923

Jarhead Corporation wholesales oil and grease products to equipment manufacturers. On March 1, 2008, Jarhead Corporation issued $2,500,000 of five-year, 13% bonds at an effective interest rate of 11%, receiving cash of $2,688,440. Interest is payable semiannually on March 1 and September 1. Jarhead Corporation's fiscal year begins on March 1.

a. Journalize the entries to record the following:
1. Sale of the bonds.
2. First interest payment on September 1, 2008. (Amortization of premium is to be recorded annually.)
3. Second interest payment on March 1, 2009.
4. Amortization of premium at the end of the first year, using the interest method. (Round to the nearest dollar.)
b. Determine the bond interest expense for the first year.

APPENDIX EX 15-23
Compute bond proceeds, amortizing premium by interest method, and interest expense

✓ a. $24,487,410
✓ c. $203,818

Ti-Pod Co. produces and sells advanced electronic equipment. On the first day of its fiscal year, Ti-Pod Co. issued $22,000,000 of five-year, 14% bonds at an effective interest rate of 11%, with interest payable semiannually. Compute the following, presenting figures used in your computations.

a. The amount of cash proceeds from the sale of the bonds. (Use the tables of present values in Exhibits 3 and 4. Round to the nearest dollar.)
b. The amount of premium to be amortized for the first semiannual interest payment period, using the interest method. (Round to the nearest dollar.)
c. The amount of premium to be amortized for the second semiannual interest payment period, using the interest method. (Round to the nearest dollar.)
d. The amount of the bond interest expense for the first year.

APPENDIX EX 15-24
Compute bond proceeds, amortizing discount by interest method, and interest expense

✓ a. $25,376,439
✓ b. $168,822

Little Chicken Co. produces and sells restaurant equipment. On the first day of its fiscal year, Little Chicken Co. issued $27,500,000 of five-year, 8% bonds at an effective interest rate of 10%, with interest payable semiannually. Compute the following, presenting figures used in your computations.

a. The amount of cash proceeds from the sale of the bonds. (Use the tables of present values in Exhibits 3 and 4.)
b. The amount of discount to be amortized for the first semiannual interest payment period, using the interest method. (Round to the nearest dollar.)
c. The amount of discount to be amortized for the second semiannual interest payment period, using the interest method. (Round to the nearest dollar.)
d. The amount of the bond interest expense for the first year.

Problems Series A

PR 15-1A
Effect of financing on earnings per share

obj. **1**

✓ 1. Plan 3: $10.64

Three different plans for financing a $30,000,000 corporation are under consideration by its organizers. Under each of the following plans, the securities will be issued at their par or face amount, and the income tax rate is estimated at 40% of income.

	Plan 1	Plan 2	Plan 3
8% bonds	—	—	$20,000,000
Preferred $2 stock, $50 par	—	$20,000,000	10,000,000
Common stock, $10 par	$40,000,000	20,000,000	10,000,000
Total	$40,000,000	$40,000,000	$40,000,000

Instructions
1. Determine for each plan the earnings per share of common stock, assuming that the income before bond interest and income tax is $20,000,000.
2. Determine for each plan the earnings per share of common stock, assuming that the income before bond interest and income tax is $2,600,000.
3. Discuss the advantages and disadvantages of each plan.

PR 15-2A
Present value; bond premium; entries for bonds payable transactions

objs. **2, 3**

✓ 3. $53,796

Atlantis Inc. produces and sells voltage regulators. On July 1, 2007, Atlantis Inc. issued $800,000 of 10-year, 14% bonds at an effective interest rate of 13%. Interest on the bonds is payable semiannually on December 31 and June 30. The fiscal year of the company is the calendar year.

Instructions
1. Journalize the entry to record the amount of the cash proceeds from the sale of the bonds. Use the tables of present values in Appendix A to compute the cash proceeds, rounding to the nearest dollar.

(continued)

2. Journalize the entries to record the following:
   a. The first semiannual interest payment on December 31, 2007, including the amortization of the bond premium, using the straight-line method. (Round to the nearest dollar.)
   b. The interest payment on June 30, 2008, and the amortization of the bond premium, using the straight-line method. (Round to the nearest dollar.)
3. Determine the total interest expense for 2007.
4. Will the bond proceeds always be greater than the face amount of the bonds when the contract rate is greater than the market rate of interest? Explain.

PR 15-3A
Present value; bond discount; entries for bonds payable transactions

objs. 2, 3

✓ 3. $723,347

On July 1, 2007, Iaket Equipment Inc. issued $12,500,000 of 10-year, 11% bonds at an effective interest rate of 12%. Interest on the bonds is payable semiannually on December 31 and June 30. The fiscal year of the company is the calendar year.

Instructions

1. Journalize the entry to record the amount of the cash proceeds from the sale of the bonds. Use the tables of present values in Appendix A to compute the cash proceeds, rounding to the nearest dollar.
2. Journalize the entries to record the following:
   a. The first semiannual interest payment on December 31, 2007, and the amortization of the bond discount, using the straight-line method. (Round to the nearest dollar.)
   b. The interest payment on June 30, 2008, and the amortization of the bond discount, using the straight-line method. (Round to the nearest dollar.)
3. Determine the total interest expense for 2007.
4. Will the bond proceeds always be less than the face amount of the bonds when the contract rate is less than the market rate of interest? Explain.

PR 15-4A
Entries for bonds payable transactions

objs. 3, 4

✓ 2. a. $1,005,659

Kornet Co. produces and sells graphite for golf clubs. The following transactions were completed by Kornet Co., whose fiscal year is the calendar year:

2007
July 1. Issued $19,000,000 of seven-year, 12% callable bonds dated July 1, 2007, at an effective rate of 10%, receiving cash of $20,880,780. Interest is payable semiannually on December 31 and June 30.
Dec. 31. Paid the semiannual interest on the bonds.
     31. Recorded bond premium amortization of $134,341, which was determined by using the straight-line method.
     31. Closed the interest expense account.

2008
June 30. Paid the semiannual interest on the bonds.
Dec. 31. Paid the semiannual interest on the bonds.
Dec. 31. Recorded bond premium amortization of $268,682, which was determined by using the straight-line method.
     31. Closed the interest expense account.

2009
July 1. Recorded the redemption of the bonds, which were called at 101.5. The balance in the bond premium account is $1,343,416 after the payment of interest and amortization of premium have been recorded. (Record the redemption only.)

Instructions

1. Journalize the entries to record the foregoing transactions.
2. Indicate the amount of the interest expense in (a) 2007 and (b) 2008.
3. Determine the carrying amount of the bonds as of December 31, 2008.

PR 15-5A
Entries for bond investments

obj. 5

The following selected transactions relate to certain securities acquired by Wildflower Blueprints Inc., whose fiscal year ends on December 31:

2007
Sept. 1. Purchased $600,000 of Wilson Company 20-year, 10% bonds dated July 1, 2007, directly from the issuing company, for $578,580 plus accrued interest of $10,000.

Dec. 31. Received the semiannual interest on the Wilson Company bonds.
     31. Recorded bond discount amortization of $360 on the Wilson Company bonds. The amortization amount was determined by using the straight-line method.

(Assume that all intervening transactions and adjustments have been properly recorded and that the number of bonds owned has not changed from December 31, 2007, to December 31, 2011.)

2012
June 30. Received the semiannual interest on the Wilson Company bonds.
Oct. 31. Sold one-half of the Wilson Company bonds at 97 plus accrued interest. The broker deducted $400 for commission, etc., remitting the balance. Prior to the sale, $450 of discount on one-half of the bonds was amortized, reducing the carrying amount of those bonds to $292,080.
Dec. 31. Received the semiannual interest on the Wilson Company bonds.
     31. Recorded bond discount amortization of $540 on the Wilson Company bonds.

Instructions
Journalize the entries to record the foregoing transactions.

APPENDIX PR 15-6A
Entries for bonds payable transactions; interest method of amortizing bond premium

✓ 2. $54,865

Atlantis Inc. produces and sells voltage regulators. On July 1, 2007, Atlantis Inc. issued $800,000 of 10-year, 14% bonds at an effective interest rate of 13%, receiving proceeds of $844,077. Interest on the bonds is payable semiannually on December 31 and June 30. The fiscal year of the company is the calendar year.

Instructions
1. Journalize the entries to record the following:
   a. The first semiannual interest payment on December 31, 2007, and the amortization of the bond premium, using the interest method. (Round to the nearest dollar.)
   b. The interest payment on June 30, 2008, and the amortization of the bond premium, using the interest method. (Round to the nearest dollar.)
2. Determine the total interest expense for 2007.

APPENDIX PR 15-7A
Entries for bonds payable transactions; interest method of amortizing bond discount

✓ 2. $706,984

On July 1, 2007, Iaket Equipment Inc. issued $12,500,000 of 10-year, 11% bonds at an effective interest rate of 12%, receiving proceeds of $11,783,070. Interest on the bonds is payable semiannually on December 31 and June 30. The fiscal year of the company is the calendar year.

Instructions
1. Journalize the entries to record the following:
   a. The first semiannual interest payment on December 31, 2007, and the amortization of the bond discount, using the interest method.
   b. The interest payment on June 30, 2008, and the amortization of the bond discount, using the interest method.
2. Determine the total interest expense for 2007.

Problems Series B

PR 15-1B
Effect of financing on earnings per share
obj. 1

✓ 1. Plan 3: $9.06

Three different plans for financing a $30,000,000 corporation are under consideration by its organizers. Under each of the following plans, the securities will be issued at their par or face amount, and the income tax rate is estimated at 40% of income.

	Plan 1	Plan 2	Plan 3
8% bonds	—	—	$15,000,000
Preferred 4% stock, $100 par	—	$15,000,000	7,500,000
Common stock, $4 par	$30,000,000	15,000,000	7,500,000
Total	$30,000,000	$30,000,000	$30,000,000

Instructions

1. Determine for each plan the earnings per share of common stock, assuming that the income before bond interest and income tax is $30,000,000.
2. Determine for each plan the earnings per share of common stock, assuming that the income before bond interest and income tax is $1,800,000.
3. Discuss the advantages and disadvantages of each plan.

PR 15-2B

Present value; bond premium; entries for bonds payable transactions

objs. 2, 3

✔ 3. $870,307

Bobblehead Corporation produces and sells basketball jerseys. On July 1, 2008, Bobblehead Corporation issued $16,000,000 of seven-year, 13% bonds at an effective interest rate of 10%. Interest on the bonds is payable semiannually on December 31 and June 30. The fiscal year of the company is the calendar year.

Instructions

1. Journalize the entry to record the amount of the cash proceeds from the sale of the bonds. Use the tables of present values in Appendix A to compute the cash proceeds, rounding to the nearest dollar.
2. Journalize the entries to record the following:
   a. The first semiannual interest payment on December 31, 2008, and the amortization of the bond premium, using the straight-line method. (Round to the nearest dollar.)
   b. The interest payment on June 30, 2009, and the amortization of the bond premium, using the straight-line method. (Round to the nearest dollar.)
3. Determine the total interest expense for 2008.
4. Will the bond proceeds always be greater than the face amount of the bonds when the contract rate is greater than the market rate of interest? Explain.

PR 15-3B

Present value; bond discount; entries for bonds payable transactions

objs. 2, 3

✔ 3. $1,251,378

On July 1, 2007, Austin Corporation, a wholesaler of electronic circuits, issued $22,000,000 of 20-year, 11% bonds at an effective interest rate of 12%. Interest on the bonds is payable semiannually on December 31 and June 30. The fiscal year of the company is the calendar year.

Instructions

1. Journalize the entry to record the amount of the cash proceeds from the sale of the bonds. Use the tables of present values in Appendix A to compute the cash proceeds, rounding to the nearest dollar.
2. Journalize the entries to record the following:
   a. The first semiannual interest payment on December 31, 2007, and the amortization of the bond discount, using the straight-line method. (Round to the nearest dollar.)
   b. The interest payment on June 30, 2008, and the amortization of the bond discount, using the straight-line method. (Round to the nearest dollar.)
3. Determine the total interest expense for 2007.
4. Will the bond proceeds always be less than the face amount of the bonds when the contract rate is less than the market rate of interest? Explain.

PR 15-4B

Entries for bonds payable transactions

objs. 3, 4

✔ 2. a. $577,386

The following transactions were completed by Michura Inc., whose fiscal year is the calendar year:

2007

July   1. Issued $12,000,000 of 10-year, 9% callable bonds dated July 1, 2007, at an effective rate of 11%, receiving cash of $11,252,273. Interest is payable semiannually on December 31 and June 30.

Dec. 31. Paid the semiannual interest on the bonds.
    31. Recorded bond discount amortization of $37,386, which was determined by using the straight-line method.
    31. Closed the interest expense account.

2008

June 30. Paid the semiannual interest on the bonds.
Dec. 31. Paid the semiannual interest on the bonds.
    31. Recorded bond discount amortization of $74,772, which was determined by using the straight-line method.
    31. Closed the interest expense account.

2009

June 30. Recorded the redemption of the bonds, which were called at 98. The balance in the bond discount account is $598,183 after payment of interest and amortization of discount have been recorded. (Record the redemption only.)

Instructions

1. Journalize the entries to record the foregoing transactions.
2. Indicate the amount of the interest expense in (a) 2007 and (b) 2008.
3. Determine the carrying amount of the bonds as of December 31, 2008.

PR 15-5B
Entries for bond investments
obj. 5

Valent Inc. leases motor vehicles. The following selected transactions relate to certain securities acquired as a long-term investment by Valent Inc., whose fiscal year ends on December 31:

2007

Sept. 1. Purchased $800,000 of Ivan Company 10-year, 9% bonds dated July 1, 2007, directly from the issuing company, for $853,100 plus accrued interest of $12,000.
Dec. 31. Received the semiannual interest on the Ivan Company bonds.
     31. Recorded bond premium amortization of $1,800 on the Ivan Company bonds. The amortization amount was determined by using the straight-line method.

(Assume that all intervening transactions and adjustments have been properly recorded and that the number of bonds owned has not changed from December 31, 2007, to December 31, 2012.)

2013

June 30. Received the semiannual interest on the Ivan Company bonds.
Aug. 31. Sold one-half of the Ivan Company bonds at 102 plus accrued interest. The broker deducted $500 for commission, etc., remitting the balance. Prior to the sale, $1,800 of premium on one-half of the bonds is to be amortized, reducing the carrying amount of those bonds to $405,600.
Dec. 31. Received the semiannual interest on the Ivan Company bonds.
     31. Recorded bond premium amortization of $2,700 on the Ivan Company bonds.

Instructions

Journalize the entries to record the foregoing transactions.

APPENDIX PR 15-6B
Entries for bonds payable transactions; interest method of amortizing bond premium

✓ 2. $918,785

Bobblehead Corporation produces and sells basketball jerseys. On July 1, 2008, Bobblehead Corporation issued $16,000,000 of seven-year, 13% bonds at an effective interest rate of 10%, receiving proceeds of $18,375,706. Interest on the bonds is payable semiannually on December 31 and June 30. The fiscal year of the company is the calendar year.

Instructions

1. Journalize the entries to record the following:
   a. The first semiannual interest payment on December 31, 2008, and the amortization of the bond premium, using the interest method. (Round to the nearest dollar.)
   b. The interest payment on June 30, 2009, and the amortization of the bond premium, using the interest method. (Round to the nearest dollar.)
2. Determine the total interest expense for 2008.

APPENDIX PR 15-7B
Entries for bonds payable transactions; interest method of amortizing bond discount

✓ 2. $1,220,692

On July 1, 2007, Austin Corporation, a wholesaler of electronic circuits, issued $22,000,000 of 20-year, 11% bonds at an effective interest rate of 12%, receiving proceeds of $20,344,863. Interest on the bonds is payable semiannually on December 31 and June 30. The fiscal year of the company is the calendar year.

Instructions

1. Journalize the entries to record the following:
   a. The first semiannual interest payment on December 31, 2007, and the amortization of the bond discount, using the interest method. (Round to the nearest dollar.)
   b. The interest payment on June 30, 2008, and the amortization of the bond discount, using the interest method. (Round to the nearest dollar.)
2. Determine the total interest expense for 2007.

Comprehensive Problem 4

✓ 2.a. Net income, $229,000

Selected transactions completed by Delhome Products Inc. during the fiscal year ending July 31, 2008, were as follows:

a. Issued 12,500 shares of $30 par common stock at $65, receiving cash.
b. Issued 10,000 shares of $125 par preferred 8% stock at $160, receiving cash.
c. Issued $15,000,000 of 10-year, 12% bonds at an effective interest rate of 10%, with interest payable semiannually. Use the present value tables in Appendix A to determine the bond proceeds. (Round to the nearest dollar.)
d. Declared a dividend of $0.25 per share on common stock and $2.50 per share on preferred stock. On the date of record, 125,000 shares of common stock were outstanding, no treasury shares were held, and 18,750 shares of preferred stock were outstanding.
e. Paid the cash dividends declared in (d).
f. Redeemed $500,000 of 8-year, 15% bonds at 101. The balance in the bond premium account is $6,150 after the payment of interest and amortization of premium have been recorded. (Record only the redemption of the bonds payable.)
g. Purchased 6,250 shares of treasury common stock at $62.50 per share.
h. Declared a 2% stock dividend on common stock and a $2.50 cash dividend per share on preferred stock. On the date of declaration, the market value of the common stock was $63.75 per share. On the date of record, 125,000 shares of common stock had been issued, 6,250 shares of treasury common stock were held, and 18,750 shares of preferred stock had been issued. (Round to the nearest dollar.)
i. Issued the stock certificates for the stock dividends declared in (h) and paid the cash dividends to the preferred stockholders.
j. Purchased $150,000 of Lewis Sports Inc. 10-year, 15% bonds, directly from the issuing company, for $145,500 plus accrued interest of $5,625.
k. Sold, at $72.50 per share, 3,750 shares of treasury common stock purchased in (g).
l. Recorded the payment of semiannual interest on the bonds issued in (c) and the amortization of the premium for six months. The amortization was determined using the straight-line method. (Round the amortization to the nearest dollar.)
m. Accrued interest for four months on the Lewis Sports Inc. bonds purchased in (j). Also recorded amortization of $120.

Instructions

1. Journalize the selected transactions.
2. After all of the transactions for the year ended July 31, 2008, had been posted (including the transactions recorded in (1) and all adjusting entries), the data below and on the following page were taken from the records of Delhome Products Inc.
   a. Prepare a multiple-step income statement for the year ended July 31, 2008, concluding with earnings per share. In computing earnings per share, assume that the average number of common shares outstanding was 125,000 and preferred dividends were $131,250. (Round earnings per share to the nearest cent.)
   b. Prepare a retained earnings statement for the year ended July 31, 2008.
   c. Prepare a balance sheet in report form as of July 31, 2008.

Income statement data:	
Advertising expense	$ 150,000
Cost of merchandise sold	3,498,750
Delivery expense	27,000
Depreciation expense—office buildings and equipment	25,000
Depreciation expense—store buildings and equipment	90,000
Gain on redemption of bonds	1,150
Income tax:	
Applicable to continuing operations	247,509
Applicable to loss from discontinued operations	100,000
Applicable to gain from redemption of bonds	150
Interest expense	778,266
Interest revenue	2,025
Loss from disposal of discontinued operations	250,000

Loss from fixed asset impairment	$ 187,500
Miscellaneous administrative expenses	7,500
Miscellaneous selling expenses	13,750
Office rent expense	50,000
Office salaries expense	170,000
Office supplies expense	10,000
Restructuring charges	93,750
Sales	6,300,000
Sales commissions	195,000
Sales salaries expense	360,000
Store supplies expense	20,000
Retained earnings and balance sheet data:	
Accounts payable	212,000
Accounts receivable	562,500
Accumulated depreciation—office buildings and equipment	1,670,650
Accumulated depreciation—store buildings and equipment	4,428,750
Allowance for doubtful accounts	43,750
Bonds payable, 11%, due 2018	14,500,000
Cash	250,000
Common stock, $30 par (400,000 shares authorized;	
124,875 shares outstanding)	3,746,250
Deferred income tax payable (current portion, $17,500)	51,375
Dividends:	
Cash dividends for common stock	122,815
Cash dividends for preferred stock	187,500
Stock dividends for common stock	151,406
Dividends payable	37,500
Employee termination obligation (current)	81,250
Goodwill	540,000
Income tax payable	40,000
Interest receivable	7,500
Investment in Lewis Sports Inc. bonds (long-term)	145,620
Merchandise inventory (July 31, 2008), at lower of	
cost (fifo) or market	850,000
Notes receivable	156,250
Office buildings and equipment	7,412,500
Paid-in capital from sale of treasury stock	37,500
Paid-in capital in excess of par—common stock	700,000
Paid-in capital in excess of par—preferred stock	300,000
Preferred 8% stock, $125 par (30,000 shares authorized;	
18,750 shares issued)	2,343,750
Premium on bonds payable	1,769,722
Prepaid expenses	31,250
Retained earnings, August 1, 2007	2,302,970
Store buildings and equipment	21,920,876
Treasury stock (2,500 shares of common stock at cost	
of $62.50 per share)	156,250

Special Activities

SA 15-1
General Electric bond issuance

General Electric Capital, a division of General Electric, uses long-term debt extensively. In early 2002, GE Capital issued $11 billion in long-term debt to investors, then within days filed legal documents to prepare for another $50 billion long-term debt issue. As a result of the $50 billion filing, the price of the initial $11 billion offering declined (due to higher risk of more debt).

Bill Gross, a manager of a bond investment fund, "denounced a 'lack in candor' related to GE's recent debt deal. 'It was the most recent and most egregious example of how bondholders are mistreated.' Gross argued that GE was not forthright when GE Capital recently issued $11 billion *in bonds, one of the largest issues ever from a U.S. corporation. What bothered Gross is that three days after the issue the company announced its intention to sell as much as $50 billion in additional debt, warrants, preferred stock, guarantees, letters of credit and promissory notes at some future date."*

In your opinion, did GE Capital act unethically by selling $11 billion of long-term debt without telling those investors that a few days later it would be filing documents to prepare for another $50 billion debt offering?

Source: Jennifer Ablan, "Gross Shakes the Bond Market; GE Calms It, a Bit," *Barron's,* March 25, 2002.

SA 15-2
Ethics and professional conduct in business

ETHICS

Jenkins Pharmaceuticals develops and produces prescription medications primarily for use in hospitals. The company has an outstanding $100,000,000, 30-year, 12% bond issued dated July 1, 2001. The bond issue is due June 30, 2031. The bond indenture requires a bond sinking fund, which has a balance of $12,000,000 as of July 1, 2007. The company is currently experiencing a shortage of funds due to a recent acquisition. Bob Snapple, the company's treasurer, is considering using the funds from the bond sinking fund to cover payroll and other bills that are coming due at the end of the month. Bob's brother-in-law is a trustee in a sinking fund, who has indicated willingness to allow Bob to use the funds from the sinking fund to temporarily meet the company's cash needs.

Discuss whether Bob's proposal is appropriate.

SA 15-3
Present values

Kristen Nash recently won the jackpot in the New Jersey lottery while she was visiting her parents. When she arrived at the lottery office to collect her winnings, she was offered the following three payout options:

a. Receive $5,000,000 in cash today.
b. Receive $2,000,000 today and $600,000 per year for 10 years, with the first $600,000 payment being received one year from today.
c. Receive $1,000,000 per year for 10 years, with the first payment being received one year from today.

Assuming that the effective rate of interest is 9%, which payout option should Kristen select? Explain your answer and provide any necessary supporting calculations.

SA 15-4
Preferred stock vs. bonds

Beacon Inc. has decided to expand its operations to owning and operating long-term health care facilities. The following is an excerpt from a conversation between the chief executive officer, Terry Clark, and the vice president of finance, Frank Mills.

Terry: Frank, have you given any thought to how we're going to finance the acquisition of St. Seniors Health Care?
Frank: Well, the two basic options, as I see it, are to issue either preferred stock or bonds. The equity market is a little depressed right now. The rumor is that the Federal Reserve Bank's going to increase the interest rates either this month or next.
Terry: Yes, I've heard the rumor. The problem is that we can't wait around to see what's going to happen. We'll have to move on this next week if we want any chance to complete the acquisition of St. Seniors.
Frank: Well, the bond market is strong right now. Maybe we should issue debt this time around.
Terry: That's what I would have guessed as well. St. Seniors's financial statements look pretty good, except for the volatility of its income and cash flows. But that's characteristic of the industry.

Discuss the advantages and disadvantages of issuing preferred stock versus bonds.

SA 15-5
Investing in bonds

REAL WORLD

During fiscal year 2004, Georgia-Pacific called the following bond issuances:

$243 million	9.875% bonds	due November 1, 2021
$250 million	9.625% bonds	due March 15, 2022
$250 million	9.500% bonds	due May 15, 2022

Group Project

$240 million	9.125% bonds	due July 1, 2022
$250 million	8.250% bonds	due March 1, 2023
$250 million	8.125% bonds	due June 15, 2023

In groups of three or four:

1. Identify the face value, coupon rate, and maturity of each bond issue.
2. Discuss some of the potential reasons that Georgia-Pacific may have had for deciding to call these bond issues early.

SA 15-6
Investing in bonds

Group Project

Select a bond from listings that appear daily in *The Wall Street Journal*, and summarize the information related to the bond you select. Include the following information in your summary:

1. Contract rate of interest
2. Year when the bond matures
3. Current yield (effective rate of interest)
4. Closing price of bond (indicate date)
5. Other information noted about the bond, such as whether it is a zero-coupon bond (see the Explanatory Notes to the listings)

   In groups of three or four, share the information you developed about the bond you selected. As a group, select one bond to invest $100,000 in and prepare a justification for your choice for presentation to the class. For example, your justification should include a consideration of risk and return.

SA 15-7
Financing business expansion

You hold a 25% common stock interest in the family-owned business, a vending machine company. Your sister, who is the manager, has proposed an expansion of plant facilities at an expected cost of $5,000,000. Two alternative plans have been suggested as methods of financing the expansion. Each plan is briefly described as follows:

Plan 1. Issue $5,000,000 of 20-year, 7% notes at face amount.
Plan 2. Issue an additional 87,500 shares of $5 par common stock at $20 per share, and $3,250,000 of 20-year, 7% notes at face amount.

The balance sheet as of the end of the previous fiscal year is as follows:

Vendco, Inc.
Balance Sheet
December 31, 2008

Assets	
Current assets	$2,350,000
Property, plant, and equipment	5,150,000
Total assets	$7,500,000

Liabilities and Stockholders' Equity	
Liabilities	$2,000,000
Common stock, $5	800,000
Paid-in capital in excess of par	80,000
Retained earnings	4,620,000
Total liabilities and stockholders' equity	$7,500,000

Net income has remained relatively constant over the past several years. The expansion program is expected to increase yearly income before bond interest and income tax from $500,000 in the previous year to $700,000 for this year. Your sister has asked you, as the company treasurer, to prepare an analysis of each financing plan.

1. Prepare a table indicating the expected earnings per share on the common stock under each plan. Assume an income tax rate of 40%. Round to the nearest cent.
2. a. Discuss the factors that should be considered in evaluating the two plans.
   b. Which plan offers the greater benefit to the present stockholders? Give reasons for your opinion.

SA 15-8
Bond ratings

Internet Project

Moody's Investors Service maintains a Web site at **http://www.Moodys.com**. One of the services offered at this site is a listing of announcements of recent bond rating changes. Visit this site and read over some of these announcements. Write down several of the reasons provided for rating downgrades and upgrades. If you were a bond investor or bond issuer, would you care if Moody's changed the rating on your bonds? Why or why not?

SA 15-9
Bonds payable in the financial statements

Refer to the financial statements of Williams-Sonoma, Inc., given in Appendix D at the end of this book.

1. How much interest expense did Williams-Sonoma record in 2003, 2004, and 2005?
2. What is the number of times interest charges are earned for Williams-Sonoma in 2003, 2004, and 2005? Evaluate this ratio for Williams-Sonoma. (Round your answer to one decimal place.)

Answers to Self-Examination Questions

1. **B** Since the contract rate on the bonds is higher than the prevailing market rate, a rational investor would be willing to pay more than the face amount, or a premium (answer B), for the bonds. If the contract rate and the market rate were equal, the bonds could be expected to sell at their face amount (answer A). Likewise, if the market rate is higher than the contract rate, the bonds would sell at a price below their face amount (answer D) or at a discount (answer C).

2. **A** The bond carrying amount is the face amount plus unamortized premium or less unamortized discount. For this question, the carrying amount is $900,000 less $72,000, or $828,000 (answer A).

3. **B** Although the sinking fund may consist of cash as well as securities, the fund is listed on the balance sheet as an investment (answer B) because it is to be used to pay the long-term liability at maturity.

4. **B** The amount debited to the investment account is the cost of the bonds, which includes the amount paid to the seller for the bonds (101% × $150,000) plus broker's commissions ($50), or $151,550 (answer B). The $2,000 of accrued interest that is paid to the seller should be debited to Interest Revenue, since it is an offset against the amount that will be received as interest at the next interest date.

5. **C** The balance of Discount on Bonds Payable is usually reported as a deduction from Bonds Payable in the Long-Term Liabilities section (answer C) of the balance sheet. Likewise, a balance in a premium on bonds payable account would usually be reported as an addition to Bonds Payable in the Long-Term Liabilities section of the balance sheet.

chapter 16

Statement of Cash Flows

© ELAINE THOMPSON/ASSOCIATED PRESS

After studying this chapter, you should be able to:

1 *Summarize the types of cash flow activities reported in the statement of cash flows.*

2 *Prepare a statement of cash flows, using the indirect method.*

3 *Prepare a statement of cash flows, using the direct method.*

Jones Soda Co.

uppose you were to receive $100 as a result of some event. Would it make a difference what the event was? Yes, it would! If you received $100 for your birthday, then it's a gift. If you received $100 as a result of working part time for a week, then it's the result of your effort. If you received $100 as a loan, then it's money that you will have to pay back in the future. If you received $100 as a result of selling your CD player, then it's the result of giving up something tangible. Thus, the same $100 received can be associated with different types of events, and these events have different meanings to you. You would much rather receive a $100 gift than take out a $100 loan. Likewise, company stakeholders would also view events such as these differently.

Companies are required to report information about the events causing a change in cash over a period time. This information is reported in the statement of cash flows. One such company is Jones Soda Co. Jones began in the late 1980s as an alternative

beverage company, known for its customer provided labels, unique flavors, and support for extreme sports. You have probably seen Jones Soda at Barnes & Noble, Panera Bread, or Starbucks, or maybe sampled some of its unique flavors, such as Fufu Berry®, Blue Bubblegum®, or Lemon Drop®. As with any company, cash is important to Jones Soda. Without cash, Jones would be unable to expand its brands, distribute its product, support extreme sports, or provide a return for its owners. Thus, its managers are concerned about the sources and uses of cash.

In previous chapters, we have used the income statement, balance sheet, retained earnings statement, and other information to analyze the effects of management decisions on a business's financial position and operating performance. In this chapter, we focus on the events causing a change in cash by presenting the preparation and use of the statement of cash flows.

Reporting Cash Flows

objective 1

Summarize the types of cash flow activities reported in the statement of cash flows.

In Chapter 1, we introduced the statement of cash flows as one of the basic financial statements of a business. The **statement of cash flows** reports a firm's major cash inflows and outflows for a period.[1] It provides useful information about a firm's ability to generate cash from operations, maintain and expand its operating capacity, meet its financial obligations, and pay dividends. As a result, it is used by managers in evaluating past operations and in planning future investing and financing activities. It is also used by investors, creditors, and others in assessing a firm's profit potential. In addition, it is a basis for assessing the firm's ability to pay its maturing debt.

The statement of cash flows reports cash flows by three types of activities:

1. **Cash flows from operating activities** are cash flows from transactions that affect net income. Examples of such transactions include the purchase and sale of merchandise by a retailer.
2. **Cash flows from investing activities** are cash flows from transactions that affect the investments in noncurrent assets. Examples of such transactions include the sale and purchase of fixed assets, such as equipment and buildings.
3. **Cash flows from financing activities** are cash flows from transactions that affect the debt and equity of the business. Examples of such transactions include issuing or retiring equity and debt securities.

---

1 As used in this chapter, *cash* refers to cash and cash equivalents. Examples of cash equivalents include short-term, highly liquid investments, such as money market funds, certificates of deposit, and commercial paper.

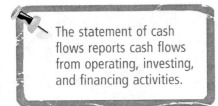

The statement of cash flows reports cash flows from operating, investing, and financing activities.

@netsolutions

The cash flows from operating activities are normally presented first, followed by the cash flows from investing activities and financing activities. The total of the net cash flow from these activities is the net increase or decrease in cash for the period. The cash balance at the beginning of the period is added to the net increase or decrease in cash, resulting in the cash balance at the end of the period. The ending cash balance on the statement of cash flows equals the cash reported on the balance sheet. Exhibit 1 illustrates a simple statement of cash flows that is reproduced from Chapter 1 (Exhibit 6) for NetSolutions.

EXHIBIT 1

Statement of Cash Flows—NetSolutions

NetSolutions Statement of Cash Flows For the Month Ended November 30, 2007			
Cash flows from operating activities:			
Cash received from customers		$ 7,500	
Deduct cash payments for expenses and			
payments to creditors		4,600	
Net cash flow from operating activities			$ 2,900
Cash flows from investing activities:			
Cash payments for purchase of land			(20,000)
Cash flows from financing activities:			
Cash received as owner's investment		$25,000	
Deduct cash withdrawal by owner		2,000	
Net cash flow provided by financing activities			23,000
Net cash flow and November 30, 2007, cash balance			$ 5,900

We have not discussed the statement of cash flows since introducing the statement in Chapter 1. We did this because a more complete understanding of operating, investing, and financing activities is helpful prior to developing and interpreting this statement. Previous chapters have introduced and described these activities so that you now have a foundation for the discussion that follows.

Exhibit 2 shows the major sources and uses of cash according to the three cash flow activities reported in the statement of cash flows. A *source* of cash causes the cash flow to increase, also called a *cash inflow*. For example, in Exhibit 1, the $25,000 cash received as owner's investment from Chris Clark is a financing activity that is a source of cash. A *use* of cash causes cash flow to decrease, also called a *cash outflow*. In Exhibit 1, NetSolutions' $20,000 cash payment for purchase of land is a use of cash. By reporting cash flows by operating, investing, and financing activities, significant relationships within and among the activities can be evaluated. For example, the cash receipts from issuing bonds can be related to repayments of borrowings when both are reported as financing activities. Also, the impact of each of the three activities (operating, investing, and financing) on cash flows can be identified. This allows investors and creditors to evaluate the effects of a firm's profits on cash flows and its ability to generate cash flows for dividends and for paying debts.

CASH FLOWS FROM OPERATING ACTIVITIES

The most important cash flows of a business often relate to operating activities. There are two alternative methods for reporting cash flows from operating activities in the statement of cash flows. These methods are (1) the direct method and (2) the indirect method.

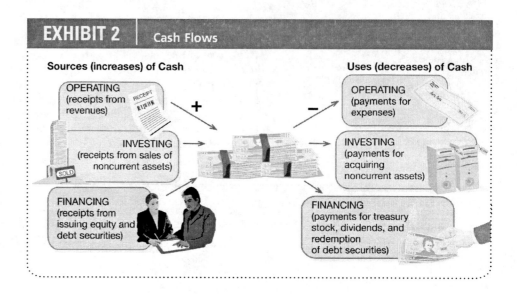

EXHIBIT 2 | Cash Flows

Sources (increases) of Cash   **Uses (decreases) of Cash**

OPERATING (receipts from revenues)   **+**   **−**   OPERATING (payments for expenses)

INVESTING (receipts from sales of noncurrent assets)   INVESTING (payments for acquiring noncurrent assets)

FINANCING (receipts from issuing equity and debt securities)   FINANCING (payments for treasury stock, dividends, and redemption of debt securities)

Cash Flows from Operating Activities

Direct Method **=** Indirect Method

The **direct method** reports the sources of operating cash and the uses of operating cash. The major source of operating cash is cash received from customers. The major uses of operating cash include cash paid to suppliers for merchandise and services and cash paid to employees for wages. The difference between these operating cash receipts and cash payments is the net cash flow from operating activities. The direct method is illustrated in Exhibit 1 for NetSolutions.

The primary advantage of the direct method is that it reports the sources and uses of operating cash flows in the statement of cash flows. Its primary disadvantage is that the necessary data may not be readily available and may be costly to gather.

The **indirect method** reports the operating cash flows by beginning with net income and adjusting it for revenues and expenses that do not involve the receipt or payment of cash. In other words, accrual net income is adjusted to determine the net amount of cash flows from operating activities.

A major advantage of the indirect method is that it focuses on the differences between net income and cash flows from operations. Thus, it shows the relationship between the income statement, the balance sheet, and the statement of cash flows. Because the data are readily available, the indirect method is normally less costly to use than the direct method. Because of these advantages, over 99% of all firms use the indirect method to report cash flows from operations.[2] We have not discussed the indirect method until this point, because it assumes an understanding of the accrual accounting concepts discussed in the prior chapters.

Exhibit 3 illustrates the cash flows from operating activities section of the statement of cash flows under the direct and indirect methods. Both statements are for Net-Solutions for the month ended November 2007. The methods show the same amount of net cash flow from operating activities, regardless of the method. We will illustrate both methods in detail later in this chapter.

REAL WORLD

The Walt Disney Company recently invested $1.4 billion in parks, resorts, and other properties, including the development of Hong Kong Disneyland.

CASH FLOWS FROM INVESTING ACTIVITIES

Cash inflows from investing activities normally arise from selling fixed assets, investments, and intangible assets. Cash outflows normally include payments to acquire fixed assets, investments, and intangible assets.

---

2 *Accounting Trends & Techniques*, AICPA, 2005 edition.

| | | EXHIBIT 3 | Cash Flow from Operations: Direct and Indirect Methods—NetSolutions |

Direct Method (from Exhibit 1)

Cash flows from operating activities:

Cash received from customers	$7,500
Deduct cash payments for expenses and payments to creditors	4,600
Net cash flow from operating activities	$2,900

Indirect Method

Cash flows from operating activities:

Net income	$3,050
Add increase in accounts payable	400
	$3,450
Deduct increase in supplies	550
Net cash flow from operating activities	$2,900

the same

Cash flows from investing activities are reported on the statement of cash flows by first listing the cash inflows. The cash outflows are then presented. If the inflows are greater than the outflows, *net cash flow provided by investing activities* is reported. If the inflows are less than the outflows, *net cash flow used for investing activities* is reported.

The cash flows from investing activities section in the statement of cash flows for NetSolutions from Exhibit 1 is shown below.

Cash flows from investing activities:
Cash payments for purchase of land . . . . $(20,000)

CASH FLOWS FROM FINANCING ACTIVITIES

Cash inflows from financing activities normally arise from issuing debt or equity securities. Examples of such inflows include issuing bonds, notes payable, and preferred and common stocks. Cash outflows from financing activities include paying cash dividends, repaying debt, and acquiring treasury stock.

Cash flows from financing activities are reported on the statement of cash flows by first listing the cash inflows. The cash outflows are then presented. If the inflows are greater than the outflows, *net cash flow provided by financing activities* is reported. If the inflows are less than the outflows, *net cash flow used for financing activities* is reported.

The cash flows from financing activities section in the statement of cash flows for NetSolutions from Exhibit 1 is shown below.

Cash flows from financing activities:
Cash received as owner's investment	$25,000
Deduct cash withdrawal by owner	2,000
Net cash flow provided by financing activities	$23,000

NONCASH INVESTING AND FINANCING ACTIVITIES

A business may enter into investing and financing activities that do not directly involve cash. For example, it may issue common stock to retire long-term debt. Such a transaction does not have a direct effect on cash. However, the transaction does eliminate the need for future cash payments to pay interest and retire the bonds. Thus, because of their future effect on cash flows, such transactions should be reported to readers of the financial statements.

When noncash investing and financing transactions occur during a period, their effect is reported in a separate schedule. This schedule usually appears at the bottom of the statement of cash flows. For example, in such a schedule, Google recently disclosed the issuance of over $25 million in common stock for business acquisitions. Other examples of noncash investing and financing transactions include acquiring fixed assets by issuing bonds or capital stock and issuing common stock in exchange for convertible preferred stock.

REAL WORLD

Business Connections

TOO MUCH CASH!

Is it possible to have too much cash? Clearly, most of us would answer no. However, a business views cash differently than an individual. Naturally, a business needs cash to develop and launch new products, expand markets, purchase plant and equipment, and acquire other businesses. However, some businesses have built up huge cash balances beyond even these needs. For example, both Microsoft Corporation and Dell Inc. have accumulated billions of dollars in cash and temporary investments, totaling in excess of 60% of their total assets. Such large cash balances can lower

the return on total assets. As stated by one analyst, "When a company sits on cash (which earns 1% or 2%) and leaves equity outstanding . . . , it is tantamount to taking a loan at 15% and investing in a passbook savings account that earns 2%—it destroys value." So while having too much cash is a good problem to have, companies like Microsoft, Cisco Systems, Inc., IBM, Apple Computer Inc., and Dell are under pressure to pay dividends or repurchase common stock. For example, Microsoft recently declared a $32 billion special dividend to return cash to its shareholders.

NO CASH FLOW PER SHARE

The term *cash flow per share* is sometimes reported in the financial press. Often, the term is used to mean "cash flow from operations per share." Such reporting may be misleading to users of the financial statements. For example, users might interpret cash flow per share as the amount available for dividends. This would not be the case if most of the cash generated by operations is required for repaying loans or for reinvesting in the business. Users might also think that cash flow per share is equivalent or perhaps superior to earnings per share. For these reasons, the financial statements, including the statement of cash flows, should not report cash flow per share.

Example Exercise 16-1   objective 1

Identify whether each of the following would be reported as an operating, investing, or financing activity in the statement of cash flows.

a. Purchase of patent
b. Payment of cash dividend
c. Disposal of equipment
d. Cash sales
e. Purchase of treasury stock
f. Payment of wages expense

Follow My Example 16-1

a. Investing
b. Financing
c. Investing
d. Operating
e. Financing
f. Operating

For Practice: PE 16-1A, PE 16-1B

Statement of Cash Flows—The Indirect Method

objective 2

Prepare a statement of cash flows, using the indirect method.

The indirect method of reporting cash flows from operating activities is normally less costly and more efficient than the direct method. In addition, when the direct method is used, the indirect method must also be used in preparing a supplemental reconciliation of net income with cash flows from operations. The 2005 edition of *Accounting Trends & Techniques* reported that 99% of the companies surveyed used the indirect method. For these reasons, we will first discuss the indirect method of preparing the statement of cash flows.

To collect the data for the statement of cash flows, all the cash receipts and cash payments for a period could be analyzed. However, this procedure is expensive and time consuming. A more efficient approach is to analyze the changes in the noncash balance sheet accounts. The logic of this approach is that a change in any balance sheet account (including cash) can be analyzed in terms of changes in the other balance sheet accounts. To illustrate, the accounting equation is rewritten below to focus on the cash account.

$$\text{Assets} = \text{Liabilities} + \text{Stockholders' Equity}$$
$$\text{Cash} + \text{Noncash Assets} = \text{Liabilities} + \text{Stockholders' Equity}$$
$$\text{Cash} = \text{Liabilities} + \text{Stockholders' Equity} - \text{Noncash Assets}$$

Any change in the cash account results in a change in one or more noncash balance sheet accounts. That is, if the cash account changes, then a liability, stockholders' equity, or noncash asset account must also change.

Additional data are also obtained by analyzing the income statement accounts and supporting records. For example, since the net income or net loss for the period is closed to *Retained Earnings*, a change in the retained earnings account can be partially explained by the net income or net loss reported on the income statement.

There is no order in which the noncash balance sheet accounts must be analyzed. However, it is usually more efficient to analyze the accounts in the reverse order in which they appear on the balance sheet. Thus, the analysis of retained earnings provides the starting point for determining the cash flows from operating activities, which is the first section of the statement of cash flows.

The comparative balance sheet for Rundell Inc. on December 31, 2008 and 2007, is used to illustrate the indirect method. This balance sheet is shown in Exhibit 4. Selected ledger accounts and other data are presented as needed.[3]

RETAINED EARNINGS

The comparative balance sheet for Rundell Inc. shows that retained earnings increased $80,000 during the year. Analyzing the entries posted to the retained earnings account indicates how this change occurred. The retained earnings account for Rundell Inc. is shown below.

ACCOUNT *Retained Earnings*				ACCOUNT NO.	
				Balance	
Date	Item	Debit	Credit	Debit	Credit
2008 Jan. 1	Balance				202 3 0 0 00
Dec. 31	Net income		108 0 0 0 00		310 3 0 0 00
31	Cash dividends	28 0 0 0 00			282 3 0 0 00

The retained earnings account must be carefully analyzed because some of the entries to retained earnings may not affect cash. For example, a decrease in retained earnings resulting from issuing a stock dividend does not affect cash. Such transactions are not reported on the statement of cash flows.

For Rundell Inc., the retained earnings account indicates that the $80,000 change resulted from net income of $108,000 and cash dividends declared of $28,000. The effect of each of these items on cash flows is discussed in the following sections.

CASH FLOWS FROM OPERATING ACTIVITIES—INDIRECT METHOD

The net income of $108,000 reported by Rundell Inc. normally is not equal to the amount of cash generated from operations during the period. This is because net income is determined using the accrual method of accounting.

---

3 An appendix that discusses using a spreadsheet (work sheet) as an aid in assembling data for the statement of cash flows is presented at the end of this chapter. This appendix illustrates the use of this spreadsheet in reporting cash flows from operating activities using the indirect method.

EXHIBIT 4

Comparative
Balance Sheet

Rundell Inc.
Comparative Balance Sheet
December 31, 2008 and 2007

Assets	2008	2007	Increase Decrease*
Cash.	$ 97,500	$ 26,000	$ 71,500
Accounts receivable (net).	74,000	65,000	9,000
Inventories.	172,000	180,000	8,000*
Land.	80,000	125,000	45,000*
Building.	260,000	200,000	60,000
Accumulated depreciation—building.	(65,300)	(58,300)	7,000
Total assets.	$618,200	$537,700	$ 80,500
Liabilities			
Accounts payable (merchandise			
creditors).	$ 43,500	$ 46,700	$ 3,200*
Accrued expenses payable			
(operating expenses).	26,500	24,300	2,200
Income taxes payable.	7,900	8,400	500*
Dividends payable.	14,000	10,000	4,000
Bonds payable.	100,000	150,000	50,000*
Total liabilities.	$191,900	$239,400	$ 47,500*
Stockholders' Equity			
Common stock ($2 par).	$ 24,000	$ 16,000	$ 8,000
Paid-in capital in excess of par.	120,000	80,000	40,000
Retained earnings.	282,300	202,300	80,000
Total stockholders' equity.	$426,300	$298,300	$128,000
Total liabilities and stockholders' equity. . . .	$618,200	$537,700	$ 80,500

Under the accrual method of accounting, revenues and expenses are recorded at different times from when cash is received or paid. For example, merchandise may be sold on account and the cash received at a later date. Likewise, insurance expense represents the amount of insurance expired during the period. The premiums for the insurance may have been paid in a prior period.

Under the indirect method, these differences are used to reconcile the net income to cash flows from operating activities. The typical adjustments to net income under the indirect method are reported in the statement of cash flows, as shown in Exhibit 5.[4]

In practice, the list of adjustments often begins with expenses that do not affect cash. Common examples are depreciation of fixed assets and amortization of intangible assets. Thus, in Exhibit 5, these two items are *added* to net income in determining cash flows from operating activities.

Typically, the next adjustments to net income are for gains and losses from disposal of assets. These adjustments arise because cash flows from operating activities should not include investing or financing transactions. For example, assume that land costing $50,000 was sold for $90,000 (a gain of $40,000). The sale should be reported as an investing activity: "Cash receipts from the sale of land, $90,000." However, the $40,000 gain on the disposal of the land is included in net income on the income statement. Thus, the $40,000 gain is *deducted* from net income in determining cash flows from operations to

---

4 Other items that also require adjustments to net income to obtain cash flows from operating activities include amortization of bonds payable discounts (add), losses on debt retirement (add), amortization of bonds payable premium (deduct), and gains on retirement of debt (deduct).

EXHIBIT 5

Adjustments to Net
Income (Loss) Using
the Indirect Method

	Increase (Decrease)
Net income (loss)	$ XXX
Adjustments to reconcile net income to net cash flow from operating activities:	
Depreciation of fixed assets	XXX
Amortization of intangible assets	XXX
Losses on disposal of assets	XXX
Gains on disposal of assets	(XXX)
Changes in current operating assets and liabilities:	
Increases in noncash current operating assets	(XXX)
Decreases in noncash current operating assets	XXX
Increases in current operating liabilities	XXX
Decreases in current operating liabilities	(XXX)
Net cash flow from operating activities	$ XXX
	or
	$(XXX)

Subtract   Add

Increases in accounts receivable	Decreases in accounts receivable
Increases in inventory	Decreases in inventory
Increases in prepaid expenses	Decreases in prepaid expenses
Decreases in accounts payable	Increases in accounts payable
Decreases in accrued expenses payable	Increases in accrued expenses payable

avoid "double counting" the cash flow from the gain. Likewise, losses from the disposal of fixed assets are *added* to net income in determining cash flows from operations.

Net income is also adjusted for changes in noncash current assets and current liabilities that support operations. Under the indirect method, these items are often listed last as "changes in current operating assets and liabilities." Under this heading, current assets are listed first, followed by current liabilities. Changes in noncash current assets and current liabilities are the result of revenue or expense transactions that may or may not affect cash flow. For example, a sale of $10,000 on account increases accounts receivable by $10,000. However, cash is not affected. Thus, the increase in accounts receivable of $10,000 between two balance sheet dates is *deducted* from net income in arriving at cash flows from operating activities. In contrast, a decrease in accounts receivable indicates the collection of cash that may have been reported as revenues in a prior period. Thus, a decrease in accounts receivable is added to net income in arriving at cash flows from operating activities.

Similar adjustments to net income are required for the changes in the other current asset and liability accounts supporting operations, such as inventory, prepaid expenses, accounts payable, and other accrued expenses. The direction of the adjustment is shown at the bottom of Exhibit 5. For example, an increase in accounts payable from the beginning to the end of the period would be added to net income in determining cash flows from operating activities.

The effect of dividends payable, though a current liability, is not included in the operating activity section of the statement of cash flows. Dividends payable is omitted from Exhibit 5 because dividends are not an operating activity that affects net income. Later in the chapter, we will discuss how dividends are reported in the statement of cash flows as a part of financing activities. In the following paragraphs, we will discuss each of the adjustments that convert Rundell Inc.'s net income to "Cash flows from operating activities."

Depreciation The comparative balance sheet in Exhibit 4 indicates that Accumulated Depreciation—Building increased by $7,000. As shown at the top of the following page, this account indicates that depreciation for the year was $7,000 for the building.

ACCOUNT *Accumulated Depreciation—Building*   ACCOUNT NO.

Date		Item	Debit	Credit	Balance Debit	Balance Credit
2008 Jan.	1	Balance				58 3 0 0 00
Dec.	31	Depreciation for year		7 0 0 0 00		65 3 0 0 00

The $7,000 of depreciation expense reduced net income but did not require an outflow of cash. Thus, the $7,000 is added to net income in determining cash flows from operating activities, as follows:

Cash flows from operating activities:		
Net income	$108,000	
Add depreciation	7,000	$115,000

Gain on Sale of Land   The ledger or income statement of Rundell Inc. indicates that the sale of land resulted in a gain of $12,000. As we discussed previously, the sale proceeds, which include the gain and the carrying value of the land, are included in cash flows from investing activities.[5] The gain is also included in net income. Thus, to avoid double reporting, the gain of $12,000 is deducted from net income in determining cash flows from operating activities, as shown below.

Cash flows from operating activities:	
Net income	$108,000
Deduct gain on sale of land	12,000

Example Exercise 16-2   objective **2**

Omni Corporation's accumulated depreciation increased by $12,000, while patents decreased by $3,400 between balance sheet dates. There were no purchases or sales of depreciable or intangible assets during the year. In addition, the income statement showed a gain of $4,100 from the sale of land. Reconcile a net income of $50,000 to net cash flow from operating activities.

Follow My Example 16-2

Net income	$50,000
Adjustments to reconcile net income to net cash flow from operating activities:	
Depreciation	12,000
Amortization	3,400
Gain from sale of land	(4,100)
Net cash flow from operating activities	$61,300

For Practice: PE 16-2A, PE 16-2B

Changes in Current Operating Assets and Liabilities   As shown in Exhibit 5, decreases in noncash current assets and increases in current liabilities are added to net income. In contrast, increases in noncash current assets and decreases in current liabilities are deducted from net income. The current asset and current liability accounts of Rundell Inc. are as follows:

---

5 The reporting of the proceeds (cash flows) from the sale of land as part of investing activities is discussed later in this chapter.

Accounts	December 31		Increase Decrease*
	2008	2007	
Accounts receivable (net)	$ 74,000	$ 65,000	$9,000
Inventories	172,000	180,000	8,000*
Accounts payable (merchandise creditors)	43,500	46,700	3,200*
Accrued expenses payable (operating expenses) ..	26,500	24,300	2,200
Income taxes payable	7,900	8,400	500*

REAL WORLD

Continental Airlines had a net loss of $363 million but a positive cash flow from operating activities of $373 million. This difference was mostly due to $414 million of depreciation expenses and $417 million from changes in operating assets and liabilities.

As discussed previously, the $9,000 increase in *accounts receivable* indicates that the sales on account during the year are $9,000 more than collections from customers on account. The amount reported as sales on the income statement therefore includes $9,000 that did not result in a cash inflow during the year. Thus, $9,000 is deducted from net income.

The $8,000 decrease in *inventories* indicates that the merchandise sold exceeds the cost of the merchandise purchased by $8,000. The amount deducted as cost of merchandise sold on the income statement therefore includes $8,000 that did not require a cash outflow during the year. Thus, $8,000 is added to net income.

The $3,200 decrease in *accounts payable* indicates that the amount of cash payments for merchandise exceeds the merchandise purchased on account by $3,200. The amount reported on the income statement for cost of merchandise sold therefore excludes $3,200 that required a cash outflow during the year. Thus, $3,200 is deducted from net income.

The $2,200 increase in *accrued expenses payable* indicates that the amount incurred during the year for operating expenses exceeds the cash payments by $2,200. The amount reported on the income statement for operating expenses therefore includes $2,200 that did not require a cash outflow during the year. Thus, $2,200 is added to net income.

The $500 decrease in *income taxes payable* indicates that the amount paid for taxes exceeds the amount incurred during the year by $500. The amount reported on the income statement for income tax therefore is less than the amount paid by $500. Thus, $500 is deducted from net income.

Example Exercise 16-3

objective 2

Victor Corporation's comparative balance sheet for current assets and liabilities was as follows:

	Dec. 31, 2009	Dec. 31, 2008
Accounts receivable	$ 6,500	$ 4,900
Inventory	12,300	15,000
Accounts payable	4,800	5,200
Dividends payable	5,000	4,000

Adjust net income of $70,000 for changes in operating assets and liabilities to arrive at cash flows from operating activities.

Follow My Example 16-3

Net income	$70,000
Adjustments to reconcile net income to net cash flow from operating activities:	
Changes in current operating assets and liabilities:	
Increase in accounts receivable	(1,600)
Decrease in inventory	2,700
Decrease in accounts payable	(400)
Net cash flow from operating activities	$70,700

For Practice: PE 16-3A, PE 16-3B

Integrity, Objectivity, and Ethics in Business

CREDIT POLICY AND CASH FLOW

One would expect customers to pay for products and services sold on account. Unfortunately, that is not always the case. Collecting accounts receivable efficiently is the key to turning a current asset into positive cash flow. Most entrepreneurs would rather think about the exciting aspects of their business—such as product development, marketing, sales, and advertising—rather than credit collection. This can be a mistake. Hugh McHugh of Overhill Flowers, Inc., decided that he would have no more trade accounts after dealing with Christmas orders that weren't paid for until late February, or sometimes not paid at all. As stated by one collection service, "One thing business owners always tell me is that they never thought about [collections] when they started their own business." To the small business owner, the collected receivable is often their paycheck, so it pays to pay attention.

Source: Paulette Thomas, "Making Them Pay: The Last Thing Most Entrepreneurs Want to Think About Is Bill Collection; It Should Be One of the First Things," *The Wall Street Journal*, September 19, 2005, p. R6.

Reporting Cash Flows from Operating Activities   We have now presented all the necessary adjustments to convert the net income to cash flows from operating activities for Rundell Inc. These adjustments are summarized in Exhibit 6 for the statement of cash flows.

EXHIBIT 6   Cash Flows from Operating Activities—Indirect Method

Cash flows from operating activities:		
Net income	$108,000	
Adjustments to reconcile net income to net cash flow from operating activities:		
Depreciation	7,000	
Gain on sale of land	(12,000)	
Changes in current operating assets and liabilities:		
Increase in accounts receivable	(9,000)	
Decrease in inventory	8,000	
Decrease in accounts payable	(3,200)	
Increase in accrued expenses	2,200	
Decrease in income taxes payable	(500)	
Net cash flow from operating activities		$100,500

Example Exercise 16-4

objective *2*

Omicron Inc. reported the following data:

Net income	$120,000
Depreciation expense	12,000
Loss on disposal of equipment	15,000
Increase in accounts receivable	5,000
Decrease in accounts payable	2,000

Prepare the cash flows from operating activities section of the statement of cash flows using the indirect method.

(continued)

703

Follow My Example 16-4

Cash flows from operating activities:	
Net income	$120,000
Adjustments to reconcile net income to net cash flow from operating activities:	
Depreciation	12,000
Loss from disposal of equipment	15,000
Changes in current operating assets and liabilities:	
Increase in accounts receivable	(5,000)
Decrease in accounts payable	(2,000)
Net cash flow from operating activities	$140,000

For Practice: PE 16-4A, PE 16-4B

CASH FLOWS USED FOR PAYMENT OF DIVIDENDS

According to the retained earnings account of Rundell Inc., shown earlier in the chapter, cash dividends of $28,000 were declared during the year. However, the dividends payable account, shown below, indicates that dividends of only $24,000 were paid during the year.

ACCOUNT *Dividends Payable*   **ACCOUNT NO.**

Date		Item	Debit	Credit	Balance Debit	Balance Credit
2008 Jan.	1	Balance				10 0 0 0 00
	10	Cash paid	10 0 0 0 00		—	—
June	20	Dividends declared		14 0 0 0 00		14 0 0 0 00
July	10	Cash paid	14 0 0 0 00		—	—
Dec.	20	Dividends declared		14 0 0 0 00		14 0 0 0 00

The $24,000 of dividend payments represents a cash outflow that is reported in the financing activities section as follows:

Cash flows from financing activities:	
Cash paid for dividends	$24,000

COMMON STOCK

REAL WORLD

XM Satellite Radio has had negative cash flows from operations for most of its young corporate life. However, it has been able to grow by obtaining cash from the sale of common stock and issuing debt. Investors are willing to purchase the common stock and debt on the belief that XM will have a very profitable future as satellite radio matures.

The common stock account increased by $8,000, and the paid-in capital in excess of par—common stock account increased by $40,000, as shown below. These increases result from issuing 4,000 shares of common stock for $12 per share.

ACCOUNT *Common Stock*   **ACCOUNT NO.**

Date		Item	Debit	Credit	Balance Debit	Balance Credit
2008 Jan.	1	Balance				16 0 0 0 00
Nov.	1	4,000 shares issued for cash		8 0 0 0 00		24 0 0 0 00

ACCOUNT *Paid-In Capital in Excess of Par—Common Stock*   **ACCOUNT NO.**

Date		Item	Debit	Credit	Balance Debit	Balance Credit
2008 Jan.	1	Balance				80 0 0 0 00
Nov.	1	4,000 shares issued for cash		40 0 0 0 00		120 0 0 0 00

This cash inflow is reported in the financing activities section as follows:

Cash flows from financing activities:
Cash received from sale of common stock $48,000

BONDS PAYABLE

The bonds payable account decreased by $50,000, as shown below. This decrease results from retiring the bonds by a cash payment for their face amount.

					Balance	
ACCOUNT Bonds Payable						**ACCOUNT NO.**
Date	Item	Debit	Credit	Debit	Credit
2008 Jan. 1	Balance				150 0 0 0 00
June 30	Retired by payment of cash				
	at face amount	50 0 0 0 00			100 0 0 0 00

This cash outflow is reported in the financing activities section as follows:

Cash flows from financing activities:
Cash paid to retire bonds payable $50,000

BUILDING

The building account increased by $60,000, and the accumulated depreciation—building account increased by $7,000, as shown below.

ACCOUNT Building   **ACCOUNT NO.**

				Balance	
Date	Item	Debit	Credit	Debit	Credit
2008 Jan. 1	Balance			200 0 0 0 00	
Dec. 27	Purchased for cash	60 0 0 0 00		260 0 0 0 00	

ACCOUNT Accumulated Depreciation—Building   **ACCOUNT NO.**

				Balance	
Date	Item	Debit	Credit	Debit	Credit
2008 Jan. 1	Balance				58 3 0 0 00
Dec. 31	Depreciation for the year		7 0 0 0 00		65 3 0 0 00

The purchase of a building for cash of $60,000 is reported as an outflow of cash in the investing activities section, as follows:

Cash flows from investing activities:
Cash paid for purchase of building $60,000

The credit in the accumulated depreciation—building account, shown earlier, represents depreciation expense for the year. This depreciation expense of $7,000 on the building has already been considered as an addition to net income in determining cash flows from operating activities, as reported in Exhibit 6.

LAND

The $45,000 decline in the land account resulted from two separate transactions, as shown below.

						Balance	
ACCOUNT *Land*					**ACCOUNT NO.**		
Date		**Item**	**Debit**	**Credit**	**Debit**	**Credit**
2008 Jan.	1	Balance			125 00 0 00	
June	8	Sold for $72,000 cash		60 0 0 0 00	65 0 0 0 00	
Oct.	12	Purchased for $15,000 cash	15 0 0 0 00		80 0 0 0 00	

The first transaction is the sale of land with a cost of $60,000 for $72,000 in cash. The $72,000 proceeds from the sale are reported in the investing activities section, as follows:

> Cash flows from investing activities:
> Cash received from sale of land (includes
> $12,000 gain reported in net income) $72,000

The proceeds of $72,000 include the $12,000 gain on the sale of land and the $60,000 cost (book value) of the land. As shown in Exhibit 6, the $12,000 gain is also deducted from net income in the cash flows from operating activities section. This is necessary so that the $12,000 cash inflow related to the gain is not included twice as a cash inflow.

The second transaction is the purchase of land for cash of $15,000. This transaction is reported as an outflow of cash in the investing activities section, as follows:

> Cash flows from investing activities:
> Cash paid for purchase of land $15,000

Example Exercise 16-5
objective 2

Alpha Corporation purchased land for $125,000. Later in the year, the company sold land with a book value of $165,000 for $200,000. How are the effects of these transactions reported on the statement of cash flows?

Follow My Example 16-5

The gain on sale of land is deducted from net income as shown below:
Gain on sale of land . . . . $ (35,000)

The purchase and sale of land is reported as part of cash flows from investing activities as shown below:
Cash received for sale of land   200,000
Cash paid for purchase of land . . . .   (125,000)

For Practice: PE 16-5A, PE 16-5B

PREPARING THE STATEMENT OF CASH FLOWS

The statement of cash flows for Rundell Inc. is prepared from the data assembled and analyzed above, using the indirect method. Exhibit 7 shows the statement of cash flows prepared by Rundell Inc. The statement indicates that the cash position increased by $71,500 during the year. The most significant increase in net cash flows, $100,500, was from operating activities. The most significant use of cash, $26,000, was for financing activities.

<table>
<tr><td>**EXHIBIT 7**

Statement of Cash
Flows—Indirect
Method</td></tr>
</table>

Rundell Inc.
Statement of Cash Flows
For the Year Ended December 31, 2008

Cash flows from operating activities:		
Net income	$108,000	
Adjustments to reconcile net income to net cash flow from operating activities:		
Depreciation	7,000	
Gain on sale of land	(12,000)	
Changes in current operating assets and liabilities:		
Increase in accounts receivable	(9,000)	
Decrease in inventory	8,000	
Decrease in accounts payable	(3,200)	
Increase in accrued expenses.	2,200	
Decrease in income taxes payable	(500)	
Net cash flow from operating activities		$100,500
Cash flows from investing activities:		
Cash from sale of land	$ 72,000	
Less: Cash paid to purchase land . . . . $ 15,000		
Cash paid for purchase of building 60,000	75,000	
Net cash flow used for investing activities		(3,000)
Cash flows from financing activities:		
Cash received from sale of common stock	$ 48,000	
Less: Cash paid to retire bonds payable . . . . . . $ 50,000		
Cash paid for dividends 24,000	74,000	
Net cash flow used for financing activities		(26,000)
Increase in cash		$ 71,500
Cash at the beginning of the year		26,000
Cash at the end of the year		$ 97,500

Statement of Cash Flows—The Direct Method

objective   **3**

*Prepare a
statement of cash
flows, using the
direct method.*

As we discussed previously, the manner of reporting cash flows from investing and financing activities is the same under the direct and indirect methods. In addition, the direct method and the indirect method will report the same amount of cash flows from operating activities. However, the methods differ in how the cash flows from operating activities data are obtained, analyzed, and reported.

To illustrate the direct method, we will use the comparative balance sheet and the income statement for Rundell Inc. In this way, we can compare the statement of cash flows under the direct method and the indirect method.

Exhibit 8 shows the changes in the current asset and liability account balances for Rundell Inc. The income statement in Exhibit 8 shows additional data for Rundell Inc.

The direct method reports cash flows from operating activities by major classes of operating cash receipts and operating cash payments. The difference between the major classes of total operating cash receipts and total operating cash payments is the net cash flow from operating activities.

CASH RECEIVED FROM CUSTOMERS

The $1,180,000 of sales for Rundell Inc. is reported by using the accrual method. To determine the cash received from sales to customers, the $1,180,000 must be adjusted.

EXHIBIT 8

Balance Sheet and
Income Statement
Data for Direct
Method

Rundell Inc.
Schedule of Changes in Current Accounts

Accounts	December 31		Increase Decrease*
	2008	2007	
Cash	$ 97,500	$ 26,000	$71,500
Accounts receivable (net)	74,000	65,000	9,000
Inventories	172,000	180,000	8,000*
Accounts payable (merchandise creditors)	43,500	46,700	3,200*
Accrued expenses payable (operating expenses) ..	26,500	24,300	2,200
Income taxes payable	7,900	8,400	500*
Dividends payable	14,000	10,000	4,000

Rundell Inc.
Income Statement
For the Year Ended December 31, 2008

Sales		$1,180,000
Cost of merchandise sold		790,000
Gross profit		$ 390,000
Operating expenses:		
Depreciation expense	$ 7,000	
Other operating expenses	196,000	
Total operating expenses		203,000
Income from operations		$ 187,000
Other income:		
Gain on sale of land	$ 12,000	
Other expense:		
Interest expense	8,000	4,000
Income before income tax		$ 191,000
Income tax expense		83,000
Net income		$ 108,000

The adjustment necessary to convert the sales reported on the income statement to the cash received from customers is summarized below.

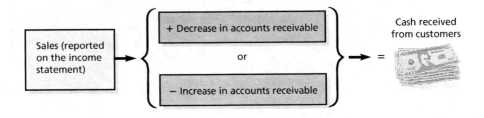

For Rundell Inc., the cash received from customers is $1,171,000, as shown below.

Sales	$1,180,000
Less increase in accounts receivable	9,000
Cash received from customers	$1,171,000

The additions to *accounts receivable* for sales on account during the year were $9,000 more than the amounts collected from customers on account. Sales reported on the income statement therefore included $9,000 that did not result in a cash inflow during the year. In other words, the increase of $9,000 in accounts receivable during 2008 indicates that sales on account exceeded cash received from customers by $9,000. Thus, $9,000 is deducted from sales to determine the cash received from customers. The $1,171,000 of cash received from customers is reported in the cash flows from operating activities section of the cash flow statement.

Example Exercise 16-6
objective 3

Sales reported on the income statement were $350,000. The accounts receivable balance declined $8,000 over the year. Determine the amount of cash received from customers.

Follow My Example 16-6

Sales	$350,000
Add decrease in accounts receivable	8,000
Cash received from customers	$358,000

For Practice: PE 16-6A, PE 16-6B

CASH PAYMENTS FOR MERCHANDISE

The $790,000 of cost of merchandise sold is reported on the income statement for Rundell Inc., using the accrual method. The adjustments necessary to convert the cost of merchandise sold to cash payments for merchandise during 2008 are summarized below.

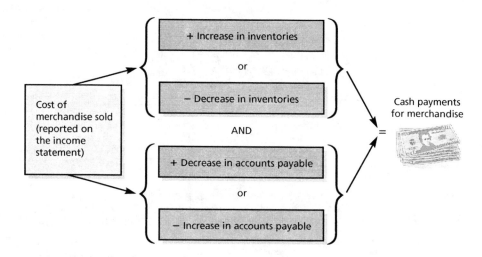

For Rundell Inc., the amount of cash payments for merchandise is $785,200, as determined below.

Cost of merchandise sold	$790,000
Deduct decrease in inventories	(8,000)
Add decrease in accounts payable	3,200
Cash payments for merchandise	$785,200

The $8,000 decrease in *inventories* indicates that the merchandise sold exceeded the cost of the merchandise purchased by $8,000. The amount reported on the income statement for cost of merchandise sold therefore includes $8,000 that did not require a cash outflow during the year. Thus, $8,000 is deducted from the cost of merchandise sold in determining the cash payments for merchandise.

The $3,200 decrease in *accounts payable* (merchandise creditors) indicates a cash outflow that is excluded from cost of merchandise sold. That is, the decrease in accounts payable indicates that cash payments for merchandise were $3,200 more than the purchases on account during 2008. Thus, $3,200 is added to the cost of merchandise sold in determining the cash payments for merchandise.

Example Exercise 16-7   objective **3**

Cost of merchandise sold reported on the income statement was $145,000. The accounts payable balance increased $4,000, and the inventory balance increased by $9,000 over the year. Determine the amount of cash paid for merchandise.

Follow My Example 16-7

Cost of merchandise sold	$145,000
Add increase in inventories	9,000
Deduct increase in accounts payable	(4,000)
Cash paid for merchandise	$150,000

For Practice: PE 16-7A, PE 16-7B

CASH PAYMENTS FOR OPERATING EXPENSES

The $7,000 of depreciation expense reported on the income statement did not require a cash outflow. Thus, under the direct method, it is not reported on the statement of cash flows. The $196,000 reported for other operating expenses is adjusted to reflect the cash payments for operating expenses, as summarized below.

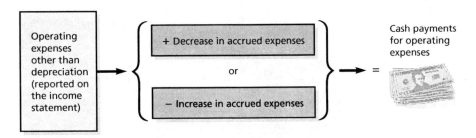

For Rundell Inc., the amount of cash payments for operating expenses is $193,800, determined as follows:

Operating expenses other than depreciation	$196,000
Deduct increase in accrued expenses	2,200
Cash payments for operating expenses	$193,800

The increase in *accrued expenses* (operating expenses) indicates that operating expenses include $2,200 for which there was no cash outflow (payment) during the year. That is, the increase in accrued expenses indicates that the cash payments for operating expenses were $2,200 less than the amount reported as an expense during the year. Thus, $2,200 is deducted from the operating expenses on the income statement in determining the cash payments for operating expenses.

GAIN ON SALE OF LAND

The income statement for Rundell Inc. in Exhibit 8 reports a gain of $12,000 on the sale of land. As we discussed previously, the gain is included in the proceeds from the sale of land, which is reported as part of the cash flows from investing activities.

INTEREST EXPENSE

The income statement for Rundell Inc. in Exhibit 8 reports interest expense of $8,000. The interest expense is related to the bonds payable that were outstanding during the year. We assume that interest on the bonds is paid on June 30 and December 31. Thus, $8,000 cash outflow for interest expense is reported on the statement of cash flows as an operating activity.

If interest payable had existed at the end of the year, the interest expense would be adjusted for any increase or decrease in interest payable from the beginning to the end of the year. That is, a decrease in interest payable would be added to interest expense and an increase in interest payable would be subtracted from interest expense. This is similar to the adjustment for changes in income taxes payable, which we will illustrate in the following paragraphs.

CASH PAYMENTS FOR INCOME TAXES

The adjustment to convert the income tax reported on the income statement to the cash basis is summarized below.

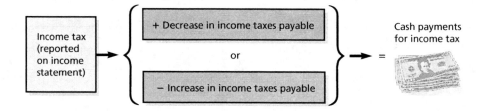

For Rundell Inc., cash payments for income tax are $83,500, determined as follows:

Income tax	$83,000
Add decrease in income taxes payable	500
Cash payments for income tax	$83,500

The cash outflow for income taxes exceeded the income tax deducted as an expense during the period by $500. Thus, $500 is added to the amount of income tax reported on the income statement in determining the cash payments for income tax.

REPORTING CASH FLOWS FROM OPERATING ACTIVITIES—DIRECT METHOD

Exhibit 9 is a complete statement of cash flows for Rundell Inc., using the direct method for reporting cash flows from operating activities. The portions of this statement that differ from the indirect method are highlighted in color. Exhibit 9 also includes the separate schedule reconciling net income and net cash flow from operating activities. This schedule must accompany the statement of cash flows when the direct method is used. This schedule is similar to the cash flows from operating activities section of the statement of cash flows prepared using the indirect method.

EXHIBIT 9

Statement of Cash
Flows—Direct Method

Rundell Inc.
Statement of Cash Flows
For the Year Ended December 31, 2008

Cash flows from operating activities:			
Cash received from customers		$1,171,000	
Deduct: Cash payments for merchandise.	$785,200		
Cash payments for operating expenses. . . .	193,800		
Cash payments for interest	8,000		
Cash payments for income taxes	83,500	1,070,500	
Net cash flow from operating activities			$100,500
Cash flows from investing activities:			
Cash from sale of land		$ 72,000	
Less: Cash paid to purchase land	$ 15,000		
Cash paid for purchase of building	60,000	75,000	
Net cash flow used for investing activities			(3,000)
Cash flows from financing activities:			
Cash received from sale of common stock		$ 48,000	
Less: Cash paid to retire bonds payable	$ 50,000		
Cash paid for dividends	24,000	74,000	
Net cash flow used for financing activities			(26,000)
Increase in cash			$ 71,500
Cash at the beginning of the year			26,000
Cash at the end of the year			$ 97,500
Schedule Reconciling Net Income with Cash			
Flows from Operating Activities:			
Cash flows from operating activities:			
Net income			$108,000
Adjustments to reconcile net income to net cash			
flow from operating activities:			
Depreciation			7,000
Gain on sale of land			(12,000)
Changes in current operating assets and liabilities:			
Increase in accounts receivable			(9,000)
Decrease in inventory			8,000
Decrease in accounts payable			(3,200)
Increase in accrued expenses			2,200
Decrease in income taxes payable			(500)
Net cash flow from operating activities			$100,500

Financial Analysis and Interpretation

A valuable tool for evaluating the cash flows of a business is free cash flow. **Free cash flow** is a measure of operating cash flow available for corporate purposes after providing sufficient fixed asset additions to maintain current productive capacity and dividends. Thus, free cash flow can be calculated as follows:

Cash flow from operating activities	$XXX
Less: Investments in fixed assets to maintain current production	XXX
Free cash flow	$XXX

Analysts often use free cash flow, rather than cash flows from operating activities, to measure the financial strength of a business. Many high-technology firms must aggressively reinvest in new technology to remain competitive. This can reduce free cash flow. For example, Motorola Inc.'s free cash flow is less than 10% of the cash flow from operating activities. In contrast, The Coca-Cola Company's free cash flow is approximately 75% of the cash flow from operating activities. The top three nonfinancial companies with the largest free cash flows for a recent year were as follows:

	Free Cash Flow (in millions)
General Electric Company	$25,598
ExxonMobil Corporation	18,705
Microsoft Corporation	14,289

To illustrate, the cash flow from operating activities for Intuit Inc., the developer of TurboTax®, was $590 million in a recent fiscal year. The statement of cash flows indicated that the cash invested in property, plant, and equipment was $38 million. Assuming that the amount invested in property, plant, and equipment maintained existing operations, free cash flow would be calculated as follows (in millions):

Cash flow from operating activities	$590
Less: Investments in fixed assets to maintain current production	38
Free cash flow	$552

During this period, Intuit generated free cash flow in excess of $500 million, which was 94% of cash flows from operations and over 27% of sales.

Positive free cash flow is considered favorable. A company that has free cash flow is able to fund internal growth, retire debt, pay dividends, and enjoy financial flexibility. A company with no free cash flow is unable to maintain current productive capacity. Lack of free cash flow can be an early indicator of liquidity problems. As stated by one analyst, "Free cash flow gives the company firepower to reduce debt and ultimately generate consistent, actual income."[6]

Source: "CFO Free Cash Flow Scorecard," *CFO Magazine*, January 1, 2005.

Appendix

Spreadsheet (Work Sheet) for Statement of Cash Flows—The Indirect Method

A spreadsheet (work sheet) may be useful in assembling data for the statement of cash flows. Whether or not a spreadsheet (work sheet) is used, the concepts of cash flow and the statements of cash flows presented in this chapter are not affected. In this appendix, we will describe and illustrate the use of the spreadsheet (work sheet) for the indirect method.

6 Jill Krutick, *Fortune*, March 30, 1998, p. 106.

We will use the data for Rundell Inc., presented in Exhibit 4, as a basis for illustrating the spreadsheet (work sheet) for the indirect method. The procedures used in preparing this spreadsheet (work sheet), shown in Exhibit 10, are outlined below.

1. List the title of each balance sheet account in the Accounts column. For each account, enter its balance as of December 31, 2007, in the first column and its balance as of December 31, 2008, in the last column. Place the credit balances in parentheses. The column totals should equal zero, since the total of the debits in a column should equal the total of the credits in a column.
2. Analyze the change during the year in each account to determine the net increase (decrease) in cash and the cash flows from operating activities, investing activities, financing activities, and the noncash investing and financing activities. Show the effect of the change on cash flows by making entries in the Transactions columns.

ANALYZING ACCOUNTS

An efficient method of analyzing cash flows is to determine the type of cash flow activity that led to changes in balance sheet accounts during the period. As we analyze each noncash account, we will make entries on the spreadsheet (work sheet) for specific types of cash flow activities related to the noncash accounts. After we have analyzed all the noncash accounts, we will make an entry for the increase (decrease) in cash during the period. These entries, however, are not posted to the ledger. They only aid in assembling the data on the spreadsheet.

The order in which the accounts are analyzed is unimportant. However, it is more efficient to begin with the retained earnings account and proceed upward in the account listing.

RETAINED EARNINGS

The spreadsheet (work sheet) shows a Retained Earnings balance of $202,300 at December 31, 2007, and $282,300 at December 31, 2008. Thus, Retained Earnings increased $80,000 during the year. This increase resulted from two factors: (1) net income of $108,000 and (2) declaring cash dividends of $28,000. To identify the cash flows by activity, we will make two entries on the spreadsheet. These entries also serve to account for or explain, in terms of cash flows, the increase of $80,000.

In closing the accounts at the end of the year, the retained earnings account was credited for the net income of $108,000. The $108,000 is reported on the statement of cash flows as "cash flows from operating activities." The following entry is made in the Transactions columns on the spreadsheet. This entry (1) accounts for the credit portion of the closing entry (to Retained Earnings) and (2) identifies the cash flow in the bottom portion of the spreadsheet.

(a)	Operating Activities—Net Income	108,000	
	Retained Earnings		108,000

In closing the accounts at the end of the year, the retained earnings account was debited for dividends declared of $28,000. The $28,000 is reported as a financing activity on the statement of cash flows. The following entry on the spreadsheet (1) accounts for the debit portion of the closing entry (to Retained Earnings) and (2) identifies the cash flow in the bottom portion of the spreadsheet.

(b)	Retained Earnings	28,000	
	Financing Activities—Declared Cash Dividends		28,000

The $28,000 of declared dividends will be adjusted later for the actual amount of cash dividends paid during the year.

EXHIBIT 10   End-of-Period Spreadsheet (Work Sheet) for Statement of Cash Flows—Indirect Method

Rundell Inc.
End-of-Period Spreadsheet (Work Sheet) for Statement of Cash Flows
For the Year Ended December 31, 2008

	A Accounts	B Balance, Dec. 31, 2007	C	D Transactions Debit	E	F Credit	G Balance, Dec. 31, 2008	
1	Cash	26,000	(o)	71,500			97,500	1
2	Accounts receivable (net)	65,000	(n)	9,000			74,000	2
3	Inventories	180,000			(m)	8,000	172,000	3
4	Land	125,000	(k)	15,000	(l)	60,000	80,000	4
5	Building	200,000	(j)	60,000			260,000	5
6	Accumulated depreciation—building	(58,300)			(i)	7,000	(65,300)	6
7	Accounts payable (merchandise creditors)	(46,700)	(h)	3,200			(43,500)	7
8	Accrued expenses payable (operating expenses)	(24,300)			(g)	2,200	(26,500)	8
9	Income taxes payable	(8,400)	(f)	500			(7,900)	9
10	Dividends payable	(10,000)			(e)	4,000	(14,000)	10
11	Bonds payable	(150,000)	(d)	50,000			(100,000)	11
12	Common stock	(16,000)			(c)	8,000	(24,000)	12
13	Paid-in capital in excess of par	(80,000)			(c)	40,000	(120,000)	13
14	Retained earnings	(202,300)	(b)	28,000	(a)	108,000	(282,300)	14
15	Totals	0		237,200		237,200	0	15
16	Operating activities:							16
17	Net income		(a)	108,000				17
18	Depreciation of building		(i)	7,000				18
19	Gain on sale of land				(l)	12,000		19
20	Increase in accounts receivable				(n)	9,000		20
21	Decrease in inventories		(m)	8,000				21
22	Decrease in accounts payable				(h)	3,200		22
23	Increase in accrued expenses		(g)	2,200				23
24	Decrease in income taxes payable				(f)	500		24
25	Investing activities:							25
26	Sale of land		(l)	72,000				26
27	Purchase of land				(k)	15,000		27
28	Purchase of building				(j)	60,000		28
29	Financing activities:							29
30	Issued common stock		(c)	48,000				30
31	Retired bonds payable				(d)	50,000		31
32	Declared cash dividends				(b)	28,000		32
33	Increase in dividends payable		(e)	4,000				33
34	Net increase in cash				(o)	71,500		34
35	Totals			249,200		249,200		35

OTHER ACCOUNTS

The entries for the other accounts are made in the spreadsheet in a manner similar to entries (a) and (b). A summary of these entries is as follows:

(c)	Financing Activities—Issued Common Stock	48,000	
	Common Stock		8,000
	Paid-In Capital in Excess of Par—Common Stock		40,000
(d)	Bonds Payable	50,000	
	Financing Activities—Retired Bonds Payable		50,000
(e)	Financing Activities—Increase in Dividends Payable	4,000	
	Dividends Payable		4,000
(f)	Income Taxes Payable	500	
	Operating Activities—Decrease in Income Taxes Payable		500

(g)	Operating Activities—Increase in Accrued Expenses	2,200	
	Accrued Expenses Payable		2,200
(h)	Accounts Payable	3,200	
	Operating Activities—Decrease in Accounts Payable		3,200
(i)	Operating Activities—Depreciation of Building	7,000	
	Accumulated Depreciation—Building		7,000
(j)	Building	60,000	
	Investing Activities—Purchase of Building		60,000
(k)	Land	15,000	
	Investing Activities—Purchase of Land		15,000
(l)	Investing Activities—Sale of Land	72,000	
	Operating Activities—Gain on Sale of Land		12,000
	Land		60,000
(m)	Operating Activities—Decrease in Inventories	8,000	
	Inventories		8,000
(n)	Accounts Receivable	9,000	
	Operating Activities—Increase in Accounts Receivable		9,000
(o)	Cash	71,500	
	Net Increase in Cash		71,500

After we have analyzed all the balance sheet accounts and made the entries on the spreadsheet (work sheet), all the operating, investing, and financing activities are identified in the bottom portion of the spreadsheet. The accuracy of the spreadsheet entries is verified by the equality of each pair of the totals of the debit and credit Transactions columns.

PREPARING THE STATEMENT OF CASH FLOWS

The statement of cash flows prepared from the spreadsheet is identical to the statement in Exhibit 7. The data for the three sections of the statement are obtained from the bottom portion of the spreadsheet.

At a Glance

1. Summarize the types of cash flow activities reported in the statement of cash flows.

Key Points	Key Learning Outcomes	Example Exercises	Practice Exercises
The statement of cash flows reports cash receipts and cash payments by three types of activities: operating activities, investing activities, and financing activities. Investing and financing for a business may be affected by transactions that do not involve cash. The effect of such transactions should be reported in a separate schedule accompanying the statement of cash flows.	• Classify transactions that either provide or use cash into either operating, investing, or financing activities.	16-1	16-1A, 16-1B

(continued)

2. Prepare a statement of cash flows, using the indirect method.

Key Points	Key Learning Outcomes	Example Exercises	Practice Exercises
The changes in the noncash balance sheet accounts are used to develop the statement of cash flows, beginning with the cash flows from operating activities.			
Determine the cash flows from operating activities using the indirect method by adjusting net income for expenses that do not require cash and for gains and losses from disposal of fixed assets.	• Adjust net income for non-cash expenses and gains and losses from asset disposals under the indirect method.	16-2	16-2A, 16-2B
Determine the cash flows from operating activities using the indirect method by adjusting net income for changes in current operating assets and liabilities.	• Adjust net income for changes in current operating assets and liabilities under the indirect method.	16-3	16-3A, 16-3B
Report cash flows from operating activities under the indirect method.	• Prepare the cash flows from operating activities under the indirect method in proper form.	16-4	16-4A, 16-4B
Report investing and financing activities on the statement of cash flows.	• Prepare the remainder of the statement of cash flows by reporting investing and financing activities.	16-5	16-5A, 16-5B

3. Prepare a statement of cash flows, using the direct method.

Key Points	Key Learning Outcomes	Example Exercises	Practice Exercises
The direct method reports cash flows from operating activities by major classes of operating cash receipts and cash payments. The difference between the major classes of total operating cash receipts and total operating cash payments is the net cash flow from operating activities. The investing and financing activities sections of the statement are the same as under the indirect method.	• Prepare the cash flows from operating activities and the remainder of the statement of cash flows under the direct method.	16-6 16-7	16-6A, 16-6B 16-7A, 16-7B

Key Terms

cash flows from financing
   activities (692)
cash flows from investing
   activities (692)

cash flows from operating
   activities (692)
direct method (694)
free cash flow (712)

indirect method (694)
statement of cash flows (692)

Illustrative Problem

The comparative balance sheet of Dowling Company for December 31, 2008 and 2007, is as follows:

Dowling Company
Comparative Balance Sheet
December 31, 2008 and 2007

Assets	2008	2007
Cash	$ 140,350	$ 95,900
Accounts receivable (net)	95,300	102,300
Inventories	165,200	157,900
Prepaid expenses	6,240	5,860
Investments (long-term)	35,700	84,700
Land	75,000	90,000
Buildings	375,000	260,000
Accumulated depreciation—buildings	(71,300)	(58,300)
Machinery and equipment	428,300	428,300
Accumulated depreciation—machinery and equipment	(148,500)	(138,000)
Patents	58,000	65,000
Total assets	$1,159,290	$1,093,660
Liabilities and Stockholders' Equity		
Accounts payable (merchandise creditors)	$ 43,500	$ 46,700
Accrued expenses (operating expenses)	14,000	12,500
Income taxes payable	7,900	8,400
Dividends payable	14,000	10,000
Mortgage note payable, due 2019	40,000	0
Bonds payable	150,000	250,000
Common stock, $30 par	450,000	375,000
Excess of issue price over par—common stock	66,250	41,250
Retained earnings	373,640	349,810
Total liabilities and stockholders' equity	$1,159,290	$1,093,660

The income statement for Dowling Company is shown here:

Dowling Company
Income Statement
For the Year Ended December 31, 2008

Sales		$1,100,000
Cost of merchandise sold		710,000
Gross profit		$ 390,000
Operating expenses:		
Depreciation expense	$ 23,500	
Patent amortization	7,000	
Other operating expenses	196,000	
Total operating expenses		226,500
Income from operations		$ 163,500
Other income:		
Gain on sale of investments	$ 11,000	
Other expense:		
Interest expense	26,000	(15,000)
Income before income tax		$ 148,500
Income tax expense		50,000
Net income		$ 98,500

An examination of the accounting records revealed the following additional information applicable to 2008:

a. Land costing $15,000 was sold for $15,000.
b. A mortgage note was issued for $40,000.
c. A building costing $115,000 was constructed.
d. 2,500 shares of common stock were issued at 40 in exchange for the bonds payable.
e. Cash dividends declared were $74,670.

Instructions

1. Prepare a statement of cash flows, using the indirect method of reporting cash flows from operating activities.
2. Prepare a statement of cash flows, using the direct method of reporting cash flows from operating activities.

Solution

1.

Dowling Company
Statement of Cash Flows—Indirect Method
For the Year Ended December 31, 2008

Cash flows from operating activities:		
Net income	$ 98,500	
Adjustments to reconcile net income to net cash flow from operating activities:		
Depreciation	23,500	
Amortization of patents	7,000	
Gain on sale of investments	(11,000)	
Changes in current operating assets and liabilities:		
Decrease in accounts receivable	7,000	
Increase in inventories	(7,300)	
Increase in prepaid expenses	(380)	
Decrease in accounts payable	(3,200)	
Increase in accrued expenses	1,500	
Decrease in income taxes payable	(500)	
Net cash flow from operating activities		$115,120
Cash flows from investing activities:		
Cash received from sale of:		
Investments	$60,000	
Land	15,000	$ 75,000
Less: Cash paid for construction of building	115,000	
Net cash flow used for investing activities		(40,000)
Cash flows from financing activities:		
Cash received from issuing mortgage note payable	$ 40,000	
Less: Cash paid for dividends	70,670	
Net cash flow used for financing activities		(30,670)
Increase in cash		$ 44,450
Cash at the beginning of the year		95,900
Cash at the end of the year		$140,350
Schedule of Noncash Investing and Financing Activities:		
Issued common stock to retire bonds payable		$100,000

2.

Dowling Company Statement of Cash Flows—Direct Method For the Year Ended December 31, 2008			
Cash flows from operating activities:			
Cash received from customers[1]		$1,107,000	
Deduct: Cash paid for merchandise[2]	$720,500		
Cash paid for operating expenses[3]	194,880		
Cash paid for interest expense	26,000		
Cash paid for income tax[4]	50,500	991,880	
Net cash flow from operating activities			$115,120
Cash flows from investing activities:			
Cash received from sale of:			
Investments	$ 60,000		
Land	15,000	$ 75,000	
Less: Cash paid for construction of building . . .		115,000	
Net cash flow used for investing activities			(40,000)
Cash flows from financing activities:			
Cash received from issuing mortgage			
note payable		$ 40,000	
Less: Cash paid for dividends[5]		70,670	
Net cash flow used for financing activities			(30,670)
Increase in cash			$ 44,450
Cash at the beginning of the year			95,900
Cash at the end of the year			$140,350
Schedule of Noncash Investing and			
Financing Activities:			
Issued common stock to retire bonds payable . .			$100,000
Schedule Reconciling Net Income with Cash Flows			
from Operating Activities[6]			

Computations:
[1]$1,100,000 + $7,000 = $1,107,000
[2]$710,000 + $3,200 + $7,300 = $720,500
[3]$196,000 + $380 − $1,500 = $194,880
[4]$50,000 + $500 = $50,500

[5]$74,670 + $10,000 − $14,000 = $70,670
[6]The content of this schedule is the same as the
operating activities section of Part 1 of this
solution and is not reproduced here for the sake
of brevity.

Self-Examination Questions

(Answers at End of Chapter)

1. An example of a cash flow from an operating activity is:
   A. receipt of cash from the sale of stock.
   B. receipt of cash from the sale of bonds.
   C. payment of cash for dividends.
   D. receipt of cash from customers on account.

2. An example of a cash flow from an investing activity is:
   A. receipt of cash from the sale of equipment.
   B. receipt of cash from the sale of stock.
   C. payment of cash for dividends.
   D. payment of cash to acquire treasury stock.

3. An example of a cash flow from a financing activity is:
   A. receipt of cash from customers on account.
   B. receipt of cash from the sale of equipment.

C. payment of cash for dividends.
D. payment of cash to acquire land.

4. Which of the following methods of reporting cash flows from operating activities adjusts net income for revenues and expenses not involving the receipt or payment of cash?
   A. Direct method   C. Reciprocal method
   B. Purchase method   D. Indirect method

5. The net income reported on the income statement for the year was $55,000, and depreciation of fixed assets for the year was $22,000. The balances of the current asset and current liability accounts at the beginning and end of the year are shown at the top of the following page.

	End	Beginning
Cash	$ 65,000	$ 70,000
Accounts receivable	100,000	90,000
Inventories	145,000	150,000
Prepaid expenses	7,500	8,000
Accounts payable (merchandise creditors)	51,000	58,000

The total amount reported for cash flows from operating activities in the statement of cash flows, using the indirect method, is:

A. $33,000.   C. $65,500.
B. $55,000.   D. $77,000.

Eye Openers

1. What is the principal disadvantage of the direct method of reporting cash flows from operating activities?
2. What are the major advantages of the indirect method of reporting cash flows from operating activities?
3. A corporation issued $300,000 of common stock in exchange for $300,000 of fixed assets. Where would this transaction be reported on the statement of cash flows?
4. a. What is the effect on cash flows of declaring and issuing a stock dividend?
   b. Is the stock dividend reported on the statement of cash flows?
5. A retail business, using the accrual method of accounting, owed merchandise creditors (accounts payable) $290,000 at the beginning of the year and $315,000 at the end of the year. How would the $25,000 increase be used to adjust net income in determining the amount of cash flows from operating activities by the indirect method? Explain.
6. If salaries payable was $75,000 at the beginning of the year and $60,000 at the end of the year, should $15,000 be added to or deducted from income to determine the amount of cash flows from operating activities by the indirect method? Explain.
7. A long-term investment in bonds with a cost of $75,000 was sold for $84,000 cash. (a) What was the gain or loss on the sale? (b) What was the effect of the transaction on cash flows? (c) How should the transaction be reported in the statement of cash flows if cash flows from operating activities are reported by the indirect method?
8. A corporation issued $4,000,000 of 20-year bonds for cash at 105. How would the transaction be reported on the statement of cash flows?
9. Fully depreciated equipment costing $65,000 was discarded. What was the effect of the transaction on cash flows if (a) $12,000 cash is received, (b) no cash is received?
10. For the current year, Bearings Company decided to switch from the indirect method to the direct method for reporting cash flows from operating activities on the statement of cash flows. Will the change cause the amount of net cash flow from operating activities to be (a) larger, (b) smaller, or (c) the same as if the indirect method had been used? Explain.
11. Name five common major classes of operating cash receipts or operating cash payments presented on the statement of cash flows when the cash flows from operating activities are reported by the direct method.
12. In a recent annual report, eBay Inc. reported that during the year it issued stock of $128 million for acquisitions. How would this be reported on the statement of cash flows?

Practice Exercises

PE 16-1A
Classifying cash flows
obj. 1

Identify whether each of the following would be reported as an operating, investing, or financing activity in the statement of cash flows.

a. Issuance of bonds payable   d. Disposal of equipment
b. Collection of accounts receivable   e. Payment for selling expenses
c. Purchase of investments   f. Cash sales

PE 16-1B
Classifying cash flows
obj. 1

Identify whether each of the following would be reported as an operating, investing, or financing activity in the statement of cash flows.

a. Payment for administrative expenses
b. Retirement of bonds payable
c. Purchase of land

d. Issuance of common stock
e. Cash received from customers
f. Payment of accounts payable

PE 16-2A
Adjustments to net income—indirect method
obj. 2

Zale Corporation's accumulated depreciation—equipment increased by $8,000, while patents decreased by $5,200 between balance sheet dates. There were no purchases or sales of depreciable or intangible assets during the year. In addition, the income statement showed a loss of $6,000 from the sale of investments. Reconcile a net income of $90,000 to net cash flow from operating activities.

PE 16-2B
Adjustments to net income—indirect method
obj. 2

Nordic Corporation's accumulated depreciation—furniture increased by $3,500, while patents decreased by $1,800 between balance sheet dates. There were no purchases or sales of depreciable or intangible assets during the year. In addition, the income statement showed a gain of $12,500 from the sale of land. Reconcile a net income of $125,000 to net cash flow from operating activities.

PE 16-3A
Changes in current operating assets and liabilities—indirect method
obj. 2

Sage Corporation's comparative balance sheet for current assets and liabilities was as follows:

	Dec. 31, 2008	Dec. 31, 2007
Accounts receivable	$12,000	$14,000
Inventory	9,000	6,500
Accounts payable	8,500	7,200
Dividends payable	24,000	26,000

Adjust net income of $110,000 for changes in operating assets and liabilities to arrive at cash flows from operating activities.

PE 16-3B
Changes in current operating assets and liabilities—indirect method
obj. 2

Lanier Corporation's comparative balance sheet for current assets and liabilities was as follows:

	Dec. 31, 2008	Dec. 31, 2007
Accounts receivable	$32,500	$25,000
Inventory	69,000	48,000
Accounts payable	51,500	32,000
Dividends payable	15,000	16,400

Adjust net income of $290,000 for changes in operating assets and liabilities to arrive at cash flows from operating activities.

PE 16-4A
Reporting cash flows from operating activities—indirect method
obj. 2

Texas Holdem Inc. reported the following data:

Net income	$85,000
Depreciation expense	14,000
Gain on disposal of equipment	10,500
Decrease in accounts receivable	6,000
Decrease in accounts payable	1,800

Prepare the cash flows from operating activities section of the statement of cash flows using the indirect method.

PE 16-4B
Reporting cash flows from operating activities—indirect method
obj. 2

Pier Inc. reported the following data:

Net income	$150,000
Depreciation expense	25,000
Loss on disposal of equipment	14,300
Increase in accounts receivable	9,400
Increase in accounts payable	4,300

Prepare the cash flows from operating activities section of the statement of cash flows using the indirect method.

PE 16-5A
Reporting land transactions on the statement of cash flows
obj. 2

Gamma Corporation purchased land for $200,000. Later in the year, the company sold land with a book value of $105,000 for $90,000. How are the effects of these transactions reported on the statement of cash flows?

PE 16-5B
Reporting land transactions on the statement of cash flows
obj. 2

Sunrise Corporation purchased land for $500,000. Later in the year, the company sold land with a book value of $320,000 for $375,000. How are the effects of these transactions reported on the statement of cash flows?

PE 16-6A
Cash received from customers—direct method
obj. 3

Sales reported on the income statement were $623,000. The accounts receivable balance increased $48,000 over the year. Determine the amount of cash received from customers.

PE 16-6B
Cash received from customers—direct method
obj. 3

Sales reported on the income statement were $58,400. The accounts receivable balance decreased $2,100 over the year. Determine the amount of cash received from customers.

PE 16-7A
Cash payments for merchandise—direct method
obj. 3

Cost of merchandise sold reported on the income statement was $568,000. The accounts payable balance decreased $28,000, and the inventory balance decreased by $39,000 over the year. Determine the amount of cash paid for merchandise.

PE 16-7B
Cash payments for merchandise—direct method
obj. 3

Cost of merchandise sold reported on the income statement was $111,000. The accounts payable balance increased $5,700, and the inventory balance increased by $8,400 over the year. Determine the amount of cash paid for merchandise.

Exercises

EX 16-1
Cash flows from operating activities—net loss
obj. 1

On its income statement for a recent year, Northwest Airlines Corporation reported a net *loss* of $862 million from operations. On its statement of cash flows, it reported $271 million of cash flows from operating activities.

 Explain this apparent contradiction between the loss and the positive cash flows.

EX 16-2
Effect of transactions on cash flows
obj. 1

✓ *b. Cash receipt, $36,000*

State the effect (cash receipt or payment and amount) of each of the following transactions, considered individually, on cash flows:

a. Sold 5,000 shares of $30 par common stock for $90 per share.
b. Sold equipment with a book value of $42,500 for $36,000.
c. Purchased land for $250,000 cash.
d. Purchased 5,000 shares of $30 par common stock as treasury stock at $60 per share.
e. Sold a new issue of $100,000 of bonds at 98.
f. Paid dividends of $1.50 per share. There were 40,000 shares issued and 5,000 shares of treasury stock.

g. Retired $500,000 of bonds, on which there was $2,500 of unamortized discount, for $500,500.
h. Purchased a building by paying $40,000 cash and issuing a $90,000 mortgage note payable.

EX 16-3
Classifying cash flows
obj. 1

Identify the type of cash flow activity for each of the following events (operating, investing, or financing):

a. Issued preferred stock.
b. Net income.
c. Sold equipment.
d. Purchased treasury stock.
e. Purchased buildings.
f. Purchased patents.

g. Issued bonds.
h. Issued common stock.
i. Sold long-term investments.
j. Paid cash dividends.
k. Redeemed bonds.

EX 16-4
Cash flows from operating activities—indirect method
obj. 2

Indicate whether each of the following would be added to or deducted from net income in determining net cash flow from operating activities by the indirect method:

a. Gain on retirement of long-term debt
b. Increase in merchandise inventory
c. Amortization of patent
d. Decrease in accounts receivable
e. Depreciation of fixed assets
f. Decrease in prepaid expenses
g. Decrease in salaries payable

h. Increase in notes receivable due in 90 days from customers
i. Decrease in accounts payable
j. Loss on disposal of fixed assets
k. Increase in notes payable due in 90 days to vendors

EX 16-5
Cash flows from operating activities—indirect method
obj. 2

✓ Net cash flow from operating activities, $111,700

The net income reported on the income statement for the current year was $92,000. Depreciation recorded on store equipment for the year amounted to $18,600. Balances of the current asset and current liability accounts at the beginning and end of the year are as follows:

	End of Year	Beginning of Year
Cash	$46,700	$44,200
Accounts receivable (net)	32,300	31,100
Merchandise inventory	54,800	56,700
Prepaid expenses	4,000	3,500
Accounts payable (merchandise creditors)	46,000	42,900
Wages payable	21,400	23,600

Prepare the cash flows from operating activities section of the statement of cash flows, using the indirect method.

EX 16-6
Cash flows from operating activities—indirect method
objs. 1, 2

✓ a. Cash flows from operating activities, $203,100

The net income reported on the income statement for the current year was $165,300. Depreciation recorded on equipment and a building amounted to $46,700 for the year. Balances of the current asset and current liability accounts at the beginning and end of the year are as follows:

	End of Year	Beginning of Year
Cash	$ 42,000	$ 43,500
Accounts receivable (net)	65,400	69,200
Inventories	125,900	115,100
Prepaid expenses	5,800	6,400
Accounts payable (merchandise creditors)	61,400	64,200
Salaries payable	8,300	8,000

a. Prepare the cash flows from operating activities section of the statement of cash flows, using the indirect method.
b. ▸ If the direct method had been used, would the net cash flow from operating activities have been the same? Explain.

EX 16-7
Cash flows from operating activities—indirect method
objs. 1, 2

The income statement disclosed the following items for 2008:

Depreciation expense	$ 24,500
Gain on disposal of equipment	10,200
Net income	186,000

Balances of the current assets and current liability accounts changed between December 31, 2007, and December 31, 2008, as follows:

Accounts receivable	$4,400
Inventory	2,000*
Prepaid insurance	800*
Accounts payable	2,700*
Income taxes payable	900
Dividends payable	500

*Decrease

Prepare the cash flows from operating activities section of the statement of cash flows, using the indirect method.

EX 16-8
Determining cash payments to stockholders
obj. 2

The board of directors declared cash dividends totaling $120,000 during the current year. The comparative balance sheet indicates dividends payable of $35,000 at the beginning of the year and $30,000 at the end of the year. What was the amount of cash payments to stockholders during the year?

EX 16-9
Reporting changes in equipment on statement of cash flows
obj. 2

An analysis of the general ledger accounts indicates that office equipment, which cost $60,000 and on which accumulated depreciation totaled $15,000 on the date of sale, was sold for $41,000 during the year. Using this information, indicate the items to be reported on the statement of cash flows.

EX 16-10
Reporting changes in equipment on statement of cash flows
obj. 2

An analysis of the general ledger accounts indicates that delivery equipment, which cost $45,000 and on which accumulated depreciation totaled $32,000 on the date of sale, was sold for $15,000 during the year. Using this information, indicate the items to be reported on the statement of cash flows.

EX 16-11
Reporting land transactions on statement of cash flows
obj. 2

On the basis of the details of the following fixed asset account, indicate the items to be reported on the statement of cash flows:

ACCOUNT *Land*   **ACCOUNT NO.**

Date		Item	Debit	Credit	Balance Debit	Balance Credit
2008						
Jan.	1	Balance			900,000	
Feb.	5	Purchased for cash	400,000		1,300,000	
Oct.	30	Sold for $365,000		250,000	1,050,000	

EX 16-12
Reporting stockholders' equity items on statement of cash flows
obj. 2

On the basis of the following stockholders' equity accounts, indicate the items, exclusive of net income, to be reported on the statement of cash flows. There were no unpaid dividends at either the beginning or the end of the year.

ACCOUNT *Common Stock, $10 par*   **ACCOUNT NO.**

Date		Item	Debit	Credit	Balance Debit	Balance Credit
2008						
Jan.	1	Balance, 70,000 shares				700,000
Feb.	11	16,000 shares issued for cash		160,000		860,000
June	30	4,100-share stock dividend		41,000		901,000

ACCOUNT *Paid-In Capital in Excess of Par—Common Stock*				ACCOUNT NO.
2008				
Jan.	1	Balance		140,000
Feb.	11	16,000 shares issued for cash	336,000	476,000
June	30	Stock dividend	102,500	578,500

ACCOUNT *Retained Earnings*				ACCOUNT NO.
2008				
Jan.	1	Balance		1,000,000
June	30	Stock dividend	143,500	856,500
Dec.	30	Cash dividend	124,000	732,500
	31	Net income		630,000	1,362,500

EX 16-13
Reporting land acquisition for cash and mortgage note on statement of cash flows
obj. 2

On the basis of the details of the following fixed asset account, indicate the items to be reported on the statement of cash flows:

ACCOUNT *Land*					ACCOUNT NO.	
					Balance	
Date		Item	Debit	Credit	Debit	Credit
2008						
Jan.	1	Balance			160,000	
Feb.	10	Purchased for cash	326,000		486,000	
Nov.	20	Purchased with long-term mortgage note	400,000		886,000	

EX 16-14
Reporting issuance and retirement of long-term debt
obj. 2

On the basis of the details of the following bonds payable and related discount accounts, indicate the items to be reported in the financing section of the statement of cash flows, assuming no gain or loss on retiring the bonds:

ACCOUNT *Bonds Payable*					ACCOUNT NO.	
					Balance	
Date		Item	Debit	Credit	Debit	Credit
2008						
Jan.	1	Balance				150,000
Jan.	3	Retire bonds	70,000			80,000
July	30	Issue bonds		350,000		430,000

ACCOUNT *Discount on Bonds Payable*					ACCOUNT NO.	
2008						
Jan.	1	Balance			12,000	
Jan.	3	Retire bonds		5,600	6,400	
July	30	Issue bonds	20,000		26,400	
Dec.	31	Amortize discount		1,600	24,800	

EX 16-15
Determining net income from net cash flow from operating activities
obj. 2

Emerald Golf Inc. reported a net cash flow from operating activities of $86,700 on its statement of cash flows for the year ended December 31, 2008. The following information was reported in the cash flows from operating activities section of the statement of cash flows, using the indirect method:

Decrease in income taxes payable	$2,000
Decrease in inventories	5,600
Depreciation	8,500
Gain on sale of investments	3,400
Increase in accounts payable	1,200
Increase in prepaid expenses	700
Increase in accounts receivable	4,300

Determine the net income reported by Emerald Golf Inc. for the year ended December 31, 2008.

EX 16-16
Cash flows from operating activities— indirect method

obj. 2

✓ *Net cash flow used in operating activities, ($773)*

Selected data derived from the income statement and balance sheet of Jones Soda Co. for a recent year are as follows:

Income statement data (in thousands):	
Net earnings	$1,330
Depreciation expense	193
Stock-based compensation expense (noncash)	20
Balance sheet data (in thousands):	
Increase in accounts receivable	$1,328
Increase in inventory	1,550
Increase in prepaid expenses	124
Increase in accounts payable	686

a. Prepare the cash flows from operating activities section of the statement of cash flows using the indirect method for Jones Soda Co. for the year.
b. ▭▭▭▶ Interpret your results in part (a).

EX 16-17
Statement of cash flows—indirect method

obj. 2

✓ *Net cash flow from operating activities, $50*

The comparative balance sheet of Alliance Structures Inc. for December 31, 2008 and 2007, is as follows:

	Dec. 31, 2008	Dec. 31, 2007
Assets		
Cash	$ 90	$ 23
Accounts receivable (net)	30	27
Inventories	24	21
Land	35	55
Equipment	32	22
Accumulated depreciation—equipment	(9)	(5)
Total	$202	$143
Liabilities and Stockholders' Equity		
Accounts payable (merchandise creditors)	$ 17	$ 10
Dividends payable	1	—
Common stock, $1 par	6	3
Paid-in capital in excess of par—common stock	30	10
Retained earnings	148	120
Total	$202	$143

The following additional information is taken from the records:

a. Land was sold for $15.
b. Equipment was acquired for cash.
c. There were no disposals of equipment during the year.
d. The common stock was issued for cash.
e. There was a $40 credit to Retained Earnings for net income.
f. There was a $12 debit to Retained Earnings for cash dividends declared.

Prepare a statement of cash flows, using the indirect method of presenting cash flows from operating activities.

EX 16-18
Statement of cash flows—indirect method

obj. 2

List the errors you find in the following statement of cash flows. The cash balance at the beginning of the year was $83,600. All other amounts are correct, except the cash balance at the end of the year.

Whole Life Nutrition Products Inc.
Statement of Cash Flows
For the Year Ended December 31, 2008

Cash flows from operating activities:			
Net income		$123,400	
Adjustments to reconcile net income to net cash flow from operating activities:			
Depreciation		35,000	
Gain on sale of investements		6,000	
Changes in current operating assets and liabilities:			
Increase in accounts receivable		9,500	
Increase in inventories		(12,300)	
Increase in accounts payable		(3,700)	
Decrease in accrued expenses		(900)	
Net cash flow from operating activities			$157,000
Cash flows from investing activities:			
Cash received from sale of investments		$ 85,000	
Less: Cash paid for purchase of land	$ 90,000		
Cash paid for purchase of equipment	150,100	240,100	
Net cash flow used for investing activities			(155,100)
Cash flows from financing activities:			
Cash received from sale of common stock		$107,000	
Cash paid for dividends		45,000	
Net cash flow provided by financing activities			152,000
Increase in cash			$153,900
Cash at the end of the year			105,300
Cash at the beginning of the year			$259,200

EX 16-19
Cash flows from operating activities— direct method

obj. 3

✓ a. $471,000

The cash flows from operating activities are reported by the direct method on the statement of cash flows. Determine the following:

a. If sales for the current year were $450,000 and accounts receivable decreased by $21,000 during the year, what was the amount of cash received from customers?
b. If income tax expense for the current year was $35,000 and income tax payable decreased by $3,100 during the year, what was the amount of cash payments for income tax?

EX 16-20
Cash paid for merchandise purchases

obj. 3

The cost of merchandise sold for Kohl's Corporation for a recent year was $8,639 million. The balance sheet showed the following current account balances (in millions):

	Balance, End of Year	Balance, Beginning of Year
Merchandise inventories	$2,238	$1,947
Accounts payable	830	705

Determine the amount of cash payments for merchandise.

EX 16-21
Determining selected amounts for cash flows from operating activities—direct method

obj. 3

✓ b. $59,900

Selected data taken from the accounting records of Extravaganza Inc. for the current year ended December 31 are as follows:

	Balance, December 31	Balance, January 1
Accrued expenses (operating expenses)	$ 4,300	$ 4,700
Accounts payable (merchandise creditors)	32,100	35,400
Inventories	59,500	64,700
Prepaid expenses	2,500	3,000

During the current year, the cost of merchandise sold was $345,000, and the operating expenses other than depreciation were $60,000. The direct method is used for presenting the cash flows from operating activities on the statement of cash flows.

Determine the amount reported on the statement of cash flows for (a) cash payments for merchandise and (b) cash payments for operating expenses.

EX 16-22
Cash flows from operating activities—direct method

obj. 3

✓ *Net cash flow from operating activities, $87,200*

The income statement of Country Kitchen Bakeries Inc. for the current year ended June 30 is as follows:

Sales		$456,000
Cost of merchandise sold		259,000
Gross profit		$197,000
Operating expenses:		
Depreciation expense	$35,000	
Other operating expenses	92,400	
Total operating expenses		127,400
Income before income tax		$ 69,600
Income tax expense		19,300
Net income		$ 50,300

Changes in the balances of selected accounts from the beginning to the end of the current year are as follows:

	Increase Decrease*
Accounts receivable (net)	$10,500*
Inventories	3,500
Prepaid expenses	3,400*
Accounts payable (merchandise creditors)	7,200*
Accrued expenses (operating expenses)	1,100
Income tax payable	2,400*

Prepare the cash flows from operating activities section of the statement of cash flows, using the direct method.

EX 16-23
Cash flows from operating activities—direct method

obj. 3

✓ *Net cash flow from operating activities, $47,600*

The income statement for Wholly Bagel Company for the current year ended June 30 and balances of selected accounts at the beginning and the end of the year are as follows:

Sales		$184,000
Cost of merchandise sold		67,000
Gross profit		$117,000
Operating expenses:		
Depreciation expense	$14,500	
Other operating expenses	49,000	
Total operating expenses		63,500
Income before income tax		$ 53,500
Income tax expense		15,400
Net income		$ 38,100

	End of Year	Beginning of Year
Accounts receivable (net)	$14,800	$12,900
Inventories	38,100	33,100
Prepaid expenses	6,000	6,600
Accounts payable (merchandise creditors)	27,900	25,900
Accrued expenses (operating expenses)	7,900	8,600
Income tax payable	1,500	1,500

Prepare the cash flows from operating activities section of the statement of cash flows, using the direct method.

EX 16-24
Free cash flow

Mediterranean Tile Company has cash flows from operating activities of $120,000. Cash flows used for investments in property, plant, and equipment totaled $45,000, of which 60% of this investment was used to replace existing capacity.
    Determine the free cash flow for Mediterranean Tile Company.

EX 16-25
Free cash flow

The financial statements for Williams-Sonoma, Inc., are provided in Appendix D at the end of the text.
    Determine the free cash flow for the year ended January 29, 2006. Assume that 70% of purchases of property and equipment were for new store openings, and the remaining was for remodeling and updating existing stores.

Problems Series A

PR 16-1A
Statement of cash flows—indirect method
obj. 2

✓ *Net cash flow from operating activities, $72,200*

The comparative balance sheet of Oak and Tile Flooring Co. for June 30, 2008 and 2007, is as follows:

	June 30, 2008	June 30, 2007
Assets		
Cash	$ 34,700	$ 23,500
Accounts receivable (net)	101,600	92,300
Inventories	146,300	142,100
Investments	0	50,000
Land	145,000	0
Equipment	215,000	175,500
Accumulated depreciation	(48,600)	(41,300)
	$594,000	$442,100
Liabilities and Stockholders' Equity		
Accounts payable (merchandise creditors)	$100,900	$ 95,200
Accrued expenses (operating expenses)	15,000	13,200
Dividends payable	12,500	10,000
Common stock, $1 par	56,000	50,000
Paid-in capital in excess of par—common stock	220,000	100,000
Retained earnings	189,600	173,700
	$594,000	$442,100

    The following additional information was taken from the records of Oak and Tile Flooring Co.:

a. Equipment and land were acquired for cash.
b. There were no disposals of equipment during the year.
c. The investments were sold for $45,000 cash.
d. The common stock was issued for cash.
e. There was a $65,900 credit to Retained Earnings for net income.
f. There was a $50,000 debit to Retained Earnings for cash dividends declared.

Instructions
Prepare a statement of cash flows, using the indirect method of presenting cash flows from operating activities.

PR 16-2A
Statement of cash flows—indirect method
obj. 2

The comparative balance sheet of Portable Luggage Company at December 31, 2008 and 2007, is as follows:

✓ *Net cash flow from operating activities, $221,700*

	Dec. 31, 2008	Dec. 31, 2007
Assets		
Cash	$ 175,900	$ 143,200
Accounts receivable (net)	264,100	235,000
Inventories	352,300	405,800
Prepaid expenses	12,500	10,000
Land	120,000	120,000
Buildings	680,000	450,000
Accumulated depreciation—buildings	(185,000)	(164,500)
Machinery and equipment	310,000	310,000
Accumulated depreciation—machinery & equipment	(85,000)	(76,000)
Patents	42,500	48,000
	$1,687,300	$1,481,500
Liabilities and Stockholders' Equity		
Accounts payable (merchandise creditors)	$ 332,300	$ 367,900
Dividends payable	13,000	10,000
Salaries payable	30,200	34,600
Mortgage note payable, due 2015	90,000	—
Bonds payable	—	154,000
Common stock, $1 par	24,000	20,000
Paid-in capital in excess of par—common stock	200,000	50,000
Retained earnings	997,800	845,000
	$1,687,300	$1,481,500

An examination of the income statement and the accounting records revealed the following additional information applicable to 2008:

a. Net income, $204,800.
b. Depreciation expense reported on the income statement: buildings, $20,500; machinery and equipment, $9,000.
c. Patent amortization reported on the income statement, $5,500.
d. A building was constructed for $230,000.
e. A mortgage note for $90,000 was issued for cash.
f. 4,000 shares of common stock were issued at $38.50 in exchange for the bonds payable.
g. Cash dividends declared, $52,000.

Instructions
Prepare a statement of cash flows, using the indirect method of presenting cash flows from operating activities.

PR 16-3A
Statement of cash flows—indirect method

obj. 2

✓ *Net cash flow from operating activities, $4,100*

The comparative balance sheet of Reston Supply Co. at December 31, 2008 and 2007, is as follows:

	Dec. 31, 2008	Dec. 31, 2007
Assets		
Cash	$ 45,500	$ 51,200
Accounts receivable (net)	106,700	92,400
Inventories	139,200	131,200
Prepaid expenses	2,800	4,000
Land	150,000	210,000
Buildings	300,000	150,000
Accumulated depreciation—buildings	(60,200)	(55,500)
Equipment	100,100	80,300
Accumulated depreciation—equipment	(20,200)	(24,500)
	$763,900	$639,100
Liabilities and Stockholders' Equity		
Accounts payable (merchandise creditors)	$ 90,000	$ 95,600
Income tax payable	4,000	3,200
Bonds payable	50,000	0
Common stock, $1 par	33,000	30,000
Paid-in capital in excess of par—common stock	180,000	120,000
Retained earnings	406,900	390,300
	$763,900	$639,100

The noncurrent asset, noncurrent liability, and stockholders' equity accounts for 2008 are as follows:

ACCOUNT *Land* ACCOUNT NO.

Date		Item	Debit	Credit	Balance Debit	Balance Credit
2008						
Jan.	1	Balance			210,000	
Apr.	20	Realized $69,000 cash from sale		60,000	150,000	

ACCOUNT *Buildings* ACCOUNT NO.

Date		Item	Debit	Credit	Balance Debit	Balance Credit
2008						
Jan.	1	Balance			150,000	
Apr.	20	Acquired for cash	150,000		300,000	

ACCOUNT *Accumulated Depreciation—Buildings* ACCOUNT NO.

Date		Item	Debit	Credit	Balance Debit	Balance Credit
2008						
Jan.	1	Balance				55,500
Dec.	31	Depreciation for year		4,700		60,200

ACCOUNT *Equipment* ACCOUNT NO.

Date		Item	Debit	Credit	Balance Debit	Balance Credit
2008						
Jan.	1	Balance			80,300	
	26	Discarded, no salvage		10,000	70,300	
Aug.	11	Purchased for cash	29,800		100,100	

ACCOUNT *Accumulated Depreciation—Equipment* ACCOUNT NO.

Date		Item	Debit	Credit	Balance Debit	Balance Credit
2008						
Jan.	1	Balance				24,500
	26	Equipment discarded	10,000			14,500
Dec.	31	Depreciation for year		5,700		20,200

ACCOUNT *Bonds Payable* ACCOUNT NO.

Date		Item	Debit	Credit	Balance Debit	Balance Credit
2008						
May	1	Issued 20-year bonds		50,000		50,000

ACCOUNT *Common Stock, $1 par* ACCOUNT NO.

Date		Item	Debit	Credit	Balance Debit	Balance Credit
2008						
Jan.	1	Balance				30,000
Dec.	7	Issued 3,000 shares of common stock for $21 per share		3,000		33,000

ACCOUNT *Paid-In Capital in Excess of Par—Common Stock* ACCOUNT NO.

Date		Item	Debit	Credit	Balance Debit	Balance Credit
2008						
Jan.	1	Balance				120,000
Dec.	7	Issued 3,000 shares of common stock for $21 per share		60,000		180,000

ACCOUNT *Retained Earnings* ACCOUNT NO.

Date		Item	Debit	Credit	Balance Debit	Balance Credit
2008						
Jan.	1	Balance				390,300
Dec.	31	Net income		28,600		418,900
	31	Cash dividends	12,000			406,900

Instructions

Prepare a statement of cash flows, using the indirect method of presenting cash flows from operating activities.

PR 16-4A
Statement of cash flows—direct method

obj. 3

✓ *Net cash flow from operating activities, $107,900*

The comparative balance sheet of Green Earth Lawn and Garden Inc. for December 31, 2008 and 2009, is as follows:

	Dec. 31, 2009	Dec. 31, 2008
Assets		
Cash	$ 137,900	$142,300
Accounts receivable (net)	206,800	190,500
Inventories	290,500	284,100
Investments	0	90,000
Land	200,000	0
Equipment	255,000	205,000
Accumulated depreciation	(100,300)	(76,700)
	$ 989,900	$835,200
Liabilities and Stockholders' Equity		
Accounts payable (merchandise creditors)	$ 224,900	$201,400
Accrued expenses (operating expenses)	14,100	16,500
Dividends payable	21,000	19,000
Common stock, $1 par	10,000	8,000
Paid-in capital in excess of par—common stock	200,000	100,000
Retained earnings	519,900	490,300
	$ 989,900	$835,200

The income statement for the year ended December 31, 2009, is as follows:

Sales		$940,000
Cost of merchandise sold		489,300
Gross profit		$450,700
Operating expenses:		
Depreciation expense	$ 23,600	
Other operating expenses	278,900	
Total operating expenses		302,500
Operating income		$148,200
Other income:		
Gain on sale of investments		32,000
Income before income tax		$180,200
Income tax expense		62,300
Net income		$117,900

The following additional information was taken from the records:

a. Equipment and land were acquired for cash.
b. There were no disposals of equipment during the year.
c. The investments were sold for $122,000 cash.
d. The common stock was issued for cash.
e. There was a $88,300 debit to Retained Earnings for cash dividends declared.

Instructions
Prepare a statement of cash flows, using the direct method of presenting cash flows from operating activities.

PR 16-5A
Statement of cash flows—direct method applied to PR 16-1A

obj. 3

✓ *Net cash flow from operating activities, $72,200*

The comparative balance sheet of Oak and Tile Flooring Co. for June 30, 2008 and 2007, is as follows:

	June 30, 2008	June 30, 2007
Assets		
Cash	$ 34,700	$ 23,500
Accounts receivable (net)	101,600	92,300
Inventories	146,300	142,100
Investments	0	50,000
Land	145,000	0
Equipment	215,000	175,500
Accumulated depreciation	(48,600)	(41,300)
	$594,000	$442,100

Liabilities and Stockholders' Equity

Accounts payable (merchandise creditors)	$100,900	$ 95,200
Accrued expenses (operating expenses)	15,000	13,200
Dividends payable	12,500	10,000
Common stock, $1 par	56,000	50,000
Paid-in capital in excess of par—common stock	220,000	100,000
Retained earnings	189,600	173,700
	$594,000	$442,100

The income statement for the year ended June 30, 2008, is as follows:

Sales		$963,400
Cost of merchandise sold		662,100
Gross profit		$301,300
Operating expenses:		
Depreciation expense	$ 7,300	
Other operating expenses	195,000	
Total operating expenses		202,300
Operating income		$ 99,000
Other expenses:		
Loss on sale of investments		(5,000)
Income before income tax		$ 94,000
Income tax expense		28,100
Net income		$ 65,900

The following additional information was taken from the records:

a. Equipment and land were acquired for cash.
b. There were no disposals of equipment during the year.
c. The investments were sold for $45,000 cash.
d. The common stock was issued for cash.
e. There was a $50,000 debit to Retained Earnings for cash dividends declared.

Instructions
Prepare a statement of cash flows, using the direct method of presenting cash flows from operating activities.

Problems Series B

PR 16-1B
Statement of cash flows—indirect method
obj. **2**

✓ *Net cash flow from operating activities, $61,900*

The comparative balance sheet of Gold Medal Sporting Goods Inc. for December 31, 2008 and 2007, is shown as follows:

	Dec. 31, 2008	Dec. 31, 2007
Assets		
Cash	$ 391,100	$ 366,200
Accounts receivable (net)	142,400	130,600
Inventories	401,100	385,700
Investments	0	150,000
Land	205,000	0
Equipment	440,700	345,700
Accumulated depreciation—equipment	(104,000)	(92,500)
	$1,476,300	$1,285,700
Liabilities and Stockholders' Equity		
Accounts payable (merchandise creditors)	$ 267,800	$ 253,100
Accrued expenses (operating expenses)	26,400	32,900
Dividends payable	15,000	12,000
Common stock, $10 par	80,000	60,000
Paid-in capital in excess of par—common stock	300,000	175,000
Retained earnings	787,100	752,700
	$1,476,300	$1,285,700

The following additional information was taken from the records:

a. The investments were sold for $175,000 cash.
b. Equipment and land were acquired for cash.
c. There were no disposals of equipment during the year.
d. The common stock was issued for cash.
e. There was a $94,400 credit to Retained Earnings for net income.
f. There was a $60,000 debit to Retained Earnings for cash dividends declared.

Instructions

Prepare a statement of cash flows, using the indirect method of presenting cash flows from operating activities.

PR 16-2B
Statement of cash flows—indirect method
obj. 2

✓ *Net cash flow from operating activities, $108,500*

The comparative balance sheet of Air Glide Athletic Apparel Co. at December 31, 2008 and 2007, is as follows:

	Dec. 31, 2008	Dec. 31, 2007
Assets		
Cash	$ 45,800	$ 56,200
Accounts receivable (net)	70,200	75,600
Merchandise inventory	100,500	93,500
Prepaid expenses	4,200	3,000
Equipment	204,700	167,800
Accumulated depreciation—equipment	(53,400)	(41,300)
	$372,000	$354,800
Liabilities and Stockholders' Equity		
Accounts payable (merchandise creditors)	$ 78,200	$ 74,300
Mortgage note payable	0	105,000
Common stock, $1 par	15,000	10,000
Paid-in capital in excess of par—common stock	180,000	100,000
Retained earnings	98,800	65,500
	$372,000	$354,800

Additional data obtained from the income statement and from an examination of the accounts in the ledger for 2008 are as follows:

a. Net income, $81,300.
b. Depreciation reported on the income statement, $26,100.
c. Equipment was purchased at a cost of $50,900, and fully depreciated equipment costing $14,000 was discarded, with no salvage realized.
d. The mortgage note payable was not due until 2011, but the terms permitted earlier payment without penalty.
e. 5,000 shares of common stock were issued at $17 for cash.
f. Cash dividends declared and paid, $48,000.

Instructions

Prepare a statement of cash flows, using the indirect method of presenting cash flows from operating activities.

PR 16-3B
Statement of cash flows—indirect method
obj. 2

✓ *Net cash flow from operating activities, ($68,400)*

The comparative balance sheet of Rise N' Shine Juice Co. at December 31, 2008 and 2007, is as follows:

	Dec. 31, 2008	Dec. 31, 2007
Assets		
Cash	$ 392,300	$ 412,300
Accounts receivable (net)	354,200	325,600
Inventories	542,100	497,000
Prepaid expenses	12,500	15,000
Land	135,000	205,000
Buildings	625,000	385,000
Accumulated depreciation—buildings	(174,600)	(163,400)
Equipment	218,900	194,300
Accumulated depreciation—equipment	(60,400)	(67,800)
	$2,045,000	$1,803,000

Liabilities and Stockholders' Equity

Accounts payable (merchandise creditors)	$ 394,200	$ 409,500
Bonds payable	115,000	0
Common stock, $1 par	58,000	50,000
Paid-in capital in excess of par—common stock	400,000	240,000
Retained earnings	1,077,800	1,103,500
	$2,045,000	$1,803,000

The noncurrent asset, noncurrent liability, and stockholders' equity accounts for 2008 are as follows:

ACCOUNT *Land* ACCOUNT NO.

Date		Item	Debit	Credit	Balance Debit	Balance Credit
2008						
Jan.	1	Balance			205,000	
Apr.	20	Realized $64,000 cash from sale		70,000	135,000	

ACCOUNT *Buildings* ACCOUNT NO.

Date		Item	Debit	Credit	Balance Debit	Balance Credit
2008						
Jan.	1	Balance			385,000	
Apr.	20	Acquired for cash	240,000		625,000	

ACCOUNT *Accumulated Depreciation—Buildings* ACCOUNT NO.

Date		Item	Debit	Credit	Balance Debit	Balance Credit
2008						
Jan.	1	Balance				163,400
Dec.	31	Depreciation for year		11,200		174,600

ACCOUNT *Equipment* ACCOUNT NO.

Date		Item	Debit	Credit	Balance Debit	Balance Credit
2008						
Jan.	1	Balance			194,300	
	26	Discarded, no salvage		20,000	174,300	
Aug.	11	Purchased for cash	44,600		218,900	

ACCOUNT *Accumulated Depreciation—Equipment* ACCOUNT NO.

Date		Item	Debit	Credit	Balance Debit	Balance Credit
2008						
Jan.	1	Balance				67,800
	26	Equipment discarded	20,000			47,800
Dec.	31	Depreciation for year		12,600		60,400

ACCOUNT *Bonds Payable* ACCOUNT NO.

Date		Item	Debit	Credit	Balance Debit	Balance Credit
2008						
May	1	Issued 20-year bonds		115,000		115,000

ACCOUNT *Common Stock, $1 Par* ACCOUNT NO.

Date		Item	Debit	Credit	Balance Debit	Balance Credit
2008						
Jan.	1	Balance				50,000
Dec.	7	Issued 8,000 shares of common stock for $21 per share		8,000		58,000

ACCOUNT *Paid-In Capital in Excess of Par—Common Stock* ACCOUNT NO.

Date		Item	Debit	Credit	Balance Debit	Balance Credit
2008						
Jan.	1	Balance				240,000
Dec.	7	Issued 8,000 shares of common stock for $21 per share		160,000		400,000

(continued)

ACCOUNT *Retained Earnings*   **ACCOUNT NO.**

Date		Item	Debit	Credit	Balance Debit	Balance Credit
2008						
Jan.	1	Balance				1,103,500
Dec.	31	Net loss	11,700			1,091,800
	31	Cash dividends	14,000			1,077,800

Instructions

Prepare a statement of cash flows, using the indirect method of presenting cash flows from operating activities.

PR 16-4B
Statement of cash flows—direct method
obj. 3

✓ *Net cash flow from operating activities, $193,600*

The comparative balance sheet of Home and Hearth Inc. for December 31, 2009 and 2008, is as follows:

	Dec. 31, 2009	Dec. 31, 2008
Assets		
Cash	$ 402,100	$ 424,600
Accounts receivable (net)	354,200	342,100
Inventories	631,900	614,200
Investments	0	150,000
Land	325,000	0
Equipment	550,000	425,000
Accumulated depreciation	(152,700)	(125,300)
	$2,110,500	$1,830,600
Liabilities and Stockholders' Equity		
Accounts payable (merchandise creditors)	$ 482,400	$ 467,800
Accrued expenses (operating expenses)	39,600	44,200
Dividends payable	5,500	4,000
Common stock, $1 par	24,000	20,000
Paid-in capital in excess of par—common stock	260,000	120,000
Retained earnings	1,299,000	1,174,600
	$2,110,500	$1,830,600

The income statement for the year ended December 31, 2009, is as follows:

Sales		$3,745,700
Cost of merchandise sold		1,532,500
Gross profit		$2,213,200
Operating expenses:		
Depreciation expense	$ 27,400	
Other operating expenses	1,936,800	
Total operating expenses		1,964,200
Operating income		$ 249,000
Other expense:		
Loss on sale of investments		(40,000)
Income before income tax		$ 209,000
Income tax expense		63,000
Net income		$ 146,000

The following additional information was taken from the records:

a. Equipment and land were acquired for cash.
b. There were no disposals of equipment during the year.
c. The investments were sold for $110,000 cash.
d. The common stock was issued for cash.
e. There was a $21,600 debit to Retained Earnings for cash dividends declared.

Instructions

Prepare a statement of cash flows, using the direct method of presenting cash flows from operating activities.

PR 16-5B
Statement of cash flows—direct method applied to PR 16-1B

obj. 3

✓ *Net cash flow from operating activities, $61,900*

The comparative balance sheet of Gold Medal Sporting Goods Inc. for December 31, 2008 and 2007, is as follows:

	Dec. 31, 2008	Dec. 31, 2007
Assets		
Cash	$ 391,100	$ 366,200
Accounts receivable (net)	142,400	130,600
Inventories	401,100	385,700
Investments	0	150,000
Land	205,000	0
Equipment	440,700	345,700
Accumulated depreciation—equipment	(104,000)	(92,500)
	$1,476,300	$1,285,700
Liabilities and Stockholders' Equity		
Accounts payable (merchandise creditors)	$ 267,800	$ 253,100
Accrued expenses (operating expenses)	26,400	32,900
Dividends payable	15,000	12,000
Common stock, $10 par	80,000	60,000
Paid-in capital in excess of par—common stock	300,000	175,000
Retained earnings	787,100	752,700
	$1,476,300	$1,285,700

The income statement for the year ended December 31, 2008, is as follows:

Sales		$1,632,500
Cost of merchandise sold		908,300
Gross profit		$ 724,200
Operating expenses:		
Depreciation expense	$ 11,500	
Other operating expenses	609,000	
Total operating expenses		620,500
Operating income		$ 103,700
Other income:		
Gain on sale of investments		25,000
Income before income tax		$ 128,700
Income tax expense		34,300
Net income		$ 94,400

The following additional information was taken from the records:

a. The investments were sold for $175,000 cash.
b. Equipment and land were acquired for cash.
c. There were no disposals of equipment during the year.
d. The common stock was issued for cash.
e. There was a $60,000 debit to Retained Earnings for cash dividends declared.

Instructions

Prepare a statement of cash flows, using the direct method of presenting cash flows from operating activities.

Special Activities

SA 16-1
Ethics and professional conduct in business

ETHICS

Linda Stern, president of Venician Fashions Inc., believes that reporting operating cash flow per share on the income statement would be a useful addition to the company's just completed financial statements. The following discussion took place between Linda Stern and Venician Fashions' controller, Ben Trotter, in January, after the close of the fiscal year.

Linda: I have been reviewing our financial statements for the last year. I am disappointed that our net income per share has dropped by 10% from last year. This is not going to look good to our shareholders. Isn't there anything we can do about this?

Ben: What do you mean? The past is the past, and the numbers are in. There isn't much that can be done about it. Our financial statements were prepared according to generally accepted accounting principles, and I don't see much leeway for significant change at this point.

Linda: No, no. I'm not suggesting that we "cook the books." But look at the cash flow from operating activities on the statement of cash flows. The cash flow from operating activities has increased by 20%. This is very good news—and, I might add, useful information. The higher cash flow from operating activities will give our creditors comfort.

Ben: Well, the cash flow from operating activities is on the statement of cash flows, so I guess users will be able to see the improved cash flow figures there.

Linda: This is true, but somehow I feel that this information should be given a much higher profile. I don't like this information being "buried" in the statement of cash flows. You know as well as I do that many users will focus on the income statement. Therefore, I think we ought to include an operating cash flow per share number on the face of the income statement—someplace under the earnings per share number. In this way users will get the complete picture of our operating performance. Yes, our earnings per share dropped this year, but our cash flow from operating activities improved! And all the information is in one place where users can see and compare the figures. What do you think?

Ben: I've never really thought about it like that before. I guess we could put the operating cash flow per share on the income statement, under the earnings per share. Users would really benefit from this disclosure. Thanks for the idea—I'll start working on it.

Linda: Glad to be of service.

How would you interpret this situation? Is Ben behaving in an ethical and professional manner?

SA 16-2
Using the statement of cash flows

You are considering an investment in a new start-up company, Aspen Technologies Inc., an Internet service provider. A review of the company's financial statements reveals a negative retained earnings. In addition, it appears as though the company has been running a negative cash flow from operating activities since the company's inception.

How is the company staying in business under these circumstances? Could this be a good investment?

SA 16-3
Analysis of cash flow from operations

The Retailing Division of Bargain Buyer Inc. provided the following information on its cash flow from operations:

Net income	$ 450,000
Increase in accounts receivable	(540,000)
Increase in inventory	(600,000)
Decrease in accounts payable	(90,000)
Depreciation	100,000
Cash flow from operating activities	$(680,000)

The manager of the Retailing Division provided the accompanying memo with this report:

From: Senior Vice President, Retailing Division

I am pleased to report that we had earnings of $450,000 over the last period. This resulted in a return on invested capital of 10%, which is near our targets for this division. I have been aggressive in building the revenue volume in the division. As a result, I am happy to report that we have increased the number of new credit card customers as a result of an aggressive marketing campaign. In addition, we have found some excellent merchandise opportunities. Some of our suppliers have made some of their apparel merchandise available at a deep discount. We have purchased as much of these goods as possible in order to improve profitability. I'm also happy to report that our vendor payment problems have improved. We are nearly caught up on our overdue payables balances.

Comment on the senior vice president's memo in light of the cash flow information.

SA 16-4
Analysis of statement of cash flows

Jabari Daniels is the president and majority shareholder of Cabinet Craft Inc., a small retail store chain. Recently, Daniels submitted a loan application for Cabinet Craft Inc. to Montvale National Bank. It called for a $200,000, 9%, 10-year loan to help finance the construction of a building and the purchase of store equipment, costing a total of $250,000, to enable Cabinet Craft Inc. to open a store in Montvale. Land for this purpose was acquired last year. The bank's loan officer requested a statement of cash flows in addition to the most recent income statement, balance sheet, and retained earnings statement that Daniels had submitted with the loan application.

As a close family friend, Daniels asked you to prepare a statement of cash flows. From the records provided, you prepared the following statement.

Cabinet Craft Inc.
Statement of Cash Flows
For the Year Ended December 31, 2008

Cash flows from operating activities:		
Net income	$ 94,500	
Adjustments to reconcile net income to net cash flow from operating activities:		
Depreciation	26,000	
Gain on sale of investments	(8,000)	
Changes in current operating assets and liabilities:		
Decrease in accounts receivable	5,000	
Increase in inventories	(12,000)	
Increase in accounts payable	8,500	
Decrease in accrued expenses	(1,200)	
Net cash flow from operating activities		$112,800
Cash flows from investing activities:		
Cash received from investments sold	$ 50,000	
Less cash paid for purchase of store equipment	(30,000)	
Net cash flow provided by investing activities		20,000
Cash flows from financing activities:		
Cash paid for dividends	$ 35,000	
Net cash flow used for financing activities		(35,000)
Increase in cash		$ 97,800
Cash at the beginning of the year		34,800
Cash at the end of the year		$132,600
Schedule of Noncash Financing and Investing Activities:		
Issued common stock for land		$ 75,000

After reviewing the statement, Daniels telephoned you and commented, "Are you sure this statement is right?" Daniels then raised the following questions:

1. "How can depreciation be a cash flow?"
2. "Issuing common stock for the land is listed in a separate schedule. This transaction has nothing to do with cash! Shouldn't this transaction be eliminated from the statement?"

(continued)

3. "How can the gain on sale of investments be a deduction from net income in determining the cash flow from operating activities?"
4. "Why does the bank need this statement anyway? They can compute the increase in cash from the balance sheets for the last two years."

After jotting down Daniels' questions, you assured him that this statement was "right." However, to alleviate Daniels' concern, you arranged a meeting for the following day.

a. ⬤▬▶ How would you respond to each of Daniels' questions?
b. ⬤▬▶ Do you think that the statement of cash flows enhances the chances of Cabinet Craft Inc. receiving the loan? Discuss.

SA 16-5
Statement of cash flows

Group Project

Internet Project

This activity will require two teams to retrieve cash flow statement information from the Internet. One team is to obtain the most recent year's statement of cash flows for Johnson & Johnson, and the other team the most recent year's statement of cash flows for AMR Corp. (American Airlines).

The statement of cash flows is included as part of the annual report information that is a required disclosure to the Securities and Exchange Commission (SEC). The SEC, in turn, provides this information online through its EDGAR service. EDGAR (Electronic Data Gathering, Analysis, and Retrieval) is the electronic archive of financial statements filed with the Securities and Exchange Commission (SEC). SEC documents can be retrieved using the EdgarScan service from PricewaterhouseCoopers at **http://edgarscan.pwcglobal.com**.

To obtain annual report information, type in a company name in the appropriate space. EdgarScan will list the reports available to you for the company you've selected. Select the most recent annual report filing, identified as a 10-K or 10-K405. EdgarScan provides an outline of the report, including the separate financial statements. You can double-click the income statement and balance sheet for the selected company into an Excel™ spreadsheet for further analysis.

As a group, compare the two statements of cash flows.

a. How are Johnson & Johnson and AMR similar or different regarding cash flows?
b. Compute and compare the free cash flow for each company, assuming additions to property, plant, and equipment replace current capacity.

Answers to Self-Examination Questions

1. **D** Cash flows from operating activities affect transactions that enter into the determination of net income, such as the receipt of cash from customers on account (answer D). Receipts of cash from the sale of stock (answer A) and the sale of bonds (answer B) and payments of cash for dividends (answer C) are cash flows from financing activities.
2. **A** Cash flows from investing activities include receipts from the sale of noncurrent assets, such as equipment (answer A), and payments to acquire noncurrent assets. Receipts of cash from the sale of stock (answer B) and payments of cash for dividends (answer C) and to acquire treasury stock (answer D) are cash flows from financing activities.
3. **C** Payment of cash for dividends (answer C) is an example of a financing activity. The receipt of cash from customers on account (answer A) is an operating activity. The receipt of cash from the sale of equipment (answer B) is an investing activity. The payment of cash to acquire land (answer D) is an example of an investing activity.

4. **D** The indirect method (answer D) reports cash flows from operating activities by beginning with net income and adjusting it for revenues and expenses not involving the receipt or payment of cash.
5. **C** The cash flows from operating activities section of the statement of cash flows would report net cash flow from operating activities of $65,500, determined as follows:

Cash flows from operating activities:		
Net income		$ 55,000
Adjustments to reconcile net income to net cash flow from operating activities:		
Depreciation		22,000
Changes in current operating assets and liabilities:		
Increase in accounts receivable	(10,000)	
Decrease in inventories	5,000	
Decrease in prepaid expenses	500	
Decrease in accounts payable	(7,000)	
Net cash flow from operating activities		$65,500

chapter 17

Financial Statement Analysis

© CHITOSE SUZUKI/ASSOCIATED PRESS

objectives

After studying this chapter, you should be able to:

1 List basic financial statement analytical procedures.

2 Apply financial statement analysis to assess the solvency of a business.

3 Apply financial statement analysis to assess the profitability of a business.

4 Describe the contents of corporate annual reports.

Williams-Sonoma, Inc.

During a recent year, Williams-Sonoma, Inc., reported revenues of over $3.1 billion and net income of over $190 million. The common stock of Williams-Sonoma is traded on the New York Stock Exchange (symbol WSM) and closed on February 17, 2006, at $39.80 per share. Based upon current market values, Williams-Sonoma is worth almost $4.6 billion. Do you wish you could have invested in Williams-Sonoma 15 years ago?

Williams-Sonoma is a specialty retailer in the United States, well-known for its home furnishings. The company began in 1956, when owner Chuck Williams opened a store selling restaurant-quality cookware from France in Sonoma, California. The business expanded quickly, and Williams soon moved his store to Sutter Street in San Francisco. From there, the company expanded into catalogs, the Internet, and additional brands, such as Pottery Barn.

The success of Williams-Sonoma shows that reputation and the popularity of a company's product are important indicators of success. However, these are not the *only* factors that determine a company's success. A business needs to combine product offerings with proper financial, marketing, and sales strategies to be successful. Clearly, Williams-Sonoma has accomplished this. If you had invested in its common stock back in 1990, the stock price would have risen from $3 per share to nearly $40 per share today.

How, then, should you select companies in which to invest? Like any significant purchase, you should do some research to guide your investment decision. If you were buying a car, for example, you might go to Edmunds.com to obtain reviews, ratings, prices, specifications, options, and fuel economy across a number of vehicle alternatives. In deciding whether to invest in a company, you can use financial analysis to gain insight into a company's past performance and future prospects. This chapter describes and illustrates common financial data that can be analyzed to assist you in making investment decisions such as whether or not to invest in Williams-Sonoma stock. The contents of corporate annual reports are also discussed.

Source: Walter Nicholls, "The 90-Year-Old Pioneer Behind Williams-Sonoma," *The Seattle Times*, October 5, 2005.

Basic Analytical Procedures

objective   1

List basic financial statement analytical procedures.

The basic financial statements provide much of the information users need to make economic decisions about businesses. In this chapter, we illustrate how to perform a complete analysis of these statements by integrating individual analytical measures.

Analytical procedures may be used to compare items on a current statement with related items on earlier statements. For example, cash of $150,000 on the current balance sheet may be compared with cash of $100,000 on the balance sheet of a year earlier. The current year's cash may be expressed as 1.5 or 150% of the earlier amount, or as an increase of 50% or $50,000.

Analytical procedures are also widely used to examine relationships within a financial statement. To illustrate, assume that cash of $50,000 and inventories of $250,000 are included in the total assets of $1,000,000 on a balance sheet. In relative terms, the cash balance is 5% of the total assets, and the inventories are 25% of the total assets.

In this chapter, we will illustrate a number of common analytical measures. The measures are not ends in themselves. They are only guides in evaluating financial and operating data. Many other factors, such as trends in the industry and general economic conditions, should also be considered.

HORIZONTAL ANALYSIS

The percentage analysis of increases and decreases in related items in comparative financial statements is called **horizontal analysis**. The amount of each item on the most recent statement is compared with the related item on one or more earlier statements. The amount of increase or decrease in the item is listed, along with the percent of increase or decrease.

Horizontal analysis may compare two statements. In this case, the earlier statement is used as the base. Horizontal analysis may also compare three or more statements. In this case, the earliest date or period may be used as the base for comparing all later dates or periods. Alternatively, each statement may be compared to the immediately preceding statement. Exhibit 1 is a condensed comparative balance sheet for two years for Lincoln Company, with horizontal analysis.

EXHIBIT 1

Comparative Balance Sheet—Horizontal Analysis

Lincoln Company
Comparative Balance Sheet
December 31, 2008 and 2007

	2008	2007	Increase (Decrease) Amount	Percent
Assets				
Current assets	$ 550,000	$ 533,000	$ 17,000	3.2%
Long-term investments	95,000	177,500	(82,500)	(46.5%)
Property, plant, and				
equipment (net)	444,500	470,000	(25,500)	(5.4%)
Intangible assets	50,000	50,000	—	—
Total assets	$1,139,500	$1,230,500	$ (91,000)	(7.4%)
Liabilities				
Current liabilities	$ 210,000	$ 243,000	$ (33,000)	(13.6%)
Long-term liabilities	100,000	200,000	(100,000)	(50.0%)
Total liabilities	$ 310,000	$ 443,000	$(133,000)	(30.0%)
Stockholders' Equity				
Preferred 6% stock, $100 par . . .	$ 150,000	$ 150,000	—	—
Common stock, $10 par	500,000	500,000	—	—
Retained earnings	179,500	137,500	$ 42,000	30.5%
Total stockholders' equity	$ 829,500	$ 787,500	$ 42,000	5.3%
Total liabilities and				
stockholders' equity	$1,139,500	$1,230,500	$ (91,000)	(7.4%)

We cannot fully evaluate the significance of the various increases and decreases in the items shown in Exhibit 1 without additional information. Although total assets at the end of 2008 were $91,000 (7.4%) less than at the beginning of the year, liabilities were reduced by $133,000 (30%), and stockholders' equity increased $42,000 (5.3%). It appears that the reduction of $100,000 in long-term liabilities was achieved mostly through the sale of long-term investments.

The balance sheet in Exhibit 1 may be expanded to include the details of the various categories of assets and liabilities. An alternative is to present the details in separate schedules. Exhibit 2 is a supporting schedule with horizontal analysis.

The decrease in accounts receivable may be due to changes in credit terms or improved collection policies. Likewise, a decrease in inventories during a period of increased sales may indicate an improvement in the management of inventories.

EXHIBIT 2

Comparative Schedule
of Current Assets—
Horizontal Analysis

			Increase (Decrease)	
	2008	**2007**	**Amount**	**Percent**
Cash	$ 90,500	$ 64,700	$ 25,800	39.9%
Marketable securities	75,000	60,000	15,000	25.0%
Accounts receivable (net)	115,000	120,000	(5,000)	(4.2%)
Inventories	264,000	283,000	(19,000)	(6.7%)
Prepaid expenses	5,500	5,300	200	3.8%
Total current assets	$550,000	$533,000	$ 17,000	3.2%

Lincoln Company
Comparative Schedule of Current Assets
December 31, 2008 and 2007

The changes in the current assets in Exhibit 2 appear favorable. This assessment is supported by the 24.8% increase in net sales shown in Exhibit 3.

EXHIBIT 3

Comparative Income
Statement—
Horizontal Analysis

Lincoln Company
Comparative Income Statement
For the Years Ended December 31, 2008 and 2007

			Increase (Decrease)	
	2008	**2007**	**Amount**	**Percent**
Sales	$1,530,500	$1,234,000	$296,500	24.0%
Sales returns and allowances . . .	32,500	34,000	(1,500)	(4.4%)
Net sales	$1,498,000	$1,200,000	$298,000	24.8%
Cost of goods sold	1,043,000	820,000	223,000	27.2%
Gross profit	$ 455,000	$ 380,000	$ 75,000	19.7%
Selling expenses	$ 191,000	$ 147,000	$ 44,000	29.9%
Administrative expenses	104,000	97,400	6,600	6.8%
Total operating expenses	$ 295,000	$ 244,400	$ 50,600	20.7%
Income from operations	$ 160,000	$ 135,600	$ 24,400	18.0%
Other income	8,500	11,000	(2,500)	(22.7%)
	$ 168,500	$ 146,600	$ 21,900	14.9%
Other expense (interest)	6,000	12,000	(6,000)	(50.0%)
Income before income tax	$ 162,500	$ 134,600	$ 27,900	20.7%
Income tax expense	71,500	58,100	13,400	23.1%
Net income	$ 91,000	$ 76,500	$ 14,500	19.0%

An increase in net sales may not have a favorable effect on operating performance. The percentage increase in Lincoln Company's net sales is accompanied by a greater percentage increase in the cost of goods (merchandise) sold.[1] This has the effect of reducing gross profit as a percentage of sales. Selling expenses increased significantly, and administrative expenses increased slightly. Overall, operating expenses increased by 20.7%, whereas gross profit increased by only 19.7%.

The increase in income from operations and in net income is favorable. However, a study of the expenses and additional analyses and comparisons should be made before reaching a conclusion as to the cause.

Exhibit 4 illustrates a comparative retained earnings statement with horizontal analysis. It reveals that retained earnings increased 30.5% for the year. The increase is due to net income of $91,000 for the year, less dividends of $49,000.

---

1 The term *cost of goods sold* is often used in practice in place of *cost of merchandise sold*. Such usage is followed in this chapter.

EXHIBIT 4

Comparative Retained
Earnings Statement—
Horizontal Analysis

Lincoln Company
Comparative Retained Earnings Statement
December 31, 2008 and 2007

	2008	2007	Increase (Decrease) Amount	Percent
Retained earnings, January 1	$137,500	$100,000	$37,500	37.5%
Net income for the year	91,000	76,500	14,500	19.0%
Total	$228,500	$176,500	$52,000	29.5%
Dividends:				
On preferred stock	$ 9,000	$ 9,000	—	—
On common stock	40,000	30,000	$10,000	33.3%
Total	$ 49,000	$ 39,000	$10,000	25.6%
Retained earnings, December 31 . . .	$179,500	$137,500	$42,000	30.5%

Example Exercise 17-1   objective 1

The comparative cash and accounts receivable balances for a company are provided below.

	2008	2007
Cash	$62,500	$50,000
Accounts receivable (net)	74,400	80,000

Based on this information, what is the amount and percentage of increase or decrease that would be shown in a balance sheet with horizontal analysis?

Follow My Example 17-1

Cash $12,500 increase ($62,500 − $50,000), or 25%
Accounts receivable $5,600 decrease ($74,400 − $80,000), or −7%

For Practice: PE 17-1A, PE 17-1B

VERTICAL ANALYSIS

A percentage analysis may also be used to show the relationship of each component to the total within a single statement. This type of analysis is called **vertical analysis**. Like horizontal analysis, the statements may be prepared in either detailed or condensed form. In the latter case, additional details of the changes in individual items may be presented in supporting schedules. In such schedules, the percentage analysis may be based on either the total of the schedule or the statement total. Although vertical analysis is limited to an individual statement, its significance may be improved by preparing comparative statements.

In vertical analysis of the balance sheet, each asset item is stated as a percent of the total assets. Each liability and stockholders' equity item is stated as a percent of the total liabilities and stockholders' equity. Exhibit 5 is a condensed comparative balance sheet with vertical analysis for Lincoln Company.

The major percentage changes in Lincoln Company's assets are in the current asset and long-term investment categories. Current assets increased from 43.3% to 48.3% of total assets, and long-term investments decreased from 14.4% to 8.3% of total assets. In the Liabilities and Stockholders' Equity sections of the balance sheet, the greatest percentage changes are in long-term liabilities and retained earnings. Stockholders' equity increased from 64% to 72.8% of total liabilities and stockholders' equity in 2008. There is a comparable decrease in liabilities.

EXHIBIT 5

Comparative Balance
Sheet—Vertical
Analysis

Lincoln Company
Comparative Balance Sheet
December 31, 2008 and 2007

	2008 Amount	Percent	2007 Amount	Percent
Assets				
Current assets	$ 550,000	48.3%	$ 533,000	43.3%
Long-term investments	95,000	8.3	177,500	14.4
Property, plant, and equipment (net)	444,500	39.0	470,000	38.2
Intangible assets	50,000	4.4	50,000	4.1
Total assets	$1,139,500	100.0%	$1,230,500	100.0%
Liabilities				
Current liabilities	$ 210,000	18.4%	$ 243,000	19.7%
Long-term liabilities	100,000	8.8	200,000	16.3
Total liabilities	$ 310,000	27.2%	$ 443,000	36.0%
Stockholders' Equity				
Preferred 6% stock, $100 par	$ 150,000	13.2%	$ 150,000	12.2%
Common stock, $10 par	500,000	43.9	500,000	40.6
Retained earnings	179,500	15.7	137,500	11.2
Total stockholders' equity	$ 829,500	72.8%	$ 787,500	64.0%
Total liabilities and stockholders' equity	$1,139,500	100.0%	$1,230,500	100.0%

In a vertical analysis of the income statement, each item is stated as a percent of net sales. Exhibit 6 is a condensed comparative income statement with vertical analysis for Lincoln Company.

EXHIBIT 6

Comparative Income
Statement—Vertical
Analysis

Lincoln Company
Comparative Income Statement
For the Years Ended December 31, 2008 and 2007

	2008 Amount	Percent	2007 Amount	Percent
Sales	$1,530,500	102.2%	$1,234,000	102.8%
Sales returns and allowances	32,500	2.2	34,000	2.8
Net sales	$1,498,000	100.0%	$1,200,000	100.0%
Cost of goods sold	1,043,000	69.6	820,000	68.3
Gross profit	$ 455,000	30.4%	$ 380,000	31.7%
Selling expenses	$ 191,000	12.8%	$ 147,000	12.3%
Administrative expenses	104,000	6.9	97,400	8.1
Total operating expenses	$ 295,000	19.7%	$ 244,400	20.4%
Income from operations	$ 160,000	10.7%	$ 135,600	11.3%
Other income	8,500	0.6	11,000	0.9
	$ 168,500	11.3%	$ 146,600	12.2%
Other expense (interest)	6,000	0.4	12,000	1.0
Income before income tax	$ 162,500	10.9%	$ 134,600	11.2%
Income tax expense	71,500	4.8	58,100	4.8
Net income	$ 91,000	6.1%	$ 76,500	6.4%

REAL WORLD

The percentages of gross profit and net income to sales for a recent fiscal year for Target and Wal-Mart are shown below.

	Target	Wal-Mart
Gross profit to sales	31.2%	22.9%
Net income to sales	6.8%	3.6%

Wal-Mart has a significantly lower gross profit margin percentage than does Target, which is likely due to Wal-Mart's aggressive pricing strategy. However, Target's gross profit margin advantage shrinks when comparing the net income to sales ratio. Target must have larger selling and administrative expenses to sales than does Wal-Mart. Even so, Target's net income to sales is still 3.2 percentage points better than Wal-Mart's net income to sales.

We must be careful when judging the significance of differences between percentages for the two years. For example, the decline of the gross profit rate from 31.7% in 2007 to 30.4% in 2008 is only 1.3 percentage points. In terms of dollars of potential gross profit, however, it represents a decline of approximately $19,500 (1.3% × $1,498,000).

COMMON-SIZE STATEMENTS

Horizontal and vertical analyses with both dollar and percentage amounts are useful in assessing relationships and trends in financial conditions and operations of a business. Vertical analysis with both dollar and percentage amounts is also useful in comparing one company with another or with industry averages. Such comparisons are easier to make with the use of common-size statements. In a **common-size statement**, all items are expressed in percentages.

Common-size statements are useful in comparing the current period with prior periods, individual businesses, or one business with industry percentages. Industry data are often available from trade associations and financial information services. Exhibit 7 is a comparative common-size income statement for two businesses.

Exhibit 7 indicates that Lincoln Company has a slightly higher rate of gross profit than Madison Corporation. However, this advantage is more than offset by Lincoln Company's higher percentage of selling and administrative expenses. As a result, the income from operations of Lincoln Company is 10.7% of net sales, compared with 14.4% for Madison Corporation—an unfavorable difference of 3.7 percentage points.

EXHIBIT 7

Common-Size Income Statement

Lincoln Company and Madison Corporation
Condensed Common-Size Income Statement
For the Year Ended December 31, 2008

	Lincoln Company	Madison Corporation
Sales	102.2%	102.3%
Sales returns and allowances	2.2	2.3
Net sales	100.0%	100.0%
Cost of goods sold	69.6	70.0
Gross profit	30.4%	30.0%
Selling expenses	12.8%	11.5%
Administrative expenses	6.9	4.1
Total operating expenses	19.7%	15.6%
Income from operations	10.7%	14.4%
Other income	0.6	0.6
	11.3%	15.0%
Other expense (interest)	0.4	0.5
Income before income tax	10.9%	14.5%
Income tax expense	4.8	5.5
Net income	6.1%	9.0%

OTHER ANALYTICAL MEASURES

In addition to the preceding analyses, other relationships may be expressed in ratios and percentages. Often, these items are taken from the financial statements and thus are a type of vertical analysis. Comparing these items with items from earlier periods is a type of horizontal analysis.

Example Exercise 17-2

Income statement information for Lee Corporation is provided below.

Sales	$100,000
Cost of goods sold	65,000
Gross profit	$ 35,000

Prepare a vertical analysis of the income statement for Lee Corporation.

Follow My Example 17-2

	Amount	Percentage	
Sales	$100,000	100%	($100,000/$100,000)
Cost of goods sold	65,000	65	($65,000/$100,000)
Gross profit	$ 35,000	35%	($35,000/$100,000)

For Practice: PE 17-2A, PE 17-2B

Solvency Analysis

Apply financial statement analysis to assess the solvency of a business.

Two popular printed sources for industry ratios are *Annual Statement Studies* from Robert Morris Associates and *Industry Norms & Key Business Ratios* from Dun's Analytical Services. Online analysis is available from Zacks Investment Research site or Market Guide's site, both of which are linked to the text's Web site at **www.thomson edu.com/accounting/warren**.

Some aspects of a business's financial condition and operations are of greater importance to some users than others. However, all users are interested in the ability of a business to pay its debts as they are due and to earn income. The ability of a business to meet its financial obligations (debts) is called **solvency**. The ability of a business to earn income is called **profitability**.

The factors of solvency and profitability are interrelated. A business that cannot pay its debts on a timely basis may experience difficulty in obtaining credit. A lack of available credit may, in turn, lead to a decline in the business's profitability. Eventually, the business may be forced into bankruptcy. Likewise, a business that is less profitable than its competitors is likely to be at a disadvantage in obtaining credit or new capital from stockholders.

In the following paragraphs, we discuss various types of financial analyses that are useful in evaluating the solvency of a business. In the next section, we discuss various types of profitability analyses. The examples in both sections are based on Lincoln Company's financial statements presented earlier. In some cases, data from Lincoln Company's financial statements of the preceding year and from other sources are also used. These historical data are useful in assessing the past performance of a business and in forecasting its future performance. The results of financial analyses may be even more useful when they are compared with those of competing businesses and with industry averages.

Solvency analysis focuses on the ability of a business to pay or otherwise satisfy its current and noncurrent liabilities. It is normally assessed by examining balance sheet relationships, using the following major analyses:

1. Current position analysis
2. Accounts receivable analysis
3. Inventory analysis
4. The ratio of fixed assets to long-term liabilities
5. The ratio of liabilities to stockholders' equity
6. The number of times interest charges are earned

CURRENT POSITION ANALYSIS

To be useful in assessing solvency, a ratio or other financial measure must relate to a business's ability to pay or otherwise satisfy its liabilities. Using measures to assess a

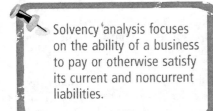

Solvency analysis focuses on the ability of a business to pay or otherwise satisfy its current and noncurrent liabilities.

business's ability to pay its current liabilities is called *current position analysis*. Such analysis is of special interest to short-term creditors.

An analysis of a firm's current position normally includes determining the working capital, the current ratio, and the quick ratio. The current and quick ratios are most useful when analyzed together and compared to previous periods and other firms in the industry.

Working Capital The excess of the current assets of a business over its current liabilities is called *working capital*. The working capital is often used in evaluating a company's ability to meet currently maturing debts. It is especially useful in making monthly or other period-to-period comparisons for a company. However, amounts of working capital are difficult to assess when comparing companies of different sizes or in comparing such amounts with industry figures. For example, working capital of $250,000 may be adequate for a small kitchenware store, but it would be inadequate for all of Williams-Sonoma, Inc.

Current Ratio Another means of expressing the relationship between current assets and current liabilities is the **current ratio**. This ratio is sometimes called the *working capital ratio* or *bankers' ratio*. The ratio is computed by dividing the total current assets by the total current liabilities. For Lincoln Company, working capital and the current ratio for 2008 and 2007 are as follows:

	2008	2007
a. Current assets	$550,000	$533,000
b. Current liabilities	210,000	243,000
Working capital (a − b)	$340,000	$290,000
Current ratio (a/b)	2.6	2.2

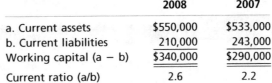

Microsoft Corporation maintains a high current ratio—4.7 for a recent year. Microsoft's stable and profitable software business has allowed it to develop a strong cash position coupled with no short-term notes payable.

The current ratio is a more reliable indicator of solvency than is working capital. To illustrate, assume that as of December 31, 2008, the working capital of a competitor is much greater than $340,000, but its current ratio is only 1.3. Considering these facts alone, Lincoln Company, with its current ratio of 2.6, is in a more favorable position to obtain short-term credit than the competitor, which has the greater amount of working capital.

Quick Ratio The working capital and the current ratio do not consider the makeup of the current assets. To illustrate the importance of this consideration, the current position data for Lincoln Company and Jefferson Corporation as of December 31, 2008, are as follows:

	Lincoln Company	Jefferson Corporation
Current assets:		
Cash	$ 90,500	$ 45,500
Marketable securities	75,000	25,000
Accounts receivable (net)	115,000	90,000
Inventories	264,000	380,000
Prepaid expenses	5,500	9,500
a. Total current assets	$550,000	$550,000
b. Current liabilities	210,000	210,000
Working capital (a − b)	$340,000	$340,000
Current ratio (a/b)	2.6	2.6

Both companies have a working capital of $340,000 and a current ratio of 2.6. But the ability of each company to pay its current debts is significantly different. Jefferson Corporation has more of its current assets in inventories. Some of these inventories must be sold and the receivables collected before the current liabilities can be paid in full. Thus, a large amount of time may be necessary to convert these inventories into cash. Declines in market prices and a reduction in demand could also impair its ability to pay current liabilities. In contrast, Lincoln Company has cash and current assets (marketable securities and accounts receivable) that can generally be converted to cash rather quickly to meet its current liabilities.

A ratio that measures the "instant" debt-paying ability of a company is called the **quick ratio** or *acid-test ratio*. It is the ratio of the total quick assets to the total current liabilities. **Quick assets** are cash and other current assets that can be quickly converted to cash. Quick assets normally include cash, marketable securities, and receivables. The quick ratio data for Lincoln Company are as follows:

	2008	2007
Quick assets:		
Cash	$ 90,500	$ 64,700
Marketable securities	75,000	60,000
Accounts receivable (net)	115,000	120,000
a. Total quick assets	$280,500	$244,700
b. Current liabilities	$210,000	$243,000
Quick ratio (a/b)	1.3	1.0

Example Exercise 17-3 objective 2

The following items are reported on a company's balance sheet:

Cash	$300,000
Marketable securities	100,000
Accounts receivable (net)	200,000
Inventory	200,000
Accounts payable	400,000

Determine (a) the current ratio and (b) the quick ratio.

Follow My Example 17-3

a. Current Ratio = Current Assets /Current Liabilities
    Current Ratio = ($300,000 + $100,000 + $200,000 + $200,000)/$400,000
    Current Ratio = 2.0

b. Quick Ratio = Quick Assets /Current Liabilities
    Quick Ratio = ($300,000 + $100,000 + $200,000)/$400,000
    Quick Ratio = 1.5

For Practice: PE 17-3A, PE 17-3B

ACCOUNTS RECEIVABLE ANALYSIS

The size and makeup of accounts receivable change constantly during business operations. Sales on account increase accounts receivable, whereas collections from customers decrease accounts receivable. Firms that grant long credit terms usually have larger accounts receivable balances than those granting short credit terms. Increases or decreases in the volume of sales also affect the balance of accounts receivable.

It is desirable to collect receivables as promptly as possible. The cash collected from receivables improves solvency. In addition, the cash generated by prompt collections from customers may be used in operations for such purposes as purchasing merchandise in large quantities at lower prices. The cash may also be used for payment of dividends to stockholders or for other investing or financing purposes. Prompt collection also lessens the risk of loss from uncollectible accounts.

Accounts Receivable Turnover The relationship between sales and accounts receivable may be stated as the **accounts receivable turnover**. This ratio is computed by dividing net sales by the average net accounts receivable.[2] It is desirable to base the average on monthly balances, which allows for seasonal changes in sales. When such data are not available, it may be necessary to use the average of the accounts receivable balance at the beginning and the end of the year. If there are trade notes receivable as well as accounts, the two may be combined. The accounts receivable turnover data for Lincoln Company are as follows.

	2008	2007
a. Net sales	$1,498,000	$1,200,000
Accounts receivable (net):		
Beginning of year	$ 120,000	$ 140,000
End of year	115,000	120,000
Total	$ 235,000	$ 260,000
b. Average (Total/2)	$ 117,500	$ 130,000
Accounts receivable turnover (a/b)	12.7	9.2

The increase in the accounts receivable turnover for 2008 indicates that there has been an improvement in the collection of receivables. This may be due to a change in the granting of credit or in collection practices or both.

Number of Days' Sales in Receivables Another measure of the relationship between sales and accounts receivable is the **number of days' sales in receivables**. This ratio is computed by dividing the average accounts receivable by the average daily sales. Average daily sales is determined by dividing net sales by 365 days. The number of days' sales in receivables is computed for Lincoln Company as follows:

	2008	2007
a. Average (Total/2)	$ 117,500	$ 130,000
Net sales	$1,498,000	$1,200,000
b. Average daily sales (Sales/365)	$4,104	$3,288
Number of days' sales in receivables (a/b)	28.6	39.5

The number of days' sales in receivables is an estimate of the length of time (in days) the accounts receivable have been outstanding. Comparing this measure with the credit terms provides information on the efficiency in collecting receivables. For example, assume that the number of days' sales in receivables for Grant Inc. is 40. If Grant Inc.'s credit terms are n/45, then its collection process appears to be efficient. On the other hand, if Grant Inc.'s credit terms are n/30, its collection process does not appear to be efficient. A comparison with other firms in the same industry and with prior years also provides useful information. Such comparisons may indicate efficiency of collection procedures and trends in credit management.

2 If known, *credit* sales should be used in the numerator. Because credit sales are not normally known by external users, we use net sales in the numerator.

Example Exercise 17-4

objective 2

A company reports the following:

Net sales	$960,000
Average accounts receivable (net)	48,000

Determine (a) the accounts receivable turnover and (b) the number of days' sales in receivables. Round to one decimal place.

Follow My Example 17-4

a. Accounts Receivable Turnover = Sales/Average Accounts Receivable
   Accounts Receivable Turnover = $960,000/$48,000
   Accounts Receivable Turnover = 20.0

b. Number of Days' Sales in Receivables = Average Accounts Receivable/Average Daily Sales
   Number of Days' Sales in Receivables = $48,000/($960,000/365) = $48,000/$2,630
   Number of Days' Sales in Receivables = 18.3 days

For Practice: PE 17-4A, PE 17-4B

INVENTORY ANALYSIS

A business should keep enough inventory on hand to meet the needs of its customers and its operations. At the same time, however, an excessive amount of inventory reduces solvency by tying up funds. Excess inventories also increase insurance expense, property taxes, storage costs, and other related expenses. These expenses further reduce funds that could be used elsewhere to improve operations. Finally, excess inventory also increases the risk of losses because of price declines or obsolescence of the inventory. Two measures that are useful for evaluating the management of inventory are the inventory turnover and the number of days' sales in inventory.

Inventory Turnover   The relationship between the volume of goods (merchandise) sold and inventory may be stated as the **inventory turnover**. It is computed by dividing the cost of goods sold by the average inventory. If monthly data are not available, the average of the inventories at the beginning and the end of the year may be used. The inventory turnover for Lincoln Company is computed as follows:

	2008	2007
a. Cost of goods sold	$1,043,000	$820,000
Inventories:		
Beginning of year	$ 283,000	$311,000
End of year	264,000	283,000
Total	$ 547,000	$594,000
b. Average (Total/2)	$ 273,500	$297,000
Inventory turnover (a/b)	3.8	2.8

The inventory turnover improved for Lincoln Company because of an increase in the cost of goods sold and a decrease in the average inventories. Differences across inventories, companies, and industries are too great to allow a general statement on what is a good inventory turnover. For example, a firm selling food should have a higher turnover than a firm selling furniture or jewelry. Likewise, the perishable foods department of a supermarket should have a higher turnover than the soaps and cleansers department. However, for each business or each department within a business, there is a reasonable turnover rate. A turnover lower than this rate could mean that inventory is not being managed properly.

Number of Days' Sales in Inventory   Another measure of the relationship between the cost of goods sold and inventory is the **number of days' sales in inventory**. This measure is computed by dividing the average inventory by the average daily cost of goods sold (cost of goods sold divided by 365). The number of days' sales in inventory for Lincoln Company is computed as follows:

	2008	2007
a. Average (Total/2)	$ 273,500	$297,000
Cost of goods sold	$1,043,000	$820,000
b. Average daily cost of goods sold (COGS/365 days)	$2,858	$2,247
Number of days' sales in inventory (a/b)	95.7	132.2

The number of days' sales in inventory is a rough measure of the length of time it takes to acquire, sell, and replace the inventory. For Lincoln Company, there is a major improvement in the number of days' sales in inventory during 2008. However, a comparison with earlier years and similar firms would be useful in assessing Lincoln Company's overall inventory management.

Example Exercise 17-5   objective 2

A company reports the following:

Cost of goods sold	$560,000
Average inventory	112,000

Determine (a) the inventory turnover and (b) the number of days' sales in inventory. Round to one decimal place.

Follow My Example 17-5

a. Inventory Turnover = Cost of Goods Sold/Average Inventory
Inventory Turnover = $560,000/$112,000
Inventory Turnover = 5.0

b. Number of Days' Sales in Inventory = Average Inventory/Average Daily Cost of Goods Sold
Number of Days' Sales in Inventory = $112,000/($560,000/365) = $112,000/$1,534
Number of Days' Sales in Inventory = 73.0 days

For Practice: PE 17-5A, PE 17-5B

RATIO OF FIXED ASSETS TO LONG-TERM LIABILITIES

Long-term notes and bonds are often secured by mortgages on fixed assets. The **ratio of fixed assets to long-term liabilities** is a solvency measure that indicates the margin of safety of the noteholders or bondholders. It also indicates the ability of the business to borrow additional funds on a long-term basis. The ratio of fixed assets to long-term liabilities for Lincoln Company is as follows:

	2008	2007
a. Fixed assets (net)	$444,500	$470,000
b. Long-term liabilities	$100,000	$200,000
Ratio of fixed assets to long-term liabilities (a/b)	4.4	2.4

The major increase in this ratio at the end of 2008 is mainly due to liquidating one-half of Lincoln Company's long-term liabilities. If the company needs to borrow additional funds on a long-term basis in the future, it is in a strong position to do so.

RATIO OF LIABILITIES TO STOCKHOLDERS' EQUITY

Claims against the total assets of a business are divided into two groups: (1) claims of creditors and (2) claims of owners. The relationship between the total claims of the creditors and owners—the **ratio of liabilities to stockholders' equity**—is a solvency measure that indicates the margin of safety for creditors. It also indicates the ability of the business to withstand adverse business conditions. When the claims of creditors are large in relation to the equity of the stockholders, there are usually significant interest payments. If earnings decline to the point where the company is unable to meet its interest payments, the business may be taken over by the creditors.

The ratio of liabilities to stock-holders' equity varies across industries. For example, recent annual reports of some selected companies showed the following ratio of liabilities to stock-holders' equity:

Continental Airlines	66.8
Procter & Gamble	2.5
Circuit City Stores, Inc.	0.8

The airline industry generally uses more debt financing than the consumer product or retail industries. Thus, the airline industry is generally considered more risky.

The relationship between creditor and stockholder equity is shown in the vertical analysis of the balance sheet. For example, the balance sheet of Lincoln Company in Exhibit 5 indicates that on December 31, 2008, liabilities represented 27.2% and stockholders' equity represented 72.8% of the total liabilities and stockholders' equity (100.0%). Instead of expressing each item as a percent of the total, this relationship may be expressed as a ratio of one to the other, as follows:

	2008	2007
a. Total liabilities	$310,000	$443,000
b. Total stockholders' equity	$829,500	$787,500
Ratio of liabilities to stockholders' equity (a/b)	0.4	0.6

The balance sheet of Lincoln Company shows that the major factor affecting the change in the ratio was the $100,000 decrease in long-term liabilities during 2008. The ratio at the end of both years shows a large margin of safety for the creditors.

Example Exercise 17-6
objective 2

The following information was taken from Acme Company's balance sheet:

Fixed assets (net)	$1,400,000
Long-term liabilities	400,000
Total liabilities	560,000
Total stockholders' equity	1,400,000

Determine the company's (a) ratio of fixed assets to long-term liabilities and (b) ratio of liabilities to total stockholders' equity.

Follow My Example 17-6

a. Ratio of Fixed Assets to Long-Term Liabilities = Fixed Assets/Long-Term Liabilities
    Ratio of Fixed Assets to Long-Term Liabilities = $1,400,000/$400,000
    Ratio of Fixed Assets to Long-Term Liabilities = 3.5

b. Ratio of Liabilities to Total Stockholders' Equity = Total Liabilities/Total Stockholders' Equity
    Ratio of Liabilities to Total Stockholders' Equity = $560,000/$1,400,000
    Ratio of Liabilities to Total Stockholders' Equity = 0.4

For Practice: PE 17-6A, PE 17-6B

NUMBER OF TIMES INTEREST CHARGES EARNED

Corporations in some industries, such as airlines, normally have high ratios of debt to stockholders' equity. For such corporations, the relative risk of the debtholders is normally measured as the **number of times interest charges are earned**, sometimes called the *fixed charge coverage ratio*, during the year. The higher the ratio, the lower the risk that interest payments will not be made if earnings decrease. In other words, the higher the ratio, the greater the assurance that interest payments will be made on a continuing basis. This measure also indicates the general financial strength of the business, which is of interest to stockholders and employees as well as creditors.

The amount available to meet interest charges is not affected by taxes on income. This is because interest is deductible in determining taxable income. Thus, the number of times interest charges are earned for Lincoln Company is computed as shown below, rounded to one decimal place.

	2008	2007
Income before income tax	$162,500	$134,600
a. Add interest expense	6,000	12,000
b. Amount available to meet interest charges	$168,500	$146,600
Number of times interest charges earned (b/a)	28.1	12.2

These calculations indicate Lincoln Company has very high coverage of its interest charges for both years. Analysis such as this can also be applied to dividends on preferred stock. In such a case, net income is divided by the amount of preferred dividends to yield the *number of times preferred dividends are earned*. This measure indicates the risk that dividends to preferred stockholders may not be paid.

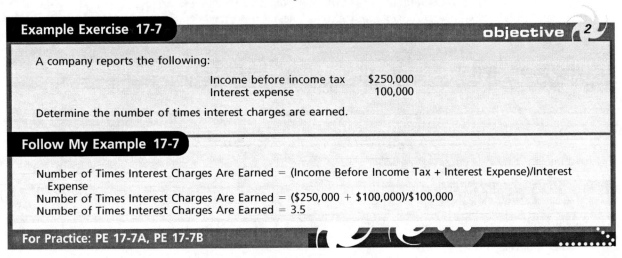

Example Exercise 17-7 objective 2

A company reports the following:

Income before income tax	$250,000
Interest expense	100,000

Determine the number of times interest charges are earned.

Follow My Example 17-7

Number of Times Interest Charges Are Earned = (Income Before Income Tax + Interest Expense)/Interest Expense
Number of Times Interest Charges Are Earned = ($250,000 + $100,000)/$100,000
Number of Times Interest Charges Are Earned = 3.5

For Practice: PE 17-7A, PE 17-7B

Profitability Analysis

objective 3

Apply financial statement analysis to assess the profitability of a business.

The ability of a business to earn profits depends on the effectiveness and efficiency of its operations as well as the resources available to it. Profitability analysis, therefore, focuses primarily on the relationship between operating results as reported in the income statement and resources available to the business as reported in the balance sheet. Major analyses used in assessing profitability include the following:

1. Ratio of net sales to assets
2. Rate earned on total assets
3. Rate earned on stockholders' equity
4. Rate earned on common stockholders' equity
5. Earnings per share on common stock
6. Price-earnings ratio
7. Dividends per share
8. Dividend yield

> Profitability analysis focuses on the relationship between operating results and the resources available to a business.

RATIO OF NET SALES TO ASSETS

The ratio of net sales to assets is a profitability measure that shows how effectively a firm utilizes its assets. For example, two competing businesses have equal amounts of assets. If the sales of one are twice the sales of the other, the business with the higher sales is making better use of its assets.

In computing the ratio of net sales to assets, any long-term investments are excluded from total assets, because such investments are unrelated to normal operations involving the sale of goods or services. Assets may be measured as the total at the end of the year, the average at the beginning and end of the year, or the average of monthly totals. The basic data and the computation of this ratio for Lincoln Company are as follows:

	2008	2007
a. Net sales	$1,498,000	$1,200,000
Total assets (excluding long-term investments):		
Beginning of year	$1,053,000	$1,010,000
End of year	1,044,500	1,053,000
Total	$2,097,500	$2,063,000
b. Average (Total/2)	$1,048,750	$1,031,500
Ratio of net sales to assets (a/b)	1.4	1.2

This ratio improved during 2008, primarily due to an increase in sales volume. A comparison with similar companies or industry averages would be helpful in assessing the effectiveness of Lincoln Company's use of its assets.

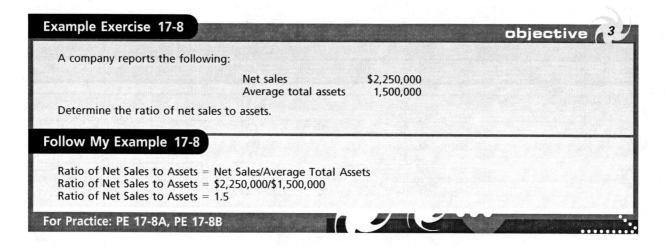

Example Exercise 17-8   objective **3**

A company reports the following:

Net sales	$2,250,000
Average total assets	1,500,000

Determine the ratio of net sales to assets.

Follow My Example 17-8

Ratio of Net Sales to Assets = Net Sales/Average Total Assets
Ratio of Net Sales to Assets = $2,250,000/$1,500,000
Ratio of Net Sales to Assets = 1.5

For Practice: PE 17-8A, PE 17-8B

RATE EARNED ON TOTAL ASSETS

The **rate earned on total assets** measures the profitability of total assets, without considering how the assets are financed. This rate is therefore not affected by whether the assets are financed primarily by creditors or stockholders.

The rate earned on total assets is computed by adding interest expense to net income and dividing this sum by the average total assets. Adding interest expense to net income eliminates the effect of whether the assets are financed by debt or equity. The rate earned by Lincoln Company on total assets is computed as follows:

	2008	2007
Net income	$ 91,000	$ 76,500
Plus interest expense	6,000	12,000
a. Total	$ 97,000	$ 88,500
Total assets:		
Beginning of year	$1,230,500	$1,187,500
End of year	1,139,500	1,230,500
Total	$2,370,000	$2,418,000
b. Average (Total/2)	$1,185,000	$1,209,000
Rate earned on total assets (a/b)	8.2%	7.3%

The rate earned on total assets of Lincoln Company during 2008 improved over that of 2007. A comparison with similar companies and industry averages would be useful in evaluating Lincoln Company's profitability on total assets.

Sometimes it may be desirable to compute the *rate of income from operations to total assets*. This is especially true if significant amounts of nonoperating income and expense are reported on the income statement. In this case, any assets related to the nonoperating income and expense items should be excluded from total assets in computing the rate. In addition, using income from operations (which is before tax) has the advantage of eliminating the effects of any changes in the tax structure on the rate of earnings. When evaluating published data on rates earned on assets, you should be careful to determine the exact nature of the measure that is reported.

Example Exercise 17-9   **objective** 3

A company reports the following income statement and balance sheet information for the current year:

Net income	$ 125,000
Interest expense	25,000
Average total assets	2,000,000

Determine the rate earned on total assets.

Follow My Example 17-9

Rate Earned on Total Assets = (Net Income + Interest Expense)/Average Total Assets
Rate Earned on Total Assets = ($125,000 + $25,000)/$2,000,000
Rate Earned on Total Assets = $150,000/$2,000,000
Rate Earned on Total Assets = 7.5%

For Practice: PE 17-9A, PE 17-9B

RATE EARNED ON STOCKHOLDERS' EQUITY

Another measure of profitability is the **rate earned on stockholders' equity**. It is computed by dividing net income by average total stockholders' equity. In contrast to the rate earned on total assets, this measure emphasizes the rate of income earned on the amount invested by the stockholders.

The total stockholders' equity may vary throughout a period. For example, a business may issue or retire stock, pay dividends, and earn net income. If monthly amounts are not available, the average of the stockholders' equity at the beginning and the end of the year is normally used to compute this rate. For Lincoln Company, the rate earned on stockholders' equity is computed as follows:

	2008	2007
a. Net income	$ 91,000	$ 76,500
Stockholders' equity:		
Beginning of year	$ 787,500	$ 750,000
End of year	829,500	787,500
Total	$1,617,000	$1,537,500
b. Average (Total/2)	$ 808,500	$ 768,750
Rate earned on stockholders' equity (a/b)	11.3%	10.0%

The rate earned by a business on the equity of its stockholders is usually higher than the rate earned on total assets. This occurs when the amount earned on assets acquired with creditors' funds is more than the interest paid to creditors. This difference in the rate on stockholders' equity and the rate on total assets is called **leverage**.

Lincoln Company's rate earned on stockholders' equity for 2008, 11.3%, is greater than the rate of 8.2% earned on total assets. The leverage of 3.1% (11.3% − 8.2%) for 2008 compares favorably with the 2.7% (10.0% − 7.3%) leverage for 2007. Exhibit 8 shows the 2008 and 2007 leverages for Lincoln Company.

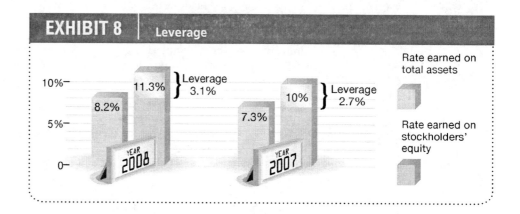

EXHIBIT 8 | Leverage

RATE EARNED ON COMMON STOCKHOLDERS' EQUITY

The approximate rates earned on assets and stockholders' equity for Molson Coors Brewing Company and Anheuser-Busch Companies, Inc., for a recent fiscal year are shown below.

	Molson Coors	Anheuser-Busch
Rate earned on assets	4%	15%
Rate earned on stockholders' equity	12%	83%

Anheuser-Busch has been more profitable and has benefited from a greater use of leverage than has Molson Coors.

A corporation may have both preferred and common stock outstanding. In this case, the common stockholders have the residual claim on earnings. The **rate earned on common stockholders' equity** focuses only on the rate of profits earned on the amount invested by the common stockholders. It is computed by subtracting preferred dividend requirements from the net income and dividing by the average common stockholders' equity.

Lincoln Company has $150,000 of 6% nonparticipating preferred stock outstanding on December 31, 2008 and 2007. Thus, the annual preferred dividend requirement is $9,000 ($150,000 × 6%). The common stockholders' equity equals the total stockholders' equity, including retained earnings, less the par of the preferred stock ($150,000). The basic data and the rate earned on common stockholders' equity for Lincoln Company are as follows:

	2008	2007
Net income	$ 91,000	$ 76,500
Preferred dividends	9,000	9,000
a. Remainder—identified with common stock	$ 82,000	$ 67,500
Common stockholders' equity:		
Beginning of year	$ 637,500	$ 600,000
End of year	679,500	637,500
Total	$1,317,000	$1,237,500
b. Average (Total/2)	$ 658,500	$ 618,750
Rate earned on common stockholders' equity (a/b)	12.5%	10.9%

The rate earned on common stockholders' equity differs from the rates earned by Lincoln Company on total assets and total stockholders' equity. This occurs if there are borrowed funds and also preferred stock outstanding, which rank ahead of the common shares in their claim on earnings. Thus, the concept of leverage, as we discussed in the preceding section, can also be applied to the use of funds from the sale of preferred stock as well as borrowing. Funds from both sources can be used in an attempt to increase the return on common stockholders' equity.

Example Exercise 17-10 objective 3

A company reports the following:

Net income	$ 125,000
Preferred dividends	5,000
Average stockholders' equity	1,000,000
Average common stockholders' equity	800,000

Determine (a) the rate earned on stockholders' equity and (b) the rate earned on common stockholders' equity.

Follow My Example 17-10

a. Rate Earned on Stockholders' Equity = Net Income/Average Stockholders' Equity
Rate Earned on Stockholders' Equity = $125,000/$1,000,000
Rate Earned on Stockholders' Equity = 12.5%

b. Rate Earned on Common Stockholders' Equity = (Net Income − Preferred Dividends)/Average
Common Stockholders' Equity
Rate Earned on Common Stockholders' Equity = ($125,000 − $5,000)/$800,000
Rate Earned on Common Stockholders' Equity = 15%

For Practice: PE 17-10A, PE 17-10B

EARNINGS PER SHARE ON COMMON STOCK

One of the profitability measures often quoted by the financial press is **earnings per share (EPS) on common stock**. It is also normally reported in the income statement in corporate annual reports. If a company has issued only one class of stock, the earnings per share is computed by dividing net income by the number of shares of stock outstanding. If preferred and common stock are outstanding, the net income is first reduced by the amount of preferred dividend requirements.[3]

The data on the earnings per share of common stock for Lincoln Company are as follows:

	2008	2007
Net income	$91,000	$76,500
Preferred dividends	9,000	9,000
a. Remainder—identified with common stock	$82,000	$67,500
b. Shares of common stock outstanding	50,000	50,000
Earnings per share on common stock (a/b)	$1.64	$1.35

PRICE-EARNINGS RATIO

Another profitability measure quoted by the financial press is the **price-earnings (P/E) ratio** on common stock. The price-earnings ratio is an indicator of a firm's future earnings prospects. It is computed by dividing the market price per share of common stock at a specific date by the annual earnings per share. To illustrate, assume that the market prices per common share are 41 at the end of 2008 and 27 at the end of 2007. The price-earnings ratio on common stock of Lincoln Company is computed as follows:

	2008	2007
Market price per share of common stock	$41.00	$27.00
Earnings per share on common stock	÷ 1.64	÷ 1.35
Price-earnings ratio on common stock	25	20

---

3 Additional details related to earnings per share were discussed in Chapter 14.

The price-earnings ratio indicates that a share of common stock of Lincoln Company was selling for 20 times the amount of earnings per share at the end of 2007. At the end of 2008, the common stock was selling for 25 times the amount of earnings per share.

Example Exercise 17-11   objective **3**

A company reports the following:

Net income	$250,000
Preferred dividends	$15,000
Shares of common stock outstanding	20,000
Market price per share of common stock	$35.00

a. Determine the company's earnings per share on common stock.
b. Determine the company's price-earnings ratio. Round to one decimal place.

Follow My Example 17-11

a. Earnings per Share on Common Stock = (Net Income − Preferred Dividends)/Shares of Common Stock Outstanding
    Earnings per Share = ($250,000 − $15,000)/20,000
    Earnings per Share = $11.75

b. Price-Earnings Ratio = Market Price per Share of Common Stock/Earnings per Share on Common Stock
    Price-Earnings Ratio = $35.00/$11.75
    Price-Earnings Ratio = 3.0

For Practice: PE 17-11A, PE 17-11B

The dividend per share, dividend yield, and P/E ratio of a common stock are normally quoted on the daily listing of stock prices in *The Wall Street Journal* and on Yahoo!'s finance Web site.

DIVIDENDS PER SHARE AND DIVIDEND YIELD

Since the primary basis for dividends is earnings, dividends per share and earnings per share on common stock are commonly used by investors in assessing alternative stock investments. The dividends per share for Lincoln Company were $0.80 ($40,000/50,000 shares) for 2008 and $0.60 ($30,000/50,000 shares) for 2007.

Dividends per share can be reported with earnings per share to indicate the relationship between dividends and earnings. Comparing these two per share amounts indicates the extent to which the corporation is retaining its earnings for use in operations. Exhibit 9 shows these relationships for Lincoln Company.

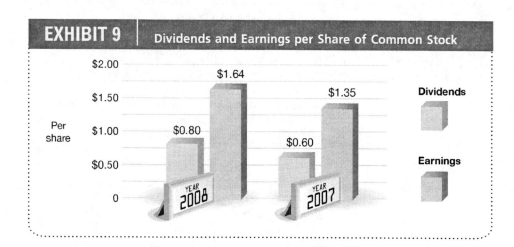

EXHIBIT 9 | Dividends and Earnings per Share of Common Stock

The **dividend yield** on common stock is a profitability measure that shows the rate of return to common stockholders in terms of cash dividends. It is of special interest to investors whose main investment objective is to receive current returns (dividends) on an investment rather than an increase in the market price of the investment. The dividend yield is computed by dividing the annual dividends paid per share of common stock by the market price per share on a specific date. To illustrate, assume that the market price was 41 at the end of 2008 and 27 at the end of 2007. The dividend yield on common stock of Lincoln Company is as follows:

	2008	2007
Dividends per share of common stock	$ 0.80	$ 0.60
Market price per share of common stock	÷ 41.00	÷ 27.00
Dividend yield on common stock	2.0%	2.2%

SUMMARY OF ANALYTICAL MEASURES

Exhibit 10 presents a summary of the analytical measures that we have discussed. These measures can be computed for most medium-size businesses. Depending on the specific business being analyzed, some measures might be omitted or additional measures could be developed. The type of industry, the capital structure, and the diversity of the business's operations usually affect the measures used. For example, analysis for an airline might include revenue per passenger mile and cost per available seat as measures. Likewise, analysis for a hotel might focus on occupancy rates.

Percentage analyses, ratios, turnovers, and other measures of financial position and operating results are useful analytical measures. They are helpful in assessing a business's past performance and predicting its future. They are not, however, a substitute for sound judgment. In selecting and interpreting analytical measures, conditions peculiar to a business or its industry should be considered. In addition, the influence of the general economic and business environment should be considered.

In determining trends, the interrelationship of the measures used in assessing a business should be carefully studied. Comparable indexes of earlier periods should also be studied. Data from competing businesses may be useful in assessing the efficiency of operations for the firm under analysis. In making such comparisons, however, the effects of differences in the accounting methods used by the businesses should be considered.

EXHIBIT 10   Summary of Analytical Measures

	Method of Computation	Use
Solvency measures:		
Working Capital	Current Assets − Current Liabilities	To indicate the ability to meet currently maturing obligations
Current Ratio	$\dfrac{\text{Current Assets}}{\text{Current Liabilities}}$	
Quick Ratio	$\dfrac{\text{Quick Assets}}{\text{Current Liabilities}}$	To indicate instant debt-paying ability
Accounts Receivable Turnover	$\dfrac{\text{Net Sales}}{\text{Average Accounts Receivable}}$	To assess the efficiency in collecting receivables and in the management of credit
Numbers of Days' Sales in Receivables	$\dfrac{\text{Average Accounts Receivable}}{\text{Average Daily Sales}}$	
Inventory Turnover	$\dfrac{\text{Cost of Goods Sold}}{\text{Average Inventory}}$	To assess the efficiency in the management of inventory
Number of Days' Sales in Inventory	$\dfrac{\text{Average Inventory}}{\text{Average Daily Cost of Goods Sold}}$	
Ratio of Fixed Assets to Long-Term Liabilities	$\dfrac{\text{Fixed Assets (net)}}{\text{Long-Term Liabilities}}$	To indicate the margin of safety to long-term creditors
Ratio of Liabilities to Stockholders' Equity	$\dfrac{\text{Total Liabilities}}{\text{Total Stockholders' Equity}}$	To indicate the margin of safety to creditors
Number of Times Interest Charges Earned	$\dfrac{\text{Income Before Income Tax} + \text{Interest Expense}}{\text{Interest Expense}}$	To assess the risk to debtholders in terms of number of times interest charges were earned
Profitability measures:		
Ratio of Net Sales to Assets	$\dfrac{\text{Net Sales}}{\text{Average Total Assets (excluding long-term investments)}}$	To assess the effectiveness in the use of assets
Rate Earned on Total Assets	$\dfrac{\text{Net Income} + \text{Interest Expense}}{\text{Average Total Assets}}$	To assess the profitability of the assets
Rate Earned on Stockholders' Equity	$\dfrac{\text{Net Income}}{\text{Average Total Stockholders' Equity}}$	To assess the profitability of the investment by stockholders
Rate Earned on Common Stockholders' Equity	$\dfrac{\text{Net Income} - \text{Preferred Dividends}}{\text{Average Common Stockholders' Equity}}$	To assess the profitability of the investment by common stockholders
Earnings per Share on Common Stock	$\dfrac{\text{Net Income} - \text{Preferred Dividends}}{\text{Shares of Common Stock Outstanding}}$	
Price-Earnings Ratio	$\dfrac{\text{Market Price per Share of Common Stock}}{\text{Earnings per Share of Common Stock}}$	To indicate future earnings prospects, based on the relationship between market value of common stock and earnings
Dividends per Share of Common Stock	$\dfrac{\text{Dividends}}{\text{Shares of Common Stock Outstanding}}$	To indicate the extent to which earnings are being distributed to common stockholders
Dividend Yield	$\dfrac{\text{Dividends per Share of Common Stock}}{\text{Market Price per Share of Common Stock}}$	To indicate the rate of return to common stockholders in terms of dividends

Integrity, Objectivity, and Ethics in Business

ETHICS

ONE BAD APPLE

A recent survey by *CFO* magazine reported that 47% of chief financial officers have been pressured by the chief executive officer to use questionable accounting. In addition, only 38% of those surveyed feel less pressure to use aggressive accounting today than in years past, while 20% believe there is more pressure. Perhaps more troublesome is the chief financial officers' confidence in the quality of financial information, with only 27% being "very confident" in the quality of financial information presented by public companies.

Source: D. Durfee, "It's Better (and Worse) Than You Think," *CFO*, May 3, 2004.

Corporate Annual Reports

objective 4

Describe the contents of corporate annual reports.

Public corporations are required to issue annual reports to their stockholders and other interested parties. Such reports summarize the corporation's operating activities for the past year and plans for the future. There are many variations in the order and form for presenting the major sections of annual reports. However, one section of the annual report is devoted to the financial statements, including the accompanying notes. In addition, annual reports usually include the following sections:

1. Management discussion and analysis
2. Report on adequacy of internal control
3. Report on fairness of financial statements

In the following paragraphs, we describe these sections. Each section, as well as the financial statements, is illustrated in the annual report for Williams-Sonoma, Inc., in Appendix D.

MANAGEMENT DISCUSSION AND ANALYSIS

A required disclosure in the annual report filed with the Securities and Exchange Commission is the **Management's Discussion and Analysis (MD&A)**. The MD&A provides critical information in interpreting the financial statements and assessing the future of the company.

The MD&A includes an analysis of the results of operations and discusses management's opinion about future performance. It compares the prior year's income statement with the current year's to explain changes in sales, significant expenses, gross profit, and income from operations. For example, an increase in sales may be explained by referring to higher shipment volume or stronger prices.

The MD&A also includes an analysis of the company's financial condition. It compares significant balance sheet items between successive years to explain changes in liquidity and capital resources. In addition, the MD&A discusses significant risk exposure.

A new subsection of the MD&A required by the Sarbanes-Oxley Act must now include a section describing any "off-balance-sheet" arrangements. Such arrangements are discussed in advanced accounting courses.

REPORT ON ADEQUACY OF INTERNAL CONTROL

As discussed in Chapter 8, the Sarbanes-Oxley Act of 2002 requires management to provide a report stating their responsibility for establishing and maintaining internal control. In addition, the report must state management's conclusion concerning the effectiveness of internal controls over financial reporting. The act also requires a public accounting firm to examine and verify management's conclusions regarding internal control. Thus, public companies must provide two reports, one by management and one by a public accounting firm, certifying the management report as accurate. In some situations, the auditor may combine these reports into a single report. The combined report for Williams-Sonoma, Inc., is included in the annual report in Appendix D.

REPORT ON FAIRNESS OF FINANCIAL STATEMENTS

In addition to a public accounting firm's internal control report, all publicly held corporations are also required to have an independent audit (examination) of their financial statements. For the financial statements of most companies, the CPAs who conduct the audit render an opinion on the fairness of the statements. An opinion stating that the financial statements fairly represent the financial condition of a public company is said to be an unqualified, or "clean," opinion. The Independent Auditors' Report for Williams-Sonoma, Inc., is an unqualified opinion.

Business Connections

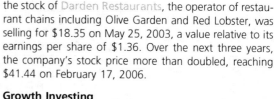

INVESTING STRATEGIES

How do people make investment decisions? Investment decisions, like any major purchase, must meet the needs of the buyer. For example, if you have a family of five and are thinking about buying a new car, you probably wouldn't buy a two-seat sports car. It just wouldn't meet your objectives or fit your lifestyle. Alternatively, if you are a young single person, a minivan might not meet your immediate needs. Investors buy stocks in the same way, buying stocks that match their investment style and their financial needs. Two common approaches are value and growth investing.

Value Investing

Value investors search for undervalued stocks. That is, the investor tries to find companies whose value is not reflected in their stock price. These are typically quiet, "boring" companies with excellent financial performance that are temporarily out of favor in the stock market. This investment approach assumes that the stock's price will eventually rise to match the company's value. The most successful investor of all time, Warren Buffett, uses this approach almost exclusively. Naturally, the key to successful value investing is to accurately determine a stock's value. This will often include analyzing a company's financial ratios, as discussed in this chapter, compared to target ratios and industry norms. For example,

the stock of Darden Restaurants, the operator of restaurant chains including Olive Garden and Red Lobster, was selling for $18.35 on May 25, 2003, a value relative to its earnings per share of $1.36. Over the next three years, the company's stock price more than doubled, reaching $41.44 on February 17, 2006.

Growth Investing

The growth investor tries to identify companies that have the potential to grow sales and earnings through new products, markets, or opportunities. Growth companies are often newer companies that are still unproven but that possess unique technologies or capabilities. The strategy is to purchase these companies before their potential becomes obvious, hoping to profit from relatively large increases in the company's stock price. This approach, however, carries the risk that the growth may not occur. Growth investors use many of the ratios discussed in this chapter to identify high-potential growth companies. For example, in March 2003, Research in Motion Limited, maker of the popular BlackBerry® handheld mobile device, reported earnings per share of −$0.96, and the company's stock price was trading near $5 per share. In the following two years, the company's sales increased by 340%, earnings increased to $1.14 per share, and the company's stock price rose above $75 per share.

© ORATIVE CORPORATION/PRNEWSFOTO

At a Glance ↘

1. List basic financial statement analytical procedures.

Key Points	Key Learning Outcomes	Example Exercises	Practice Exercises
The basic financial statements provide much of the information users need to make economic decisions. Analytical procedures are used to compare items on a current financial statement with related items on earlier statements, or to examine relationships within a financial statement.	• Prepare a horizontal analysis from a company's financial statements. • Prepare a vertical analysis from a company's financial statements.	17-1	17-1A, 17-1B
	• Prepare common-size financial statements.	17-2	17-2A, 17-2B

2. Apply financial statement analysis to assess the solvency of a business.

Key Points	Key Learning Outcomes	Example Exercises	Practice Exercises
All users of financial statements are interested in the ability of a business to pay its debts (solvency) and earn income (profitability). Solvency and profitability are interrelated. Solvency analysis is normally assessed by examining the following balance sheet relationships: (1) current position analysis, (2) accounts receivable analysis, (3) inventory analysis, (4) the ratio of fixed assets to long term liabilities, (5) the ratio of liabilities to stockholders' equity, and (6) the number of times interest charges are earned.	• Determine working capital. • Calculate and interpret the current ratio.	17-3	17-3A, 17-3B
	• Calculate and interpret the quick ratio.	17-3	17-3A, 17-3B
	• Calculate and interpret accounts receivable turnover.	17-4	17-4A, 17-4B
	• Calculate and interpret number of days' sales in receivables.	17-4	17-4A, 17-4B
	• Calculate and interpret inventory turnover.	17-5	17-5A, 17-5B
	• Calculate and interpret number of days' sales in inventory.	17-5	17-5A, 17-5B
	• Calculate and interpret the ratio of fixed assets to long-term liabilities.	17-6	17-6A, 17-6B
	• Calculate and interpret the ratio of liabilities to stockholders' equity.	17-6	17-6A, 17-6B
	• Calculate and interpret the number of times interest charges are earned.	17-7	17-7A, 17-7B

(continued)

3. Apply financial statement analysis to assess the profitability of a business.

Key Points	Key Learning Outcomes	Example Exercises	Practice Exercises
Profitability analysis focuses mainly on the relationship between operating results (income statement) and resources available (balance sheet). Major analyses include (1) the ratio of net sales to assets, (2) the rate earned on total assets, (3) the rate earned on stockholders' equity, (4) the rate earned on common stockholders' equity, (5) earnings per share on common stock, (6) the price-earnings ratio, (7) dividends per share, and (8) dividend yield.	• Calculate and interpret the ratio of net sales to assets.	17-8	17-8A, 17-8B
	• Calculate and interpret the rate earned on total assets.	17-9	17-9A, 17-9B
	• Calculate and interpret the rate earned on stockholders' equity.	17-10	17-10A, 17-10B
	• Calculate and interpret the rate earned on common stockholders' equity.	17-10	17-10A, 17-10B
	• Calculate and interpret the earnings per share on common stock.	17-11	17-11A, 17-11B
	• Calculate and interpret the price-earnings ratio.	17-11	17-11A, 17-11B
	• Calculate and interpret the dividends per share and dividend yield.		
	• Describe the uses and limitations of analytical measures.		

4. Describe the contents of corporate annual reports.

Key Points	Key Learning Outcomes	Example Exercises	Practice Exercises
Corporations normally issue annual reports to their stockholders and other interested parties. Such reports summarize the corporation's operating activities for the past year and plans for the future.	• Describe the elements of a corporate annual report.		

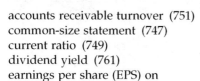

Key Terms

accounts receivable turnover (751)
common-size statement (747)
current ratio (749)
dividend yield (761)
earnings per share (EPS) on common stock (759)
horizontal analysis (742)
inventory turnover (752)
leverage (757)
Management's Discussion and Analysis (MD&A) (763)
number of days' sales in inventory (753)

number of days' sales in receivables (751)
number of times interest charges are earned (754)
price-earnings (P/E) ratio (759)
profitability (748)
quick assets (750)
quick ratio (750)
rate earned on common stockholders' equity (758)
rate earned on stockholders' equity (757)
rate earned on total assets (756)

ratio of fixed assets to long-term liabilities (753)
ratio of liabilities to stockholders' equity (754)
solvency (748)
vertical analysis (745)

Illustrative Problem

Rainbow Paint Co.'s comparative financial statements for the years ending December 31, 2008 and 2007, are as follows. The market price of Rainbow Paint Co.'s common stock was $30 on December 31, 2007, and $25 on December 31, 2008.

Rainbow Paint Co.
Comparative Income Statement
For the Years Ended December 31, 2008 and 2007

	2008	2007
Sales	$5,125,000	$3,257,600
Sales returns and allowances	125,000	57,600
Net sales	$5,000,000	$3,200,000
Cost of goods sold	3,400,000	2,080,000
Gross profit	$1,600,000	$1,120,000
Selling expenses	$ 650,000	$ 464,000
Administrative expenses	325,000	224,000
Total operating expenses	$ 975,000	$ 688,000
Income from operations	$ 625,000	$ 432,000
Other income	25,000	19,200
	$ 650,000	$ 451,200
Other expense (interest)	105,000	64,000
Income before income tax	$ 545,000	$ 387,200
Income tax expense	300,000	176,000
Net income	$ 245,000	$ 211,200

Rainbow Paint Co.
Comparative Retained Earnings Statement
For the Years Ended December 31, 2008 and 2007

	2008	2007
Retained earnings, January 1	$723,000	$581,800
Add net income for year	245,000	211,200
Total	$968,000	$793,000
Deduct dividends:		
On preferred stock	$ 40,000	$ 40,000
On common stock	45,000	30,000
Total	$ 85,000	$ 70,000
Retained earnings, December 31	$883,000	$723,000

(continued)

	2008	2007

Rainbow Paint Co.
Comparative Balance Sheet
December 31, 2008 and 2007

	2008	2007
Assets		
Current assets:		
Cash	$ 175,000	$ 125,000
Marketable securities	150,000	50,000
Accounts receivable (net)	425,000	325,000
Inventories	720,000	480,000
Prepaid expenses	30,000	20,000
Total current assets	$1,500,000	$1,000,000
Long-term investments	250,000	225,000
Property, plant, and equipment (net)	2,093,000	1,948,000
Total assets	$3,843,000	$3,173,000
Liabilities		
Current liabilities	$ 750,000	$ 650,000
Long-term liabilities:		
Mortgage note payable, 10%, due 2011	$ 410,000	—
Bonds payable, 8%, due 2014	800,000	$ 800,000
Total long-term liabilities	$1,210,000	$ 800,000
Total liabilities	$1,960,000	$1,450,000
Stockholders' Equity		
Preferred 8% stock, $100 par	$ 500,000	$ 500,000
Common stock, $10 par	500,000	500,000
Retained earnings	883,000	723,000
Total stockholders' equity	$1,883,000	$1,723,000
Total liabilities and stockholders' equity	$3,843,000	$3,173,000

Instructions
Determine the following measures for 2008:

1. Working capital
2. Current ratio
3. Quick ratio
4. Accounts receivable turnover
5. Number of days' sales in receivables
6. Inventory turnover
7. Number of days' sales in inventory
8. Ratio of fixed assets to long-term liabilities
9. Ratio of liabilities to stockholders' equity
10. Number of times interest charges earned
11. Number of times preferred dividends earned
12. Ratio of net sales to assets
13. Rate earned on total assets
14. Rate earned on stockholders' equity
15. Rate earned on common stockholders' equity
16. Earnings per share on common stock
17. Price-earnings ratio
18. Dividends per share of common stock
19. Dividend yield

Solution

(Ratios are rounded to the nearest single digit after the decimal point.)

1. Working capital: $750,000
   $1,500,000 − $750,000

2. Current ratio: 2.0
   $1,500,000/$750,000

3. Quick ratio: 1.0
   $750,000/$750,000

4. Accounts receivable turnover: 13.3
   $5,000,000/[($425,000 + $325,000)/2]

5. Number of days' sales in receivables: 27.4 days
   $5,000,000/365 = $13,699
   $375,000/$13,699

6. Inventory turnover: 5.7
   $3,400,000/[($720,000 + $480,000)/2]

7. Number of days' sales in inventory: 64.4 days
   $3,400,000/365 = $9,315
   $600,000/$9,315

8. Ratio of fixed assets to long-term liabilities: 1.7
   $2,093,000/$1,210,000

9. Ratio of liabilities to stockholders' equity: 1.0
   $1,960,000/$1,883,000

10. Number of times interest charges earned: 6.2
    ($545,000 + $105,000)/$105,000

11. Number of times preferred dividends earned: 6.1
    $245,000/$40,000

12. Ratio of net sales to assets: 1.5
    $5,000,000/[($3,593,000 + $2,948,000)/2]

13. Rate earned on total assets: 10.0%
    ($245,000 + $105,000)/[($3,843,000 + $3,173,000)/2]

14. Rate earned on stockholders' equity: 13.6%
    $245,000/[($1,883,000 + $1,723,000)/2]

15. Rate earned on common stockholders' equity: 15.7%
    ($245,000 − $40,000)/[($1,383,000 + $1,223,000)/2]

16. Earnings per share on common stock: $4.10
    ($245,000 − $40,000)/50,000

17. Price-earnings ratio: 6.1
    $25/$4.10

18. Dividends per share of common stock: $0.90
    $45,000/50,000 shares

19. Dividend yield: 3.6%
    $0.90/$25

Self-Examination Questions (Answers at End of Chapter)

1. What type of analysis is indicated by the following?

	Amount	Percent
Current assets	$100,000	20%
Property, plant, and equipment	400,000	80
Total assets	$500,000	100%

   A. Vertical analysis   C. Profitability analysis
   B. Horizontal analysis   D. Contribution margin
                                         analysis

2. Which of the following measures indicates the ability of a firm to pay its current liabilities?
   A. Working capital   C. Quick ratio
   B. Current ratio   D. All of the above

3. The ratio determined by dividing total current assets by total current liabilities is:
   A. current ratio.   C. bankers' ratio.
   B. working capital ratio.   D. all of the above.

4. The ratio of the quick assets to current liabilities, which indicates the "instant" debt-paying ability of a firm, is the:
   A. current ratio.   C. quick ratio.
   B. working capital ratio.   D. bankers' ratio.

5. A measure useful in evaluating efficiency in the management of inventories is the:
   A. working capital ratio.
   B. quick ratio.
   C. number of days' sales in inventory.
   D. ratio of fixed assets to long-term liabilities.

Eye Openers

1. What is the difference between horizontal and vertical analysis of financial statements?
2. What is the advantage of using comparative statements for financial analysis rather than statements for a single date or period?
3. The current year's amount of net income (after income tax) is 20% larger than that of the preceding year. Does this indicate an improved operating performance? Discuss.
4. How would you respond to a horizontal analysis that showed an expense increasing by over 80%?
5. How would the current and quick ratios of a service business compare?
6. For Lindsay Corporation, the working capital at the end of the current year is $8,000 less than the working capital at the end of the preceding year, reported as follows:

	Current Year	Preceding Year
Current assets:		
Cash, marketable securities, and receivables	$35,000	$36,000
Inventories	55,000	42,000
Total current assets	$90,000	$78,000
Current liabilities	50,000	30,000
Working capital	$40,000	$48,000

Has the current position improved? Explain.
7. Why would the accounts receivable turnover ratio be different between Wal-Mart and Procter & Gamble?
8. A company that grants terms of n/45 on all sales has a yearly accounts receivable turnover, based on monthly averages, of 5. Is this a satisfactory turnover? Discuss.
9. a. Why is it advantageous to have a high inventory turnover?
   b. Is it possible for the inventory turnover to be too high? Discuss.
   c. Is it possible to have a high inventory turnover and a high number of days' sales in inventory? Discuss.
10. What do the following data taken from a comparative balance sheet indicate about the company's ability to borrow additional funds on a long-term basis in the current year as compared to the preceding year?

	Current Year	Preceding Year
Fixed assets (net)	$300,000	$300,000
Total long-term liabilities	100,000	120,000

11. a. How does the rate earned on total assets differ from the rate earned on stockholders' equity?
    b. Which ratio is normally higher? Explain.
12. a. Why is the rate earned on stockholders' equity by a thriving business ordinarily higher than the rate earned on total assets?
    b. Should the rate earned on common stockholders' equity normally be higher or lower than the rate earned on total stockholders' equity? Explain.
13. The net income (after income tax) of Choi Inc. was $15 per common share in the latest year and $60 per common share for the preceding year. At the beginning of the latest year, the number of shares outstanding was doubled by a stock split. There were no other changes in the amount of stock outstanding. What were the earnings per share in the preceding year, adjusted for comparison with the latest year?
14. The price-earnings ratio for the common stock of Cotter Company was 10 at December 31, the end of the current fiscal year. What does the ratio indicate about the selling price of the common stock in relation to current earnings?
15. Why would the dividend yield differ significantly from the rate earned on common stockholders' equity?
16. Favorable business conditions may bring about certain seemingly unfavorable ratios, and unfavorable business operations may result in apparently favorable ratios. For example, Trivec Company increased its sales and net income substantially for the current year, yet the current ratio at the end of the year is lower than at the beginning of the year. Discuss some possible causes of the apparent weakening of the current position, while sales and net income have increased substantially.

Practice Exercises

PE 17-1A
Horizontal analysis
obj. 1

The comparative marketable securities and inventory balances for a company are provided below.

	2008	2007
Marketable securities	$68,200	$55,000
Inventory	63,700	65,000

Based on this information, what is the amount and percentage of increase or decrease that would be shown in a balance sheet with horizontal analysis?

PE 17-1B
Horizontal analysis
obj. 1

The comparative accounts payable and long-term debt balances of a company are provided below.

	2008	2007
Accounts payable	$141,600	$120,000
Long-term debt	150,000	125,000

Based on this information, what is the amount and percentage of increase or decrease that would be shown in a balance sheet with horizontal analysis?

PE 17-2A
Common-size financial statements
obj. 1

Income statement information for Washburn Corporation is provided below.

Sales	$400,000
Cost of goods sold	340,000
Gross profit	$ 60,000

Prepare a vertical analysis of the income statement for Washburn Corporation.

PE 17-2B
Common-size financial statements
obj. **1**

Income statement information for Lewis Corporation is provided below.

Sales	$250,000
Gross profit	100,000
Net income	50,000

Prepare a vertical analysis of the income statement for Lewis Corporation.

PE 17-3A
Current position analysis
obj. **2**

The following items are reported on a company's balance sheet:

Cash	$125,000
Marketable securities	40,000
Accounts receivable (net)	30,000
Inventory	120,000
Accounts payable	150,000

Determine (a) the current ratio and (b) the quick ratio. Round to one decimal place.

PE 17-3B
Current position analysis
obj. **2**

The following items are reported on a company's balance sheet:

Cash	$275,000
Marketable securities	200,000
Accounts receivable (net)	625,000
Inventory	300,000
Accounts payable	800,000

Determine (a) the current ratio and (b) the quick ratio. Round to one decimal place.

PE 17-4A
Accounts receivable analysis
obj. **2**

A company reports the following:

Net sales	$450,000
Average accounts receivable (net)	37,500

Determine (a) the accounts receivable turnover and (b) the number of days' sales in receivables. Round to one decimal place.

PE 17-4B
Accounts receivable analysis
obj. **2**

A company reports the following:

Net sales	$225,000
Average accounts receivable (net)	25,000

Determine (a) the accounts receivable turnover and (b) the number of days' sales in receivables. Round to one decimal place.

PE 17-5A
Inventory analysis
obj. **2**

A company reports the following:

Cost of goods sold	$465,000
Average inventory	71,500

Determine (a) the inventory turnover and (b) the number of days' sales in inventory. Round to one decimal place.

PE 17-5B
Inventory analysis
obj. **2**

A company reports the following:

Cost of goods sold	$330,000
Average inventory	55,000

Determine (a) the inventory turnover and (b) the number of days' sales in inventory. Round to one decimal place.

PE 17-6A
Ratio of fixed assets to long-term liabilities and ratio of liabilities to stockholders' equity
obj. 2

The following information was taken from Straub Company's balance sheet:

Fixed assets (net)	$700,000
Long-term liabilities	218,750
Total liabilities	235,000
Total stockholders' equity	940,000

Determine the company's (a) ratio of fixed assets to long-term liabilities and (b) ratio of liabilities to stockholders' equity.

PE 17-6B
Ratio of fixed assets to long-term liabilities and ratio of liabilities to stockholders' equity
obj. 2

The following information was taken from Tristar Company's balance sheet:

Fixed assets (net)	$900,000
Long-term liabilities	625,000
Total liabilities	850,000
Total stockholders' equity	500,000

Determine the company's (a) ratio of fixed assets to long-term liabilities and (b) ratio of liabilities to stockholders' equity.

PE 17-7A
Number of times interest charges are earned
obj. 2

A company reports the following:

Income before income tax	$375,000
Interest expense	120,000

Determine the number of times interest charges are earned.

PE 17-7B
Number of times interest charges are earned
obj. 2

A company reports the following:

Income before income tax	$625,000
Interest expense	160,000

Determine the number of times interest charges are earned.

PE 17-8A
Ratio of net sales to assets
obj. 3

A company reports the following:

Net sales	$1,170,000
Average total assets	650,000

Determine the ratio of net sales to assets.

PE 17-8B
Ratio of net sales to assets
obj. 3

A company reports the following:

Net sales	$1,520,000
Average total assets	950,000

Determine the ratio of net sales to assets.

PE 17-9A
Rate earned on total assets
obj. 3

A company reports the following income statement and balance sheet information for the current year:

Net income	$ 225,000
Interest expense	20,000
Average total assets	3,250,000

Determine the rate earned on total assets.

PE 17-9B
Rate earned on total assets
obj. 3

A company reports the following income statement and balance sheet information for the current year:

Net income	$ 115,000
Interest expense	10,000
Average total assets	1,250,000

Determine the rate earned on total assets.

PE 17-10A
*Rate earned on
stockholders' equity and
rate earned on common
stockholders' equity*

obj. **3**

A company reports the following:

Net income	$ 225,000
Preferred dividends	20,000
Average stockholders' equity	1,750,000
Average common stockholders' equity	1,000,000

Determine (a) the rate earned on stockholders' equity and (b) the rate earned on common stockholders' equity. Round to one decimal place.

PE 17-10B
*Rate earned on
stockholders' equity and
rate earned on common
stockholders' equity*

obj. **3**

A company reports the following:

Net income	$115,000
Preferred dividends	10,000
Average stockholders' equity	850,000
Average common stockholders' equity	750,000

Determine (a) the rate earned on stockholders' equity and (b) the rate earned on common stockholders' equity.

PE 17-11A
*Earnings per share on
common stock and price
earnings ratio*

obj. **3**

A company reports the following:

Net income	$115,000
Preferred dividends	$15,000
Shares of common stock outstanding	20,000
Market price per share of common stock	$65.00

a. Determine the company's earnings per share on common stock.
b. Determine the company's price-earnings ratio.

PE 17-11B
*Earnings per share on
common stock and price
earnings ratio*

obj. **3**

A company reports the following:

Net income	$525,000
Preferred dividends	$25,000
Shares of common stock outstanding	50,000
Market price per share of common stock	$75.00

a. Determine the company's earnings per share on common stock.
b. Determine the company's price-earnings ratio.

Exercises

EX 17-1
*Vertical analysis of
income statement*

obj. **1**

✓ *a. 2008 net income:
$37,500; 5% of sales*

Revenue and expense data for Jazz-Tech Communications Co. are as follows:

	2008	2007
Sales	$750,000	$600,000
Cost of goods sold	450,000	312,000
Selling expenses	120,000	126,000
Administrative expenses	105,000	84,000
Income tax expense	37,500	30,000

a. Prepare an income statement in comparative form, stating each item for both 2008 and 2007 as a percent of sales. Round to one decimal place.

b. Comment on the significant changes disclosed by the comparative income statement.

EX 17-2
Vertical analysis of income statement
obj. 1

✓ *a. Fiscal year 2004 income from continuing operations, 26.7% of revenues*

The following comparative income statement (in thousands of dollars) for the fiscal years 2003 and 2004 was adapted from the annual report of Speedway Motorsports, Inc., owner and operator of several major motor speedways, such as the Atlanta, Texas, and Las Vegas Motor Speedways.

	Fiscal Year 2004	Fiscal Year 2003
Revenues:		
Admissions	$156,718	$150,253
Event-related revenue	137,074	127,055
NASCAR broadcasting revenue	110,016	90,682
Other operating revenue	42,711	36,539
Total revenue	$446,519	$404,529
Expenses and other:		
Direct expense of events	$ 81,432	$ 77,962
NASCAR purse and sanction fees	78,473	69,691
Other direct expenses	102,053	101,408
General and administrative	65,152	58,698
Total expenses and other	$327,110	$307,759
Income from continuing operations	$119,409	$ 96,770

a. Prepare a comparative income statement for fiscal years 2003 and 2004 in vertical form, stating each item as a percent of revenues. Round to one decimal place.

b. Comment on the significant changes.

EX 17-3
Common-size income statement
obj. 1

✓ *a. Jaribo net income: $85,000; 6.8% of sales*

Revenue and expense data for the current calendar year for Jaribo Communications Company and for the communications industry are as follows. The Jaribo Communications Company data are expressed in dollars. The communications industry averages are expressed in percentages.

	Jaribo Communications Company	Communications Industry Average
Sales	$1,265,000	101.0%
Sales returns and allowances	15,000	1.0
Cost of goods sold	450,000	41.0
Selling expenses	525,000	38.0
Administrative expenses	143,750	10.5
Other income	22,500	1.2
Other expense (interest)	18,750	1.7
Income tax expense	50,000	4.0

a. Prepare a common-size income statement comparing the results of operations for Jaribo Communications Company with the industry average. Round to one decimal place.

b. As far as the data permit, comment on significant relationships revealed by the comparisons.

EX 17-4
Vertical analysis of balance sheet
obj. 1

Balance sheet data for the Dover Hot Tub Company on December 31, the end of the fiscal year, are shown at the top of the following page.

✓ *Retained earnings,*
Dec. 31, 2008, 47.5%

	2008	2007
Current assets	$768,000	$250,000
Property, plant, and equipment	336,000	650,000
Intangible assets	96,000	100,000
Current liabilities	270,000	175,000
Long-term liabilities	300,000	255,000
Common stock	60,000	70,000
Retained earnings	570,000	500,000

Prepare a comparative balance sheet for 2008 and 2007, stating each asset as a percent of total assets and each liability and stockholders' equity item as a percent of the total liabilities and stockholders' equity. Round to one decimal place.

EX 17-5
Horizontal analysis of the income statement

obj. 1

✓ *a. Net income decrease,*
53.3%

Income statement data for Web-pics Company for the years ended December 31, 2008 and 2007, are as follows:

	2008	2007
Sales	$117,000	$150,000
Cost of goods sold	56,000	70,000
Gross profit	$ 61,000	$ 80,000
Selling expenses	$ 36,000	$ 37,500
Administrative expenses	12,500	10,000
Total operating expenses	$ 48,500	$ 47,500
Income before income tax	$ 12,500	$ 32,500
Income tax expense	2,000	10,000
Net income	$ 10,500	$ 22,500

a. Prepare a comparative income statement with horizontal analysis, indicating the increase (decrease) for 2008 when compared with 2007. Round to one decimal place.
b. ➤ What conclusions can be drawn from the horizontal analysis?

EX 17-6
Current position analysis

obj. 2

✓ *a. 2008 working capital,*
$1,265,000

The following data were taken from the balance sheet of Outdoor Suppliers Company:

	Dec. 31, 2008	Dec. 31, 2007
Cash	$325,000	$300,000
Marketable securities	270,000	256,000
Accounts and notes receivable (net)	440,000	430,000
Inventories	675,000	557,000
Prepaid expenses	130,000	81,000
Accounts and notes payable (short-term)	425,000	450,000
Accrued liabilities	150,000	130,000

a. Determine for each year (1) the working capital, (2) the current ratio, and (3) the quick ratio. Round ratios to one decimal place.
b. ➤ What conclusions can be drawn from these data as to the company's ability to meet its currently maturing debts?

EX 17-7
Current position analysis

obj. 2

✓ *a. (1) Dec. 25, 2004*
current ratio, 1.2

PepsiCo, Inc., the parent company of Frito-Lay snack foods and Pepsi beverages, had the following current assets and current liabilities at the end of two recent years:

	Dec. 31, 2005 (in millions)	Dec. 25, 2004 (in millions)
Cash and cash equivalents	$1,716	$1,280
Short-term investments, at cost	3,166	2,165
Accounts and notes receivable, net	3,261	2,999
Inventories	1,693	1,541
Prepaid expenses and other current assets	618	654
Short-term obligations	2,889	1,054
Accounts payable and other current liabilities	5,971	5,999
Income taxes payable	546	99

a. Determine the (1) current ratio and (2) quick ratio for both years. Round to one decimal place.

b. ➤ What conclusions can you draw from these data?

EX 17-8
Current position analysis
obj. 2

The bond indenture for the 20-year, 11% debenture bonds dated January 2, 2007, required working capital of $560,000, a current ratio of 1.5, and a quick ratio of 1.2 at the end of each calendar year until the bonds mature. At December 31, 2008, the three measures were computed as follows:

1. Current assets:

Cash	$190,000
Marketable securities	95,000
Accounts and notes receivable (net)	171,000
Inventories	20,000
Prepaid expenses	4,500
Intangible assets	55,000
Property, plant & equipment	65,000
Total current assets (net)	$600,500

Current liabilities:

Accounts and short-term notes payable	$250,000
Accrued liabilities	150,000
Total current liabilities	400,000
Working capital	$200,500

2. Current Ratio = 1.50 ($600,500/$400,000)
3. Quick Ratio = 2.04 ($511,000/$250,000)

a. List the errors in the determination of the three measures of current position analysis.

b. ➤ Is the company satisfying the terms of the bond indenture?

EX 17-9
Accounts receivable analysis
obj. 2

✓a. Accounts receivable turnover, 2008, 6.9

The following data are taken from the financial statements of Creekside Technology Inc. Terms of all sales are 2/10, n/60.

	2008	2007	2006
Accounts receivable, end of year	$ 75,452	$ 85,500	$81,624
Monthly average accounts receivable (net)	78,261	80,645	—
Net sales	540,000	500,000	—

a. Determine for each year (1) the accounts receivable turnover and (2) the number of days' sales in receivables. Round to nearest dollar and one decimal place.

b. ➤ What conclusions can be drawn from these data concerning accounts receivable and credit policies?

EX 17-10
Accounts receivable analysis
obj. 2

REAL WORLD

✓a. (1) May's accounts receivable turnover, 7.1

The May Department Stores Company (Marshall Field's, Hecht's, Lord & Taylor) and Federated Department Stores, Inc. (Macy's and Bloomingdale's) are two of the largest department store chains in the United States. Both companies offer credit to their customers through their own credit card operations. Information from the financial statements for both companies for two recent years is as follows (all numbers are in millions):

	May	Federated
Merchandise sales	$14,441	$15,630
Credit card receivables—beginning	2,294	3,418
Credit card receivables—ending	1,788	3,213

a. Determine the (1) accounts receivable turnover and (2) the number of days' sales in receivables for both companies. Round to one decimal place.

b. ➤ Compare the two companies with regard to their credit card policies.

EX 17-11
Inventory analysis

obj. 2

✓ *a. Inventory turnover,*
current year, 7.5

The following data were extracted from the income statement of Clear View Systems Inc.:

	Current Year	Preceding Year
Sales	$756,000	$950,760
Beginning inventories	67,200	44,000
Cost of goods sold	492,000	528,200
Ending inventories	64,000	67,200

a. Determine for each year (1) the inventory turnover and (2) the number of days' sales in inventory. Round to nearest dollar and one decimal place.

b. ⬛⬛⬛➤ What conclusions can be drawn from these data concerning the inventories?

EX 17-12
Inventory analysis

obj. 2

REAL WORLD

✓ *a. Dell inventory*
turnover, 88.2

Dell Inc. and Hewlett-Packard Company (HP) compete with each other in the personal computer market. Dell's strategy is to assemble computers to customer orders, rather than for inventory. Thus, for example, Dell will build and deliver a computer within four days of a customer entering an order on a Web page. Hewlett-Packard, on the other hand, builds some computers prior to receiving an order, then sells from this inventory once an order is received. Below is selected financial information for both companies from a recent year's financial statements (in millions):

	Dell Inc.	Hewlett-Packard Company
Sales	$55,908	$86,696
Cost of goods sold	45,620	66,440
Inventory, beginning of period	459	7,071
Inventory, end of period	576	6,877

a. Determine for both companies (1) the inventory turnover and (2) the number of days' sales in inventory. Round to one decimal place.

b. ⬛⬛⬛➤ Interpret the inventory ratios by considering Dell's and Hewlett-Packard's operating strategies.

EX 17-13
Ratio of liabilities to stockholders' equity and number of times interest charges earned

obj. 2

✓ *a. Ratio of liabilities to stockholders' equity, Dec. 31, 2008, 0.5*

The following data were taken from the financial statements of Quality Construction Inc. for December 31, 2008 and 2007:

	December 31, 2008	December 31, 2007
Accounts payable	$ 240,000	$ 224,000
Current maturities of serial bonds payable	320,000	320,000
Serial bonds payable, 10%, issued 2004, due 2014	1,600,000	1,920,000
Common stock, $1 par value	160,000	160,000
Paid-in capital in excess of par	800,000	800,000
Retained earnings	3,404,800	2,560,000

The income before income tax was $844,800 and $537,600 for the years 2008 and 2007, respectively.

a. Determine the ratio of liabilities to stockholders' equity at the end of each year. Round to one decimal place.

b. Determine the number of times the bond interest charges are earned during the year for both years. Round to one decimal place.

c. ⬛⬛⬛➤ What conclusions can be drawn from these data as to the company's ability to meet its currently maturing debts?

EX 17-14
Ratio of liabilities to stockholders' equity and number of times interest charges earned

obj. 2

Hasbro and Mattel, Inc., are the two largest toy companies in North America. Condensed liabilities and stockholders' equity from a recent balance sheet are shown for each company as follows:

✓ a. Hasbro, 1.0

	Hasbro	Mattel, Inc.
Current liabilities	$1,148,611,000	$1,727,171,000
Long-term debt	302,698,000	400,000,000
Deferred liabilities	149,627,000	243,509,000
Total liabilities	$1,600,936,000	$2,370,680,000
Shareholders' equity:		
Common stock, $0.50 par value	$ 104,847,000	$ 441,369,000
Additional paid-in capital	380,745,000	1,594,332,000
Retained earnings	1,721,209,000	1,093,288,000
Accumulated other comprehensive loss		
and other equity items	82,290,000	(269,828,000)
Treasury stock, at cost	(649,367,000)	(473,349,000)
Total stockholders' equity	$1,639,724,000	$2,385,812,000
Total liabilities and stockholders' equity	$3,240,660,000	$4,756,492,000

The income from operations and interest expense from the income statement for both companies were as follows:

	Hasbro	Mattel, Inc.
Income from operations	$293,012,000	$730,817,000
Interest expense	31,698,000	77,764,000

a. Determine the ratio of liabilities to stockholders' equity for both companies. Round to one decimal place.
b. Determine the number of times interest charges are earned for both companies. Round to one decimal place.
c. Interpret the ratio differences between the two companies.

EX 17-15
Ratio of liabilities to stockholders' equity and ratio of fixed assets to long-term liabilities

obj. 2

✓ a. H.J. Heinz, 3.1

Recent balance sheet information for two companies in the food industry, H.J. Heinz Company and The Hershey Company, are as follows (in thousands of dollars):

	H.J. Heinz	Hershey
Net property, plant, and equipment	$2,163,938	$1,659,138
Current liabilities	2,587,068	1,518,223
Long-term debt	4,121,984	942,755
Other liabilities (pensions, deferred taxes)	1,266,093	813,182
Stockholders' equity	2,602,573	1,021,076

a. Determine the ratio of liabilities to stockholders' equity for both companies. Round to one decimal place.
b. Determine the ratio of fixed assets to long-term liabilities for both companies. Round to one decimal place.
c. Interpret the ratio differences between the two companies.

EX 17-16
Ratio of net sales to assets

obj. 3

✓ a. YRC Worldwide, 1.9

Three major segments of the transportation industry are motor carriers, such as YRC Worldwide; railroads, such as Union Pacific; and transportation arrangement services, such as C.H. Robinson Worldwide Inc. Recent financial statement information for these three companies is shown as follows (in thousands of dollars):

	YRC Worldwide	Union Pacific	C.H. Robinson Worldwide
Net sales	$6,767,485	$12,215,000	$4,341,538
Average total assets	3,545,199	34,041,500	994,423

a. Determine the ratio of net sales to assets for all three companies. Round to one decimal place.
b. Assume that the ratio of net sales to assets for each company represents their respective industry segment. Interpret the differences in the ratio of net sales to assets in terms of the operating characteristics of each of the respective segments.

EX 17-17
Profitability ratios
obj. 3

✓ *a. Rate earned on total assets, 2008, 11.6%*

The following selected data were taken from the financial statements of Berry Group Inc. for December 31, 2008, 2007, and 2006:

	December 31, 2008	December 31, 2007	December 31, 2006
Total assets	$1,160,000	$1,040,000	$880,000
Notes payable (10% interest)	150,000	150,000	150,000
Common stock	360,000	360,000	360,000
Preferred $8 stock, $100 par			
(no change during year)	160,000	160,000	160,000
Retained earnings	426,900	327,200	205,000

The 2008 net income was $112,500, and the 2007 net income was $135,000. No dividends on common stock were declared between 2006 and 2008.

a. Determine the rate earned on total assets, the rate earned on stockholders' equity, and the rate earned on common stockholders' equity for the years 2007 and 2008. Round to one decimal place.
b. ⬛⬛⬛▶ What conclusions can be drawn from these data as to the company's profitability?

EX 17-18
Profitability ratios
obj. 3

✓ *a. 2005 rate earned on total assets, 6.0%*

Ann Taylor Retail, Inc., sells professional women's apparel through company-owned retail stores. Recent financial information for Ann Taylor is provided below (all numbers in thousands):

	Fiscal Year Ended	
	Jan. 28, 2006	Jan. 29, 2005
Net income	$81,872	$63,276
Interest expense	2,083	3,641

	Jan. 28, 2006	Jan. 29, 2005	Jan. 31, 2004
Total assets	$1,492,906	$1,327,338	$1,256,397
Total stockholders' equity	1,034,482	926,744	818,856

Assume the apparel industry average rate earned on total assets is 8.2%, and the average rate earned on stockholders' equity is 16.7% for fiscal 2005.

a. Determine the rate earned on total assets for Ann Taylor for the fiscal years ended January 28, 2006, and January 29, 2005. Round to one digit after the decimal place.
b. Determine the rate earned on stockholders' equity for Ann Taylor for the fiscal years ended January 28, 2006, and January 29, 2005. Round to one decimal place.
c. ⬛⬛⬛▶ Evaluate the two-year trend for the profitability ratios determined in (a) and (b).
d. ⬛⬛⬛▶ Evaluate Ann Taylor's profit performance relative to the industry.

EX 17-19
Six measures of solvency or profitability
objs. 2, 3

✓ *c. Ratio of net sales to assets, 1.5*

The following data were taken from the financial statements of Bendax Enterprises Inc. for the current fiscal year. Assuming that long-term investments totaled $240,000 throughout the year and that total assets were $2,525,000 at the beginning of the year, determine the following: (a) ratio of fixed assets to long-term liabilities, (b) ratio of liabilities to stockholders' equity, (c) ratio of net sales to assets, (d) rate earned on total assets, (e) rate earned on stockholders' equity, and (f) rate earned on common stockholders' equity. Round to one decimal place.

Property, plant, and equipment (net)		$1,200,000
Liabilities:		
Current liabilities	$ 60,000	
Mortgage note payable, 8%, issued 1997, due 2013	825,000	
Total liabilities		$ 885,000

Stockholders' equity:			
Preferred $9 stock, $100 par (no change during year) ...			$ 250,000
Common stock, $20 par (no change during year)			800,000
Retained earnings:			
Balance, beginning of year	$600,000		
Net income	216,000	$816,000	
Preferred dividends	$ 22,500		
Common dividends	57,600	80,100	
Balance, end of year			735,900
Total stockholders' equity			$1,785,900
Net sales			$3,600,000
Interest expense			$ 66,000

EX 17-20
Six measures of solvency or profitability
objs. 2, 3

✓ *d. Price-earnings ratio, 16.1*

The balance sheet for Chaney Resources Inc. at the end of the current fiscal year indicated the following:

Bonds payable, 10% (issued in 1995, due in 2015)	$2,250,000
Preferred $25 stock, $200 par	500,000
Common stock, $10 par	2,500,000

Income before income tax was $625,000, and income taxes were $175,000 for the current year. Cash dividends paid on common stock during the current year totaled $125,000. The common stock was selling for $25 per share at the end of the year. Determine each of the following: (a) number of times bond interest charges are earned, (b) number of times preferred dividends are earned, (c) earnings per share on common stock, (d) price-earnings ratio, (e) dividends per share of common stock, and (f) dividend yield. Round to one decimal place except earnings per share, which should be rounded to two decimal places.

EX 17-21
Earnings per share, price-earnings ratio, dividend yield
obj. 3

✓ *b. Price-earnings ratio, 14.8*

The following information was taken from the financial statements of Royer Medical Inc. for December 31 of the current fiscal year:

Common stock, $5 par value (no change during the year)	$1,500,000
Preferred $5 stock, $50 par (no change during the year)	450,000

The net income was $450,000, and the declared dividends on the common stock were $75,000 for the current year. The market price of the common stock is $20 per share.

For the common stock, determine (a) the earnings per share, (b) the price-earnings ratio, (c) the dividends per share, and (d) the dividend yield. Round to one decimal place except earnings per share, which should be rounded to two decimal places.

EX 17-22
Earnings per share
obj. 3

✓ *b. Earnings per share on common stock, $3.00*

The net income reported on the income statement of Ground Hog Co. was $1,250,000. There were 250,000 shares of $40 par common stock and 50,000 shares of $10 preferred stock outstanding throughout the current year. The income statement included two extraordinary items: a $360,000 gain from condemnation of land and a $235,000 loss arising from flood damage, both after applicable income tax. Determine the per share figures for common stock for (a) income before extraordinary items and (b) net income.

EX 17-23
Price-earnings ratio; dividend yield
obj. 3

The table below shows the stock price, earnings per share, and dividends per share for three companies as of February 10, 2006:

	Price	Earnings per Share	Dividends per Share
Bank of America Corporation	$44.47	$4.15	$2.00
eBay Inc.	41.60	0.78	0.00
The Coca-Cola Company	41.19	2.04	1.12

a. Determine the price-earnings ratio and dividend yield for the three companies. Round to one decimal place.

b. Explain the differences in these ratios across the three companies.

Problems Series A

PR 17-1A
Horizontal analysis for income statement
obj. 1

✓1. Net sales, 25.1% increase

For 2008, Doane Inc. reported its most significant increase in net income in years. At the end of the year, Jeff Newton, the president, is presented with the following condensed comparative income statement:

Doane Inc.
Comparative Income Statement
For the Years Ended December 31, 2008 and 2007

	2008	2007
Sales	$91,500	$73,200
Sales returns and allowances	1,440	1,200
Net sales	$90,060	$72,000
Cost of goods sold	50,400	42,000
Gross profit	$39,660	$30,000
Selling expenses	$16,560	$14,400
Administrative expenses	10,800	9,600
Total operating expenses	$27,360	$24,000
Income from operations	$12,300	$ 6,000
Other income	600	600
Income before income tax	$12,900	$ 6,600
Income tax expense	2,880	1,440
Net income	$10,020	$ 5,160

Instructions

1. Prepare a comparative income statement with horizontal analysis for the two-year period, using 2007 as the base year. Round to one decimal place.
2. To the extent the data permit, comment on the significant relationships revealed by the horizontal analysis prepared in (1).

PR 17-2A
Vertical analysis for income statement
obj. 1

✓1. Net income, 2007, 8.0%

For 2008, Dusan Water Supplies Inc. initiated a sales promotion campaign that included the expenditure of an additional $21,000 for advertising. At the end of the year, Ivana Novatna, the president, is presented with the following condensed comparative income statement:

Dusan Water Supplies Inc.
Comparative Income Statement
For the Years Ended December 31, 2008 and 2007

	2008	2007
Sales	$255,000	$214,000
Sales returns and allowances	5,000	4,000
Net sales	$250,000	$210,000
Cost of goods sold	142,500	121,800
Gross profit	$107,500	$ 88,200
Selling expenses	$100,000	$ 50,400
Administrative expenses	20,000	16,800
Total operating expenses	$120,000	$ 67,200
Income from operations	$ (12,500)	$ 21,000
Other income	6,250	4,200
Income before income tax	$ (6,250)	$ 25,200
Income tax expense (benefit)	(2,500)	8,400
Net income (loss)	$ (3,750)	$ 16,800

Instructions

1. Prepare a comparative income statement for the two-year period, presenting an analysis of each item in relationship to net sales for each of the years. Round to one decimal place.
2. To the extent the data permit, comment on the significant relationships revealed by the vertical analysis prepared in (1).

PR 17-3A
Effect of transactions on current position analysis

obj. 2

✓1. c. Quick ratio, 1.4

Data pertaining to the current position of Tsali Industries, Inc., are as follows:

Cash	$195,000
Marketable securities	92,500
Accounts and notes receivable (net)	293,000
Inventories	357,500
Prepaid expenses	15,000
Accounts payable	295,000
Notes payable (short-term)	92,000
Accrued expenses	42,500

Instructions

1. Compute (a) the working capital, (b) the current ratio, and (c) the quick ratio. Round to one decimal place.
2. List the following captions on a sheet of paper:

Transaction   Working Capital   Current Ratio   Quick Ratio

Compute the working capital, the current ratio, and the quick ratio after each of the following transactions, and record the results in the appropriate columns. Consider each transaction separately and assume that only that transaction affects the data given above. Round to one decimal place.
a. Sold marketable securities at no gain or loss, $37,500.
b. Paid accounts payable, $84,000.
c. Purchased goods on account, $55,000.
d. Paid notes payable, $32,500.
e. Declared a cash dividend, $38,000.
f. Declared a common stock dividend on common stock, $21,500.
g. Borrowed cash from bank on a long-term note, $185,000.
h. Received cash on account, $93,500.
i. Issued additional shares of stock for cash, $175,000.
j. Paid cash for prepaid expenses, $15,000.

PR 17-4A
Nineteen measures of solvency and profitability

objs. 2, 3

✓9. Ratio of liabilities to stockholders' equity, 0.5

The comparative financial statements of Triad Images Inc. are as follows. The market price of Triad Images Inc. common stock was $55 on December 31, 2008.

Triad Images Inc.
Comparative Retained Earnings Statement
For the Years Ended December 31, 2008 and 2007

	Dec. 31, 2008	Dec. 31, 2007
Retained earnings, January 1	$1,006,500	$ 781,500
Add net income for year	430,000	277,500
Total	$1,436,500	$1,059,000
Deduct dividends:		
On preferred stock	$ 12,500	$ 12,500
On common stock	40,000	40,000
Total	$ 52,500	$ 52,500
Retained earnings, December 31	$1,384,000	$1,006,500

(continued)

Triad Images Inc.
Comparative Income Statement
For the Years Ended December 31, 2008 and 2007

	2008	2007
Sales	$3,395,000	$3,062,500
Sales returns and allowances	35,000	22,500
Net sales	$3,360,000	$3,040,000
Cost of goods sold	1,500,000	1,437,500
Gross profit	$1,860,000	$1,602,500
Selling expenses	$ 726,000	$ 718,750
Administrative expenses	486,000	475,000
Total operating expenses	$1,212,000	$1,193,750
Income from operations	$ 648,000	$ 408,750
Other income	48,000	37,500
	$ 696,000	$ 446,250
Other expense (interest)	98,000	50,000
Income before income tax	$ 598,000	$ 396,250
Income tax expense	168,000	118,750
Net income	$ 430,000	$ 277,500

Triad Images Inc.
Comparative Balance Sheet
December 31, 2008 and 2007

	Dec. 31, 2008	Dec. 31, 2007
Assets		
Current assets:		
Cash	$ 132,000	$ 120,000
Marketable securities	387,000	157,500
Accounts receivable (net)	260,000	196,500
Inventories	425,000	332,500
Prepaid expenses	27,500	35,000
Total current assets	$1,231,500	$ 841,500
Long-term investments	319,500	250,000
Property, plant, and equipment (net)	2,575,000	2,000,000
Total assets	$4,126,000	$3,091,500
Liabilities		
Current liabilities	$ 342,000	$ 285,000
Long-term liabilities:		
Mortgage note payable, 8%, due 2013	$ 600,000	—
Bonds payable, 10%, due 2017	500,000	$ 500,000
Total long-term liabilities	$1,100,000	$ 500,000
Total liabilities	$1,442,000	$ 785,000
Stockholders' Equity		
Preferred $2.50 stock, $100 par	$ 500,000	$ 500,000
Common stock, $20 par	800,000	800,000
Retained earnings	1,384,000	1,006,500
Total stockholders' equity	$2,684,000	$2,306,500
Total liabilities and stockholders' equity	$4,126,000	$3,091,500

Instructions

Determine the following measures for 2008, rounding to one decimal place:

1. Working capital
2. Current ratio
3. Quick ratio
4. Accounts receivable turnover
5. Number of days' sales in receivables
6. Inventory turnover
7. Number of days' sales in inventory
8. Ratio of fixed assets to long-term liabilities

9. Ratio of liabilities to stockholders' equity
10. Number of times interest charges earned
11. Number of times preferred dividends earned
12. Ratio of net sales to assets
13. Rate earned on total assets
14. Rate earned on stockholders' equity
15. Rate earned on common stockholders' equity
16. Earnings per share on common stock
17. Price-earnings ratio
18. Dividends per share of common stock
19. Dividend yield

PR 17-5A
Solvency and profitability trend analysis
objs. 2, 3

Shore Company has provided the following comparative information:

	2008	2007	2006	2005	2004
Net income	$ 42,000	$ 70,000	$ 140,000	$ 210,000	$ 210,000
Interest expense	142,800	133,000	119,000	112,000	105,000
Income tax expense	12,600	21,000	42,000	63,000	63,000
Total assets (ending balance)	2,240,000	2,100,000	1,890,000	1,680,000	1,400,000
Total stockholders' equity (ending balance)	812,000	770,000	700,000	560,000	350,000
Average total assets	2,170,000	1,995,000	1,785,000	1,540,000	1,260,000
Average stockholders' equity	791,000	735,000	630,000	455,000	315,000

You have been asked to evaluate the historical performance of the company over the last five years.

Selected industry ratios have remained relatively steady at the following levels for the last five years:

	2004–2008
Rate earned on total assets	14%
Rate earned on stockholders' equity	20%
Number of times interest charges earned	3.0
Ratio of liabilities to stockholders' equity	2.0

Instructions
1. Prepare four line graphs with the ratio on the vertical axis and the years on the horizontal axis for the following four ratios (rounded to one decimal place):
   a. Rate earned on total assets
   b. Rate earned on stockholders' equity
   c. Number of times interest charges earned
   d. Ratio of liabilities to stockholders' equity
   Display both the company ratio and the industry benchmark on each graph. That is, each graph should have two lines.
2. Prepare an analysis of the graphs in (1).

Problems Series B

PR 17-1B
Horizontal analysis for income statement
obj. 1

For 2008, Phoenix Technology Company reported its most significant decline in net income in years. At the end of the year, Hai Chow, the president, is presented with the following condensed comparative income statement:

✓ *1. Net sales, 11.8%
increase*

Phoenix Technology Company
Comparative Income Statement
For the Years Ended December 31, 2008 and 2007

	2008	2007
Sales	$385,000	$343,200
Sales returns and allowances	4,800	3,200
Net sales	$380,200	$340,000
Cost of goods sold	180,000	144,000
Gross profit	$200,200	$196,000
Selling expenses	$ 87,400	$ 76,000
Administrative expenses	30,000	24,000
Total operating expenses	$117,400	$100,000
Income from operations	$ 82,800	$ 96,000
Other income	1,600	1,600
Income before income tax	$ 84,400	$ 97,600
Income tax expense	36,800	32,000
Net income	$ 47,600	$ 65,600

Instructions
1. Prepare a comparative income statement with horizontal analysis for the two-year period, using 2007 as the base year. Round to one decimal place.
2. ➡ To the extent the data permit, comment on the significant relationships revealed by the horizontal analysis prepared in (1).

PR 17-2B
*Vertical analysis for
income statement*

obj. 1

✓ *1. Net income, 2008,
20.0%*

For 2008, Acedia Technology Company initiated a sales promotion campaign that included the expenditure of an additional $10,000 for advertising. At the end of the year, Gordon Kincaid, the president, is presented with the following condensed comparative income statement:

Acedia Technology Company
Comparative Income Statement
For the Years Ended December 31, 2008 and 2007

	2008	2007
Sales	$755,000	$676,000
Sales returns and allowances	5,000	6,000
Net sales	$750,000	$670,000
Cost of goods sold	292,500	274,700
Gross profit	$457,500	$395,300
Selling expenses	$172,500	$160,800
Administrative expenses	82,500	80,400
Total operating expenses	$255,000	$241,200
Income from operations	$202,500	$154,100
Other income	7,500	6,700
Income before income tax	$210,000	$160,800
Income tax expense	60,000	53,600
Net income	$150,000	$107,200

Instructions
1. Prepare a comparative income statement for the two-year period, presenting an analysis of each item in relationship to net sales for each of the years. Round to one decimal place.
2. ➡ To the extent the data permit, comment on the significant relationships revealed by the vertical analysis prepared in (1).

PR 17-3B
*Effect of transactions on
current position analysis*

obj. 2

✓ *1. b. Current ratio, 2.1*

Data pertaining to the current position of Spruce Pine Medical Company are as follows:

Cash	$384,000
Marketable securities	176,000
Accounts and notes receivable (net)	608,000
Inventories	792,000
Prepaid expenses	48,000
Accounts payable	624,000
Notes payable (short-term)	240,000
Accrued expenses	80,000

Instructions

1. Compute (a) the working capital, (b) the current ratio, and (c) the quick ratio. Round to one decimal place.
2. List the following captions on a sheet of paper:

Transaction	Working Capital	Current Ratio	Quick Ratio

Compute the working capital, the current ratio, and the quick ratio after each of the following transactions, and record the results in the appropriate columns. Consider each transaction separately and assume that only that transaction affects the data given above. Round to one decimal place.

a. Sold marketable securities at no gain or loss, $65,000.
b. Paid accounts payable, $90,000.
c. Purchased goods on account, $120,000.
d. Paid notes payable, $65,000.
e. Declared a cash dividend, $32,500.
f. Declared a common stock dividend on common stock, $34,000.
g. Borrowed cash from bank on a long-term note, $160,000.
h. Received cash on account, $125,000.
i. Issued additional shares of stock for cash, $425,000.
j. Paid cash for prepaid expenses, $16,000.

PR 17-4B
Nineteen measures of solvency and profitability
objs. 2, 3

✓ *5. Number of days' sales in receivables, 50.8*

The comparative financial statements of Dental Innovations Inc. are as follows. The market price of Dental Innovations Inc. common stock was $15 on December 31, 2008.

Dental Innovations Inc.
Comparative Retained Earnings Statement
For the Years Ended December 31, 2008 and 2007

	Dec. 31, 2008	Dec. 31, 2007
Retained earnings, January 1	$265,000	$ 31,000
Add net income for year	321,500	244,000
Total	$586,500	$275,000
Deduct dividends:		
On preferred stock	$ 10,000	$ 5,000
On common stock	7,000	5,000
Total	$ 17,000	$ 10,000
Retained earnings, December 31	$569,500	$265,000

Dental Innovations Inc.
Comparative Income Statement
For the Years Ended December 31, 2008 and 2007

	2008	2007
Sales	$1,055,000	$966,000
Sales returns and allowances	5,000	6,000
Net sales	$1,050,000	$960,000
Cost of goods sold	300,000	312,000
Gross profit	$ 750,000	$648,000
Selling expenses	$ 202,500	$220,000
Administrative expenses	146,250	132,000
Total operating expenses	$ 348,750	$352,000
Income from operations	$ 401,250	$296,000
Other income	15,000	12,000
	$ 416,250	$308,000
Other expense (interest)	64,000	40,000
Income before income tax	$ 352,250	$268,000
Income tax expense	30,750	24,000
Net income	$ 321,500	$244,000

(continued)

Dental Innovations Inc.
Comparative Balance Sheet
December 31, 2008 and 2007

	Dec. 31, 2008	Dec. 31, 2007
Assets		
Current assets:		
Cash	$ 165,000	$ 101,500
Marketable securities	335,000	205,500
Accounts receivable (net)	160,000	132,000
Inventories	67,500	41,500
Prepaid expenses	27,000	14,500
Total current assets	$ 754,500	$ 495,000
Long-term investments	310,000	160,000
Property, plant, and equipment (net)	950,000	610,000
Total assets	$2,014,500	$1,265,000
Liabilities		
Current liabilities	$ 225,000	$ 200,000
Long-term liabilities:		
Mortgage note payable, 10%, due 2013	$ 240,000	—
Bonds payable, 8%, due 2017	500,000	$ 500,000
Total long-term liabilities	$ 740,000	$ 500,000
Total liabilities	$ 965,000	$ 700,000
Stockholders' Equity		
Preferred $2.50 stock, $50 par	$ 200,000	$ 100,000
Common stock, $10 par	280,000	200,000
Retained earnings	569,500	265,000
Total stockholders' equity	$1,049,500	$ 565,000
Total liabilities and stockholders' equity	$2,014,500	$1,265,000

Instructions

Determine the following measures for 2008, rounding to one decimal place:

1. Working capital
2. Current ratio
3. Quick ratio
4. Accounts receivable turnover
5. Number of days' sales in receivables
6. Inventory turnover
7. Number of days' sales in inventory
8. Ratio of fixed assets to long-term liabilities
9. Ratio of liabilities to stockholders' equity
10. Number of times interest charges earned
11. Number of times preferred dividends earned
12. Ratio of net sales to assets
13. Rate earned on total assets
14. Rate earned on stockholders' equity
15. Rate earned on common stockholders' equity
16. Earnings per share on common stock
17. Price-earnings ratio
18. Dividends per share of common stock
19. Dividend yield

PR 17-5B
Solvency and profitability
trend analysis

objs. 2, 3

Van DeKamp Company has provided the following comparative information:

	2008	2007	2006	2005	2004
Net income	$1,815,000	$1,200,000	$ 900,000	$ 600,000	$ 450,000
Interest expense	271,800	234,000	202,500	162,000	135,000
Income tax expense	635,250	420,000	315,000	210,000	157,500
Total assets (ending balance)	9,035,000	6,800,000	5,250,000	3,900,000	3,000,000
Total stockholders' equity (ending balance)	6,015,000	4,200,000	3,000,000	2,100,000	1,500,000
Average total assets	7,917,500	6,025,000	4,575,000	3,450,000	2,700,000
Average stockholders' equity	5,107,500	3,600,000	2,550,000	1,800,000	1,350,000

You have been asked to evaluate the historical performance of the company over the last five years.

Selected industry ratios have remained relatively steady at the following levels for the last five years:

	2004–2008
Rate earned on total assets	13%
Rate earned on stockholders' equity	20%
Number of times interest charges earned	4.0
Ratio of liabilities to stockholders' equity	1.3

Instructions

1. Prepare four line graphs with the ratio on the vertical axis and the years on the horizontal axis for the following four ratios (rounded to one decimal place):
   a. Rate earned on total assets
   b. Rate earned on stockholders' equity
   c. Number of times interest charges earned
   d. Ratio of liabilities to stockholders' equity
   Display both the company ratio and the industry benchmark on each graph. That is, each graph should have two lines.
2. Prepare an analysis of the graphs in (1).

Williams-Sonoma, Inc., Problem

FINANCIAL STATEMENT ANALYSIS

The financial statements for Williams-Sonoma, Inc., are presented in Appendix D at the end of the text. The following additional information (in thousands) is available:

Accounts receivable at February 1, 2004	$ 31,573
Inventories at February 1, 2004	404,100
Total assets at February 1, 2004	1,470,735
Stockholders' equity at February 1, 2004	804,591

Instructions

1. Determine the following measures for the fiscal years ended January 29, 2006 and January 30, 2005, rounding to one decimal place.
   a. Working capital
   b. Current ratio
   c. Quick ratio
   d. Accounts receivable turnover
   e. Number of days' sales in receivables
   f. Inventory turnover
   g. Number of days' sales in inventory
   h. Ratio of liabilities to stockholders' equity
   i. Ratio of net sales to average total assets
   j. Rate earned on average total assets
   k. Rate earned on average common stockholders' equity
   l. Price-earnings ratio, assuming that the market price was $40.62 per share on January 29, 2006 and $34.53 on January 30, 2005.
   m. Percentage relationship of net income to net sales
2. What conclusions can be drawn from these analyses?

Special Activities

SA 17-1
Analysis of financing corporate growth

Assume that the president of Ice Mountain Brewery made the following statement in the Annual Report to Shareholders:

"The founding family and majority shareholders of the company do not believe in using debt to finance future growth. The founding family learned from hard experience during Prohibition and the Great Depression that debt can cause loss of flexibility and eventual loss of corporate control. The company will not place itself at such risk. As such, all future growth will be financed either by stock sales to the public or by internally generated resources."

As a public shareholder of this company, how would you respond to this policy?

SA 17-2
Receivables and inventory turnover

Roan Mountain Fitness Company has completed its fiscal year on December 31, 2008. The auditor, Steve Berry, has approached the CFO, Tony Brubaker, regarding the year-end receivables and inventory levels of Roan Mountain Fitness. The following conversation takes place:

Steve: We are beginning our audit of Roan Mountain Fitness and have prepared ratio analyses to determine if there have been significant changes in operations or financial position. This helps us guide the audit process. This analysis indicates that the inventory turnover has decreased from 4.5 to 2.1, while the accounts receivable turnover has decreased from 10 to 6. I was wondering if you could explain this change in operations.

Tony: There is little need for concern. The inventory represents computers that we were unable to sell during the holiday buying season. We are confident, however, that we will be able to sell these computers as we move into the next fiscal year.

Steve: What gives you this confidence?

Tony: We will increase our advertising and provide some very attractive price concessions to move these machines. We have no choice. Newer technology is already out there, and we have to unload this inventory.

Steve: . . . and the receivables?

Tony: As you may be aware, the company is under tremendous pressure to expand sales and profits. As a result, we lowered our credit standards to our commercial customers so that we would be able to sell products to a broader customer base. As a result of this policy change, we have been able to expand sales by 35%.

Steve: Your responses have not been reassuring to me.

Tony: I'm a little confused. Assets are good, right? Why don't you look at our current ratio? It has improved, hasn't it? I would think that you would view that very favorably.

Why is Steve concerned about the inventory and accounts receivable turnover ratios and Tony's responses to them? What action may Steve need to take? How would you respond to Tony's last comment?

SA 17-3
Vertical analysis

The condensed income statements through income from operations for Dell Inc. and Apple Computer, Inc., are reproduced below for recent fiscal years (numbers in millions of dollars).

	Dell Inc.	Apple Computer, Inc.
Sales (net)	$55,908	$13,931
Cost of sales	45,958	9,888
Gross profit	$ 9,950	$ 4,043
Selling, general, and administrative expenses	$ 5,140	$ 1,859
Research and development	463	534
Operating expenses	$ 5,603	$ 2,393
Income from operations	$ 4,347	$ 1,650

Prepare comparative common-size statements, rounding percents to one decimal place. Interpret the analyses.

SA 17-4
Profitability and stockholder ratios

Ford Motor Company is the second largest automobile and truck manufacturer in the United States. In addition to manufacturing motor vehicles, Ford also provides vehicle-related financing, insurance, and leasing services. Historically, people purchase automobiles when the economy is strong and delay automobile purchases when the economy is faltering. For this reason, Ford is considered a cyclical company. This means that when the economy does well, Ford usually prospers, and when the economy is down, Ford usually suffers.

The following information is available for three recent years (in millions except per-share amounts):

	2005	2004	2003
Net income (loss)	$2,024	$3,487	$495
Preferred dividends	$0	$0	$0
Shares outstanding for computing earnings per share	1,846	1,830	1,832
Cash dividend per share	$0.40	$0.40	$0.40
Average total assets	$287,669	$308,032	$293,678
Average stockholders' equity	$14,501	$13,848	$8,532
Average stock price per share	$11.22	$14.98	$11.95

1. Calculate the following ratios for each year:
   a. Rate earned on total assets
   b. Rate earned on stockholders' equity
   c. Earnings per share
   d. Dividend yield
   e. Price-earnings ratio
2. What is the ratio of average liabilities to average stockholders' equity for 2005?
3. ▬▬▶ Why does Ford have so much leverage?
4. ▬▬▶ Explain the direction of the dividend yield and price-earnings ratio in light of Ford's profitability trend.

SA 17-5
Projecting financial statements

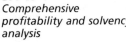

Go to Microsoft Corporation's Web site at **http://www.microsoft.com** and click on the "Investor Relations" area under "About Microsoft." Select the menu item "Stock Info and Analysis." Select the "What-if?" tool. With this tool, use horizontal and vertical information to create a full-year projection of the Microsoft income statement. Make the following assumptions:

Revenue growth	12%
Cost of goods sold as a percent of revenue	15%
Research and development growth	10%
Sales and marketing as a percent of sales	18%
General and administrative as a percent of sales	6%
Tax rate	32%
Diluted shares outstanding	12,000

SA 17-6
Comprehensive profitability and solvency analysis

Marriott International, Inc., and Hilton Hotels Corporation are two major owners and managers of lodging and resort properties in the United States. Abstracted income statement information for the two companies is as follows for a recent year:

	Marriott (in millions)	Hilton (in millions)
Operating profit before other expenses and interest	$ 477	$ 658
Other income (expenses)	318	(19)
Interest expense	(99)	(274)
Income before income taxes	$ 696	$ 365
Income tax expense	100	127
Net income	$ 596	$ 238

Balance sheet information is as follows:

	Marriott (in millions)	Hilton (in millions)
Total liabilities	$4,587	$5,674
Total stockholders' equity	4,081	2,568
Total liabilties and stockholders' equity	$8,668	$8,242

The average liabilities, stockholders' equity, and total assets were as follows:

	Marriott	Hilton
Average total liabilities	$4,210	$5,809
Average total stockholders' equity	3,960	2,404
Average total assets	8,423	8,213

1. Determine the following ratios for both companies (round to one decimal place after the whole percent):
   a. Rate earned on total assets
   b. Rate earned on total stockholders' equity
   c. Number of times interest charges are earned
   d. Ratio of liabilities to stockholders' equity
2. Analyze and compare the two companies, using the information in (1).

Answers to Self-Examination Questions

1. **A** Percentage analysis indicating the relationship of the component parts to the total in a financial statement, such as the relationship of current assets to total assets (20% to 100%) in the question, is called vertical analysis (answer A). Percentage analysis of increases and decreases in corresponding items in comparative financial statements is called horizontal analysis (answer B). An example of horizontal analysis would be the presentation of the amount of current assets in the preceding balance sheet, along with the amount of current assets at the end of the current year, with the increase or decrease in current assets between the periods expressed as a percentage. Profitability analysis (answer C) is the analysis of a firm's ability to earn income. Contribution margin analysis (answer D) is discussed in a later managerial accounting chapter.

2. **D** Various solvency measures, categorized as current position analysis, indicate a firm's ability to meet currently maturing obligations. Each measure contributes to the analysis of a firm's current position and is most useful when viewed with other measures and when compared with similar measures for other periods and for other firms. Working capital (answer A) is the excess of current assets over current liabilities; the current ratio (answer B) is the ratio of current assets to current liabilities; and the quick ratio (answer C) is the ratio of the sum of cash, receivables, and marketable securities to current liabilities.

3. **D** The ratio of current assets to current liabilities is usually called the current ratio (answer A). It is sometimes called the working capital ratio (answer B) or bankers' ratio (answer C).

4. **C** The ratio of the sum of cash, receivables, and marketable securities (sometimes called quick assets) to current liabilities is called the quick ratio (answer C) or acid-test ratio. The current ratio (answer A), working capital ratio (answer B), and bankers' ratio (answer D) are terms that describe the ratio of current assets to current liabilities.

5. **C** The number of days' sales in inventory (answer C), which is determined by dividing the average inventory by the average daily cost of goods sold, expresses the relationship between the cost of goods sold and inventory. It indicates the efficiency in the management of inventory. The working capital ratio (answer A) indicates the ability of the business to meet currently maturing obligations (debt). The quick ratio (answer B) indicates the "instant" debt-paying ability of the business. The ratio of fixed assets to long-term liabilities (answer D) indicates the margin of safety for long-term creditors.

chapter 18

Managerial Accounting Concepts and Principles

© GREG BROWN/WATERLOO COURIER/ASSOCIATED PRESS

objectives

After studying this chapter, you should be able to:

1 *Describe managerial accounting and the role of managerial accounting in a business.*

2 *Describe and illustrate the following costs: direct and indirect, direct materials, direct labor, factory overhead, and product and period costs.*

3 *Describe and illustrate the statement of cost of goods manufactured, income statement, and balance sheet for a manufacturing business.*

4 *Describe the uses of managerial accounting information.*

Washburn Guitars

Dan Donnegan, guitarist for the rock band *Disturbed*, captivates millions of fans each year playing his guitar. His guitar which was built by quality craftsmen at Washburn Guitars in Chicago. Washburn Guitars is no stranger to the music business. The company has been in business for over 120 years and is the guitar maker of choice for professional and amateur musicians.

Staying in business for 120 years requires a thorough understanding of how to manufacture high quality guitars. In addition, it requires knowledge of how to account for the costs of making guitars. For example, how much should Washburn charge for its guitars? The purchase price must be greater than the cost of producing the guitar, but how is the cost of producing the guitar determined? Moreover, how many guitars does the company have to sell in a year

to cover its costs? Would a new production facility be a good investment? How many employees should the company have working on each stage of the guitar manufacturing process?

All of these questions can be answered with the aid of managerial accounting information. In this chapter, we introduce cost concepts used in managerial accounting, which help answer questions like those above. We begin this chapter by describing managerial accounting and its relationship to financial accounting. Following this overview, we will describe the management process and the role of managerial accounting. We will also discuss characteristics of managerial accounting reports, various managerial accounting terms, and some of the uses of managerial accounting information.

Managerial Accounting

objective **1**

Describe managerial accounting and the role of managerial accounting in a business.

Managing a business isn't easy. Managers must make numerous decisions in operating a business efficiently and in preparing for the future. Managerial accounting provides much of the information used by managers in running a business. The following sections discuss the differences between financial and managerial accounting and the role of the managerial accountant in an organization. The remaining chapters of this text are dedicated to examining the various types of managerial accounting information that managers use in operating a business.

THE DIFFERENCES BETWEEN MANAGERIAL AND FINANCIAL ACCOUNTING

As we discussed in Chapter 1, accountants often divide accounting information into two types: financial and managerial. The diagram in Exhibit 1 illustrates the relationship between financial accounting and managerial accounting. Understanding this relationship is useful in understanding the information needs of management.

Financial accounting information is reported in statements that are useful for stakeholders, such as creditors, who are "outside" or external to the organization. Examples of such stakeholders include:

- Shareholders,
- Creditors,
- Government agencies, and
- The general public.

The management of a company also uses the financial statements in directing current operations and planning future operations. In planning future operations, management often begins by evaluating the results of past activities as reported in the financial state-

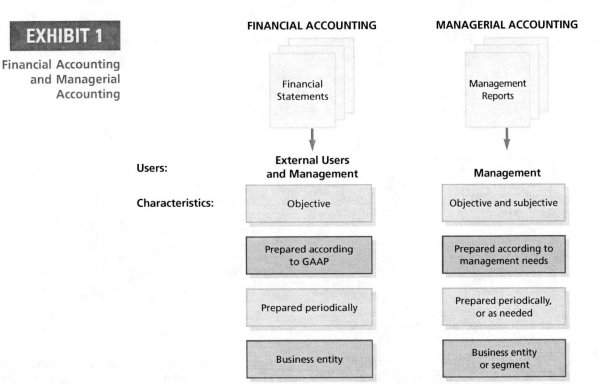

EXHIBIT 1

Financial Accounting
and Managerial
Accounting

ments. The financial statements objectively report the results of past operations at fixed periods and the financial condition of the business according to generally accepted accounting principles (GAAP).

Managerial accounting information meets the specific needs of a company's management. This information includes:

■ Historical data, which provide objective measures of past operations, and
■ Estimated data, which provide subjective estimates about future decisions.

Management uses both types of information in conducting daily operations, planning future operations, and developing overall business strategies. For example, subjective estimates in managerial accounting reports assist management in responding to business opportunities.

Unlike financial accounting statements, managerial accounting reports:

■ Are not prepared according to generally accepted accounting principles since only management uses the information;
■ Are prepared periodically, or at any time management needs information; and
■ Are prepared for the business entity as a whole or a segment of the entity, such as a division, product, project, or territory.

THE MANAGEMENT ACCOUNTANT IN THE ORGANIZATION

In most large organizations, departments or similar units are assigned responsibilities for specific functions or activities. This operating structure of an organization can be shown in an organization chart. Exhibit 2 is a partial organization chart for Callaway Golf Company, the manufacturer and distributor of Big Bertha® golf clubs.

The individual reporting units in an organization can be viewed as having either (1) line responsibilities or (2) staff responsibilities. A **line department** or unit is one directly involved in the basic objectives of the organization. For Callaway Golf, the

EXHIBIT 2   Partial Organizational Chart for Callaway Golf Company

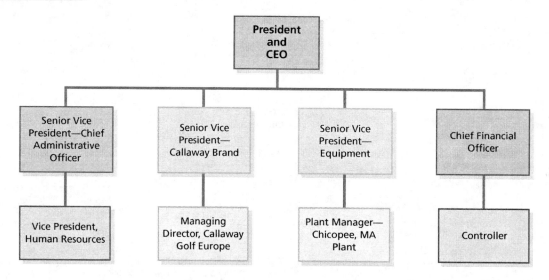

The terms *line* and *staff* may be applied to service organizations. For example, the line positions in a hospital would be the nurses, doctors, and other caregivers. Staff positions would include admissions and records. The line positions for a professional basketball team, such as the Boston Celtics, would be the basketball players and coaches, since they are directly involved in the basic objectives of the organization—playing professional basketball. Staff positions would include public relations, player development and recruiting, legal staff, and accounting. These positions serve and advise the players and coaches.

senior vice president of equipment and the manager of the Chicopee, Massachusetts, plant occupy line positions because they are responsible for manufacturing Callaway's products. Likewise, the senior vice president of the Callaway Brand and other sales managers are in line positions because they are directly responsible for generating revenues.

A **staff department** or unit is one that provides services, assistance, and advice to the departments with line or other staff responsibilities. A staff department has no direct authority over a line department. For example, the senior vice president—chief administrative officer and vice president of human resources are staff positions supporting the organization. In addition, the chief financial officer (sometimes called the vice president of finance) occupies a staff position, to which the controller reports. In most business organizations, the **controller** is the chief management accountant.

The controller's staff often consists of several management accountants. Each accountant is responsible for a specialized accounting function, such as systems and procedures, general accounting, budgets and budget analysis, special reports and analysis, taxes, and cost accounting.

Experience in managerial accounting is often an excellent training ground for senior management positions. This is not surprising, since accounting and finance bring an individual into contact with all phases of operations.

MANAGERIAL ACCOUNTING IN THE MANAGEMENT PROCESS

In its role as a staff department, managerial accounting supports management and the management process. The **management process** has five basic phases:

1. Planning
2. Directing
3. Controlling
4. Improving
5. Decision making

As shown in Exhibit 3, the five phases interact with each other as the basis for a company's strategies and operations. Management's actions in the management process are, to some extent, measured by the company's operating results.

EXHIBIT 3	The Management Process

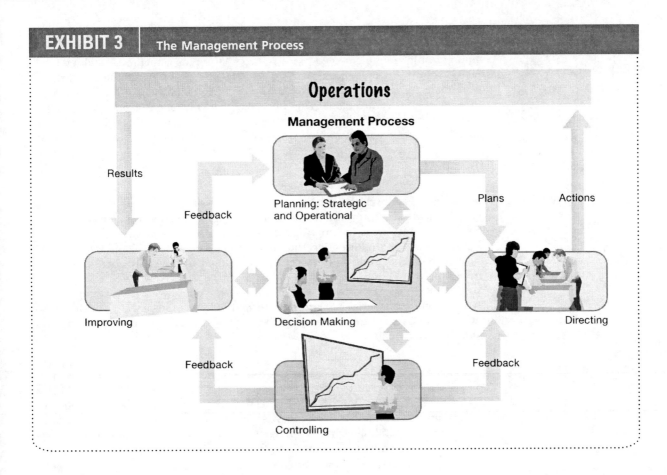

Operations

Management Process

Results

Feedback

Planning: Strategic and Operational

Plans

Actions

Improving

Decision Making

Directing

Feedback

Feedback

Controlling

Planning **Planning** is used by management to develop the company's **objectives (goals)** and to translate these objectives into courses of actions. For example, a company, as part of the planning process, may set objectives to increase market share by 15% and introduce three new products. The courses of action, or means, for achieving these objectives must be established. In this example, the company may decide to follow three courses of action: increase the advertising budget, open a new sales territory, and increase the research and development budget.

Planning can be categorized as either strategic planning or operational planning. **Strategic planning** is developing long-range courses of action to achieve goals. Long-range courses of action, called **strategies**, can often involve periods ranging from 5 to 10 years. **Operational planning** develops short term courses of action to manage the day-to-day operations of a business.

Directing **Directing** is the process by which managers, given their assigned level of responsibilities, run day-to-day operations. Examples of directing include a production supervisor's efforts to keep the production line moving smoothly throughout a work shift and the credit manager's efforts to assess the credit standing of potential customers.

Managerial accounting aids managers in directing a business by providing reports that allow managers to adjust operations for changing conditions. For example, reports on the cost of defective material by vendors may aid managers in making vendor selections or improvements. In addition, managerial accounting reports are used by management to estimate the appropriate staffing and resources necessary for achieving plans.

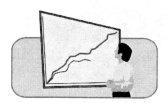

Controlling Once managers have planned goals and directed the action, how well the plan is working must be monitored. **Controlling** consists of monitoring the operating results of implemented plans and comparing the actual results with the expected results. This **feedback** allows management to isolate significant departures from plans for further investigation and possible remedial action. It may also lead to a revision of future plans. This philosophy of controlling is sometimes called **management by exception**. For example, if actual departmental costs incurred in maintaining a process significantly exceed expected costs, then an investigation may be conducted to determine the cause of the difference so that corrective action may be taken.

Improving Feedback can also be used by managers to support continuous process improvement. **Continuous process improvement** is the philosophy of continually improving employees, business processes, and products. Continuous improvement uses process information to eliminate the *source* of problems in a process, so that the right products (services) are delivered in the right quantities at the right time.

Managers use a wide variety of information sources for improving operations, including managerial accounting information. For example, a report identifying the cost of process inefficiency can be used by management to prioritize and monitor improvements.

Decision Making **Decision making** is inherent in each of the four management processes described in the preceding paragraphs. For example, in developing a future plan, managers must decide between alternative courses of action to achieve long-range goals and objectives. Likewise, in directing operations, managers must decide on an operating structure, procedures, training, staffing, and other aspects of day-to-day operations. In controlling and improving, managers must decide how to respond to unfavorable performance.

Example Exercise 18-1

objective **1**

Three phases of the management process are planning, controlling, and improving. Match the following descriptions to the proper phase.

Phase of management process	Description
Planning	a. Monitoring the operating results of implemented plans and comparing the actual results with expected results.
Controlling	b. Rejects solving individual problems with temporary solutions that fail to address the root cause of the problem.
Continuous improvement	c. Used by management to develop the company's objectives.

Follow My Example 18-1

Phase of management process

Planning (c)
Controlling (a)
Continuous improvement (b)

For Practice: PE 18-1A, PE 18-1B

Integrity, Objectivity, and Ethics in Business

ETHICS

ENVIRONMENTAL ACCOUNTING

In recent years, the environmental impact of a business has become an increasingly important issue. Multinational agreements such as the Montreal Protocol and Kyoto Protocol have acknowledged the impact that society has on the environment and raised public awareness of the impact that businesses have on the environment. As a result, environmental issues have become an important operational issue for most businesses. Managers must now consider the environmental impact of their decisions in the same way that they would consider other operational issues.

To help managers understand the environmental impact of their business decisions, new managerial accounting measures are being developed. The emerging field of environmental management accounting focuses on developing various measures of the environmental-related costs of a business. These measures can evaluate a variety of issues including the volume and level of emissions, the estimated costs of different levels of emissions, and the impact that environmental costs have on product cost. Thus, environmental managerial accounting can provide managers with important information to help them more clearly consider the environmental effects of their decisions.

A Tour of Manufacturing Operations: Costs and Terminology

objective 2

Describe and illustrate the following costs: direct and indirect, direct materials, direct labor, factory overhead, and product and period costs.

As we discussed in Chapter 1, the operations of a business can be classified as service, merchandising, or manufacturing. Most of the managerial accounting concepts and terms described in the remaining chapters of this text apply to all three types of businesses. We have described and illustrated the accounting for service and merchandising businesses in the earlier chapters of this text. For this reason, we focus primarily upon manufacturing businesses in the remainder of this text. We begin with a tour of a guitar manufacturer, Legend Guitars.

Like Washburn Guitars, Legend Guitars manufactures high-quality guitars that combine innovation with high-quality craftsmanship. Exhibit 4 provides an overview of Legend's guitar manufacturing operations. The process begins when a customer places an order for a custom-made guitar. Once the order is received, the production process is started by employees who cut the body and neck of the guitar out of raw lumber using a computerized saw. Once the wood is cut, the body and neck of the guitar are assembled. When the assembly is complete, the guitar is painted and finished.

EXHIBIT 4 | **Guitar Making Operations of Legend Guitars**

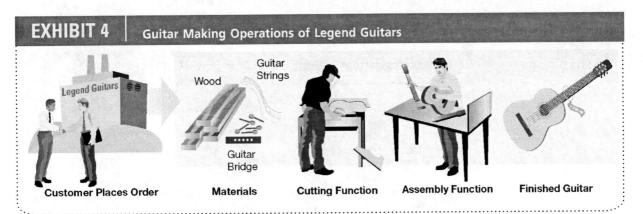

Customer Places Order   Materials   Cutting Function   Assembly Function   Finished Guitar

Next, we introduce the common cost terms associated with manufacturing operations using Legend Guitars. We begin by defining *cost*. A **cost** is a payment of cash or the commitment to pay cash in the future for the purpose of generating revenues. For example, cash (or credit) used to purchase equipment is the cost of the equipment. If equipment is purchased by exchanging assets other than cash, the current market value of the assets given up is the cost of the equipment purchased.

Costs may be classified in a number of ways. Understanding these classifications provides a basis for later discussions and illustrations of managerial decision making.

DIRECT AND INDIRECT COSTS

For management's use in making decisions, costs are often classified in terms of how they relate to an object or segment of operations, often called a **cost object**. A cost object may be a product, a sales territory, a department, or some activity, such as research and development. Costs are identified with cost objects as either **direct costs** or **indirect costs**.

Direct costs are specifically attributed to the cost object. For example, if Legend Guitars is assigning costs to guitars that are produced, the cost of materials used in the guitar would be a direct cost of the guitar.

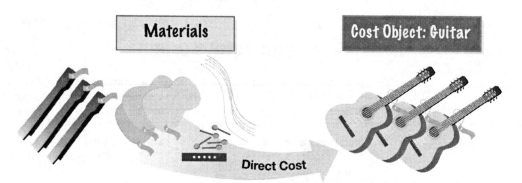

Indirect costs cannot be identified directly with a cost object. For example, the salary of the vice president of production is an indirect cost of the guitars produced by Legend Guitars. While the vice president provides an important contribution to the production of guitars produced by Legend, his salary cannot be directly identified or traced to the individual guitars produced. However, the salary of the vice president of production would be a direct cost to the overall production process. Thus, the salary of the production supervisor can be either an indirect cost (when the cost object is the guitar) or a direct cost (when the cost object is the overall production process).

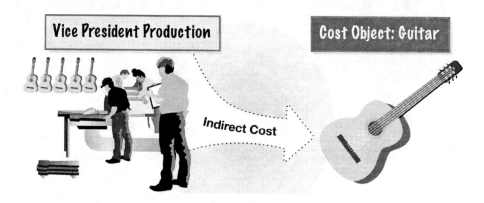

The process of classifying a cost as direct or indirect is illustrated in Exhibit 5.

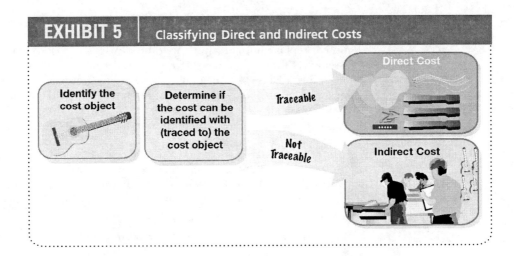

EXHIBIT 5 | Classifying Direct and Indirect Costs

MANUFACTURING COSTS

The cost of a manufactured product includes the cost of materials used in making the product, as well as the costs incurred in converting the materials into a finished product. For example, Legend Guitars uses employees, machines, and other inputs to convert wood and other materials into the finished product, guitars. The finished guitar is the cost object, and the cost of the finished guitars includes direct materials cost, direct labor cost, and factory overhead cost.

Direct Materials Cost Manufactured products convert raw materials into finished products. For example, Legend Guitars uses raw materials such as wood, guitar strings, and guitar bridges and converts them into a finished guitar. The cost of any material that is an integral part of the final guitar is classified as a **direct materials cost**. Other examples of direct materials costs are the cost of electronic components for a TV manufacturer, lumber for a furniture manufacturer, silicon wafers for a producer of microcomputer chips, and tires for an automobile manufacturer.

As a practical matter, a direct materials cost must not only be an integral part of the finished product, but it must also be a significant portion of the total cost of the product. For Legend Guitars, the cost of wood used in the body and neck is a significant portion of the total cost of each guitar.

Direct Labor Cost Most manufacturing processes need employees to convert materials into the final product. For example, Legend Guitars uses employees to assemble guitars by gluing together the neck and body and installing the guitar bridge and strings. The wages of each employee who is directly involved in converting materials

As manufacturing processes have become more automated, direct labor costs have become so small that they are often included as part of factory overhead.

into the final guitar are classified as a **direct labor cost**. Other examples of direct labor costs are carpenters' wages for a construction contractor, mechanics' wages in an automotive repair shop, machine operators' wages in a tool manufacturing plant, and assemblers' wages in a computer assembly plant.

A direct labor cost must not only be an integral part of the finished product, but it must also be a significant portion of the total cost of the product. For Legend Guitars, the wages of employees who operate the saws and cutting machines and assemble the guitars make up a significant portion of the total cost of each guitar.

Factory Overhead Cost Costs, other than direct materials cost and direct labor cost, that are incurred in the manufacturing process are combined and classified as **factory overhead cost**. Factory overhead is sometimes called **manufacturing overhead** or **factory burden**. All factory overhead costs are indirect costs and include the costs of:

- Heating and lighting the factory,
- Repairing and maintaining factory equipment,
- Property taxes,
- Insurance, and
- Depreciation on factory plant and equipment.

Factory overhead cost also includes materials and labor costs that do not enter directly into the finished product. Examples include the cost of oil used to lubricate machinery and the wages of janitorial and supervisory employees. If the costs of direct materials or direct labor are not a significant portion of the total product cost, these costs may be classified as factory overhead.

In Legend Guitars, the costs of sandpaper, buffing compound, and glue used in the assembly of guitars enter directly into the manufacture of each guitar. However, because these costs are a small cost of each guitar, they are classified as factory overhead. Other overhead costs for Legend Guitars would include the power to run the machines, the depreciation of machines, and the salary of production supervisors (including the vice president of production).

Example Exercise 18-2
objective **2**

Identify the following costs as direct materials (DM), direct labor (DL), or factory overhead (FO) for a baseball glove manufacturer.

a. Leather used to make a baseball glove
b. Coolants for machines that sew baseball gloves
c. Wages of assembly line employees
d. Ink used to print a player's autograph on a baseball glove

Follow My Example 18-2

a. DM
b. FO
c. DL
d. FO

For Practice: PE 18-2A, PE 18-2B

Prime Costs and Conversion Costs Direct materials, direct labor, and factory overhead costs are often grouped together for analysis and reporting purposes. Two common groupings of these costs are prime costs and conversion costs. Exhibit 6 summarizes the classification of manufacturing costs into prime costs and conversion costs.

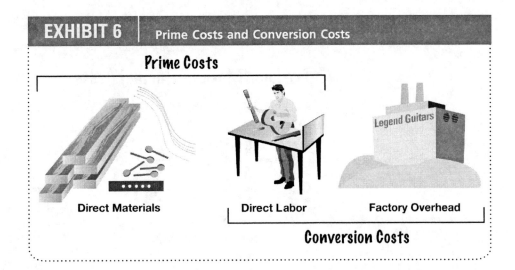

EXHIBIT 6 | Prime Costs and Conversion Costs

Prime costs consist of direct materials and direct labor costs. **Conversion costs** consist of direct labor and factory overhead costs. Conversion costs are the costs of converting the materials into a finished product. As shown in Exhibit 6, direct labor is both a prime cost and a conversion cost.

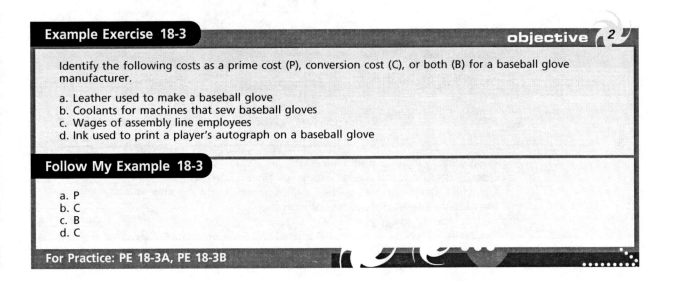

Example Exercise 18-3   objective 2

Identify the following costs as a prime cost (P), conversion cost (C), or both (B) for a baseball glove manufacturer.

a. Leather used to make a baseball glove
b. Coolants for machines that sew baseball gloves
c. Wages of assembly line employees
d. Ink used to print a player's autograph on a baseball glove

Follow My Example 18-3

a. P
b. C
c. B
d. C

For Practice: PE 18-3A, PE 18-3B

Product Costs and Period Costs For financial reporting purposes, costs are often classified as either product costs or period costs. **Product costs** consist of the three elements of manufacturing cost: direct materials, direct labor, and factory overhead. **Period costs** are generally classified into two categories: selling and administrative. Selling expenses are incurred in marketing the product and delivering the sold product to customers. Administrative expenses are incurred in the administration of the business and are not directly related to the manufacturing or selling functions. Examples of product costs and period costs for Legend Guitars are presented in Exhibit 7.

Classifying period costs as selling or administrative expenses assists management in controlling the costs of these two activities. Different levels of responsibility for these

EXHIBIT 7 | Examples of Product Costs and Period Costs—Legend Guitars

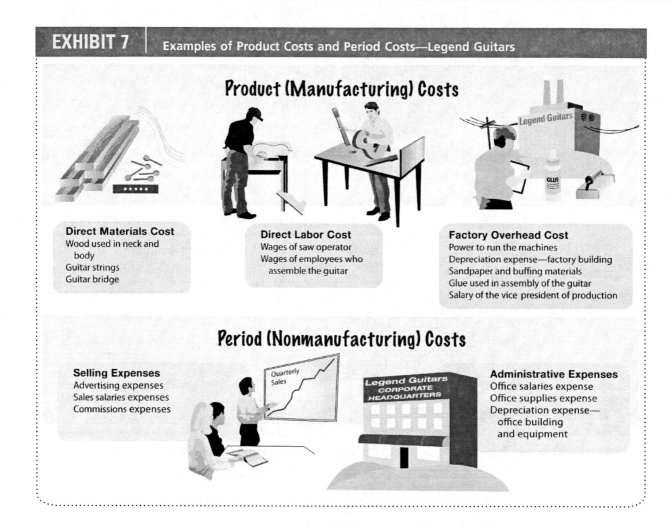

Product (Manufacturing) Costs

Direct Materials Cost
Wood used in neck and
   body
Guitar strings
Guitar bridge

Direct Labor Cost
Wages of saw operator
Wages of employees who
   assemble the guitar

Factory Overhead Cost
Power to run the machines
Depreciation expense—factory building
Sandpaper and buffing materials
Glue used in assembly of the guitar
Salary of the vice president of production

Period (Nonmanufacturing) Costs

Selling Expenses
Advertising expenses
Sales salaries expenses
Commissions expenses

Administrative Expenses
Office salaries expense
Office supplies expense
Depreciation expense—
   office building
   and equipment

activities may be shown in managerial reports. For example, selling expenses may be reported by product, salespersons, departments, divisions, or geographic territories. Likewise, administrative expenses may be reported by functional area, such as personnel, computer services, accounting, finance, or office support.

The classification of costs as product costs and period costs is summarized in Exhibit 8. As product costs are incurred in the manufacturing process, they are accounted for as assets and reported on the balance sheet as inventory. When the in-

EXHIBIT 8

**Product Costs and
Period Costs**

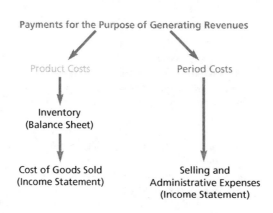

Payments for the Purpose of Generating Revenues

Product Costs   Period Costs

Inventory
(Balance Sheet)

Cost of Goods Sold   Selling and
(Income Statement)   Administrative Expenses
                           (Income Statement)

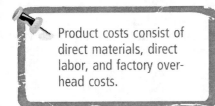

Product costs consist of direct materials, direct labor, and factory overhead costs.

ventory is sold, the direct materials, direct labor, and factory overhead costs are reported as cost of goods sold on the income statement. Period costs do not appear on the balance sheet. They are recognized as expenses in the period in which they are incurred. In the next section, we illustrate the reporting of product costs and period costs in the financial statements of manufacturing businesses.

Example Exercise 18-4 objective 2

Identify the following costs as a product cost or a period cost for a baseball glove manufacturer.

a. Leather used to make a baseball glove
b. Cost of endorsement from a professional baseball player
c. Offices supplies used at the company headquarters
d. Ink used to print a player's autograph on the baseball glove

Follow My Example 18-4

a. Product cost
b. Period cost
c. Period cost
d. Product cost

For Practice: PE 18-4A, PE 18-4B

Financial Statements for a Manufacturing Business

objective 3

Describe and illustrate the statement of cost of goods manufactured, income statement, and balance sheet for a manufacturing business.

The financial statements for a manufacturing business are more complex than those for service and merchandising businesses. This is because a manufacturer makes the products that it sells. As a result, manufacturing costs must be properly accounted for and reported in the financial statements. These manufacturing costs primarily affect the preparation of the balance sheet and the income statement. The retained earnings and cash flow statements for merchandising and manufacturing businesses are similar to those we illustrated in earlier chapters. For this reason, we focus only upon the balance sheet and income statement.

BALANCE SHEET FOR A MANUFACTURING BUSINESS

A manufacturing business reports the following three types of inventory on its balance sheet:

1. **Materials inventory** (sometimes called raw materials inventory)
   - Consists of the costs of the direct and indirect materials that have not yet entered the manufacturing process.
   - For Legend Guitars, wood used to make the body and neck of the guitar is part of the materials inventory.

2. **Work in process inventory**
   - Consists of the direct materials costs, the direct labor costs, and the factory overhead costs that have entered the manufacturing process but are associated with products that have not been completed.

- For Legend Guitars, the unassembled guitars for which the neck and body have been produced are "in process" because they have not yet been put together into a finished guitar. Thus, the cost of the direct materials, direct labor, and factory overhead incurred during the period to create any in-process guitars is part of the work in process inventory.

3. **Finished goods inventory**
   - Consists of *completed* (or finished) products that have not been sold.
   - For Legend Guitars, finished goods inventory contains all of the costs incurred to manufacture the completed, but not yet sold, guitars.

Exhibit 9 compares the balance sheet presentation of inventory for a manufacturing company, Legend Guitars, to that of a merchandising company, MusicLand Stores, Inc. In both balance sheets, inventory is shown in the Current Assets section.

EXHIBIT 9

Balance Sheet Presentation of Inventory in Manufacturing and Merchandising Companies

MusicLand Stores, Inc.
Balance Sheet
December 31, 2008

Current assets:	
Cash	$ 25,000
Accounts receivable (net)	85,000
Merchandise inventory	142,000
Supplies	10,000
Total current assets	$262,000

Legend Guitars
Balance Sheet
December 31, 2008

Current assets:		
Cash		$ 21,000
Accounts receivable (net)		120,000
Inventories:		
Finished goods	$62,500	
Work in process	24,000	
Materials	35,000	121,500
Supplies		2,000
Total current assets		$264,500

INCOME STATEMENT FOR A MANUFACTURING COMPANY

The major difference in the income statements for merchandising and manufacturing businesses is in the reporting of cost of products sold during the period. A merchandising business purchases merchandise (products) in a finished state for resale to customers. The cost of products sold is called the **cost of merchandise sold**, which we described and illustrated in earlier chapters.

A manufacturer makes the products it sells, using direct materials, direct labor, and factory overhead. The cost of the product sold is generally called the cost of goods sold. For a manufacturer, the total cost of making and finishing the product is called the **cost**

of goods manufactured. This is very similar to the cost of merchandise available for sale in a merchandising business.

The income statement of manufacturing companies is supported by a **statement of cost of goods manufactured**, which provides the details of the cost of goods manufactured. To illustrate the flow of manufacturing costs to the income statement for Legend Guitars, assume the following data for 2008:

Inventories	January 1	December 31
Materials	$65,000	$35,000
Work in process	30,000	24,000
Finished goods	60,000	62,500

Materials purchased during the year		$100,000
Direct labor incurred in production		110,000
Factory overhead incurred in production:		
Indirect labor	$24,000	
Depreciation on factory equipment	10,000	
Factory supplies and utility costs	10,000	
Total		44,000
Selling expenses		20,000
Administrative expenses		15,000
Sales		366,000

The manufacturing costs for Legend Guitars would flow to the financial statements as shown in Exhibit 10.

EXHIBIT 10 Flow of Manufacturing Costs

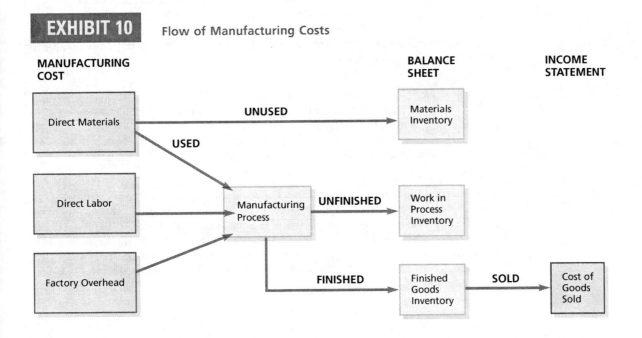

As discussed previously, three calculation steps are required to determine the cost of goods manufactured.

The cost of goods manufactured is determined by first computing the cost of direct materials used in the year as follows:

Materials inventory, January 1, 2008	$ 65,000
Add: Materials purchased during the year	100,000
Cost of materials available for use	$165,000
Less: Materials inventory, December 31, 2008	35,000
Cost of direct materials used in production	$130,000

Adding the beginning (January 1) materials inventory of $65,000 to the cost of materials purchased during the period, $100,000, yields the total cost of materials that are available for use during the period of $165,000. Deducting the ending December 31 materials inventory of $35,000 equals the cost of direct materials used in production during the year.

The total manufacturing costs incurred during the year of $284,000 is determined as follows:

Direct materials used during the year	$130,000
Direct labor	110,000
Factory overhead	44,000
Total manufacturing costs incurred during the year	$284,000

To determine the cost of goods manufactured during the year, the beginning work in process inventory of $30,000 is added to the total manufacturing costs incurred during the year of $284,000 to yield the total manufacturing costs of $314,000. The ending work in process of $24,000 is then deducted to determine the cost of goods manufactured during the year as follows:

Work in process inventory, January 1, 2008	$ 30,000
Total manufacturing costs incurred during the year	284,000
Total manufacturing costs	$314,000
Less work in process inventory, December 31, 2008	24,000
Cost of goods manufactured during the year	$290,000

The preceding computations of the cost of goods manufactured are often reported in a statement of cost of goods manufactured as shown in Exhibit 11. The statement of cost of goods manufactured supports the income statement shown in Exhibit 11. On the income statement, the cost of goods manufactured is added to the beginning finished goods inventory of $60,000 to determine the cost of finished goods available for sale of $350,000. The ending finished goods inventory of $62,500 is then deducted to determine the cost of goods sold of $287,500.

EXHIBIT 11

Manufacturing Company—Income Statement with Statement of Cost of Goods Manufactured

Legend Guitars
Income Statement
For the Year Ended December 31, 2008

Sales		$366,000
Cost of goods sold:		
Finished goods inventory, January 1, 2008	$ 60,000	
Cost of goods manufactured	290,000	
Cost of finished goods available for sale	$350,000	
Less finished goods inventory, December 31, 2008	62,500	
Cost of goods sold		287,500
Gross profit		$ 78,500
Operating expenses:		
Selling expenses	$ 20,000	
Administrative expenses	15,000	
Total operating expenses		35,000
Net income		$ 43,500

Legend Guitars
Statement of Cost of Goods Manufactured
For the Year Ended December 31, 2008

Work in process inventory, January 1, 2008			$ 30,000
Direct materials:			
Materials inventory, January 1, 2008	$ 65,000		
Purchases	100,000		
Cost of materials available for use	$165,000		
Less materials inventory, December 31, 2008	35,000		
Cost of direct materials used in production		$130,000	
Direct labor		110,000	
Factory overhead:			
Indirect labor	$ 24,000		
Depreciation on factory equipment	10,000		
Factory supplies and utility costs	10,000		
Total factory overhead		44,000	
Total manufacturing costs incurred during the year			284,000
Total manufacturing costs			$314,000
Less work in process inventory, December 31, 2008			24,000
Cost of goods manufactured			$290,000

Example Exercise 18-5   objective **3**

Gauntlet Company has the following information for January:

Cost of direct materials used in production	$25,000
Direct labor	35,000
Factory overhead	20,000
Work in process inventory, January 1	30,000
Work in process inventory, January 31	25,000
Finished goods inventory, January 1	15,000
Finished goods inventory, January 31	12,000

For January, determine (a) the cost of goods manufactured and (b) the cost of goods sold.

Follow My Example 18-5

a.

Work in process inventory, January 1		$ 30,000
Cost of direct materials used in production	$25,000	
Direct labor	35,000	
Factory overhead	20,000	
Total manufacturing costs incurred during January		80,000
Total manufacturing costs		$110,000
Less: Work in process inventory, January 31		25,000
Cost of goods manufactured		$ 85,000

b.

Finished goods inventory, January 1	$ 15,000
Cost of goods manufactured	85,000
Cost of finished goods available for sale	$100,000
Less: Finished goods inventory, January 31	12,000
Cost of goods sold	$ 88,000

For Practice: PE 18-5A, PE 18-5B

Uses of Managerial Accounting

objective **4**

Describe the uses of managerial accounting information.

As discussed in the first part of this chapter, managers need information to guide their decision making. Managerial accounting provides information and reports that help managers run the day-to-day operations of their business. For example, Legend Guitars uses managerial information to determine the cost of manufacturing each guitar. This cost can then be used to set the selling price of guitars. In addition, comparing the costs of guitars over time can aid managers in monitoring and controlling the cost of direct materials, direct labor, and factory overhead.

Managerial reports also help managers evaluate the performance of a company's operations. Managerial accounting can be used to evaluate the efficiency in using raw materials or direct labor in the manufacturing process. For example, Legend Guitars can use performance reports to identify the cause for large amounts of unusable wood remaining after the cutting process. Managers can then use this information to make the cutting process more efficient.

Companies also use managerial accounting information to support long-term planning decisions, such as investment decisions. For example, Legend Guitars management may consider buying a new computerized saw to speed up the production process while providing higher quality cuts. Managerial accounting information can help management determine if this is a good investment.

Managerial accounting data can be used to help managers understand how many guitars need to be sold in a month in order to cover recurring monthly costs. Such information can be used to set monthly selling targets.

As these examples illustrate, managerial accounting information can be used for a variety of purposes. In the remaining chapters of this text, we examine these and other areas of managerial accounting in greater detail and discuss how this information is used to aid managerial decision making.

Business Connections

REAL WORLD

NAVIGATING THE INFORMATION HIGHWAY

Dell Inc. follows a build-to-order manufacturing process, where each computer is manufactured based on a specific customer order. In a build-to-order manufacturing process like this, customers select the features they want on their computer from the company's Web site. Once the order is submitted, the manufacturing process begins. The parts required for each feature are removed from inventory, and the computer is manufactured and shipped within days of the order. Inventory items are scanned as they are removed from inventory to keep accurate track of inventory levels and help the manufacturer determine when to reorder.

But calculating the amount of materials to reorder is not the only use of these data. Data on which parts are included in each order are placed in the company's database. This information can then be used to track manufacturing patterns such as the type of features that are frequently ordered together and seasonal changes in the features that are ordered.

In recent years, information systems have become more sophisticated, making it easier and less expensive for companies to gather large amounts of data on their manufacturing processes and customers. If used effectively, these new data sources can help a business like Dell decide what features to offer for its products, what features to discontinue, and how to combine features into a package. For example, manufacturing data might indicate that the demand for DVD drives on computers increases significantly each summer right before school starts. A

© 1999–2006 DELL INC.

build-to-order manufacturer like Dell might use this information to realign the manufacturing process during that time of year, or to offer certain packages of features in July and August.

However, the ability to generate value from this information depends on a company's ability to merge these new data with existing accounting information in a meaningful manner. The managerial accountant must now be prepared to analyze and evaluate a broader set of information and determine how it will affect a company's operational performance and profitability.

Source: "Delivering Strategic Business Value: Business Intelligence Can Help Management Accounting Reclaim Its Relevance and Rightful Role," Steve Williams, *Strategic Finance*, August 2004.

At a Glance

1. Describe managerial accounting and the role of managerial accounting in a business.			
Key Points	**Key Learning Outcomes**	**Example Exercises**	**Practice Exercises**
Managerial accounting is a staff function that supports the management process by providing reports to aid management in planning, directing, controlling, improving, and decision making. This differs from financial accounting, which provides information to stakeholders outside of the organization. Managerial accounting reports are designed to meet the specific needs of management and aid management in planning long-term strategies and running the day-to-day operations.	• Describe the differences between financial accounting and managerial accounting. • Describe the role of the management accountant in the organization. • Describe the role of managerial accounting in the management process.	18-1	18-1A, 18-1B

(continued)

2. Describe and illustrate the following costs: direct and indirect, direct materials, direct labor, factory overhead, and product and period costs.

Key Points	Key Learning Outcomes	Example Exercises	Practice Exercises
Manufacturing companies use machinery and labor to convert materials into a finished product. A direct cost can be directly traced to a finished product, while an indirect cost cannot. The cost of a finished product is made up of three components: (1) the cost of materials that are directly identifiable with the final product, (2) the wages of employees that directly convert materials to a finished product, and (3) factory overhead. Costs incurred in the manufacturing process other than direct materials and direct labor are classified as factory overhead costs. These three manufacturing costs can be categorized into prime costs (direct material and direct labor) or conversion costs (direct labor and factory overhead). Product costs consist of the elements of manufacturing cost—direct materials, direct labor, and factory overhead—while period costs consist of selling and administrative expenses.	• Describe a cost object. • Classify a cost as a direct or indirect cost for a cost object. • Describe direct materials cost. • Describe direct labor cost. • Describe factory overhead cost. • Describe prime costs and conversion costs. • Describe product costs and period costs.	 18-2 18-2 18-2 18-3 18-4	 18-2A, 18-2B 18-2A, 18-2B 18-2A, 18-2B 18-3A, 18-3B 18-4A, 18-4B

3. Describe and illustrate the statement of cost of goods manufactured, income statement, and balance sheet for a manufacturing business.

Key Points	Key Learning Outcomes	Example Exercises	Practice Exercises
The financial statements of manufacturing companies differ from those of merchandising companies. Manufacturing company balance sheets report three types of inventory: materials, work in process, and finished goods. The income statement of manufacturing companies reports cost of goods sold, which is the total manufacturing cost of the goods sold. The income statement is supported by the statement of cost of goods manufactured, which provides the details of the cost of goods manufactured during the period.	• Describe materials inventory. • Describe work in process inventory. • Describe finished goods inventory. • Describe the differences between merchandising and manufacturing company balance sheets. • Prepare a statement of cost of goods manufactured. • Prepare an income statement for a manufacturing company.	 18-5 18-5	 18-5A, 18-5B 18-5A, 18-5B

4. Describe the uses of managerial accounting information.

Key Points	Key Learning Outcomes	Example Exercises	Practice Exercises
Managers need information to guide their decision making. Managerial accounting provides a variety of information and reports that help managers run the operations of their business.	• Describe examples of how managerial accounting aids managers in decision making.		

Key Terms

continuous process improvement (798)
controller (796)
controlling (798)
conversion costs (803)
cost (799)
cost object (800)
cost of goods manufactured (806)
cost of merchandise sold (806)
decision making (798)
direct costs (800)
direct labor cost (802)
direct materials cost (801)

directing (797)
factory burden (802)
factory overhead cost (802)
feedback (798)
financial accounting (794)
finished goods inventory (806)
indirect costs (800)
line department (795)
management by exception (798)
management process (796)
managerial accounting (795)
manufacturing overhead (802)
materials inventory (805)

objectives (goals) (797)
operational planning (797)
period costs (803)
planning (797)
prime costs (803)
product costs (803)
staff department (796)
statement of cost of goods
  manufactured (807)
strategic planning (797)
strategies (797)
work in process inventory (805)

Illustrative Problem

The following is a list of costs that were incurred in producing this textbook:

a. Insurance on the factory building and equipment
b. Salary of the vice president of finance
c. Hourly wages of printing press operators during production
d. Straight-line depreciation on the printing presses used to manufacture the text
e. Electricity used to run the presses during the printing of the text
f. Sales commissions paid to textbook representatives for each text sold
g. Paper on which the text is printed
h. Book covers used to bind the pages
i. Straight-line depreciation on an office building
j. Salaries of staff used to develop artwork for the text
k. Glue used to bind pages to cover

Instructions

With respect to the manufacture and sale of this text, classify each cost as either a product cost or a period cost. Indicate whether each product cost is a direct materials cost, a direct labor cost, or a factory overhead cost. Indicate whether each period cost is a selling expense or an administrative expense.

Solution

Cost	Product Cost			Period Cost	
	Direct Materials Cost	Direct Labor Cost	Factory Overhead Cost	Selling Expense	Administrative Expense
a.			X		
b.					X
c.		X			
d.			X		
e.			X		
f.				X	
g.	X				
h.	X				
i.					X
j.			X		
k.			X		

Self-Examination Questions

1. Which of the following best describes the difference between financial and managerial accounting?
   A. Managerial accounting provides information to support decisions, while financial accounting does not.
   B. Managerial accounting is not restricted to generally accepted accounting principles (GAAP), while financial accounting is restricted to GAAP.
   C. Managerial accounting does not result in financial reports, while financial accounting does result in financial reports.
   D. Managerial accounting is concerned solely with the future and does not record events from the past, while financial accounting records only events from past transactions.

2. Which of the following is *not* one of the five basic phases of the management process?
   A. Planning   C. Decision making
   B. Controlling   D. Operating

3. Which of the following is *not* considered a cost of manufacturing a product?
   A. Direct materials cost
   B. Factory overhead cost
   C. Sales salaries
   D. Direct labor cost

4. Which of the following costs would be included as part of the factory overhead costs of a microcomputer manufacturer?
   A. The cost of memory chips
   B. Depreciation of testing equipment
   C. Wages of microcomputer assemblers
   D. The cost of disk drives

5. For the month of May, Latter Company has beginning finished goods inventory of $50,000, ending finished goods inventory of $35,000, and cost of goods manufactured of $125,000. What is the cost of goods sold for May?
   A. $90,000   C. $140,000
   B. $110,000   D. $170,000

Eye Openers

1. What are the major differences between managerial accounting and financial accounting?
2. a. Differentiate between a department with line responsibility and a department with staff responsibility.
   b. In an organization that has a Sales Department and a Personnel Department, among others, which of the two departments has (1) line responsibility and (2) staff responsibility?
3. a. What is the role of the controller in a business organization?
   b. Does the controller have a line or staff responsibility?
4. What are the five basic phases of the management process?
5. What is the term for a plan that encompasses a period ranging from five or more years and that serves as a basis for long-range actions?
6. What is the process by which management runs day-to-day operations?
7. What is the process by which management assesses how well a plan is working?
8. Describe what is meant by *management by exception*.
9. What term describes a payment in cash or the commitment to pay cash in the future for the purpose of generating revenues?
10. For a company that produces desktop computers, would memory chips be considered a direct or an indirect cost of each microcomputer produced?
11. What three costs make up the cost of manufacturing a product?
12. What manufacturing cost term is used to describe the cost of materials that are an integral part of the manufactured end product?
13. If the cost of wages paid to employees who are directly involved in converting raw materials into a manufactured end product is not a significant portion of the total product cost, how would the wages cost be classified as to type of manufacturing cost?
14. Distinguish between prime costs and conversion costs.
15. What is the difference between a product cost and a period cost?
16. Name the three inventory accounts for a manufacturing business, and describe what each balance represents at the end of an accounting period.

17. In what order should the three inventories of a manufacturing business be presented on the balance sheet?
18. What are the three categories of manufacturing costs included in the cost of finished goods and the cost of work in process?
19. For a manufacturer, what is the description of the amount that is comparable to a merchandising business's cost of merchandise sold?
20. For June, Fosina Company had beginning materials inventory of $25,000, ending materials inventory of $30,000, and materials purchases of $140,000. What is the cost of direct materials used in production?
21. How does the cost of goods sold section of the income statement differ between merchandising and manufacturing companies?
22. Describe how an automobile manufacturer might use managerial accounting information to (a) evaluate the performance of the company and (b) make strategic decisions.

Practice Exercises

PE 18-1A
Managerial accounting in the management process
obj. 1

Three phases of the management process are planning, directing, and controlling (management by exception). One type of planning is strategic planning. Match the following descriptions to the proper phase.

Phase of management process	Description
Strategic planning	a. Isolating significant departures from plans for further investigation and possible remedial action. It may lead to a revision of future plans.
Directing	b. Process by which managers, given their assigned levels of responsibilities, run day-to-day operations.
Management by exception	c. Developing long-range courses of action to achieve goals.

PE 18-1B
Managerial accounting in the management process
obj. 1

Three phases of the management process are controlling, strategies, and decision making. Match the following descriptions to the proper phase.

Phase of management process	Description
Controlling	a. Inherent in planning, directing, controlling, and improving.
Strategies	b. Monitoring the operating results of implemented plans and comparing the actual results with expected results.
Decision making	c. Long-range courses of action.

PE 18-2A
Direct materials, direct labor, and factory overhead
obj. 2

Identify the following costs as direct materials (DM), direct labor (DL), or factory overhead (FO) for a textbook publisher.

a. Maintenance on printing machines
b. Glue used to bind books
c. Wages of printing machine employees
d. Paper used to make a textbook

PE 18-2B
Direct materials, direct labor, and factory overhead
obj. 2

Identify the following costs as direct materials (DM), direct labor (DL), or factory overhead (FO) for an automobile manufacturer.

a. Wages of employees that operate painting equipment
b. Steel
c. Wages of the plant manager
d. Oil used for assembly line machinery

PE 18-3A
Prime costs vs. conversion costs
obj. 2

Identify the following costs as a prime cost (P), conversion cost (C), or both (B) for a textbook publisher.

a. Maintenance on printing machines
b. Glue used to bind books
c. Wages of printing machine employees
d. Paper used to make a textbook

PE 18-3B
Prime costs vs. conversion costs
obj. 2

Identify the following costs as a prime cost (P), conversion cost (C), or both (B) for an automobile manufacturer.

a. Wages of employees that operate painting equipment
b. Steel
c. Wages of the plant manager
d. Oil used for assembly line machinery

PE 18-4A
Product costs vs. period costs
obj. 2

Identify the following costs as a product cost or a period cost for a textbook publisher.

a. Maintenance on printing machines
b. Sales salaries
c. Depreciation expense—corporate headquarters
d. Paper used to make a textbook

PE 18-4B
Product costs vs. period costs
obj. 2

Identify the following costs as a product cost or a period cost for an automobile manufacturer.

a. Wages of employees that operate painting equipment
b. Steel
c. Accounting staff salaries
d. Rent on office building

PE 18-5A
Cost of goods sold, cost of goods manufactured
obj. 3

Nantahala Company has the following information for August:

Cost of direct materials used in production	$30,000
Direct labor	45,000
Factory overhead	22,000
Work in process inventory, August 1	10,000
Work in process inventory, August 31	8,000
Finished goods inventory, August 1	18,000
Finished goods inventory, August 31	10,000

For August, determine (a) the cost of goods manufactured and (b) the cost of goods sold.

PE 18-5B
Cost of goods sold, cost of goods manufactured
obj. 3

Tsali Company has the following information for February:

Cost of direct materials used in production	$18,000
Direct labor	54,000
Factory overhead	36,000
Work in process inventory, February 1	50,000
Work in process inventory, February 28	57,000
Finished goods inventory, February 1	22,000
Finished goods inventory, February 28	26,000

For February, determine (a) the cost of goods manufactured and (b) the cost of goods sold.

Exercises

EX 18-1
Classifying costs as materials, labor, or factory overhead
obj. 2

Indicate whether each of the following costs of an airplane manufacturer would be classified as direct materials cost, direct labor cost, or factory overhead cost:

a. Steel used in landing gear
b. Controls for flight deck
c. Welding machinery lubricants
d. Salary of test pilot
e. Wages of assembly line worker
f. Tires
g. Aircraft engines
h. Depreciation of welding equipment

EX 18-2
Classifying costs as materials, labor, or factory overhead
obj. 2

Indicate whether the following costs of Colgate-Palmolive Company would be classified as direct materials cost, direct labor cost, or factory overhead cost:

a. Packaging materials
b. Depreciation on production machinery
c. Salary of process engineers
d. Depreciation on the Clarksville, Indiana, soap plant
e. Scents and fragrances
f. Wages of Marketing Department employees
g. Resins for soap and shampoo products
h. Plant manager salary for the Morristown, Tennessee, toothpaste plant
i. Maintenance supplies
j. Wages paid to Packaging Department employees

EX 18-3
Classifying costs as factory overhead
obj. 2

Which of the following items are properly classified as part of factory overhead for Caterpillar?

a. Vice president of finance's salary
b. Interest expense on debt
c. Plant manager's salary at Aurora, Illinois, manufacturing plant
d. Consultant fees for a study of production line employee productivity
e. Factory supplies used in the Morganton, North Carolina, engine parts plant
f. Amortization of patents on new assembly process
g. Steel plate
h. Depreciation on Peoria, Illinois, headquarters building
i. Property taxes on the Danville, Kentucky, tractor tread plant
j. Sales incentive fees to dealers

EX 18-4
Classifying costs as product or period costs
obj. 2

For apparel manufacturer Ann Taylor, Inc., classify each of the following costs as either a product cost or a period cost:

a. Factory janitorial supplies
b. Depreciation on office equipment
c. Advertising expenses
d. Fabric used during production
e. Depreciation on sewing machines
f. Property taxes on factory building and equipment
g. Sales commissions
h. Wages of sewing machine operators
i. Repairs and maintenance costs for sewing machines
j. Salary of production quality control supervisor
k. Factory supervisors' salaries
l. Oil used to lubricate sewing machines

(continued)

m. Travel costs of salespersons

n. Corporate controller's salary

o. Utility costs for office building

p. Research and development costs

q. Salaries of distribution center personnel

EX 18-5
Concepts and terminology

objs. 1, 2

From the choices presented in parentheses, choose the appropriate term for completing each of the following sentences:

a. Feedback is often used to (improve, direct) operations.

b. A product, sales territory, department, or activity to which costs are traced is called a (direct cost, cost object).

c. Payments of cash or the commitment to pay cash in the future for the purpose of generating revenues are (costs, expenses).

d. The balance sheet of a manufacturer would include an account for (cost of goods sold, work in process inventory).

e. Factory overhead costs combined with direct labor costs are called (prime, conversion) costs.

f. Advertising costs are usually viewed as (period, product) costs.

g. The implementation of automatic, robotic factory equipment normally (increases, decreases) the direct labor component of product costs.

EX 18-6
Concepts and terminology

objs. 1, 2

From the choices presented in parentheses, choose the appropriate term for completing each of the following sentences:

a. Direct materials costs combined with direct labor costs are called (prime, conversion) costs.

b. The wages of an assembly worker are normally considered a (period, product) cost.

c. The phase of the management process that uses process information to eliminate the source of problems in a process so that the process delivers the correct product in the correct quantities is called (directing, improving).

d. Short-term plans are called (strategic, operational) plans.

e. The plant manager's salary would be considered (direct, indirect) to the product.

f. Materials for use in production are called (supplies, materials inventory).

g. An example of factory overhead is (sales office depreciation, plant depreciation).

EX 18-7
Classifying costs in a service company

obj. 2

A partial list of the costs for Mountain Lakes Railroad, a short hauler of freight, is provided below. Classify each cost as either indirect or direct. For purposes of classifying each cost as direct or indirect, use the train as the cost object.

a. Cost to lease (rent) train locomotives.

b. Wages of switch and classification yard personnel

c. Wages of train engineers

d. Cost to lease (rent) railroad cars

e. Maintenance costs of right of way, bridges, and buildings

f. Fuel costs

g. Payroll clerk salaries

h. Safety training costs

i. Salaries of dispatching and communications personnel

j. Costs of accident cleanup

k. Cost of track and bed (ballast) replacement

l. Depreciation of terminal facilities

EX 18-8
Classifying costs

objs. 2, 3

The following report was prepared for evaluating the performance of the plant manager of Miss-Take Inc. Evaluate and correct this report.

Miss-Take Inc.
Manufacturing Costs
For the Quarter Ended March 31, 2008

Direct labor (including $80,000 maintenance salaries)	$ 430,000
Materials used in production (including	
$40,000 of indirect materials)	680,000
Factory overhead:	
Supervisor salaries	610,000
Heat, light, and power	140,000
Sales salaries	270,000
Promotional expenses	310,000
Insurance and property taxes—plant	160,000
Insurance and property taxes—corporate offices	210,000
Depreciation—plant and equipment	80,000
Depreciation—corporate offices	100,000
Total	$2,990,000

EX 18-9
Financial statements of a manufacturing firm

obj. 3

✓ a. Net income, $55,000

The following events took place for Gantt Manufacturing Company during March, the first month of its operations as a producer of digital clocks:

a. Purchased $65,000 of materials.
b. Used $50,000 of direct materials in production.
c. Incurred $75,000 of direct labor wages.
d. Incurred $105,000 of factory overhead.
e. Transferred $175,000 of work in process to finished goods.
f. Sold goods with a cost of $140,000.
g. Earned revenues of $310,000.
h. Incurred $80,000 of selling expenses.
i. Incurred $35,000 of administrative expenses.

a. Prepare the March income statement for Gantt Manufacturing Company.
b. Determine the inventory balances at the end of the first month of operations.

EX 18-10
Manufacturing company balance sheet

obj. 3

Partial balance sheet data for Ellison Company at December 31, 2008, are as follows:

Finished goods inventory	$12,500
Prepaid insurance	6,000
Accounts receivable	25,000
Work in process inventory	45,000
Supplies	15,000
Materials inventory	24,000
Cash	32,000

Prepare the Current Assets section of Ellison Company's balance sheet at December 31, 2008.

EX 18-11
Cost of direct materials used in production for a manufacturing company

obj. 3

Guzman Manufacturing Company reported the following materials data for the month ending October 31, 2008:

Materials purchased	$175,000
Materials inventory, October 1	45,000
Materials inventory, October 31	30,000

Determine the cost of direct materials used in production by Guzman during the month ended October 31, 2008.

EX 18-12
Cost of goods manufactured for a manufacturing company

obj. **3**

✓ e. $4,000

Two items are omitted from each of the following three lists of cost of goods manufactured statement data. Determine the amounts of the missing items, identifying them by letter.

Work in process inventory, December 1	$ 1,000	$ 10,000	(e)
Total manufacturing costs incurred during December	12,000	(c)	60,000
Total manufacturing costs	(a)	$120,000	$64,000
Work in process inventory, December 31	2,000	20,000	(f)
Cost of goods manufactured	(b)	(d)	$58,000

EX 18-13
Cost of goods manufactured for a manufacturing company

obj. **3**

The following information is available for Applebaum Manufacturing Company for the month ending January 31, 2008:

Cost of direct materials used in production	$165,000
Direct labor	145,000
Work in process inventory, January 1	70,000
Work in process inventory, January 31	125,000
Total factory overhead	65,000

Determine Applebaum's cost of goods manufactured for the month ended January 31, 2008.

EX 18-14
Income statement for a manufacturing company

obj. **3**

✓ d. $190,000

Two items are omitted from each of the following three lists of cost of goods sold data from a manufacturing company income statement. Determine the amounts of the missing items, identifying them by letter.

Finished goods inventory, November 1	$ 25,000	$ 40,000	(e)
Cost of goods manufactured	160,000	(c)	350,000
Cost of finished goods available for sale	(a)	$250,000	$400,000
Finished goods inventory, November 30	30,000	60,000	(f)
Cost of goods sold	(b)	(d)	$335,000

EX 18-15
Statement of cost of goods manufactured for a manufacturing company

obj. **3**

✓ a. Total manufacturing costs, $622,000

Cost data for T. Clark Manufacturing Company for the month ending April 30, 2008, are as follows:

Inventories	April 1	April 30
Materials	$125,000	$110,000
Work in process	85,000	95,000
Finished goods	65,000	75,000

Direct labor	$225,000
Materials purchased during April	240,000
Factory overhead incurred during April:	
Indirect labor	24,000
Machinery depreciation	14,000
Heat, light, and power	5,000
Supplies	4,000
Property taxes	3,500
Miscellaneous cost	6,500

a. Prepare a cost of goods manufactured statement for April 2008.
b. Determine the cost of goods sold for April 2008.

EX 18-16
Cost of goods sold, profit margin, and net income for a manufacturing company

obj. **3**

✓ a. Cost of goods sold, $270,000

The following information is available for Renteria Manufacturing Company for the month ending March 31, 2008:

Cost of goods manufactured	$265,000
Selling expenses	85,000
Administrative expenses	45,000
Sales	540,000
Finished goods inventory, March 1	60,000
Finished goods inventory, March 31	55,000

For the month ended March 31, 2008, determine Renteria's (a) cost of goods sold, (b) gross profit, and (c) net income.

EX 18-17
Cost flow relationships
obj. 3
✓ a. $250,000

The following information is available for the first month of operations of Brown Company, a manufacturer of mechanical pencils:

Sales	$600,000
Gross profit	350,000
Cost of goods manufactured	300,000
Indirect labor	130,000
Factory depreciation	20,000
Materials purchased	185,000
Total manufacturing costs for the period	345,000
Materials inventory	25,000

Using the above information, determine the following missing amounts:

a. Cost of goods sold
b. Finished goods inventory
c. Direct materials cost
d. Direct labor cost
e. Work in process inventory

Problems Series A

PR 18-1A
Classifying costs
obj. 2

The following is a list of costs that were incurred in the production and sale of boats:

a. Commissions to sales representatives, based upon the number of boats sold.
b. Cost of boat for "grand prize" promotion in local bass tournament.
c. Memberships for key executives in the Bass World Association.
d. Cost of electrical wiring for boats.
e. Cost of normal scrap from defective hulls.
f. Cost of metal hardware for boats, such as ornaments and tie-down grasps.
g. Cost of paving the employee parking lot.
h. Hourly wages of assembly line workers.
i. Annual bonus paid to top executives of the company.
j. Straight-line depreciation on factory equipment.
k. Wood paneling for use in interior boat trim.
l. Steering wheels.
m. Special advertising campaign in *Bass World*.
n. Masks for use by sanders in smoothing boat hulls.
o. Power used by sanding equipment.
p. Yearly cost maintenance contract for robotic equipment.
q. Oil to lubricate factory equipment.
r. Canvas top for boats.
s. Executive end-of-year bonuses.
t. Salary of shop supervisor.
u. Decals for boat hull.
v. Annual fee to pro-fisherman Jim Bo Wilks to promote the boats.
w. Paint for boats.
x. Legal department costs for the year.
y. Fiberglass for producing the boat hull.
z. Salary of president of company.

Instructions
Classify each cost as either a product cost or a period cost. Indicate whether each product cost is a direct materials cost, a direct labor cost, or a factory overhead cost. Indicate whether

each period cost is a selling expense or an administrative expense. Use the following tabular headings for your answer, placing an "X" in the appropriate column.

		Product Costs			Period Costs	
Cost	Direct Materials Cost	Direct Labor Cost	Factory Overhead Cost		Selling Expense	Administrative Expense

PR 18-2A
Classifying costs
obj. 2

The following is a list of costs incurred by several businesses:

a. Cost of dyes used by a clothing manufacturer.
b. Salary of the vice president of manufacturing logistics.
c. Wages of a machine operator on the production line.
d. Travel costs of marketing executives to annual sales meeting.
e. Cost of sewing machine needles used by a shirt manufacturer.
f. Depreciation of microcomputers used in the factory to coordinate and monitor the production schedules.
g. Pens, paper, and other supplies used by the Accounting Department in preparing various managerial reports.
h. Electricity used to operate factory machinery.
i. Factory janitorial supplies.
j. Fees paid to lawn service for office grounds upkeep.
k. Wages of computer programmers for production of microcomputer software.
l. Depreciation of copying machines used by the Marketing Department.
m. Telephone charges by president's office.
n. Cost of plastic for a telephone being manufactured.
o. Oil lubricants for factory plant and equipment.
p. Cost of a 30-second television commercial.
q. Depreciation of robot used to assemble a product.
r. Wages of production quality control personnel.
s. Maintenance and repair costs for factory equipment.
t. Depreciation of tools used in production.
u. Rent for a warehouse used to store finished products.
v. Maintenance costs for factory equipment.
w. Fees charged by collection agency on past-due customer accounts.
x. Charitable contribution to United Fund.

Instructions
Classify each of the preceding costs as product costs or period costs. Indicate whether each product cost is a direct materials cost, a direct labor cost, or a factory overhead cost. Indicate whether each period cost is a selling expense or an administrative expense. Use the following tabular headings for preparing your answer, placing an "X" in the appropriate column.

		Product Costs			Period Costs	
Cost	Direct Materials Cost	Direct Labor Cost	Factory Overhead Cost		Selling Expense	Administrative Expense

PR 18-3A
Cost classifications—service company
obj. 2

A partial list of Highland Medical Center's costs is provided below.

a. Depreciation of X-ray equipment.
b. Cost of drugs used for patients.
c. Nurses' salaries.
d. Cost of new heart wing.
e. Overtime incurred in the Records Department due to a computer failure.

f. Cost of patient meals.
g. General maintenance of the hospital.
h. Salary of the nutritionist.
i. Cost of maintaining the staff and visitors' cafeteria.
j. Training costs for nurses.
k. Operating room supplies used on patients (catheters, sutures, etc.).
l. Utility costs of the hospital.
m. Cost of intravenous solutions.
n. Cost of blood tests.
o. Cost of improvements on the employee parking lot.
p. Cost of laundry services for operating room personnel.
q. Depreciation on patient rooms.
r. Cost of advertising hospital services on television.
s. Cost of X-ray test.
t. Salary of intensive care personnel.
u. Doctor's fee.

Instructions
1. What would be Highland's most logical definition for the final cost object?
2. Identify how each of the costs is to be classified as either direct or indirect. Define direct costs in terms of a patient as a cost object.

PR 18-4A
Manufacturing income statement, statement of cost of goods manufactured

objs. 2, 3

✓ 2. Vinston, c. $301,000

Several items are omitted from each of the following income statement and cost of goods manufactured statement data for the month of December 2008:

	Vinston Company	Turkun Company
Materials inventory, December 1	$ 25,000	$ 32,000
Materials inventory, December 31	(a)	15,000
Materials purchased	105,000	(a)
Cost of direct materials used in production	120,000	(b)
Direct labor	145,000	95,000
Factory overhead	56,000	42,000
Total manufacturing costs incurred in December	(b)	249,000
Total manufacturing costs	336,000	283,000
Work in process inventory, December 1	45,000	34,000
Work in process inventory, December 31	65,000	(c)
Cost of goods manufactured	(c)	252,000
Finished goods inventory, December 1	84,000	44,000
Finished goods inventory, December 31	74,000	(d)
Sales	425,000	320,000
Cost of goods sold	(d)	254,000
Gross profit	(e)	(e)
Operating expenses	44,000	(f)
Net income	(f)	27,000

Instructions
1. Determine the amounts of the missing items, identifying them by letter.
2. Prepare a statement of cost of goods manufactured for Vinston Company.
3. Prepare an income statement for Vinston Company.

PR 18-5A
Statement of cost of goods manufactured and income statement for a manufacturing company

objs. 2, 3

The following information is available for Sano Instrument Manufacturing Company for 2008:

Inventories	January 1	December 31
Materials	$ 85,000	$105,000
Work in process	120,000	105,000
Finished goods	125,000	110,000

Advertising expense	$ 75,000
Depreciation expense—Office equipment	25,000
Depreciation expense—Factory equipment	16,000
Direct labor	205,000
Heat, light, and power—Factory	6,500
Indirect labor	26,000
Materials purchased during August	135,000
Office salaries expense	85,000
Property taxes—Factory	4,500
Property taxes—Headquarters building	15,000
Rent expense—Factory	7,500
Sales	950,000
Sales salaries expense	150,000
Supplies—Factory	3,500
Miscellaneous cost—Factory	4,500

Instructions

1. Prepare the 2008 statement of cost of goods manufactured.
2. Prepare the 2008 income statement.

Problems Series B

PR 18-1B
Classifying costs

obj. 2

The following is a list of costs that were incurred in the production and sale of lawn mowers:

a. Payroll taxes on hourly assembly line employees.
b. Filter for spray gun used to paint the lawn mowers.
c. Cost of boxes used in packaging lawn mowers.
d. Premiums on insurance policy for factory buildings.
e. Gasoline engines used for lawn mowers.
f. Salary of factory supervisor.
g. Tires for lawn mowers.
h. Cost of advertising in a national magazine.
i. Plastic for outside housing of lawn mowers.
j. Salary of quality control supervisor who inspects each lawn mower before it is shipped.
k. Steering wheels for lawn mowers.
l. Cash paid to outside firm for janitorial services for factory.
m. Engine oil used in mower engines prior to shipment.
n. Attorney fees for drafting a new lease for headquarters offices.
o. Maintenance costs for new robotic factory equipment, based upon hours of usage.
p. Straight-line depreciation on the robotic machinery used to manufacture the lawn mowers.
q. License fees for use of patent for lawn mower blade, based upon the number of lawn mowers produced.
r. Telephone charges for controller's office.
s. Paint used to coat the lawn mowers.
t. Steel used in producing the lawn mowers.
u. Commissions paid to sales representatives, based upon the number of lawn mowers sold.
v. Electricity used to run the robotic machinery.
w. Factory cafeteria cashier's wages.
x. Property taxes on the factory building and equipment.
y. Salary of vice president of marketing.
z. Hourly wages of operators of robotic machinery used in production.

Instructions

Classify each cost as either a product cost or a period cost. Indicate whether each product cost is a direct materials cost, a direct labor cost, or a factory overhead cost. Indicate whether each period cost is a selling expense or an administrative expense. Use the following tabular headings for your answer, placing an "X" in the appropriate column.

	Product Costs			Period Costs	
Cost	Direct Materials Cost	Direct Labor Cost	Factory Overhead Cost	Selling Expense	Administrative Expense

---

PR 18-2B
Classifying costs
obj. 2

The following is a list of costs incurred by several businesses:

a. Packing supplies for products sold.
b. Tires for an automobile manufacturer.
c. Costs for television advertisement.
d. Disk drives for a microcomputer manufacturer.
e. Executive bonus for vice president of marketing.
f. Seed for grain farmer.
g. Wages of a machine operator on the production line.
h. Wages of controller's secretary.
i. Factory operating supplies.
j. First-aid supplies for factory workers.
k. Depreciation of factory equipment.
l. Salary of quality control supervisor.
m. Sales commissions.
n. Maintenance and repair costs for factory equipment.
o. Cost of hogs for meat processor.
p. Health insurance premiums paid for factory workers.
q. Lumber used by furniture manufacturer.
r. Paper used by commercial printer.
s. Hourly wages of warehouse laborers.
t. Paper used by Computer Department in processing various managerial reports.
u. Costs of operating a research laboratory.
v. Entertainment expenses for sales representatives.
w. Cost of telephone operators for a toll-free hotline to help customers operate products.
x. Protective glasses for factory machine operators.

Instructions
Classify each of the preceding costs as product costs or period costs. Indicate whether each product cost is a direct materials cost, a direct labor cost, or a factory overhead cost. Indicate whether each period cost is a selling expense or an administrative expense. Use the following tabular headings for preparing your answer. Place an "X" in the appropriate column.

	Product Costs			Period Costs	
Cost	Direct Materials Cost	Direct Labor Cost	Factory Overhead Cost	Selling Expense	Administrative Expense

---

PR 18-3B
Cost classifications—service company
obj. 2

A partial list of Heartland Hotel's costs is provided below.

a. Salary of the hotel president.
b. Depreciation of the hotel.
c. Cost of new carpeting.
d. Cost of soaps and shampoos for rooms.
e. Cost of food.
f. Wages of desk clerks.
g. Cost to paint lobby.
h. Cost of advertising in local newspaper.
i. Utility cost.
j. Cost of valet service.
k. General maintenance supplies.
l. Wages of maids.
m. Wages of bellhops.
n. Wages of convention setup employees.
o. Pay-for-view rental costs (in rooms).

(continued)

p. Cost of room mini-bar supplies.
q. Guest room telephone costs for long-distance calls.
r. Wages of kitchen employees.
s. Cost of laundering towels and bedding.
t. Cost to replace lobby furniture.
u. Training for hotel restaurant servers.
v. Cost to mail a customer survey.
w. Champagne for guests.

Instructions
1. What would be Heartland's most logical definition for the final cost object?
2. Identify how each of the costs is to be classified as either direct or indirect. Define direct costs in terms of a hotel guest as the cost object.

PR 18-4B
Manufacturing income statement, statement of cost of goods manufactured

objs. 2, 3

Several items are omitted from each of the following income statement and cost of goods manufactured statement data for the month of December 2008:

	Washington Company	Lee Company
Materials inventory, December 1	$ 65,000	$ 85,000
Materials inventory, December 31	(a)	95,000
Materials purchased	165,000	190,000
Cost of direct materials used in production	174,000	(a)
Direct labor	245,000	(b)
Factory overhead	76,000	95,000
Total manufacturing costs incurred during December	(b)	550,000
Total manufacturing costs	620,000	755,000
Work in process inventory, December 1	125,000	205,000
Work in process inventory, December 31	105,000	(c)
Cost of goods manufactured	(c)	545,000
Finished goods inventory, December 1	110,000	95,000
Finished goods inventory, December 31	115,000	(d)
Sales	950,000	850,000
Cost of goods sold	(d)	551,000
Gross profit	(e)	(e)
Operating expenses	125,000	(f)
Net income	(f)	189,000

Instructions
1. Determine the amounts of the missing items, identifying them by letter.
2. Prepare a statement of cost of goods manufactured for Lee Company.
3. Prepare an income statement for Lee Company.

PR 18-5B
Statement of cost of goods manufactured and income statement for a manufacturing company

objs. 2, 3

The following information is available for Earp Corporation for 2008:

Inventories	January 1	December 31
Materials	$125,000	$155,000
Work in process	225,000	210,000
Finished goods	215,000	210,000

Advertising expense	$ 105,000
Depreciation expense—Office equipment	15,000
Depreciation expense—Factory equipment	20,000
Direct labor	240,000
Heat, light, and power—Factory	8,000
Indirect labor	28,000
Materials purchased during August	235,000
Office salaries expense	82,000
Property taxes—Factory	6,500
Property taxes—Office building	13,500
Rent expense—Factory	11,000
Sales	1,100,000
Sales salaries expense	135,000
Supplies—Factory	5,500
Miscellaneous cost—Factory	3,400

Instructions

1. Prepare the 2008 statement of cost of goods manufactured.
2. Prepare the 2008 income statement.

Special Activities

SA 18-1
Ethics and professional conduct in business

ETHICS

Farrar Manufacturing Company allows employees to purchase, at cost, manufacturing materials, such as metal and lumber, for personal use. To purchase materials for personal use, an employee must complete a materials requisition form, which must then be approved by the employee's immediate supervisor. Peggy Carron, an assistant cost accountant, charges the employee an amount based on Farrar's net purchase cost.

Peggy Carron is in the process of replacing a deck on her home and has requisitioned lumber for personal use, which has been approved in accordance with company policy. In computing the cost of the lumber, Peggy reviewed all the purchase invoices for the past year. She then used the lowest price to compute the amount due the company for the lumber.

Discuss whether Peggy behaved in an ethical manner.

SA 18-2
Financial vs. managerial accounting

The following statement was made by the vice president of finance of Haberman Inc.: "The managers of a company should use the same information as the shareholders of the firm. When managers use the same information in guiding their internal operations as shareholders use in evaluating their investments, the managers will be aligned with the stockholders' profit objectives."

Respond to the vice president's statement.

SA 18-3
Managerial accounting in the management process

For each of the following managers, describe how managerial accounting could be used to satisfy strategic or operational objectives:

1. The vice president of the Information Systems Division of a bank.
2. A hospital administrator.
3. The chief executive officer of a food company. The food company is divided into three divisions: Nonalcoholic Beverages, Snack Foods, and Fast Food Restaurants.
4. The manager of the local campus copy shop.

SA 18-4
Classifying costs

On-Time Computer Repairs provides computer repair services for the community. Laurie Estes's computer was not working, and she called On-Time for a home repair visit. The On-Time technician arrived at 2:00 P.M. to begin work. By 4:00 P.M. the problem was diagnosed as a failed circuit board. Unfortunately, the technician did not have a new circuit board in the truck, since the technician's previous customer had the same problem, and a board was used on that visit. Replacement boards were available back at the On-Time shop. Therefore, the technician drove back to the shop to retrieve a replacement board. From 4:00 to 5:00 P.M., the On-Time technician drove the round trip to retrieve the replacement board from the shop.

At 5:00 P.M. the technician was back on the job at Laurie's home. The replacement procedure is somewhat complex, since a variety of tests must be performed once the board is installed. The job was completed at 6:00 P.M.

Laurie's repair bill showed the following:

Circuit board	$ 80
Labor charges	190
Total	$270

Laurie was surprised at the size of the bill and asked for some greater detail supporting the calculations. On-Time responded with the following explanations.

Cost of materials:	
Purchase price of circuit board	$60
Markup on purchase price to cover storage and handling	20
Total materials charge	$80

The labor charge per hour is detailed as follows:

2:00–3:00 P.M.	$ 40
3:00–4:00 P.M.	35
4:00–5:00 P.M.	45
5:00–6:00 P.M.	70
Total labor charge	$190

Further explanations in the differences in the hourly rates are as follows:

First hour:
Base labor rate	$20
Fringe benefits	7
Overhead (other than storage and handling)	8
Total base labor rate	$35
Additional charge for first hour of any job to cover the cost of vehicle depreciation, fuel, and employee time in transit. A 30-minute transit time is assumed.	5
	$40

Third hour:
Base labor rate	$35
The trip back to the shop includes vehicle depreciation and fuel; therefore, a charge was added to the hourly rate to cover these costs. The round trip took an hour.	10
	$45

Fourth hour:
Base labor rate	$35
Overtime premium for time worked in excess of an eight-hour day (starting at 5:00 P.M.) is equal to the base rate.	35
	$70

1. If you were in Laurie's position, how would you respond to the bill? Are there parts of the bill that appear incorrect to you? If so, what argument would you employ to convince On-Time that the bill is too high?
2. Use the headings below to construct a table. Fill in the table by first listing the costs identified in the activity in the left-hand column. For each cost, place a check mark in the appropriate column identifying the correct cost classification. Assume that each service call is a job.

Cost	Direct Materials	Direct Labor	Overhead

SA 18-5
Using managerial accounting information

The following situations describe decision scenarios that could use managerial accounting information.

1. The manager of Taco Castle wishes to determine the price to charge for various lunch plates.
2. By evaluating the cost of leftover materials, the plant manager of a precision machining facility wishes to determine how effectively the plant is being run.
3. The division controller needs to determine the cost of products left in inventory.
4. The manager of the Maintenance Department wishes to plan next year's anticipated expenditures.

For each situation, discuss how managerial accounting information could be used.

SA 18-6
Classifying costs

Group Project

With a group of students, visit a local copy and graphics shop or a pizza restaurant. As you observe the operation, consider the costs associated with running the business. As a group, identify as many costs as you can and classify them according to the following table headings:

Cost	Direct Materials	Direct Labor	Overhead	Selling Expenses

Answers to Self-Examination Questions

1. **B** Managerial accounting is not restricted to generally accepted accounting principles, as is financial accounting (answer B). Both financial and managerial accounting support decision making (answer A). Financial accounting is mostly concerned with the decision making of external users, while managerial accounting supports decision making of management. Both financial and managerial accounting can result in financial reports (answer C). Managerial accounting reports are developed for internal use by managers at various levels in the organization. Both managerial and financial accounting record events from the past (answer D); however, managerial accounting can also include information about the future in the form of budgets and cash flow projections.

2. **D** The five basic phases of the management process are planning (answer A), directing (not listed), controlling (answer B), improving (not listed), and decision making (answer C). Operating (answer D) is not one of the five basic phases, but operations are the object of managers' attention.

3. **C** Sales salaries (answer C) is a selling expense and is not considered a cost of manufacturing a product. Direct materials cost (answer A), factory overhead cost (answer B), and direct labor cost (answer D) are costs of manufacturing a product.

4. **B** Depreciation of testing equipment (answer B) is included as part of the factory overhead costs of the microcomputer manufacturer. The cost of memory chips (answer A) and the cost of disk drives (answer D) are both considered a part of direct materials cost. The wages of microcomputer assemblers (answer C) are part of direct labor costs.

5. **C** Cost of goods sold is calculated as follows:

Beginning finished goods inventory	$ 50,000
Add: Cost of goods manufactured	125,000
Less: Ending finished goods inventory	35,000
Cost of goods sold	$140,000

© 2004 JIMMY CHIN/JIMMY CHIN PHOTOGRAPHY. ALL RIGHTS RESERVED.

Budgeting

objectives

After studying this chapter, you should be able to:

1 Describe budgeting, its objectives, and its impact on human behavior.

2 Describe the basic elements of the budget process, the two major types of budgeting, and the use of computers in budgeting.

3 Describe the master budget for a manufacturing business.

4 Prepare the basic income statement budgets for a manufacturing business.

5 Prepare balance sheet budgets for a manufacturing business.

The North Face

You may have financial goals for your life. To achieve these goals, it is necessary to plan for future expenses. For example, you may consider taking a part-time job to save money for school expenses for the coming school year. How much money would you need to earn and save in order to pay these expenses? One way to find an answer to this question would be to prepare a budget. For example, a budget would show an estimate of your expenses associated with school, such as tuition, fees, and books. In addition, you would have expenses for day-to-day living, such as rent, food, and clothing. You might also have expenses for travel and entertainment. Once the school year begins, you can use the budget as a tool for guiding your spending priorities during the year.

The budget is used in businesses in much the same way as it can be used in personal life. For example, The North Face sponsors mountain climbing expeditions throughout the year for professional and amateur climbers. These events require budgeting to plan for the trip expenses, much like you might use a budget to plan a vacation.

Budgeting is also used by The North Face to plan the manufacturing costs associated with its outdoor clothing and equipment production. For example, budgets would be used to determine the number of coats to be produced, number of people to be employed, and amount of material to be purchased. The budget provides the company a "game plan" for the year. In this chapter, you will see how budgets can be used for financial planning and control.

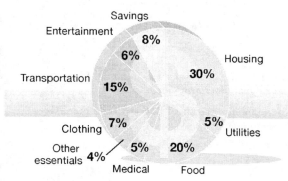

Nature and Objectives of Budgeting

objective **1**

Describe budgeting, its objectives, and its impact on human behavior.

If you were driving across the country, you might plan your trip with the aid of a road map. The road map would lay out your route across the country, identify stopovers, and reduce your chances of getting lost. In the same way, a **budget** charts a course for a business by outlining the plans of the business in financial terms. Like the road map, the budget can help a company navigate through the year and reach the destination, while minimizing bad results.

Although budgets are normally associated with profit-making businesses, they also play an important role in operating most units of government. For example, budgets are important in managing rural school districts and small villages as well as agencies of the federal government. Budgets are also important for managing the operations of churches, hospitals, and other nonprofit institutions. Individuals and families also use budgeting techniques in managing their financial affairs. In this chapter, we emphasize the principles of budgeting in the context of a business organized for profit.

OBJECTIVES OF BUDGETING

Budgeting involves (1) establishing specific goals, (2) executing plans to achieve the goals, and (3) periodically comparing actual results with the goals. These goals include both the overall business goals as well as the specific goals for the individual units within the business. Establishing specific goals for future operations is part of the *planning* function of management, while executing

The chart below shows the estimated portion of your total monthly income that should be budgeted for various living expenses.

Savings 8%
Entertainment 6%
Housing 30%
Transportation 15%
Clothing 7%
Utilities 5%
Other essentials 4%
Medical 5%
Food 20%

Source: Consumer Credit Counseling Service.

968

actions to meet the goals is the *directing* function of management. Periodically comparing actual results with these goals and taking appropriate action is the *controlling* function of management. The relationships of these functions are illustrated in Exhibit 1.

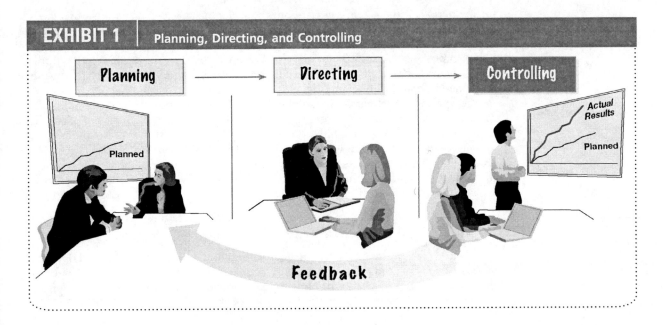

EXHIBIT 1 | Planning, Directing, and Controlling

REAL WORLD

Planning is also an important part of personal finances. Visa offers an online budget calculator and other helpful personal financial information at **http://www.practical moneyskills.com**.

Planning   A set of goals is often necessary to guide and focus individual and group actions. For example, students set academic goals, athletes set athletic goals, employees set career goals, and businesses set financial goals. In the same way, budgeting supports the planning process by requiring all organizational units to establish their goals for the upcoming period. These goals, in turn, motivate individuals and groups to perform at high levels. For example, General Motors Corporation is using its budget process to plan and execute a reduction of 25,000 manufacturing jobs through 2008 in order to better align its manufacturing capacity with the demand for vehicles.

Planning not only motivates employees to attain goals but also improves overall decision making. During the planning phase of the budget process, all viewpoints are considered, options identified, and cost reduction opportunities assessed. This effort leads to better decision making for the organization. As a result, the budget process may reveal opportunities or threats that were not known prior to the budget planning process. For example, the financial planning process helped Microsoft Corporation plan its expansion into the home and entertainment market with Xbox 360®.

Directing   Once the budget plans are in place, they can be used to direct and coordinate operations in order to achieve the stated goals. For example, your goal to receive an "A" in a course would result in certain activities, such as reading the book, completing assignments, participating in class, and studying for exams. Such actions are fairly easy to direct and coordinate. A business, however, is much more complex and requires more formal direction and coordination. The budget is one way to direct and coordinate business activities and units to achieve stated goals. The budgetary units of an organization are called **responsibility centers**. Each responsibility center is led by a manager who has the authority over and responsibility for the unit's performance.

If there is a change in the external environment, the budget process can also be used by unit managers to readjust the operations. For example, S-K-I Limited uses weather information to plan expenditures at its Killington and Mt. Snow ski resorts in Vermont. When the weather is forecasted to turn cold and dry, the company increases expenditures in snow-making activities and adds to the staff in order to serve a greater number of skiers.

Controlling As time passes, the actual performance of an operation can be compared against the planned goals. This provides prompt feedback to employees about their performance. If necessary, employees can use such *feedback* to adjust their activities in the future. For example, a salesperson may be given a quota to achieve $100,000 in sales for the period. If the actual sales are only $75,000, the salesperson can use this feedback about underperformance to change sales tactics and improve future sales. Feedback is not only helpful to individuals, but it can also redirect a complete organization. For example, Eastman Kodak Company is responding to recent declines in the traditional chemical-based photo imaging business with an ambitious strategy to expand on-demand photo printing and digital image solutions.

Comparing actual results to the plan also helps prevent unplanned expenditures. The budget encourages employees to establish their spending priorities. For example, departments in universities have budgets to support faculty travel to conferences and meetings. The travel budget communicates to the faculty the upper limit on travel. Often, desired travel exceeds the budget. Thus, the budget requires the faculty to prioritize travel-related opportunities. In the next chapter, we will discuss comparing actual costs with budgeted costs in greater detail.

HUMAN BEHAVIOR AND BUDGETING

In the budgeting process, business, team, and individual goals are established. Human behavior problems can arise if (1) the budget goal is too tight and thus is very hard for the employees to achieve, (2) the budget goal is too loose and thus is very easy for the employees to achieve, or (3) the budget goals of the business conflict with the objectives of the employees. This is illustrated in Exhibit 2.

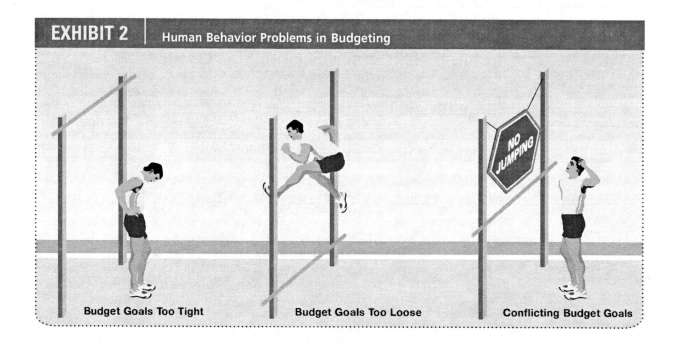

EXHIBIT 2 | Human Behavior Problems in Budgeting

Budget Goals Too Tight   Budget Goals Too Loose   Conflicting Budget Goals

Setting Budget Goals Too Tightly People can become discouraged if performance expectations are set too high. For example, would you be inspired or discouraged by a guitar instructor expecting you to play like Eric Clapton after only a few lessons? You'd probably be discouraged. This same kind of problem can occur in businesses if employees view budget goals as unrealistic or unachievable. In such a case, the budget discourages employees from achieving the goals. On the other hand, aggressive but attainable goals are likely to inspire employees to achieve the goals. Therefore, it is important that employees (managers and nonmanagers) be involved in establishing reasonable budget estimates.

Involving all employees encourages cooperation both within and among departments. It also increases awareness of each department's importance to the overall objectives of the company. Employees view budgeting more positively when they have an opportunity to participate in the budget-setting process. This is because employees with a greater sense of control over the budget process will have a greater commitment to achieving its goals. In such cases, budgets are valuable planning tools that increase the possibility of achieving business goals.

Loose budgets may be appropriate in settings involving high uncertainty, such as research and development. The loose budget acts as a "shock absorber," giving managers maneuvering room to minimize work disruptions.

The state of Illinois' budget process requires unspent budget monies to be returned to the state when the fiscal year ends. According to the state comptroller, this encourages "an orgy of spending" at the end of a fiscal year.

Setting Budget Goals Too Loosely   Although it is desirable to establish attainable goals, it is undesirable to plan lower goals than may be possible. Such budget "padding" is termed **budgetary slack**. An example of budgetary slack is including spare employees in the plan. Managers may plan slack in the budget in order to provide a "cushion" for unexpected events or improve the appearance of operations. Budgetary slack can be avoided if lower- and mid-level managers are required to support their spending requirements with operational plans.

Slack budgets can cause employees to develop a "spend it or lose it" mentality. This often occurs at the end of the budget period when actual spending is less than the budget. Employees may attempt to spend the remaining budget (purchase equipment, hire consultants, purchase supplies) in order to avoid having the budget cut next period.

Setting Conflicting Budget Goals   **Goal conflict** occurs when individual self-interest differs from business objectives or when different departments are given conflicting objectives. Often, such conflicts are subtle. For example, the Sales Department manager may be given a sales goal, while the Manufacturing Department manager may be given a cost reduction goal. It is possible for both goals to conflict. The Sales Department may increase sales by promising customers small product deviations that are difficult and unprofitable to make. This would increase sales at the expense of Manufacturing's expense reduction goal and impact the overall profitability objectives of the firm. Likewise, Manufacturing may schedule the plant for maximum manufacturing efficiency with little regard for actual customer product demand. This would reduce manufacturing costs at the expense of the sales goal and reduce the overall profitability of the firm. Goal conflict can be avoided if budget goals are carefully designed for consistency across all areas of the organization.

Integrity, Objectivity, and Ethics in Business

ETHICS

BUDGET GAMES

The budgeting system is designed to plan and control a business. However, it is common for the budget to be "gamed" by its participants. For example, managers may pad their budgets with excess resources. In this way, the managers have additional resources for unexpected events during the period. If the budget is being used to establish the incentive plan, then sales managers have incentives to understate the sales potential of a territory in order to ensure hitting their quotas. Other times, managers engage in "land grabbing," which occurs when they overstate the sales potential of a territory in order to guarantee access to resources. If managers believe that unspent resources will not roll over to future periods, then they may be encouraged to "spend it or lose it," causing wasteful expenditures. These types of problems can be partially overcome by separating the budget into planning and incentive components. This is why many organizations have two budget processes, one for resource planning and another, more challenging budget, for motivating managers.

Budgeting Systems

objective   **2**

Describe the basic elements of the budget process, the two major types of budgeting, and the use of computers in budgeting.

Western Digital Corporation, a computer hard drive manufacturer, introduced a new Web-based B&P (budget and planning) system to perform a continuous rolling budget. According to the financial executives at the company, "We're never [again] comparing results to old operating plans that were set months ago." Rather, the more frequent budget cycle enables senior managers to react to changing business conditions with revised and updated budgets.

Budgeting systems vary among businesses because of such factors as organizational structure, complexity of operations, and management philosophy. Differences in budget systems are even more significant among different types of businesses, such as manufacturers and service businesses. The details of a budgeting system used by an automobile manufacturer such as Ford Motor Company would obviously differ from a service company such as American Airlines. However, the basic budgeting concepts illustrated in the following paragraphs apply to all types of businesses and organizations.

The budgetary period for operating activities normally includes the fiscal year of a business. A year is short enough that future operations can be estimated fairly accurately, yet long enough that the future can be viewed in a broad context. However, to achieve effective control, the annual budgets are usually subdivided into shorter time periods, such as quarters of the year, months, or weeks.

A variation of fiscal-year budgeting, called **continuous budgeting**, maintains a 12-month projection into the future. The 12-month budget is continually revised by removing the data for the period just ended and adding estimated budget data for the same period next year, as shown in Exhibit 3.

Developing budgets for the next fiscal year usually begins several months prior to the end of the current year. This responsibility is normally assigned to a budget committee. Such a committee often consists of the budget director and such high-level executives as the controller, the treasurer, the production manager, and the sales manager. Once the budget has been approved, the budget process is monitored and summarized by the Accounting Department, which reports to the committee.

There are several methods of developing budget estimates. One method, termed **zero-based budgeting**, requires managers to estimate sales, production, and other operating data as though operations are being started for the first time. This approach has the benefit of taking a fresh view of operations each year. A more common approach is to start with last year's budget and revise it for actual results and expected changes for the coming year. Two major budgets using this approach are the static budget and the flexible budget.

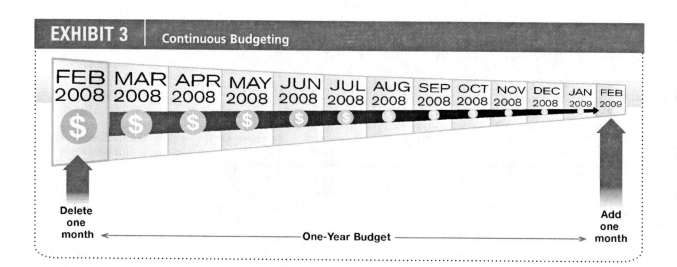

EXHIBIT 3 | **Continuous Budgeting**

STATIC BUDGET

A **static budget** shows the expected results of a responsibility center for only one activity level. Once the budget has been determined, it is not changed, even if the activity changes. Static budgeting is used by many service companies and for some administrative functions of manufacturing companies, such as purchasing, engineering, and accounting. For example, the Assembly Department manager for Colter Manufacturing Company prepared the static budget for the upcoming year, shown in Exhibit 4.

	A	B	
	Colter Manufacturing Company		
	Assembly Department Budget		
	For the Year Ending July 31, 2008		
1	Direct labor	$40,000	1
2	Electric power	5,000	2
3	Supervisor salaries	15,000	3
4	Total department costs	$60,000	4

EXHIBIT 4

Static Budget

A disadvantage of static budgets is that they do not adjust for changes in activity levels. For example, assume that the actual amounts spent by the Assembly Department of Colter Manufacturing totaled $72,000, which is $12,000 or 20% ($12,000/$60,000) more than budgeted. Is this good news or bad news? At first you might think that this is a bad result. However, this conclusion may not be valid, since static budget results may be difficult to interpret. To illustrate, assume that the assembly manager developed the budget based on plans to assemble *8,000* units during the year. However, if *10,000* units were actually produced, should the additional $12,000 in spending in excess of the budget be considered "bad news"? Maybe not. The Assembly Department provided 25% (2,000 units/8,000 units) more output for only 20% more cost.

Business Connections

BUILD VERSUS HARVEST

Budgeting systems are not "one size fits all" solutions but must adapt to the underlying business conditions. For example, a business can adopt either a build strategy or a harvest strategy. A *build* strategy is one where the business is designing, launching, and growing new products and markets. Build strategies often require short-term profit sacrifice in order to grow market share. Apple Computer, Inc.'s iPod® is an example of a product managed under a build strategy. A *harvest* strategy is often employed for business units with mature products enjoying high market share in low-growth industries. Harvest strategies maximize short-term earnings and cash flow, sometimes at the expense of market share. Often the term "cash cow" is used to describe a product managed under a harvest strategy. H.J. Heinz Company's Ketchup® and Ivory soap are examples of such products. Compared to the harvest strategy, a build strategy often has greater uncertainty, unpredictability, and change. The differences between build and harvest strategies imply different budgeting approaches.

The build strategy should employ a budget approach that is flexible to the uncertainty of the business. Thus,

budgets should adapt to changing conditions by allowing periodic revisions and flexible targets. Often the managers controlled by the budget will participate in setting budget targets, so that all uncertainties are considered. In addition, the budget will complement other, more subjective, evaluation criteria. Overall, the budget serves as a short-term planning tool to guide management in executing an uncertain and evolving product market strategy.

Under the harvest strategy, the business is often much more stable and is managed to maximize profitability and cash flow. Cost control is much more important in a harvest strategy; thus, the budget is used to restrict the actions of managers. In addition, the managers controlled by the budget often do not participate in its development. Rather, the budget is imposed. In a harvest business, the budget is the major control tool and is often not supplemented with other more subjective performance measures.

FLEXIBLE BUDGET

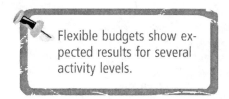

Flexible budgets show expected results for several activity levels.

Unlike static budgets, **flexible budgets** show the expected results of a responsibility center for several activity levels. You can think of a flexible budget as a series of static budgets for different levels of activity. Such budgets are especially useful in estimating and controlling factory costs and operating expenses. Exhibit 5 is a flexible budget for the annual manufacturing expense in the Assembly Department of Colter Manufacturing Company.

EXHIBIT 5

Flexible Budget

	A	B	C	D	
	Colter Manufacturing Company				
	Assembly Department Budget				
	For the Year Ending July 31, 2008				
		Level 1	Level 2	Level 3	
1	Units of production	8,000	9,000	10,000	1
2	Variable cost:				2
3	Direct labor ($5 per unit)	$40,000	$45,000	$50,000	3
4	Electric power ($0.50 per unit)	4,000	4,500	5,000	4
5	Total variable cost	$44,000	$49,500	$55,000	5
6	Fixed cost:				6
7	Electric power	$ 1,000	$ 1,000	$ 1,000	7
8	Supervisor salaries	15,000	15,000	15,000	8
9	Total fixed cost	$16,000	$16,000	$16,000	9
10	Total department costs	$60,000	$65,500	$71,000	10

Many hospitals use flexible budgeting to plan the number of nurses for patient floors. These budgets use a measure termed "relative value units," which is a measure of nursing effort. The more patients and the more severe their illnesses, the higher the total relative value units, and thus the higher the staffing budget.

When constructing a flexible budget, we first identify the relevant activity levels. In Exhibit 5, these are 8,000, 9,000, and 10,000 units of production. Alternative activity bases, such as machine hours or direct labor hours, may be used in measuring the volume of activity. Second, we identify the fixed and variable cost components of the costs being budgeted. For example, in Exhibit 5, the electric power cost is separated into its fixed cost ($1,000 per year) and variable cost ($0.50 per unit). Lastly, we prepare the budget for each activity level by multiplying the variable cost per unit by the activity level and then adding the monthly fixed cost.

With a flexible budget, the department manager can be evaluated by comparing actual expenses to the budgeted amount for actual activity. For example, if Colter Manufacturing Company's Assembly Department actually spent $72,000 to produce 10,000 units, the manager would be considered over budget by $1,000 ($72,000 − $71,000). Under the static budget in Exhibit 4, the department was $12,000 over budget. This

Example Exercise 22-1

objective **2**

At the beginning of the period, the Assembly Department budgeted direct labor of $45,000 and supervisor salaries of $30,000 for 5,000 hours of production. The department actually completed 6,000 hours of production. Determine the budget for the department, assuming that it uses flexible budgeting.

Follow My Example 22-1

Variable cost:
Direct labor (6,000 hours × $9* per hour) $54,000

Fixed cost:
Supervisor salaries 30,000
Total department costs $84,000

*$45,000/5,000 hours

For Practice: PE 22-1A, PE 22-1B

EXHIBIT 6	Static and Flexible Budgets

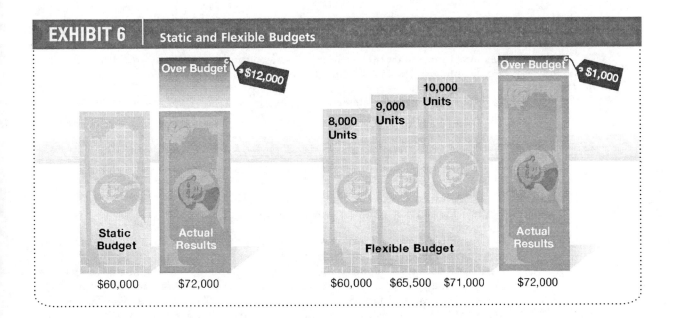

comparison is illustrated in Exhibit 6. The flexible budget for the Assembly Department is much more accurate than the static budget, because budget amounts adjust for changes in activity.

COMPUTERIZED BUDGETING SYSTEMS

In developing budgets, firms use a variety of computerized approaches. A recent survey reported that 67% of the respondents relied on spreadsheets for budgeting and planning.[1] The remaining firms use integrated computerized budget and planning (B&P) systems. Such systems speed up and reduce the cost of preparing the budget. This is especially true when large quantities of data need to be processed. The same survey reported that companies relying on spreadsheets required 30 more days to prepare the budget than those relying on integrated B&P systems. For example, Fujitsu, a major Japanese technology company, used B&P software to streamline its budgeting process from 6 to 8 weeks down to 10 to 15 days.

Integrated B&P software is also useful in continuous budgeting. The newest B&P systems are accomplishing this by using Web-based applications to link thousands of employees together. With these systems, employees can input budget information onto the Web pages that are automatically aggregated and summarized throughout the organization. In this way, an organization can link the top-level strategy to the lower-level operational goals—and do so quickly and consistently across the organization. The use of Web-based B&P systems is moving companies closer to the real-time budget, wherein the budget is being "rolled" every day and represents the best assumptions at any moment in time.[2]

Managers often use computer spreadsheets or simulation models to represent the operating and budget relationships. By using computer simulation models, the impact of various operating alternatives on the budget can be assessed. For example, the budget can be revised to show the impact of a proposed change in indirect labor wage rates. Likewise, the budgetary effect of a proposed product line can be determined. In the next section, we illustrate how a company ties its budgets together, using a master budget.

---

1 Tim Reason, "Budgeting in the Real World," *CFO Magazine,* July 1, 2005.
2 Janet Kersnar, "Rolling Along," *CFO Europe,* September 14, 2004.

Master Budget

objective   *3*

*Describe the
master budget for
a manufacturing
business.*

Manufacturing operations require a series of budgets that are linked together in a **master budget**. The major parts of the master budget are as follows:

Budgeted Income Statement	Budgeted Balance Sheet
Sales budget	Cash budget
Cost of goods sold budget:	Capital expenditures budget
Production budget	
Direct materials purchases budget	
Direct labor cost budget	
Factory overhead cost budget	
Selling and administrative expenses budget	

Exhibit 7 shows the relationship among the income statement budgets. The budget process begins by estimating sales. The sales information is then provided to the various units for estimating the production and selling and administrative expenses budgets. The production budgets are used to prepare the direct materials purchases, direct labor cost, and factory overhead cost budgets. These three budgets are used to develop the cost of goods sold budget. Once these budgets and the selling and administrative expenses budget have been completed, the budgeted income statement can be prepared, as we illustrate in the following section.

EXHIBIT 7

**Income Statement
Budgets**

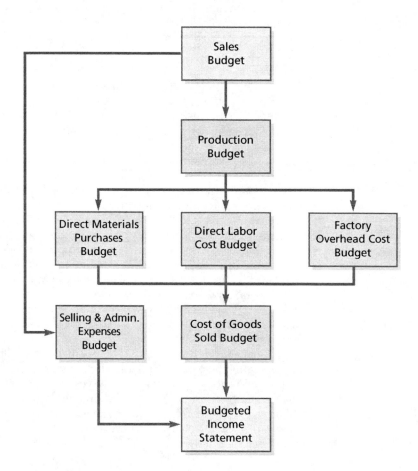

After the budgeted income statement has been developed, the budgeted balance sheet can be prepared. Two major budgets comprising the budgeted balance sheet are the cash budget and the capital expenditures budget, which we illustrate later.

Income Statement Budgets

objective **4**

Prepare the basic income statement budgets for a manufacturing business.

In the following sections, we will illustrate the major elements of the income statement budget. We will use a small manufacturing business, Elite Accessories Inc., as the basis for our illustration.

SALES BUDGET

The **sales budget** normally indicates for each product (1) the quantity of estimated sales and (2) the expected unit selling price. These data are often reported by regions or by sales representatives.

In estimating the quantity of sales for each product, past sales volumes are often used as a starting point. These amounts are revised for factors that are expected to affect future sales, such as the factors listed below.

- backlog of unfilled sales orders
- planned advertising and promotion
- expected industry and general economic conditions
- productive capacity
- projected pricing policy
- findings of market research studies

Once an estimate of the sales volume is obtained, the expected sales revenue can be determined by multiplying the volume by the expected unit sales price. Exhibit 8 is the sales budget for Elite Accessories Inc.

EXHIBIT 8

Sales Budget

	A	B	C	D	
	Elite Accessories Inc.				
	Sales Budget				
	For the Year Ending December 31, 2008				
	Product and Region	Unit Sales Volume	Unit Selling Price	Total Sales	
1	Wallet:	287,000	$12.00	$ 3,444,000	1
2	East	241,000	12.00	2,892,000	2
3	West	528,000		$ 6,336,000	3
4	Total				4
5					5
6	Handbag:				6
7	East	156,400	$25.00	$ 3,910,000	7
8	West	123,600	25.00	3,090,000	8
9	Total	280,000		$ 7,000,000	9
10					10
11	Total revenue from sales			$13,336,000	11

For control purposes, management can compare actual sales and budgeted sales by product, region, or sales representative. Management would investigate any significant differences and take possible corrective actions.

PRODUCTION BUDGET

Production should be carefully coordinated with the sales budget to ensure that production and sales are kept in balance during the period. The number of units to be manufactured to meet budgeted sales and inventory needs for each product is set forth in the **production budget**. The budgeted volume of production is determined as follows:

Expected units to be sold
+ Desired units in ending inventory
− Estimated units in beginning inventory
Total units to be produced

Exhibit 9 is the production budget for Elite Accessories Inc.

EXHIBIT 9

Production Budget

	A	B	C	
	Elite Accessories Inc. Production Budget For the Year Ending December 31, 2008			
		Units		
		Wallet	Handbag	
1	Expected units to be sold (from Exhibit 8)	528,000	280,000	1
2	Plus desired ending inventory, December 31, 2008	80,000	60,000	2
3	Total	608,000	340,000	3
4	Less estimated beginning inventory, January 1, 2008	88,000	48,000	4
5	Total units to be produced	520,000	292,000	5

Example Exercise 22-2   objective **4**

Landon Awards Co. projected sales of 45,000 brass plaques for 2008. The estimated January 1, 2008, inventory is 3,000 units, and the desired December 31, 2008, inventory is 5,000 units. What is the budgeted production (in units) for 2008?

Follow My Example 22-2

Expected units to be sold 45,000
Plus desired ending inventory, December 31, 2008   5,000
 Total 50,000
Less estimated beginning inventory, January 1, 2008   3,000
 Total units to be produced 47,000

For Practice: PE 22-2A, PE 22-2B

DIRECT MATERIALS PURCHASES BUDGET

The production budget is the starting point for determining the estimated quantities of direct materials to be purchased. Multiplying these quantities by the expected unit purchase price determines the total cost of direct materials to be purchased.

> Materials required for production
> + Desired ending materials inventory
> − Estimated beginning materials inventory
> Direct materials to be purchased

In Elite Accessories Inc.'s production operations, leather and lining are required for wallets and handbags. The quantity of direct materials expected to be used for each unit of product is as follows:

Wallet:
    Leather: 0.30 square yard per unit
    Lining: 0.10 square yard per unit

Handbag:
    Leather: 1.25 square yards per unit
    Lining: 0.50 square yard per unit

Based on these data and the production budget, the **direct materials purchases budget** is prepared. As shown in the budget in Exhibit 10, for Elite Accessories Inc. to produce 520,000 wallets, 156,000 square yards (520,000 units × 0.30 square yard per unit) of leather are needed. Likewise, to produce 292,000 handbags, 365,000 square yards (292,000 units × 1.25 square yards per unit) of leather are needed. We can compute the needs for lining in a similar manner. Then adding the desired ending inventory for each material and deducting the estimated beginning inventory determines the

EXHIBIT 10

Direct Materials
Purchases Budget

	A	B	C	D	E	
		Elite Accessories Inc.				
		Direct Materials Purchases Budget				
		For the Year Ending December 31, 2008				
			Direct Materials			
			Leather	Lining	Total	
1	Square yards required for production:					1
2	Wallet (Note A)		156,000	52,000		2
3	Handbag (Note B)		365,000	146,000		3
4	Plus desired inventory, December 31, 2008		20,000	12,000		4
5	Total		541,000	210,000		5
6	Less estimated inventory, January 1, 2008		18,000	15,000		6
7	Total square yards to be purchased		523,000	195,000		7
8	Unit price (per square yard)		× $4.50	× $1.20		8
9	Total direct materials to be purchased		$2,353,500	$234,000	$2,587,500	9
10						10
11	Note A: Leather: 520,000 units × 0.30 sq. yd. per unit = 156,000 sq. yds.					11
12	Lining: 520,000 units × 0.10 sq. yd. per unit = 52,000 sq. yds.					12
13						13
14	Note B: Leather: 292,000 units × 1.25 sq. yds. per unit = 365,000 sq. yds.					14
15	Lining: 292,000 units × 0.50 sq. yd. per unit = 146,000 sq. yds.					15

amount of each material to be purchased. Multiplying these amounts by the estimated cost per square yard yields the total materials purchase cost.

The direct materials purchases budget helps management maintain inventory levels within reasonable limits. For this purpose, the timing of the direct materials purchases should be coordinated between the purchasing and production departments.

Example Exercise 22-3   objective 4

Landon Awards Co. budgeted production of 47,000 brass plaques in 2008. Brass sheet is required to produce a brass plaque. Assume 96 square inches of brass sheet are required for each brass plaque. The estimated January 1, 2008, brass sheet inventory is 240,000 square inches. The desired December 31, 2008, brass sheet inventory is 200,000 square inches. If brass sheet costs $0.12 per square inch, determine the direct materials purchases budget for 2008.

Follow My Example 22-3

Square inches required for production:	
Brass sheet (47,000 × 96 sq. in.)	4,512,000
Plus desired ending inventory, December 31, 2008	200,000
Total	4,712,000
Less estimated beginning inventory, January 1, 2008	240,000
Total square inches to be purchased	4,472,000
Unit price (per square inch)	× $0.12
Total direct materials to be purchased	$ 536,640

For Practice: PE 22-3A, PE 22-3B

DIRECT LABOR COST BUDGET

The production budget also provides the starting point for preparing the direct labor cost budget. For Elite Accessories Inc., the labor requirements for each unit of product are estimated as follows:

Wallet:
    Cutting Department: 0.10 hour per unit
    Sewing Department: 0.25 hour per unit

Handbag:
    Cutting Department: 0.15 hour per unit
    Sewing Department: 0.40 hour per unit

Based on these data and the production budget, Elite Accessories Inc. prepares the direct labor budget. As shown in the budget in Exhibit 11, for Elite Accessories Inc. to produce 520,000 wallets, 52,000 hours (520,000 units × 0.10 hour per unit) of labor in the Cutting Department are required. Likewise, to produce 292,000 handbags, 43,800 hours (292,000 units × 0.15 hour per unit) of labor in the Cutting Department are required. In a similar manner, we can determine the direct labor hours needed in the Sewing Department to meet the budgeted production. Multiplying the direct labor hours for each department by the estimated department hourly rate yields the total direct labor cost for each department.

EXHIBIT 11

Direct Labor Cost Budget

	A	B	C	D	E	
		Elite Accessories Inc.				
		Direct Labor Cost Budget				
		For the Year Ending December 31, 2008				
			Cutting	Sewing	Total	
1	Hours required for production:					1
2	Wallet (Note A)		52,000	130,000		2
3	Handbag (Note B)		43,800	116,800		3
4	Total		95,800	246,800		4
5	Hourly rate		× $12.00	× $15.00		5
6	Total direct labor cost		$1,149,600	$3,702,000	$4,851,600	6
7						7
8	Note A:	Cutting Department: 520,000 units × 0.10 hour per unit = 52,000 hours				8
9		Sewing Department: 520,000 units × 0.25 hour per unit = 130,000 hours				9
10						10
11	Note B:	Cutting Department: 292,000 units × 0.15 hour per unit = 43,800 hours				11
12		Sewing Department: 292,000 units × 0.40 hour per unit = 116,800 hours				12

The direct labor needs should be coordinated between the production and personnel departments. This ensures that there will be enough labor available for production.

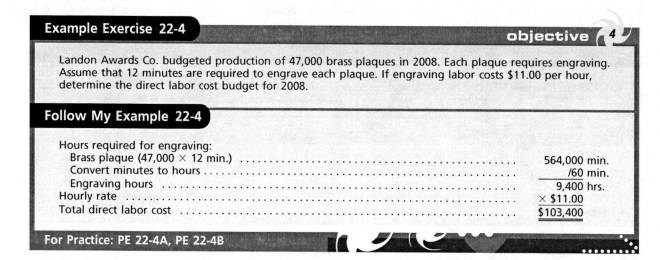

Example Exercise 22-4

objective 4

Landon Awards Co. budgeted production of 47,000 brass plaques in 2008. Each plaque requires engraving. Assume that 12 minutes are required to engrave each plaque. If engraving labor costs $11.00 per hour, determine the direct labor cost budget for 2008.

Follow My Example 22-4

Hours required for engraving:	
Brass plaque (47,000 × 12 min.)	564,000 min.
Convert minutes to hours	/60 min.
Engraving hours	9,400 hrs.
Hourly rate	× $11.00
Total direct labor cost	$103,400

For Practice: PE 22-4A, PE 22-4B

FACTORY OVERHEAD COST BUDGET

The estimated factory overhead costs necessary for production make up the factory overhead cost budget. This budget usually includes the total estimated cost for each item of factory overhead, as shown in Exhibit 12.

A business may prepare supporting departmental schedules, in which the factory overhead costs are separated into their fixed and variable cost elements. Such schedules

EXHIBIT 12

Factory Overhead
Cost Budget

	A	B	
	Elite Accessories Inc.		
	Factory Overhead Cost Budget		
	For the Year Ending December 31, 2008		
1	Indirect factory wages	$ 732,800	1
2	Supervisor salaries	360,000	2
3	Power and light	306,000	3
4	Depreciation of plant and equipment	288,000	4
5	Indirect materials	182,800	5
6	Maintenance	140,280	6
7	Insurance and property taxes	79,200	7
8	Total factory overhead cost	$2,089,080	8

enable department managers to direct their attention to those costs for which they are responsible and to evaluate performance.

COST OF GOODS SOLD BUDGET

The direct materials purchases budget, direct labor cost budget, and factory overhead cost budget are the starting point for preparing the **cost of goods sold budget**. To illustrate, these data are combined with the desired ending inventory and the estimated beginning inventory data below to determine the budgeted cost of goods sold shown in Exhibit 13.

Estimated inventories on January 1, 2008:
Finished goods $1,095,600
Work in process 214,400

Desired inventories on December 31, 2008:
Finished goods $1,565,000
Work in process 220,000

EXHIBIT 13

Cost of Goods
Sold Budget

	A	B	C	D	E	F	
	Elite Accessories Inc.						
	Cost of Goods Sold Budget						
	For the Year Ending December 31, 2008						
1	Finished goods inventory, January 1, 2008					$ 1,095,600	1
2	Work in process inventory, January 1, 2008				$ 214,400		2
3	Direct materials:						3
4	Direct materials inventory,						4
5	January 1, 2008 (Note A)			$ 99,000			5
6	Direct materials purchases (from Exhibit 10)			2,587,500			6
7	Cost of direct materials available for use			$2,686,500			7
8	Less direct materials inventory,						8
9	December 31, 2008 (Note B)			104,400			9
10	Cost of direct materials placed in production			$2,582,100			10
11	Direct labor (from Exhibit 11)			4,851,600			11
12	Factory overhead (from Exhibit 12)			2,089,080			12
13	Total manufacturing costs				9,522,780		13
14	Total work in process during period				$9,737,180		14
15	Less work in process inventory,						15
16	December 31, 2008				220,000		16
17	Cost of goods manufactured					9,517,180	17
18	Cost of finished goods available for sale					$10,612,780	18
19	Less finished goods inventory,						19
20	December 31, 2008					1,565,000	20
21	Cost of goods sold					$ 9,047,780	21
22							22
23	Note A: Leather:	18,000 sq. yds. × $4.50 per sq. yd.				$ 81,000	23
24	Lining:	15,000 sq. yds. × $1.20 per sq. yd.				18,000	24
25	Direct materials inventory, January 1, 2008					$ 99,000	25
26	Note B: Leather:	20,000 sq. yds. × $4.50 per sq. yd.				$ 90,000	26
27	Lining:	12,000 sq. yds. × $1.20 per sq. yd.				14,400	27
28	Direct materials inventory, December 31, 2008					$104,400	28

Direct materials purchases budget

Direct labor cost budget

Factory overhead cost budget

Example Exercise 22-5

objective 4

Prepare a cost of goods sold budget for Landon Awards Co. using the information in Example Exercises 22-3 and 22-4. Assume the estimated inventories on January 1, 2008, for finished goods and work in process were $54,000 and $47,000, respectively. Also assume the desired inventories on December 31, 2008, for finished goods and work in process were $50,000 and $49,000, respectively. Factory overhead was budgeted for $126,000.

Follow My Example 22-5

Finished goods inventory, January 1, 2008			$ 54,000
Work in process inventory, January 1, 2008		$ 47,000	
Direct materials:			
Direct materials inventory, January 1, 2008			
(240,000 × $0.12, from EE 22-3)	$ 28,800		
Direct materials purchases (from EE 22-3)	536,640		
Cost of direct materials available for use	$565,440		
Less direct materials inventory, December 31, 2008			
(200,000 × $0.12, from EE 22-3)	24,000		
Cost of direct materials placed in production	$541,440		
Direct labor (from EE 22-4)	103,400		
Factory overhead	126,000		
Total manufacturing costs		770,840	
Total work in process during period		$817,840	
Less work in process inventory, December 31, 2008		49,000	
Cost of goods manufactured			768,840
Cost of finished goods available for sale			$822,840
Less finished goods inventory, December 31, 2008			50,000
Cost of goods sold			$772,840

For Practice: PE 22-5A, PE 22-5B

SELLING AND ADMINISTRATIVE EXPENSES BUDGET

The sales budget is often used as the starting point for estimating the selling and administrative expenses. For example, a budgeted increase in sales may require more advertising. Exhibit 14 is a selling and administrative expenses budget for Elite Accessories Inc.

Detailed supporting schedules are often prepared for major items in the selling and administrative expenses budget. For example, an advertising expense schedule for the Marketing Department should include the advertising media to be used (newspaper, direct mail, television), quantities (column inches, number of pieces, minutes), and the cost per unit. Attention to such details results in realistic budgets. Effective control results from assigning responsibility for achieving the budget to department supervisors.

EXHIBIT 14

Selling and Administrative Expenses Budget

Elite Accessories Inc.
Selling and Administrative Expenses Budget
For the Year Ending December 31, 2008

	A	B	C	
1	Selling expenses:			1
2	Sales salaries expense	$715,000		2
3	Advertising expense	360,000		3
4	Travel expense	115,000		4
5	Total selling expenses		$1,190,000	5
6	Administrative expenses:			6
7	Officers' salaries expense	$360,000		7
8	Office salaries expense	258,000		8
9	Office rent expense	34,500		9
10	Office supplies expense	17,500		10
11	Miscellaneous administrative expenses	25,000		11
12	Total administrative expenses		695,000	12
13	Total selling and administrative expenses		$1,885,000	13

BUDGETED INCOME STATEMENT

The budgets for sales, cost of goods sold, and selling and administrative expenses, combined with the data on other income, other expense, and income tax, are used to prepare the budgeted income statement. Exhibit 15 is a budgeted income statement for Elite Accessories Inc.

EXHIBIT 15

Budgeted Income Statement

	A	B	C	
	Elite Accessories Inc.			
	Budgeted Income Statement			
	For the Year Ending December 31, 2008			
1	Revenue from sales (from Exhibit 8)		$13,336,000	1
2	Cost of goods sold (from Exhibit 13)		9,047,780	2
3				3
4	Gross profit		$ 4,288,220	4
5	Selling and administrative expenses:			5
6	Selling expenses (from Exhibit 14)	$1,190,000		6
7				7
8	Administrative expenses (from Exhibit 14)	695,000		8
9	Total selling and administrative expenses		1,885,000	9
10	Income from operations		$ 2,403,220	10
11	Other income:			11
12	Interest revenue	$ 98,000		12
13	Other expenses:			13
14	Interest expense	90,000	8,000	14
15	Income before income tax		$ 2,411,220	15
16	Income tax		600,000	16
17	Net income		$ 1,811,220	17

Sales budget / Cost of goods sold budget / Selling and administrative expenses budget

The budgeted income statement summarizes the estimates of all phases of operations. This allows management to assess the effects of the individual budgets on profits for the year. If the budgeted net income is too low, management could review and revise operating plans in an attempt to improve income.

Balance Sheet Budgets

objective 5

Prepare balance sheet budgets for a manufacturing business.

Balance sheet budgets are used by managers to plan financing, investing, and cash objectives for the firm. The balance sheet budgets illustrated for Elite Accessories Inc. in the following sections are the cash budget and the capital expenditures budget.

CASH BUDGET

The **cash budget** is one of the most important elements of the budgeted balance sheet. The cash budget presents the expected receipts (inflows) and payments (outflows) of cash for a period of time.

The cash budget presents the expected receipts and payments of cash for a period of time.

Information from the various operating budgets, such as the sales budget, the direct materials purchases budget, and the selling and administrative expenses budget, affects the cash budget. In addition, the capital expenditures budget, dividend policies, and plans for equity or long-term debt financing also affect the cash budget.

We illustrate the monthly cash budget for January, February, and March 2008, for Elite Accessories Inc. We begin by developing the estimated cash receipts and estimated cash payments portion of the cash budget.

Estimated Cash Receipts   Estimated cash receipts are planned additions to cash from sales and other sources, such as issuing securities or collecting interest. A supporting schedule can be used in determining the collections from sales. To illustrate this schedule, assume the following information for Elite Accessories Inc.:

Accounts receivable, January 1, 2008 . . . . $370,000

	January	February	March
Budgeted sales	$1,080,000	$1,240,000	$970,000

Elite Accessories Inc. expects to sell 10% of its merchandise for cash. Of the remaining 90% of the sales on account, 60% are expected to be collected in the month of the sale and the remainder in the next month. Thus, all of the accounts receivable are expected to be collectible.

Using this information, we prepare the schedule of collections from sales, shown in Exhibit 16. The cash receipts from sales on account are determined by adding the amounts collected from credit sales earned in the current period (60%) and the amounts accrued from sales in the previous period as accounts receivable (40%).

EXHIBIT 16

Schedule of Collections from Sales

	A	B	C	D	E	
		Elite Accessories Inc.				
		Schedule of Collections from Sales				
		For the Three Months Ending March 31, 2008				
			January	February	March	
1	Receipts from cash sales:					1
2	Cash sales (10% × current month's sales—					2
3	Note A)		$108,000	$ 124,000	$ 97,000	3
4						4
5	Receipts from sales on account:					5
6	Collections from prior month's sales (40% of					6
7	previous month's credit sales—Note B)		$370,000	$ 388,800	$446,400	7
8	Collections from current month's sales (60%					8
9	of current month's credit sales—Note C)		583,200	669,600	523,800	9
10	Total receipts from sales on account		$953,200	$1,058,400	$970,200	10
11						11
12	Note A:	$108,000 = $1,080,000 × 10%				12
13		$124,000 = $1,240,000 × 10%				13
14		$ 97,000 = $ 970,000 × 10%				14
15						15
16	Note B:	$370,000, given as January 1, 2008, Accounts Receivable balance				16
17		$388,800 = $1,080,000 × 90% × 40%				17
18		$446,400 = $1,240,000 × 90% × 40%				18
19						19
20	Note C:	$583,200 = $1,080,000 × 90% × 60%				20
21		$669,600 = $1,240,000 × 90% × 60%				21
22		$523,800 = $ 970,000 × 90% × 60%				22

Estimated Cash Payments   Estimated cash payments are planned reductions in cash from manufacturing costs, selling and administrative expenses, capital expenditures, and other sources, such as buying securities or paying interest or dividends. A supporting schedule can be used in estimating the cash payments for manufacturing costs. To illustrate, the schedule shown in Exhibit 17 is based on the following information for Elite Accessories:

Accounts payable, January 1, 2008 . . . . $190,000

	January	February	March
Manufacturing costs	$840,000	$780,000	$812,000

EXHIBIT 17

Schedule of Payments
for Manufacturing
Costs

	A	B	C	D	E	
		Elite Accessories Inc.				
		Schedule of Payments for Manufacturing Costs				
		For the Three Months Ending March 31, 2008				
			January	February	March	
1	Payments of prior month's manufacturing costs					1
2	{[25% × previous month's manufacturing costs					2
3	(less depreciation)]—Note A}		$190,000	$204,000	$189,000	3
4	Payments of current month's manufacturing costs					4
5	{[75% × current month's manufacturing costs					5
6	(less depreciation)]—Note B}		612,000	567,000	591,000	6
7	Total payments		$802,000	$771,000	$780,000	7
8						8
9	Note A:	$190,000, given as January 1, 2008, Accounts Payable balance				9
10		$204,000 = ($840,000 − $24,000) × 25%				10
11		$189,000 = ($780,000 − $24,000) × 25%				11
12						12
13	Note B:	$612,000 = ($840,000 − $24,000) × 75%				13
14		$567,000 = ($780,000 − $24,000) × 75%				14
15		$591,000 = ($812,000 − $24,000) × 75%				15

Depreciation expense on machines is estimated to be $24,000 per month and is included in the manufacturing costs. The accounts payable were incurred for manufacturing costs. Elite Accessories Inc. expects to pay 75% of the manufacturing costs in the month in which they are incurred and the balance in the next month.

In Exhibit 17, the cash payments are determined by adding the amounts paid from costs incurred in the current period (75%) and the amounts accrued as a liability from costs in the previous period (25%). The $24,000 of depreciation must be excluded from all calculations, since depreciation is a noncash expense that should not be included in the cash budget.

Completing the Cash Budget To complete the cash budget for Elite Accessories Inc., as shown in Exhibit 18, assume that Elite Accessories Inc. is expecting the following:

Cash balance on January 1	$280,000
Quarterly taxes paid on March 31	150,000
Quarterly interest expense paid on January 10	22,500
Quarterly interest revenue received on March 21	24,500
Sewing equipment purchased in February	274,000

In addition, monthly selling and administrative expenses, which are paid in the month incurred, are estimated as follows:

	January	February	March
Selling and administrative expenses	$160,000	$165,000	$145,000

We can compare the estimated cash balance at the end of the period with the minimum balance required by operations. Assuming that the minimum cash balance for Elite Accessories Inc. is $340,000, we can determine any expected excess or deficiency.

The minimum cash balance protects against variations in estimates and for unexpected cash emergencies. For effective cash management, much of the minimum cash balance should be deposited in income-producing securities that can be readily converted to cash. U.S. Treasury Bills or Notes are examples of such securities.

EXHIBIT 18	Cash Budget

	A	C	D	E	
	Elite Accessories Inc.				
	Cash Budget				
	For the Three Months Ending March 31, 2008				
		January	February	March	
1	Estimated cash receipts from:				1
2	Cash sales (from Exhibit 16)	$ 108,000	$ 124,000	$ 97,000	2
3	Collections of accounts receivable				3
4	(from Exhibit 16)	953,200	1,058,400	970,200	4
5	Interest revenue			24,500	5
6	Total cash receipts	$1,061,200	$1,182,400	$1,091,700	6
7	Estimated cash payments for:				7
8	Manufacturing costs (from Exhibit 17)	$ 802,000	$ 771,000	$ 780,000	8
9	Selling and administrative expenses	160,000	165,000	145,000	9
10	Capital additions		274,000		10
11	Interest expense	22,500			11
12	Income taxes			150,000	12
13	Total cash payments	$ 984,500	$1,210,000	$1,075,000	13
14	Cash increase (decrease)	$ 76,700	$ (27,600)	$ 16,700	14
15	Cash balance at beginning of month	280,000	356,700	329,100	15
16	Cash balance at end of month	$ 356,700	$ 329,100	$ 345,800	16
17	Minimum cash balance	340,000	340,000	340,000	17
18	Excess (deficiency)	$ 16,700	$ (10,900)	$ 5,800	18

Schedule of collections from sales

Schedule of cash payments for manufacturing costs

Example Exercise 22-6

objective **5**

Landon Awards Co. collects 25% of its sales on account in the month of the sale and 75% in the month following the sale. If sales on account are budgeted to be $100,000 for March and $126,000 for April, what are the budgeted cash receipts from sales on account for April?

Follow My Example 22-6

	April
Collections from March sales (75% × $100,000)	$ 75,000
Collections from April sales (25% × $126,000)	31,500
Total receipts from sales on account	$106,500

For Practice: PE 22-6A, PE 22-6B

CAPITAL EXPENDITURES BUDGET

The **capital expenditures budget** summarizes plans for acquiring fixed assets. Such expenditures are necessary as machinery and other fixed assets wear out, become obsolete, or for other reasons need to be replaced. In addition, expanding plant facilities may be necessary to meet increasing demand for a company's product.

The useful life of many fixed assets extends over long periods of time. In addition, the amount of the expenditures for such assets may vary from year to year. It is normal to project the plans for a number of periods into the future in preparing the capital expenditures budget. Exhibit 19 is a five-year capital expenditures budget for Elite Accessories Inc.

The capital expenditures budget should be considered in preparing the other operating budgets. For example, the estimated depreciation of new equipment affects the factory overhead cost budget and the selling and administrative expenses budget. The plans for financing the capital expenditures may also affect the cash budget.

EXHIBIT 19

Capital Expenditures Budget

	A	B	C	D	E	F	
	Elite Accessories Inc.						
	Capital Expenditures Budget						
	For the Five Years Ending December 31, 2012						
	Item	2008	2009	2010	2011	2012	
1	Machinery—Cutting Department	$400,000			$280,000	$360,000	1
2	Machinery—Sewing Department	274,000	$260,000	$560,000	200,000		2
3	Office equipment		90,000			60,000	3
4	Total	$674,000	$350,000	$560,000	$480,000	$420,000	4

BUDGETED BALANCE SHEET

The budgeted balance sheet estimates the financial condition at the end of a budget period. The budgeted balance sheet assumes that all operating budgets and financing plans are met. It is similar to a balance sheet based on actual data in the accounts. For this reason, we do not illustrate a budgeted balance sheet for Elite Accessories Inc. If the budgeted balance sheet indicates a weakness in financial position, revising the financing plans or other plans may be necessary. For example, a large amount of long-term debt in relation to stockholders' equity might require revising financing plans for capital expenditures. Such revisions might include issuing equity rather than debt.

At a Glance

1. Describe budgeting, its objectives, and its impact on human behavior.

Key Points	Key Learning Outcomes	Example Exercises	Practice Exercises
Budgeting involves (1) establishing plans (planning), (2) directing operations (directing), and (3) evaluating performance (controlling). In addition, budgets should be established to avoid human behavior problems.	• Describe the planning, directing, controlling, and feedback elements of the budget process. • Describe the behavioral issues associated with tight goals, loose goals, and goal conflict.		

2. Describe the basic elements of the budget process, the two major types of budgeting, and the use of computers in budgeting.

Key Points	Key Learning Outcomes	Example Exercises	Practice Exercises
The budget process is often initiated by the budget committee. The budget estimates received by the committee should be carefully studied, analyzed, revised, and integrated. The static and continuous budgets are two major budgeting approaches. Computers can be used to make the budget process more efficient and organizationally integrated.	• Describe a static budget and explain when it might be used. • Describe and prepare a flexible budget and explain when it might be used. • Describe the role of computers in the budget process.	22-1	22-1A, 22-1B

(continued)

3. Describe the master budget for a manufacturing business.

Key Points	Key Learning Outcomes	Example Exercises	Practice Exercises
The master budget consists of the budgeted income statement and budgeted balance sheet.	• Illustrate the connection between the major income statement and balance sheet budgets.		

4. Prepare the basic income statement budgets for a manufacturing business.

Key Points	Key Learning Outcomes	Example Exercises	Practice Exercises
The basic income statement budgets are the sales budget, production budget, direct materials purchases budget, direct labor cost budget, factory overhead cost budget, cost of goods sold budget, and selling and administrative expenses budget.	• Prepare a sales budget. • Prepare a production budget. • Prepare a direct materials purchases budget. • Prepare a direct labor cost budget. • Prepare a factory overhead cost budget. • Prepare a cost of goods sold budget. • Prepare a selling and administrative expenses budget.	22-2 22-3 22-4 22-5	22-2A, 22-2B 22-3A, 22-3B 22-4A, 22-4B 22-5A, 22-5B

5. Prepare balance sheet budgets for a manufacturing business.

Key Points	Key Learning Outcomes	Example Exercises	Practice Exercises
The cash budget and capital expenditures budget can be used in preparing the budgeted balance sheet.	• Prepare cash receipts and cash payments budgets. • Prepare a capital expenditures budget.	22-6	22-6A, 22-6B

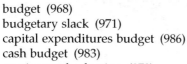

Key Terms

budget (968)
budgetary slack (971)
capital expenditures budget (986)
cash budget (983)
continuous budgeting (972)
cost of goods sold budget (981)

direct materials purchases budget (978)
flexible budget (974)
goal conflict (971)
master budget (976)
production budget (977)

responsibility center (969)
sales budget (977)
static budget (973)
zero-based budgeting (972)

Illustrative Problem

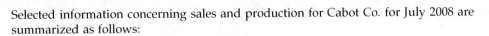

Selected information concerning sales and production for Cabot Co. for July 2008 are summarized as follows:

a. Estimated sales:

Product K: 40,000 units at $30.00 per unit
Product L: 20,000 units at $65.00 per unit

b. Estimated inventories, July 1, 2008:

Material A: 4,000 lbs.	Product K: 3,000 units at $17 per unit	$ 51,000
Material B: 3,500 lbs.	Product L: 2,700 units at $35 per unit	94,500
	Total	$145,500

There were no work in process inventories estimated for July 1, 2008.

c. Desired inventories at July 31, 2008:

Material A: 3,000 lbs.	Product K: 2,500 units at $17 per unit	$ 42,500
Material B: 2,500 lbs.	Product L: 2,000 units at $35 per unit	70,000
	Total	$112,500

There were no work in process inventories desired for July 31, 2008.

d. Direct materials used in production:

	Product K	Product L
Material A:	0.7 lb. per unit	3.5 lbs. per unit
Material B:	1.2 lbs. per unit	1.8 lbs. per unit

e. Unit costs for direct materials:

Material A: $4.00 per lb.
Material B: $2.00 per lb.

f. Direct labor requirements:

	Department 1	Department 2
Product K	0.4 hour per unit	0.15 hour per unit
Product L	0.6 hour per unit	0.25 hour per unit

g.

	Department 1	Department 2
Direct labor rate	$12.00 per hour	$16.00 per hour

h. Estimated factory overhead costs for July:

Indirect factory wages	$200,000
Depreciation of plant and equipment	40,000
Power and light	25,000
Indirect materials	34,000
Total	$299,000

Instructions
1. Prepare a sales budget for July.
2. Prepare a production budget for July.
3. Prepare a direct materials purchases budget for July.
4. Prepare a direct labor cost budget for July.
5. Prepare a cost of goods sold budget for July.

Solution

1.

	A	B	C	D	
		Cabot Co.			
		Sales Budget			
		For the Month Ending July 31, 2008			
	Product	Unit Sales Volume	Unit Selling Price	Total Sales	
1	Product K	40,000	$30.00	$1,200,000	1
2	Product L	20,000	65.00	1,300,000	2
3	Total revenue from sales			$2,500,000	3

2.

	A	C	D	
	Cabot Co.			
	Production Budget			
	For the Month Ending July 31, 2008			
		Units		
		Product K	Product L	
1	Sales	40,000	20,000	1
2	Plus desired inventories at July 31, 2008	2,500	2,000	2
3	Total	42,500	22,000	3
4	Less estimated inventories, July 1, 2008	3,000	2,700	4
5	Total production	39,500	19,300	5

3.

	A	B	C	D	E	F	G	
			Cabot Co.					
			Direct Materials Purchases Budget					
			For the Month Ending July 31, 2008					
			Direct Materials					
			Material A		Material B		Total	
1	Units required for production:							1
2	Product K (39,500 × lbs. per unit)		27,650	lbs.*	47,400	lbs.*		2
3	Product L (19,300 × lbs. per unit)		67,550	**	34,740	**		3
4	Plus desired units of inventory,							4
5	July 31, 2008		3,000		2,500			5
6	Total		98,200	lbs.	84,640	lbs.		6
7	Less estimated units of inventory,							7
8	July 1, 2008		4,000		3,500			8
9	Total units to be purchased		94,200	lbs.	81,140	lbs.		9
10	Unit price		× $4.00		× $2.00			10
11	Total direct materials purchases		$376,800		$162,280		$539,080	11
12								12
13	*27,650 = 39,500 × 0.7 47,400 = 39,500 × 1.2							13
14	**67,550 = 19,300 × 3.5 34,740 = 19,300 × 1.8							14

4.

	A	B	C	D	E	F	G	
			Cabot Co.					
			Direct Labor Cost Budget					
			For the Month Ending July 31, 2008					
			Department 1		Department 2		Total	
1	Hours required for production:							1
2	Product K (39,500 × hours per unit)		15,800	*	5,925	*		2
3	Product L (19,300 × hours per unit)		11,580	**	4,825	**		3
4	Total		27,380		10,750			4
5	Hourly rate		× $12.00		× $16.00			5
6	Total direct labor cost		$328,560		$172,000		$500,560	6
7								7
8	*15,800 = 39,500 × 0.4 5,925 = 39,500 × 0.15							8
9	**11,580 = 19,300 × 0.6 4,825 = 19,300 × 0.25							9

5.

	A	B	C	D	
	Cabot Co.				
	Cost of Goods Sold Budget				
	For the Month Ending July 31, 2008				
1	Finished goods inventory, July 1, 2008			$ 145,500	1
2	Direct materials:				2
3	Direct materials inventory, July 1, 2008—(Note A)		$ 23,000		3
4	Direct materials purchases		539,080		4
5	Cost of direct materials available for use		$562,080		5
6	Less direct materials inventory, July 31, 2008—(Note B)		17,000		6
7	Cost of direct materials placed in production		$545,080		7
8	Direct labor		500,560		8
9	Factory overhead		299,000		9
10	Cost of goods manufactured			1,344,640	10
11	Cost of finished goods available for sale			$1,490,140	11
12	Less finished goods inventory, July 31, 2008			112,500	12
13	Cost of goods sold			$1,377,640	13
14					14
15	Note A:				15
16	Material A 4,000 lbs. at $4.00 per lb.	$16,000			16
17	Material B 3,500 lbs. at $2.00 per lb.	7,000			17
18	Direct materials inventory, July 1, 2008	$23,000			18
19					19
20	Note B:				20
21	Material A 3,000 lbs. at $4.00 per lb.	$12,000			21
22	Material B 2,500 lbs. at $2.00 per lb.	5,000			22
23	Direct materials inventory, July 31, 2008	$17,000			23

Self-Examination Questions

(Answers at End of Chapter)

1. A tight budget may create:
   A. budgetary slack.
   B. discouragement.
   C. a flexible budget.
   D. a "spend it or lose it" mentality.

2. The first step of the budget process is:
   A. plan.   C. control.
   B. direct.   D. feedback.

3. Static budgets are often used by:
   A. production departments.
   B. administrative departments.
   C. responsibility centers.
   D. capital projects.

4. The total estimated sales for the coming year is 250,000 units. The estimated inventory at the beginning of the year is 22,500 units, and the desired inventory at the end of the year is 30,000 units. The total production indicated in the production budget is:
   A. 242,500 units.   C. 280,000 units.
   B. 257,500 units.   D. 302,500 units.

5. Dixon Company expects $650,000 of credit sales in March and $800,000 of credit sales in April. Dixon historically collects 70% of its sales in the month of sale and 30% in the following month. How much cash does Dixon expect to collect in April?
   A. $800,000   C. $755,000
   B. $560,000   D. $1,015,000

Eye Openers

1. What are the three major objectives of budgeting?
2. What is the manager's role in a responsibility center?
3. Briefly describe the type of human behavior problems that might arise if budget goals are set too tightly.
4. Why should all levels of management and all departments participate in preparing and submitting budget estimates?

5. Give an example of budgetary slack.
6. What behavioral problems are associated with setting a budget too loosely?
7. What behavioral problems are associated with establishing conflicting goals within the budget?
8. When would a company use zero-based budgeting?
9. Under what circumstances would a static budget be appropriate?
10. How do computerized budgeting systems aid firms in the budgeting process?
11. What is the first step in preparing a master budget?
12. Why should the production requirements set forth in the production budget be carefully coordinated with the sales budget?
13. Why should the timing of direct materials purchases be closely coordinated with the production budget?
14. In preparing the budget for the cost of goods sold, what are the three budgets from which data on relevant estimates of quantities and costs are combined with data on estimated inventories?
15. a. Discuss the purpose of the cash budget.
    b. If the cash for the first quarter of the fiscal year indicates excess cash at the end of each of the first two months, how might the excess cash be used?
16. How does a schedule of collections from sales assist in preparing the cash budget?
17. Give an example of how the capital expenditures budget affects other operating budgets.

Practice Exercises

PE 22-1A
Flexible budgeting
obj. 2

At the beginning of the period, the Assembly Department budgeted direct labor of $110,500 and property taxes of $50,000 for 8,500 hours of production. The department actually completed 10,000 hours of production. Determine the budget for the department, assuming that it uses flexible budgeting.

PE 22-1B
Flexible budgeting
obj. 2

At the beginning of the period, the Fabricating Department budgeted direct labor of $18,400 and equipment depreciation of $14,000 for 800 hours of production. The department actually completed 700 hours of production. Determine the budget for the department, assuming that it uses flexible budgeting.

PE 22-2A
Production budget
obj. 4

OnTime Publishers Inc. projected sales of 220,000 schedule planners for 2008. The estimated January 1, 2008, inventory is 15,000 units, and the desired December 31, 2008, inventory is 11,000 units. What is the budgeted production (in units) for 2008?

PE 22-2B
Production budget
obj. 4

New England Candle Co. projected sales of 95,000 candles for 2008. The estimated January 1, 2008, inventory is 2,400 units, and the desired December 31, 2008, inventory is 3,000 units. What is the budgeted production (in units) for 2008?

PE 22-3A
Direct materials purchases budget
obj. 4

OnTime Publishers Inc. budgeted production of 216,000 schedule planners in 2008. Paper is required to produce a planner. Assume 90 square feet of paper are required for each planner. The estimated January 1, 2008, paper inventory is 100,000 square feet. The desired December 31, 2008, paper inventory is 160,000 square feet. If paper costs $0.08 per square foot, determine the direct materials purchases budget for 2008.

PE 22-3B
Direct materials purchases budget
obj. 4

New England Candle, Co. budgeted production of 95,600 candles in 2008. Wax is required to produce a candle. Assume 8 ounces (one half of a pound) of wax is required for each candle. The estimated January 1, 2008, wax inventory is 1,400 pounds. The desired December 31, 2008, wax inventory is 1,100 pounds. If candle wax costs $3.60 per pound, determine the direct materials purchases budget for 2008.

PE 22-4A
Direct labor cost budget
obj. 4

OnTime Publishers Inc. budgeted production of 216,000 schedule planners in 2008. Each planner requires assembly. Assume that 15 minutes are required to assemble each planner. If assembly labor costs $12.50 per hour, determine the direct labor cost budget for 2008.

PE 22-4B
Direct labor cost budget
obj. 4

New England Candle Co. budgeted production of 95,600 candles in 2008. Each candle requires molding. Assume that 12 minutes are required to mold each candle. If molding labor costs $14.00 per hour, determine the direct labor cost budget for 2008.

PE 22-5A
Cost of goods sold budget
obj. 4

Prepare a cost of goods sold budget for OnTime Publishers Inc. using the information in Practice Exercises 22-3A and 22-4A. Assume the estimated inventories on January 1, 2008, for finished goods and work in process were $43,000 and $22,000, respectively. Also assume the desired inventories on December 31, 2008, for finished goods and work in process were $40,000 and $25,000, respectively. Factory overhead was budgeted at $245,000.

PE 22-5B
Cost of goods sold budget
obj. 4

Prepare a cost of goods sold budget for New England Candle Co. using the information in Practice Exercises 22-3B and 22-4B. Assume the estimated inventories on January 1, 2008, for finished goods and work in process were $14,000 and $6,300, respectively. Also assume the desired inventories on December 31, 2008, for finished goods and work in process were $12,000 and $7,000, respectively. Factory overhead was budgeted at $95,000.

PE 22-6A
Cash budget
obj. 5

OnTime Publishers Inc. collects 30% of its sales on account in the month of the sale and 70% in the month following the sale. If sales on account are budgeted to be $400,000 for June and $360,000 for July, what are the budgeted cash receipts from sales on account for July?

PE 22-6B
Cash budget
obj. 5

New England Candle Co. pays 10% of its purchases on account in the month of the purchase and 90% in the month following the purchase. If purchases are budgeted to be $14,000 for August and $16,000 for September, what are the budgeted cash payments for purchases on account for September?

Exercises

EX 22-1
Personal cash budget
objs. 2, 5

✓ a. December 31 cash balance, $2,900

At the beginning of the 2008 school year, Monroe Baker decided to prepare a cash budget for the months of September, October, November, and December. The budget must plan for enough cash on December 31 to pay the spring semester tuition, which is the same as the fall tuition. The following information relates to the budget:

Cash balance, September 1 (from a summer job)	$6,500
Purchase season football tickets in September	140
Additional entertainment for each month	225
Pay fall semester tuition on September 3	3,500
Pay rent at the beginning of each month	350
Pay for food each month	215
Pay apartment deposit on September 2 (to be returned Dec. 15)	600
Part-time job earnings each month (net of taxes)	800

a. Prepare a cash budget for September, October, November, and December.
b. Are the budgets prepared as static budgets or flexible budgets?
c. What are the budget implications for Monroe Baker?

EX 22-2
Flexible budget for selling and administrative expenses
objs. 2, 4

✓ Total selling and administrative expenses at $140,000 sales, $65,550

Master Electronics Company uses flexible budgets that are based on the following data:

Sales commissions	7% of sales
Advertising expense	18% of sales
Miscellaneous selling expense	$1,750 plus 4% of sales
Office salaries expense	$12,000 per month
Office supplies expense	5% of sales
Miscellaneous administrative expense	$1,400 per month plus 2% of sales

Prepare a flexible selling and administrative expenses budget for January 2008 for sales volumes of $100,000, $120,000, and $140,000. (Use Exhibit 5 as a model.)

EX 22-3
Static budget vs. flexible budget
objs. 2, 4

✓ b. Excess of actual over budget for March, $100,000

The production supervisor of the Machining Department for Landers Company agreed to the following monthly static budget for the upcoming year:

Landers Company
Machining Department
Monthly Production Budget

Wages	$ 960,000
Utilities	300,000
Depreciation	60,000
Total	$1,320,000

The actual amount spent and the actual units produced in the first three months of 2008 in the Machining Department were as follows:

	Amount Spent	Units Produced
January	$1,090,000	60,000
February	1,050,000	55,000
March	1,000,000	50,000

The Machining Department supervisor has been very pleased with this performance, since actual expenditures have been less than the monthly budget. However, the plant manager believes that the budget should not remain fixed for every month but should "flex" or adjust to the volume of work that is produced in the Machining Department. Additional budget information for the Machining Department is as follows:

Wages per hour	$16.00
Utility cost per direct labor hour	$5.00
Direct labor hours per unit	0.80
Planned unit production	75,000

a. Prepare a flexible budget for the actual units produced for January, February, and March in the Machining Department.
b. ➤ Compare the flexible budget with the actual expenditures for the first three months. What does this comparison suggest?

EX 22-4
Flexible budget for Fabrication Department
obj. 2

✓ Total department cost at 12,000 units, $957,600

Steelcase Inc. is one of the largest manufacturers of office furniture in the United States. In Grand Rapids, Michigan, it produces filing cabinets in two departments: Fabrication and Trim Assembly. Assume the following information for the Fabrication Department:

Steel per filing cabinet	50 pounds
Direct labor per filing cabinet	18 minutes
Supervisor salaries	$130,000 per month
Depreciation	$20,000 per month
Direct labor rate	$16 per hour
Steel cost	$1.25 per pound

Prepare a flexible budget for 12,000, 15,000, and 18,000 filing cabinets for the month of October 2008, similar to Exhibit 5, assuming that inventories are not significant.

EX 22-5
Sales and production budgets
obj. **4**

✓b. Model DL total production, 7,420 units

Melody Audio Company manufactures two models of speakers, DL and XL. Based on the following production and sales data for September 2007, prepare (a) a sales budget and (b) a production budget.

	DL	XL
Estimated inventory (units), September 1	380	140
Desired inventory (units), September 30	450	110
Expected sales volume (units):		
East Region	4,400	3,200
West Region	2,950	2,100
Unit sales price	$120.00	$170.00

EX 22-6
Professional fees earned budget
obj. **4**

✓Total professional fees earned, $13,956,000

Kimble and Sanchez, CPAs, offer three types of services to clients: auditing, tax, and small business accounting. Based on experience and projected growth, the following billable hours have been estimated for the year ending December 31, 2008:

	Billable Hours
Audit Department:	
Staff	34,500
Partners	5,200
Tax Department:	
Staff	27,700
Partners	4,150
Small Business Accounting Department:	
Staff	22,800
Partners	6,300

The average billing rate for staff is $120 per hour, and the average billing rate for partners is $240 per hour. Prepare a professional fees earned budget for Kimble and Sanchez, CPAs, for the year ending December 31, 2008, using the following column headings and showing the estimated professional fees by type of service rendered:

Billable Hours   Hourly Rate   Total Revenue

EX 22-7
Professional labor cost budget
obj. **4**

✓Staff total labor cost, $6,375,000

Based on the data in Exercise 22-6 and assuming that the average compensation per hour for staff is $75 and for partners is $140, prepare a professional labor cost budget for Kimble and Sanchez, CPAs, for the year ending December 31, 2008. Use the following column headings:

Staff   Partners

EX 22-8
Direct materials purchases budget
obj. **4**

✓Total cheese purchases, $131,813

Roma Frozen Pizza Inc. has determined from its production budget the following estimated production volumes for 12" and 16" frozen pizzas for November 2008:

	Units	
	12" Pizza	16" Pizza
Budgeted production volume	16,400	25,600

There are three direct materials used in producing the two types of pizza. The quantities of direct materials expected to be used for each pizza are as follows:

	12" Pizza	16" Pizza
Direct materials:		
Dough	1.00 lb. per unit	1.50 lbs. per unit
Tomato	0.60	0.90
Cheese	0.80	1.30

In addition, Roma has determined the following information about each material:

	Dough	Tomato	Cheese
Estimated inventory, November 1, 2008	675 lbs.	190 lbs.	525 lbs.
Desired inventory, November 30, 2008	480 lbs.	250 lbs.	375 lbs.
Price per pound	$1.20	$2.40	$2.85

Prepare November's direct materials purchases budget for Roma Frozen Pizza Inc.

EX 22-9
Direct materials purchases budget
obj. 4

✓ *Concentrate budgeted purchases, $90,900*

Coca-Cola Enterprises is the largest bottler of Coca-Cola® in North America. The company purchases Coke® and Sprite® concentrate from The Coca-Cola Company, dilutes and mixes the concentrate with carbonated water, and then fills the blended beverage into cans or plastic two-liter bottles. Assume that the estimated production for Coke and Sprite two-liter bottles at the Chattanooga, Tennessee, bottling plant are as follows for the month of June:

Coke	192,000 two-liter bottles
Sprite	148,000 two-liter bottles

In addition, assume that the concentrate costs $75 per pound for both Coke and Sprite and is used at a rate of 0.2 pound per 100 liters of carbonated water in blending Coke and 0.15 pound per 100 liters of carbonated water in blending Sprite. Assume that two-liter bottles cost $0.07 per bottle and carbonated water costs $0.05 per liter.

Prepare a direct materials purchases budget for June 2008, assuming no changes between beginning and ending inventories for all three materials.

EX 22-10
Direct materials purchases budget
obj. 4

✓ *Total steel belt purchases, $1,108,625*

Anticipated sales for Goodstone Tire Company were 38,000 passenger car tires and 14,000 truck tires. There were no anticipated beginning finished goods inventories for either product. The planned ending finished goods inventories were 2,750 units for each product. Rubber and steel belts are used in producing passenger car and truck tires according to the following table:

	Passenger Car	Truck
Rubber	30 lbs. per unit	65 lbs. per unit
Steel belts	4 lbs. per unit	9 lbs. per unit

The purchase prices of rubber and steel are $2.90 and $3.50 per pound, respectively. The desired ending inventories of rubber and steel belts are 45,000 and 9,000 pounds, respectively. The estimated beginning inventories for rubber and steel belts are 72,000 and 6,000 pounds, respectively.

The following direct materials purchases budget was prepared for Goodstone Tire Company:

Goodstone Tire Company
Direct Materials Purchases Budget
For the Year Ending December 31, 2008

	Rubber	Steel Belts	Total
Units required for production:			
Passenger tires	1,140,000[1] lbs.	152,000[3] lbs.	
Truck tires	910,000[2]	126,000[4]	
Total	2,050,000 lbs.	278,000 lbs.	
Unit price	× $2.90	× $3.50	
Total direct materials purchases	$5,945,000	$973,000	$6,918,000

1. 38,000 tires × 30 lbs. = 1,140,000 lbs.
2. 14,000 tires × 65 lbs. = 910,000 lbs.
3. 38,000 tires × 4 lbs. = 152,000 lbs.
4. 14,000 tires × 9 lbs. = 126,000 lbs.

Correct the direct materials purchases budget for Goodstone Tire Company.

EX 22-11
Direct labor cost budget
obj. 4

✓ *Total direct labor cost, Assembly, $186,225*

Match Point Racket Company manufactures two types of tennis rackets, the Junior and Pro Striker models. The production budget for March for the two rackets is as follows:

	Junior	Pro Striker
Production budget	7,300 units	18,400 units

Both rackets are produced in two departments, Forming and Assembly. The direct labor hours required for each racket are estimated as follows:

	Forming Department	Assembly Department
Junior	0.25 hour per unit	0.45 hour per unit
Pro Striker	0.40 hour per unit	0.60 hour per unit

The direct labor rate for each department is as follows:

Forming Department	$18.00 per hour
Assembly Department	$13.00 per hour

Prepare the direct labor cost budget for March 2008.

EX 22-12
Direct labor budget—service business
obj. 4

✓ *Average weekday total, $1,696*

Night Rest Inn Inc. operates a downtown hotel property that has 240 rooms. On average, 75% of Night Rest's rooms are occupied on weekdays, and 50% are occupied during the weekend. The manager has asked you to develop a direct labor budget for the housekeeping and restaurant staff for weekdays and weekends. You have determined that the housekeeping staff requires 45 minutes to clean each occupied room. The housekeeping staff is paid $8 per hour. The restaurant has five full-time staff (eight-hour day) on duty, regardless of occupancy. However, for every 30 occupied rooms, an additional person is brought in to work in the restaurant for the eight-hour day. The restaurant staff is paid $7 per hour.

Determine the estimated housekeeping and restaurant direct labor cost for an average weekday and weekend day. Format the budget in two columns, labeled as weekday and weekend day.

EX 22-13
Production and direct labor cost budgets
obj. 4

✓ *a. Total production of 501 Jeans, 47,000*

Levi Strauss & Co. manufactures slacks and jeans under a variety of brand names, such as Dockers® and 501 Jeans®. Slacks and jeans are assembled by a variety of different sewing operations. Assume that the sales budget for Dockers and 501 Jeans shows estimated sales of 23,800 and 46,200 pairs, respectively, for March 2008. The finished goods inventory is assumed as follows:

	Dockers	501 Jeans
March 1 estimated inventory	320	1,230
March 31 desired inventory	520	2,030

Assume the following direct labor data per 10 pairs of Dockers and 501 Jeans for four different sewing operations:

Direct Labor per 10 Pairs		
	Dockers	501 Jeans
Inseam	18 minutes	12 minutes
Outerseam	22	15
Pockets	7	9
Zipper	10	6
Total	57 minutes	42 minutes

a. Prepare a production budget for March. Prepare the budget in two columns: Dockers® and 501 Jeans®.
b. Prepare the March direct labor cost budget for the four sewing operations, assuming a $12 wage per hour for the inseam and outerseam sewing operations and a $14 wage per hour for the pocket and zipper sewing operations. Prepare the direct labor cost budget in four columns: inseam, outerseam, pockets, and zipper.

EX 22-14
Factory overhead cost budget

obj. 4

✓ *Total variable factory overhead costs, $243,000*

Fresh Mint Candy Company budgeted the following costs for anticipated production for July 2008:

Advertising expenses	$275,000	Production supervisor wages	$125,000
Manufacturing supplies	14,000	Production control salaries	33,000
Power and light	42,000	Executive officer salaries	205,000
Sales commissions	290,000	Materials management salaries	29,000
Factory insurance	23,000	Factory depreciation	17,000

Prepare a factory overhead cost budget, separating variable and fixed costs. Assume that factory insurance and depreciation are the only factory fixed costs.

EX 22-15
Cost of goods sold budget

obj. 4

✓ *Cost of goods sold, $1,269,300*

Dover Chemical Company uses oil to produce two types of plastic products, P1 and P2. Dover budgeted 30,000 barrels of oil for purchase in June for $28 per barrel. Direct labor budgeted in the chemical process was $150,000 for June. Factory overhead was budgeted $275,000 during June. The inventories on June 1 were estimated to be:

Oil	$15,300
P1	8,700
P2	9,200
Work in process	11,800

The desired inventories on June 30 were:

Oil	$12,200
P1	8,300
P2	9,500
Work in process	10,700

Use the preceding information to prepare a cost of goods sold budget for June.

EX 22-16
Cost of goods sold budget

obj. 4

✓ *Cost of goods sold, $397,320*

The controller of Moravian Ceramics Inc. wishes to prepare a cost of goods sold budget for April. The controller assembled the following information for constructing the cost of goods sold budget:

Direct materials:	Enamel	Paint	Porcelain	Total
Total direct materials purchases budgeted for April	$32,450	$4,730	$114,240	$151,420
Estimated inventory, April 1, 2008	1,150	2,800	4,330	8,280
Desired inventory, April 30, 2008	2,500	2,050	6,000	10,550

Direct labor cost:	Kiln Department	Decorating Department	Total
Total direct labor cost budgeted for April	$37,500	$134,400	$171,900

Finished goods inventories:	Dish	Bowl	Figurine	Total
Estimated inventory, April 1, 2008	$4,280	$2,970	$2,470	$ 9,720
Desired inventory, April 30, 2008	3,350	4,150	3,700	11,200

Work in process inventories:

Estimated inventory, April 1, 2008	$2,800
Desired inventory, April 30, 2008	1,750

Budgeted factory overhead costs for April:

Indirect factory wages	$55,500
Depreciation of plant and equipment	12,600
Power and light	4,900
Indirect materials	3,700
Total	$76,700

Use the preceding information to prepare a cost of goods sold budget for April 2008.

EX 22-17
Schedule of cash collections of accounts receivable

obj. 5

✓ *Total cash collected in May, $535,700*

Happy Tails Wholesale Inc., a pet wholesale supplier, was organized on March 1, 2008. Projected sales for each of the first three months of operations are as follows:

March	$450,000
April	520,000
May	560,000

The company expects to sell 10% of its merchandise for cash. Of sales on account, 50% are expected to be collected in the month of the sale, 40% in the month following the sale, and the remainder in the second month following the sale.

Prepare a schedule indicating cash collections from sales for March, April, and May.

EX 22-18
Schedule of cash collections of accounts receivable

obj. 5

✓ *Total cash collected in January, $307,600*

Office Warehouse Supplies Inc. has "cash and carry" customers and credit customers. Office Warehouse estimates that 40% of monthly sales are to cash customers, while the remaining sales are to credit customers. Of the credit customers, 30% pay their accounts in the month of sale, while the remaining 70% pay their accounts in the month following the month of sale. Projected sales for the first three months of 2008 are as follows:

January	$220,000
February	275,000
March	260,000

The Accounts Receivable balance on December 31, 2007, was $180,000.

Prepare a schedule of cash collections from sales for January, February, and March.

EX 22-19
Schedule of cash payments

obj. 5

✓ *Total cash payments in August, $107,875*

A+ Learning Systems Inc. was organized on May 31, 2009. Projected selling and administrative expenses for each of the first three months of operations are as follows:

June	$114,800
July	124,500
August	129,000

Depreciation, insurance, and property taxes represent $20,000 of the estimated monthly expenses. The annual insurance premium was paid on May 31, and property taxes for the year will be paid in December. Three-fourths of the remainder of the expenses are expected to be paid in the month in which they are incurred, with the balance to be paid in the following month.

Prepare a schedule indicating cash payments for selling and administrative expenses for June, July, and August.

EX 22-20
Schedule of cash payments

obj. 5

✓ *Total cash payments in December, $128,720*

Total Flex Physical Therapy Inc. is planning its cash payments for operations for the fourth quarter (October–December), 2009. The Accrued Expenses Payable balance on October 1 is $22,600. The budgeted expenses for the next three months are as follows:

	October	November	December
Salaries	$ 58,200	$ 63,500	$ 74,500
Utilities	5,300	5,600	7,100
Other operating expenses	44,700	52,800	62,700
Total	$108,200	$121,900	$144,300

Other operating expenses include $10,500 of monthly depreciation expense and $600 of monthly insurance expense that was prepaid for the year on March 1 of the current year. Of the remaining expenses, 80% are paid in the month in which they are incurred, with the remainder paid in the following month. The Accrued Expenses Payable balance on October 1 relates to the expenses incurred in September.

Prepare a schedule of cash payments for operations for October, November, and December.

EX 22-21
Capital expenditures budget
obj. 5

✓ *Total capital expenditures in 2008, $7,000,000*

On January 1, 2008, the controller of Garden Master Tools Inc. is planning capital expenditures for the years 2008–2011. The following interviews helped the controller collect the necessary information for the capital expenditures budget.

Director of Facilities: A construction contract was signed in late 2007 for the construction of a new factory building at a contract cost of $12,000,000. The construction is scheduled to begin in 2008 and be completed in 2009.

Vice President of Manufacturing: Once the new factory building is finished, we plan to purchase $1.5 million in equipment in late 2009. I expect that an additional $300,000 will be needed early in the following year (2010) to test and install the equipment before we can begin production. If sales continue to grow, I expect we'll need to invest another million in equipment in 2011.

Vice President of Marketing: We have really been growing lately. I wouldn't be surprised if we need to expand the size of our new factory building in 2011 by at least 40%. Fortunately, we expect inflation to have minimal impact on construction costs over the next four years.

Director of Information Systems: We need to upgrade our information systems to wireless network technology. It doesn't make sense to do this until after the new factory building is completed and producing product. During 2010, once the factory is up and running, we should equip the whole facility with wireless technology. I think it would cost us $1,600,000 today to install the technology. However, prices have been dropping by 25% per year, so it should be less expensive at a later date.

President: I am excited about our long-term prospects. My only short-term concern is financing the $7,000,000 of construction costs on the portion of the new factory building scheduled to be completed in 2008.

Use the interview information above to prepare a capital expenditures budget for Garden Master Tools Inc. for the years 2008–2011.

Problems Series A

PR 22-1A
Forecast sales volume and sales budget
obj. 4

✓ *3. Total revenue from sales, $1,869,918*

Rembrandt Frame Company prepared the following sales budget for the current year:

Rembrandt Frame Company
Sales Budget
For the Year Ending December 31, 2008

Product and Area	Unit Sales Volume	Unit Selling Price	Total Sales
8" × 10" Frame:			
East	29,000	$14.00	$ 406,000
Central	22,000	14.00	308,000
West	31,500	14.00	441,000
Total	82,500		$1,155,000
12" × 16" Frame:			
East	16,000	$24.00	$ 384,000
Central	10,500	24.00	252,000
West	15,000	24.00	360,000
Total	41,500		$ 996,000
Total revenue from sales			$2,151,000

At the end of December 2008, the following unit sales data were reported for the year:

| | Unit Sales | |
	8" × 10" Frame	12" × 16" Frame
East	29,725	16,480
Central	22,770	10,710
West	30,240	14,325

For the year ending December 31, 2009, unit sales are expected to follow the patterns established during the year ending December 31, 2008. The unit selling price for the 8" × 10" frame is expected to change to $12, and the unit selling price for the 12" × 16" frame is expected to change to $21, effective January 1, 2009.

Instructions

1. Compute the increase or decrease of actual unit sales for the year ended December 31, 2008, over budget. Place your answers in a columnar table with the following format:

	Unit Sales, Year Ended 2008		Increase (Decrease) Actual Over Budget	
	Budget	Actual Sales	Amount	Percent
8" × 10" Frame:				
East				
Central				
West				
12" × 16" Frame:				
East				
Central				
West				

2. Assuming that the trend of sales indicated in part (1) is to continue in 2009, compute the unit sales volume to be used for preparing the sales budget for the year ending December 31, 2009. Place your answers in a columnar table similar to that in part (1) above but with the following column heads. Round budgeted units to the nearest unit.

2008 Actual Units	Percentage Increase (Decrease)	2009 Budgeted Units (rounded)

3. Prepare a sales budget for the year ending December 31, 2009.

PR 22-2A
Sales, production, direct materials purchases, and direct labor cost budgets
obj. 4

✓ *3. Total direct materials purchases, $9,806,650*

The budget director of Outdoor Chef Grill Company requests estimates of sales, production, and other operating data from the various administrative units every month. Selected information concerning sales and production for October 2008 is summarized as follows:

a. Estimated sales for October by sales territory:

Maine:
    Backyard Chef ....   4,500 units at $800 per unit
    Master Chef ....   1,600 units at $1,600 per unit
Vermont:
    Backyard Chef ....   3,800 units at $900 per unit
    Master Chef ....   1,700 units at $1,450 per unit
New Hampshire:
    Backyard Chef ....   4,200 units at $850 per unit
    Master Chef ....   1,800 units at $1,700 per unit

b. Estimated inventories at October 1:

Direct materials:		Finished products:	
Grates	1,200 units	Backyard Chef	1,600 units
Stainless steel	2,300 lbs.	Master Chef	500 units
Burner subassemblies	650 units		
Shelves	500 units		

c. Desired inventories at October 31:

Direct materials:		Finished products:	
Grates	900 units	Backyard Chef	1,300 units
Stainless steel	2,000 lbs.	Master Chef	600 units
Burner subassemblies	800 units		
Shelves	450 units		

d. Direct materials used in production:

In manufacture of Backyard Chef:

Grates	3 units per unit of product
Stainless steel	25 lbs. per unit of product
Burner subassemblies	2 units per unit of product
Shelves	5 units per unit of product

In manufacture of Master Chef:

Grates	6 units per unit of product
Stainless steel	50 lbs. per unit of product
Burner subassemblies	4 units per unit of product
Shelves	6 units per unit of product

e. Anticipated purchase price for direct materials:

Grates	$18 per unit	Burner subassemblies	$115 per unit
Stainless steel	$5 per lb.	Shelves	$6 per unit

f. Direct labor requirements:

Backyard Chef:

Stamping Department	0.60 hour at $15 per hour
Forming Department	0.80 hour at $12 per hour
Assembly Department	1.50 hours at $9 per hour

Master Chef:

Stamping Department	0.80 hour at $15 per hour
Forming Department	1.60 hours at $12 per hour
Assembly Department	2.50 hours at $9 per hour

Instructions

1. Prepare a sales budget for October.
2. Prepare a production budget for October.
3. Prepare a direct materials purchases budget for October.
4. Prepare a direct labor cost budget for October.

PR 22-3A
*Budgeted income
statement and supporting
budgets*

obj. 4

✓ *4. Total direct labor
cost in Fabrication Dept.,
$282,170*

The budget director of Backyard Habitat Inc., with the assistance of the controller, treasurer, production manager, and sales manager, has gathered the following data for use in developing the budgeted income statement for December 2008:

a. Estimated sales for December:

Bird House	34,500 units at $40 per unit
Bird Feeder	25,800 units at $70 per unit

b. Estimated inventories at December 1:

Direct materials:		Finished products:	
Wood	2,600 ft.	Bird House	4,900 units at $25 per unit
Plastic	3,200 lbs.	Bird Feeder	2,500 units at $35 per unit

c. Desired inventories at December 31:

Direct materials:		Finished products:	
Wood	3,500 ft.	Bird House	5,300 units at $24 per unit
Plastic	2,800 lbs.	Bird Feeder	2,100 units at $36 per unit

d. Direct materials used in production:

In manufacture of Bird House:
Wood . . . . .   0.80 ft. per unit of product
Plastic . . . . .   0.50 lb. per unit of product

In manufacture of Bird Feeder:
Wood . . . .   1.20 ft. per unit of product
Plastic . . . .   0.75 lb. per unit of product

e. Anticipated cost of purchases and beginning and ending inventory of direct materials:

Wood . . . . $6.50 per ft.

Plastic . . . . . . $0.90 per lb.

f. Direct labor requirements:

Bird House:
Fabrication Department . . . .   0.25 hour at $14 per hour
Assembly Department . . . .   0.30 hour at $10 per hour
Bird Feeder:
Fabrication Department . . . .   0.45 hour at $14 per hour
Assembly Department . . . .   0.35 hour at $10 per hour

g. Estimated factory overhead costs for December:

Indirect factory wages	$650,000	Power and light	$42,000
Depreciation of plant and equipment	165,000	Insurance and property tax	15,400

h. Estimated operating expenses for December:

Sales salaries expense	$675,000
Advertising expense	148,600
Office salaries expense	214,800
Depreciation expense—office equipment	4,900
Telephone expense—selling	5,200
Telephone expense—administrative	1,700
Travel expense—selling	39,200
Office supplies expense	3,500
Miscellaneous administrative expense	5,000

i. Estimated other income and expense for December:

Interest revenue	$16,900
Interest expense	10,600

j. Estimated tax rate: 35%

Instructions
1. Prepare a sales budget for December.
2. Prepare a production budget for December.
3. Prepare a direct materials purchases budget for December.
4. Prepare a direct labor cost budget for December.
5. Prepare a factory overhead cost budget for December.
6. Prepare a cost of goods sold budget for December. Work in process at the beginning of December is estimated to be $27,000, and work in process at the end of December is estimated to be $32,400.
7. Prepare a selling and administrative expenses budget for December.
8. Prepare a budgeted income statement for December.

PR 22-4A
Cash budget
obj. 5

✓ 1. October deficiency, $64,500

The controller of Santa Fe Housewares Inc. instructs you to prepare a monthly cash budget for the next three months. You are presented with the following budget information:

	August	September	October
Sales	$630,000	$715,000	$845,000
Manufacturing costs	350,000	360,000	410,000
Selling and administrative expenses	170,000	205,000	235,000
Capital expenditures			150,000

The company expects to sell about 10% of its merchandise for cash. Of sales on account, 70% are expected to be collected in full in the month following the sale and the remainder the following month. Depreciation, insurance, and property tax expense represent $25,000 of the estimated monthly manufacturing costs. The annual insurance premium is paid in July, and the annual property taxes are paid in November. Of the remainder of the manufacturing costs, 80% are expected to be paid in the month in which they are incurred and the balance in the following month.

Current assets as of August 1 include cash of $50,000, marketable securities of $85,000, and accounts receivable of $635,000 ($500,000 from July sales and $135,000 from June sales). Sales on account for June and July were $450,000 and $500,000, respectively. Current liabilities as of August 1 include a $100,000, 15%, 90-day note payable due October 20 and $65,000 of accounts payable incurred in July for manufacturing costs. All selling and administrative expenses are paid in cash in the period they are incurred. It is expected that $1,800 in dividends will be received in August. An estimated income tax payment of $39,000 will be made in September. Santa Fe's regular quarterly dividend of $12,000 is expected to be declared in September and paid in October. Management desires to maintain a minimum cash balance of $40,000.

Instructions

1. Prepare a monthly cash budget and supporting schedules for August, September, and October.
2. ⬛▶ On the basis of the cash budget prepared in part (1), what recommendation should be made to the controller?

PR 22-5A
Budgeted income statement and balance sheet
objs. 4, 5

✓ *1. Budgeted net income, $175,850*

As a preliminary to requesting budget estimates of sales, costs, and expenses for the fiscal year beginning January 1, 2009, the following tentative trial balance as of December 31, 2008, is prepared by the Accounting Department of Coconut Grove Soap Co.:

Cash	$ 90,000	
Accounts Receivable	108,600	
Finished Goods	72,400	
Work in Process	27,500	
Materials	49,700	
Prepaid Expenses	3,400	
Plant and Equipment	350,000	
Accumulated Depreciation—Plant and Equipment		$130,400
Accounts Payable		57,000
Common Stock, $10 par		185,000
Retained Earnings		329,200
	$701,600	$701,600

Factory output and sales for 2009 are expected to total 215,000 units of product, which are to be sold at $4.60 per unit. The quantities and costs of the inventories at December 31, 2009, are expected to remain unchanged from the balances at the beginning of the year.

Budget estimates of manufacturing costs and operating expenses for the year are summarized as follows:

	Estimated Costs and Expenses	
	Fixed (Total for Year)	**Variable** (Per Unit Sold)
Cost of goods manufactured and sold:		
Direct materials	—	$0.80
Direct labor	—	0.45
Factory overhead:		
Depreciation of plant and equipment	$45,000	—
Other factory overhead	7,000	0.30
Selling expenses:		
Sales salaries and commissions	40,000	0.35
Advertising	55,000	—
Miscellaneous selling expense	4,500	0.15
Administrative expenses:		
Office and officers salaries	67,100	0.17
Supplies	3,000	0.06
Miscellaneous administrative expense	2,000	0.09

Balances of accounts receivable, prepaid expenses, and accounts payable at the end of the year are not expected to differ significantly from the beginning balances. Federal income tax of $80,000 on 2009 taxable income will be paid during 2009. Regular quarterly cash dividends of $0.80 a share are expected to be declared and paid in March, June, September, and December. It is anticipated that fixed assets will be purchased for $60,000 cash in May.

Instructions
1. Prepare a budgeted income statement for 2009.
2. Prepare a budgeted balance sheet as of December 31, 2009, with supporting calculations.

Problems Series B

PR 22-1B
*Forecast sales volume
and sales budget*

obj. 4

✓ *3. Total revenue from
sales, $33,161,100*

Detect and Secure Devices Inc. prepared the following sales budget for the current year:

Detect and Secure Devices Inc.
Sales Budget
For the Year Ending December 31, 2008

Product and Area	Unit Sales Volume	Unit Selling Price	Total Sales
Home Alert System:			
United States	26,400	$240	$ 6,336,000
Europe	7,100	240	1,704,000
Asia	5,200	240	1,248,000
Total	38,700		$ 9,288,000
Business Alert System:			
United States	13,500	$850	$11,475,000
Europe	5,800	850	4,930,000
Asia	3,700	850	3,145,000
Total	23,000		$19,550,000
Total revenue from sales			$28,838,000

At the end of December 2008, the following unit sales data were reported for the year:

	Unit Sales	
	Home Alert System	Business Alert System
United States	27,720	14,040
Europe	6,816	5,916
Asia	5,356	3,589

For the year ending December 31, 2009, unit sales are expected to follow the patterns established during the year ending December 31, 2008. The unit selling price for the Home Alert System is expected to increase to $290, and the unit selling price for the Business Alert System is expected to be increased to $880, effective January 1, 2009.

Instructions
1. Compute the increase or decrease of actual unit sales for the year ended December 31, 2008, over budget. Place your answers in a columnar table with the following format:

	Unit Sales, Year Ended 2008		Increase (Decrease) Actual Over Budget	
	Budget	Actual Sales	Amount	Percent
Home Alert System:				
United States				
Europe				
Asia				

(continued)

	Unit Sales, Year Ended 2008		Increase (Decrease) Actual Over Budget	
	Budget	**Actual Sales**	**Amount**	**Percent**
Business Alert System:				
United States				
Europe				
Asia				

2. Assuming that the trend of sales indicated in part (1) is to continue in 2009, compute the unit sales volume to be used for preparing the sales budget for the year ending December 31, 2009. Place your answers in a columnar table similar to that in part (1) above but with the following column heads. Round budgeted units to the nearest unit.

2008 Actual Units	Percentage Increase (Decrease)	2009 Budgeted Units (rounded)

3. Prepare a sales budget for the year ending December 31, 2009.

PR 22-2B
Sales, production, direct materials purchases, and direct labor cost budgets

obj. 4

✓ *3. Total direct materials purchases, $6,679,381*

The budget director of Kingdom Furniture Company requests estimates of sales, production, and other operating data from the various administrative units every month. Selected information concerning sales and production for May 2008 is summarized as follows:

a. Estimated sales of King and Prince chairs for May by sales territory:

Northern Domestic:
King	5,800 units at $650 per unit
Prince	6,700 units at $420 per unit

Southern Domestic:
King	3,500 units at $590 per unit
Prince	3,800 units at $480 per unit

International:
King	1,200 units at $700 per unit
Prince	1,000 units at $530 per unit

b. Estimated inventories at May 1:

Direct materials:
Fabric	5,000 sq. yds.
Wood	6,500 lineal ft.
Filler	3,000 cu. ft.
Springs	7,250 units

Finished products:
King	920 units
Prince	260 units

c. Desired inventories at May 31:

Direct materials:
Fabric	4,400 sq. yds.
Wood	5,800 lineal ft.
Filler	3,100 cu. ft.
Springs	7,500 units

Finished products:
King	800 units
Prince	400 units

d. Direct materials used in production:

In manufacture of King:
Fabric	4.6 sq. yds. per unit of product
Wood	35 lineal ft. per unit of product
Filler	3.8 cu. ft. per unit of product
Springs	14 units per unit of product

In manufacture of Prince:
Fabric	3 sq. yds. per unit of product
Wood	25 lineal ft. per unit of product
Filler	3.2 cu. ft. per unit of product
Springs	10 units per unit of product

e. Anticipated purchase price for direct materials:

Fabric	$8.00 per square yard		Filler	$3.50 per cubic foot
Wood	7.00 per lineal foot		Springs	4.50 per unit

f. Direct labor requirements:

King:
    Framing Department . . . . . .   2.5 hours at $12 per hour
    Cutting Department . . . .   1.5 hours at $9 per hour
    Upholstery Department . . . .   2.0 hours at $15 per hour
Prince:
    Framing Department . . . . . .   1.8 hours at $12 per hour
    Cutting Department . . . .   0.5 hour at $9 per hour
    Upholstery Department . . . .   2.3 hours at $15 per hour

Instructions
1. Prepare a sales budget for May.
2. Prepare a production budget for May.
3. Prepare a direct materials purchases budget for May.
4. Prepare a direct labor cost budget for May.

PR 22-3B
Budgeted income statement and supporting budgets
obj. **4**

✓*4. Total direct labor cost in Assembly Dept., $73,548*

The budget director of Safety Athletic Inc., with the assistance of the controller, treasurer, production manager, and sales manager, has gathered the following data for use in developing the budgeted income statement for January 2008:

a. Estimated sales for January:

Batting helmet	3,500 units at $65 per unit
Football helmet	6,800 units at $130 per unit

b. Estimated inventories at January 1:

Direct materials:		Finished products:	
Plastic	900 lbs.	Batting helmet	270 units at $32 per unit
Foam lining	490 lbs.	Football helmet	400 units at $52 per unit

c. Desired inventories at January 31:

Direct materials:		Finished products:	
Plastic	1,240 lbs.	Batting helmet	240 units at $34 per unit
Foam lining	470 lbs.	Football helmet	360 units at $55 per unit

d. Direct materials used in production:

In manufacture of batting helmet:
    Plastic . . . .   1.20 lbs. per unit of product
    Foam lining . . . .   0.50 lb. per unit of product
In manufacture of football helmet:
    Plastic . . . .   2.80 lbs. per unit of product
    Foam lining . . . .   1.40 lbs. per unit of product

e. Anticipated cost of purchases and beginning and ending inventory of direct materials:

Plastic	$7.00 per lb.
Foam lining	$4.00 per lb.

f. Direct labor requirements:

Batting helmet:
    Molding Department . . . .   0.20 hour at $14 per hour
    Assembly Department . . . .   0.50 hour at $12 per hour
Football helmet:
    Molding Department . . . .   0.30 hour at $14 per hour
    Assembly Department . . . .   0.65 hour at $12 per hour

g. Estimated factory overhead costs for January:

Indirect factory wages	$105,000	Power and light	$16,000
Depreciation of plant and equipment	30,000	Insurance and property tax	8,700

h. Estimated operating expenses for January:

Sales salaries expense	$265,800
Advertising expense	135,600
Office salaries expense	84,300
Depreciation expense—office equipment	5,200
Telephone expense—selling	3,500
Telephone expense—administrative	700
Travel expense—selling	43,100
Office supplies expense	4,900
Miscellaneous administrative expense	5,200

i. Estimated other income and expense for January:

Interest revenue	$14,500
Interest expense	18,700

j. Estimated tax rate: 30%

Instructions

1. Prepare a sales budget for January.
2. Prepare a production budget for January.
3. Prepare a direct materials purchases budget for January.
4. Prepare a direct labor cost budget for January.
5. Prepare a factory overhead cost budget for January.
6. Prepare a cost of goods sold budget for January. Work in process at the beginning of January is estimated to be $12,500, and work in process at the end of January is desired to be $13,500.
7. Prepare a selling and administrative expenses budget for January.
8. Prepare a budgeted income statement for January.

PR 22-4B
Cash budget
obj. 5

✓ *1. June deficiency, $10,000*

The controller of Swift Shoes Inc. instructs you to prepare a monthly cash budget for the next three months. You are presented with the following budget information:

	April	May	June
Sales	$100,000	$150,000	$180,000
Manufacturing costs	40,000	50,000	54,000
Selling and administrative expenses	32,000	38,000	45,000
Capital expenditures	—	—	30,000

The company expects to sell about 10% of its merchandise for cash. Of sales on account, 60% are expected to be collected in full in the month following the sale and the remainder the following month. Depreciation, insurance, and property tax expense represent $18,000 of the estimated monthly manufacturing costs. The annual insurance premium is paid in July, and the annual property taxes are paid in November. Of the remainder of the manufacturing costs, 80% are expected to be paid in the month in which they are incurred and the balance in the following month.

Current assets as of April 1 include cash of $40,000, marketable securities of $65,000, and accounts receivable of $117,800 ($85,000 from March sales and $32,800 from February sales). Sales on account in February and March were $82,000 and $85,000, respectively. Current liabilities as of April 1 include a $50,000, 12%, 90-day note payable due June 20 and $29,000 of accounts payable incurred in March for manufacturing costs. All selling and administrative expenses are paid in cash in the period they are incurred. It is expected that $3,500 in dividends will be received in April. An estimated income tax payment of $34,000 will be made in May. Swift Shoes' regular quarterly dividend of $8,000 is expected to be declared in May and paid in June. Management desires to maintain a minimum cash balance of $35,000.

Instructions
1. Prepare a monthly cash budget and supporting schedules for April, May, and June 2008.
2. On the basis of the cash budget prepared in part (1), what recommendation should be made to the controller?

PR 22-5B
Budgeted income statement and balance sheet
objs. 4, 5

✓ *1. Budgeted net income, $619,800*

As a preliminary to requesting budget estimates of sales, costs, and expenses for the fiscal year beginning January 1, 2009, the following tentative trial balance as of December 31, 2008, is prepared by the Accounting Department of Cornerstone Publishing Co.:

Cash	$ 122,500	
Accounts Receivable	246,700	
Finished Goods	157,800	
Work in Process	37,800	
Materials	57,800	
Prepaid Expenses	4,500	
Plant and Equipment	620,000	
Accumulated Depreciation—Plant and Equipment		$ 267,000
Accounts Payable		184,500
Common Stock, $15 par		450,000
Retained Earnings		345,600
	$1,247,100	$1,247,100

Factory output and sales for 2009 are expected to total 30,000 units of product, which are to be sold at $110 per unit. The quantities and costs of the inventories at December 31, 2009, are expected to remain unchanged from the balances at the beginning of the year.

Budget estimates of manufacturing costs and operating expenses for the year are summarized as follows:

	Estimated Costs and Expenses	
	Fixed (Total for Year)	**Variable** (Per Unit Sold)
Cost of goods manufactured and sold:		
Direct materials	—	$26.00
Direct labor	—	8.50
Factory overhead:		
Depreciation of plant and equipment	$ 40,000	—
Other factory overhead	12,000	5.00
Selling expenses:		
Sales salaries and commissions	118,000	14.00
Advertising	114,200	—
Miscellaneous selling expense	10,500	2.15
Administrative expenses:		
Office and officers salaries	83,600	6.50
Supplies	4,400	1.25
Miscellaneous administrative expense	2,000	1.45

Balances of accounts receivable, prepaid expenses, and accounts payable at the end of the year are not expected to differ significantly from the beginning balances. Federal income tax of $350,000 on 2009 taxable income will be paid during 2009. Regular quarterly cash dividends of $1.75 a share are expected to be declared and paid in March, June, September, and December. It is anticipated that fixed assets will be purchased for $180,000 cash in May.

Instructions
1. Prepare a budgeted income statement for 2009.
2. Prepare a budgeted balance sheet as of December 31, 2009, with supporting calculations.

Special Activities

SA 22-1
Ethics and professional conduct in business

ETHICS

The director of marketing for Mobile Computer Co., Sheri Keller, had the following discussion with the company controller, Isaiah Johnson, on July 26 of the current year:

Sheri: Isaiah, it looks like I'm going to spend much less than indicated on my July budget.
Isaiah: I'm glad to hear it.
Sheri: Well, I'm not so sure it's good news. I'm concerned that the president will see that I'm under budget and reduce my budget in the future. The only reason that I look good is that we've delayed an advertising campaign. Once the campaign hits in September, I'm sure my actual expenditures will go up. You see, we are also having our sales convention in September. Having the advertising campaign and the convention at the same time is going to kill my September numbers.
Isaiah: I don't think that's anything to worry about. We all expect some variation in actual spending month to month. What's really important is staying within the budgeted targets for the year. Does that look as if it's going to be a problem?
Sheri: I don't think so, but just the same, I'd like to be on the safe side.
Isaiah: What do you mean?
Sheri: Well, this is what I'd like to do. I want to pay the convention-related costs in advance this month. I'll pay the hotel for room and convention space and purchase the airline tickets in advance. In this way, I can charge all these expenditures to July's budget. This would cause my actual expenses to come close to budget for July. Moreover, when the big advertising campaign hits in September, I won't have to worry about expenditures for the convention on my September budget as well. The convention costs will already be paid. Thus, my September expenses should be pretty close to budget.
Isaiah: I can't tell you when to make your convention purchases, but I'm not too sure that it should be expensed on July's budget.
Sheri: What's the problem? It looks like "no harm, no foul" to me. I can't see that there's anything wrong with this—it's just smart management.

How should Isaiah Johnson respond to Sheri Keller's request to expense the advanced payments for convention-related costs against July's budget?

SA 22-2
Evaluating budgeting systems

REAL WORLD

Children's Hospital of the King's Daughters Health System in Norfolk, Virginia, introduced a new budgeting method that allowed the hospital's annual plan to be updated for changes in operating plans. For example, if the budget was based on 400 patient-days (number of patients × number of days in the hospital) and the actual count rose to 450 patient-days, the variable costs of staffing, lab work, and medication costs could be adjusted to reflect this change. The budget manager stated, "I work with hospital directors to turn data into meaningful information and effect change before the month ends."

a. What budgeting methods are being used under the new approach?
b. Why are these methods superior to the former approaches?

SA 22-3
Service company static decision making

A bank manager of Citizens Bank Inc. uses the managerial accounting system to track the costs of operating the various departments within the bank. The departments include Cash Management, Trust Commercial Loans, Mortgage Loans, Operations, Credit Card, and Branch Services. The budget and actual results for the Operations Department are as follows:

Resources	Budget	Actual
Salaries	$150,000	$150,000
Benefits	30,000	30,000
Supplies	45,000	42,000
Travel	20,000	30,000
Training	25,000	35,000
Overtime	25,000	20,000
Total	$295,000	$307,000
Excess of actual over budget		$ 12,000

a. What information is provided by the budget? Specifically, what questions can the bank manager ask of the Operations Department manager?

b. What information does the budget fail to provide? Specifically, could the budget information be presented differently to provide even more insight for the bank manager?

SA 22-4
Objectives of the master budget

REAL WORLD

Domino's Pizza L.L.C. operates pizza delivery and carryout restaurants. The annual report describes its business as follows:

> We offer a focused menu of high-quality, value priced pizza with three types of crust (Hand-Tossed, Thin Crust, and Deep Dish), along with buffalo wings, bread sticks, cheesy bread, CinnaStix®, and Coca-Cola® products. Our hand-tossed pizza is made from fresh dough produced in our regional distribution centers. We prepare every pizza using real cheese, pizza sauce made from fresh tomatoes, and a choice of high-quality meat and vegetable toppings in generous portions. Our focused menu and use of premium ingredients enable us to consistently and efficiently produce the highest-quality pizza.
>
> Over the 41 years since our founding, we have developed a simple, cost-efficient model. We offer a limited menu, our stores are designed for delivery and carry-out, and we do not generally offer dine-in service. As a result, our stores require relatively small, lower-rent locations and limited capital expenditures.

 How would a master budget support planning, directing, and control for Domino's?

SA 22-5
Integrity and evaluating budgeting systems

The city of Westwood has an annual budget cycle that begins on July 1 and ends on June 30. At the beginning of each budget year, an annual budget is established for each department. The annual budget is divided by 12 months to provide a constant monthly static budget. On June 30, all unspent budgeted monies for the budget year from the various city departments must be "returned" to the General Fund. Thus, if department heads fail to use their budget by year-end, they will lose it. A budget analyst prepared a chart of the difference between the monthly actual and budgeted amounts for the recent fiscal year. The chart was as follows:

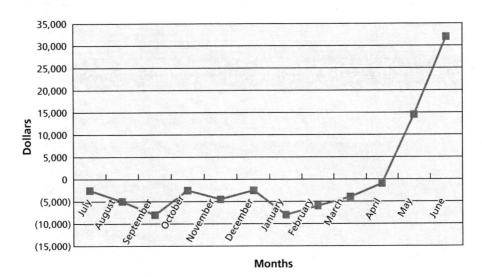

a. Interpret the chart.

b. Suggest an improvement in the budget system.

SA 22-6
Objectives of budgeting

At the beginning of the year, Kevin Frey decided to prepare a cash budget for the year, based upon anticipated cash receipts and payments. The estimates in the budget represent a "best guess." The budget is as follows:

Expected annual cash receipts:		
Salary from part-time job	$10,500	
Salary from summer job	5,000	
Total receipts		$15,500
Expected annual cash payments:		
Tuition	$ 5,000	
Books	400	
Rent	4,200	
Food	2,500	
Utilities	900	
Entertainment	4,000	
Total payments		17,000
Net change in cash		$ (1,500)

1. ⬤▭▶ What does this budget suggest? In what ways is this information useful to Kevin?
2. a. ⬤▭▶ Some items in the budget are more certain than are others. Which items are the most certain? Which items are the most uncertain? What are the implications of these different levels of certainty to Kevin's planning?
   b. ⬤▭▶ Some payment items are more controllable than others. Assuming that Kevin plans to go to school, classify the items as controllable, partially controllable, or not controllable. What are the implications of controllable items to planning?
3. ⬤▭▶ What actions could Kevin take in order to avoid having the anticipated shortfall of $1,500 at the end of the year?
4. ⬤▭▶ What does this budget fail to consider, and what are the implications of these omissions to Kevin's planning?

SA 22-7
Budget for a state government

Group Project

Internet Project

In a group, find the home page of the state in which you presently live. The home page will be of the form *statename.gov*. At the home page site, search for annual budget information.

1. What are the budgeted sources of revenue and their percentage breakdown?
2. What are the major categories of budgeted expenditures (or appropriations) and their percentage breakdown?
3. Is the projected budget in balance?

Answers to Self-Examination Questions ↘

1. **B** Individuals can be discouraged with budgets that appear too tight or unobtainable. Flexible budgeting (answer C) provides a series of budgets for varying rates of activity and thereby builds into the budgeting system the effect of fluctuations in the level of activity. Budgetary slack (answer A) comes from a loose budget, not a tight budget. A "spend it or lose it" mentality (answer D) is often associated with loose budgets.

2. **A** The first step of the budget process is to develop a plan. Once plans are established, management may direct actions (answer B). The results of actions can be controlled (answer C) by comparing them to the plan. This feedback (answer D) can be used by management to change plans or redirect actions.

3. **B** Administrative departments (answer B), such as Purchasing or Human Resources, will often use static budgeting. Production departments (answer A) fre-

quently use flexible budgets. Responsibility centers (answer C) can use either static or flexible budgeting. Capital expenditures budgets are used to plan capital projects (answer D).

4. **B** The total production indicated in the production budget is 257,500 units (answer B), which is computed as follows:

Sales	250,000 units
Plus desired ending inventory	30,000 units
Total	280,000 units
Less estimated beginning inventory	22,500 units
Total production	257,500 units

5. **C** Dixon expects to collect 70% of April sales ($560,000) plus 30% of the March sales ($195,000) in April, for a total of $755,000 (answer C). Answer A is 100% of April sales. Answer B is 70% of April sales. Answer D adds 70% of both March and April sales.

Subject Index

Discount on bonds payable, amortization of, *illus.*, 669
Discounted cash flow method, 1148
Discounting notes receivable, 410
Dishonored note receivable, *def.*, 406
Disposal of fixed assets, 447
Dividend(s), 569
   accounting for, 578
   and earnings per share of common stock, *illus.*, 760
   cash, 578
   cash flows used for payment of, 703
   liquidating, 578*fn*
   per share and dividend yield, 760
   stock, 580
   to preferred and common stock, *illus.*, 573
Dividend yield, *def.*, 587, 761
Divisional income statements, *illus.*, 1063, *illus.*, 1064
Divisions, *def.*, 1056
Double taxation, 569
Double-declining-balance method, *def.*, 443
Double-entry accounting, recording transactions, *illus.*, 59
Double-entry accounting system, *def.*, 58
Doubtful accounts, allowance for, 397
Doubtful accounts expense, 395
Drawing account, 56
Drawing, *def.*, 51
Due date, 405
DuPont formula, *def.*, 1065
Duties, rotating, 353

E

Earnings
   deductions from employee, 483
   recording employees', 489
   retained, 571
Earnings per common share (EPS)
   assuming dilution, 620
   def., 619
Earnings per share (EPS) on common stock, *def.*, 759
Earnings per share, income statement with, *illus.*, 620
Earnings record, employee's, 491
   illus., 492–493
E-commerce, *def.*, 222
Economic Research Institute, 483
Effective interest rate method, *def.*, 659
   of amortization, 668
Effective rate of interest, *def.*, 653
Electronic funds transfers (EFT)
   cash paid by, 359
   cash received by, 358
   def., 358
Elements of a computerized accounting system, *illus.*, 219
Elements of internal control, *def.*, *illus.*, 351
Employee Benefit Study, 495
Employee earnings
   deductions from, 483
   liability for, 483
Employee fraud
   def., 350
   tips on preventing, 354
Employee net pay, computing, 486

Employee theft, cost of, 273
Employee's earnings record
   def., 491
   illus., 492–493
Employee's Withholding Allowance Certificate (W-4), 483
   illus., 484
Employees
   fringe benefits, 495
   ghost, 836
   recording earnings, 489
Employer's payroll taxes, liability for, 487
End-of-period spreadsheet, 175
   illus., 146, 165
   preparing, 165
End-of-period spreadsheet for merchandising business, C-1
   using periodic inventory system, *illus.*, C-4
   using perpetual inventory system, *illus.*, C-2
Engineering change order (ECO), 1117
Entity, nontaxable, 527
Environmental accounting, 799
Equity
   owner's, 51, 150
   rate earned on common stockholders', 758
   rate earned on stockholders', 757
   ratio of liabilities to stockholders', 754
   reporting stockholders', 582
   shareholders, 571
   statement of members', 545
   statement of owner's, 255
   statement of partnership, *illus.*, 545
   statement of stockholders', 583, 585, *illus.*, 586
   stockholders', 571
Equity method, *def.*, 625
Equity securities, *def.*, 622
Equivalent units
   conversion, 880, *illus.*, 881
   cost per, 882
   determine the cost per, 881, 893
   direct materials, *illus.*, 879
   materials, 879
Equivalent units of production
   compute, 878, 893
   def., 878
Errors
   causing unequal trial balance, *illus.*, 74
   correction of, 73, 74
   discovery of, 73
   in liquidation, 544
   inventory, 322
Estimate based on analysis of receivables, 401
Estimate based on percent of sales, 400
Estimate of uncollectible accounts, *illus.*, 402
Estimated income tax payable, 511*fn*
Estimating uncollectibles, 399
Estimation methods, comparing, 403
Ethics
   def., 4
   role of in business, 4
Exchanges
   gains on, 449
   losses on, 450

Exchanges of similar fixed assets
   accounting for, *illus.*, 451
   review of accounting for, 451
Ex-dividends, 578
Expenditures
   capital, 437, 438
   revenue, 437, 438
Expense(s)
   accrued, 106, 113, 709
   administrative, 254, 843
   bad debt, 395
   cash payments for operating, 709
   def., 15, 51
   deferred, 106
   depreciation, 115
   doubtful accounts, 395
   factors in computing depreciation, 440
   general, 254
   indirect, 1061
   interest, 710
   other, 255
   prepaid, 14, 106, 108
   selling, 254, 843
   uncollectible accounts, 395
Extraordinary item, *def.*, 618
Extraordinary repairs, 438

F

Face amount
   bonds issued at, 657
   of bonds, present value of, 653
Factor, 395
Factoring, 395
Factors in computing depreciation expense, 440
Factors that complicate capital investment analysis, 1153
Factory burden, *def.*, 802
Factory labor, 835
Factory overhead
   account, 1027
   allocating, 837
   applying to work in process, 838
   assigning to jobs, *illus.*, 839
   overapplied or overabsorbed, 838
   underapplied or underabsorbed, 838
Factory overhead balance, disposal of, 840
Factory overhead cost, 837
   def., 802
   variance report, *illus.*, 1027
Factory overhead cost budget, 980
   illus., 981
   indicating standard factory overhead rate, *illus.*, 1024
Factory overhead flexible budget, 1023
Factory overhead variances, 1023, 1027
   reporting, 1027
Fair Labor Standards Act, 483
Fair value, 580
Favorable cost variance, 1018
FDA (Food and Drug Administration), 1069
Federal income tax, depreciation for, 445
Federal Insurance Contributions Act. See FICA
Federal Trade Commission, 1110
Federal unemployment compensation tax, 487

Period costs
   def., 803, 843
   examples of, *illus.*, 804
   illus., 804
Periodic inventory spreadsheet, C-3
Periodic inventory system, 276
   adjusting process under, 278
   chart of accounts, 276, *illus.*, 277
   closing entries under, 279
   cost of merchandise sold using, 276
   end-of-period spreadsheet for merchandising business, *illus.*, C-4
   financial statements under, 278
   inventory costing methods under, 315
   transactions using, *illus.*, 279
Periodic system
   def., 254
   determining cost of merchandise sold using, *illus.*, 277
Permanent differences, *def.*, 613
Perpetual inventory account (FIFO), entries and, *illus.*, 312, 314
Perpetual inventory spreadsheet, C-1
Perpetual inventory system
   computerized, 315
   end-of-period spreadsheet for merchandising business, *illus.*, C-2
   inventory costing methods, 312
   transactions using, *illus.*, 279
Perpetual system, *def.*, 254
Personnel policies, 352
Personnel, competent, 353
Petty cash fund, *def.*, 367
Physical depreciation, 440
Physical flow of merchandise, 312
Physical flows for a process manufacturer, *illus.*, 875
Physical inventory, *def.*, 309
Pirates, 21st century, 454
Planned level of production, 1017
Planning, 969
   def., 797
   function of management, 968
Plant assets, 435
   def., 115, 150
Point-to-point approach, 457
Post-closing trial balance, 155
   illus., 159, 169
   preparing, 168
Posting
   adjusting entries, 165
   cash payments journal, *illus.*, 215
   cash receipts journal, *illus.*, 211
   closing entries, 153, 168
   def., 59
   journal entries to accounts, 59
   of a debit and credit, *illus.*, 60
   purchases journal, *illus.*, 213
   to ledgers, revenue journal, *illus.*, 209
   transactions to ledger, 164
Postretirement benefits other than pensions, 498
Predetermined factory overhead rate, *def.*, 837
Preferred and common stock, dividends to, *illus.*, 573
Preferred dividends, number of times earned, 755

Preferred stock
   cumulative, 573*fn*
   def., 573*fn*
   participating, 573*fn*
Premium on bonds payable, amortization of, *illus.*, 670
Premium on stock, 575
Premium
   amortization of by interest method, 669
   bonds issued at, 659
   def., 574, 653
Prepaid expenses, 108
   def., 14, 106
Present value
   def., 653
   methods that ignore, 1143
Present value concepts, *def.*, 1146
Present value index, *def.*, 1148
Present value methods, 1146
Present value of $1, 654
   at compound interest, A-2, A-3
   illus., 655
   table, *illus.*, 1147
Present value of an amount, 1146
Present value of an annuity, *def.*, 655, 1147
Present value of an annuity of $1, *illus.*, 656
Present value of ordinary annuity of $1, A-4, A-5
Present value of periodic bond interest payments, 655
Present value of the face amount of bonds, 653
Price fixing, 1110
Price levels, changes in, 1155
Price-earnings (P/E) ratio, *def.*, 628, 759
Prime costs, 802
   def., 803
   illus., 803
Principal, 652
Principle of exceptions, 1014
Prior period adjustments, *def.*, 585
Private accounting, *def.*, 9
Private corporations, 568
Proceeds, *def.*, 481
Process cost system
   and job order cost system, comparing, 873, *illus.*, 874
   def., 832, 873
   journal entries for, 886
Process costing, overview of, 872
Process manufacturers
   cost flows for, 875, *illus.*, 876
   def., 872
   overview of, 872
   physical flows for, *illus.*, 875
Process, *def.*, 1031
Process or sell, 1106
   differential analysis report, *illus.*, 1106
Processing methods, 205
Product, 1115
   discontinue a, 1101
Product cost concept, *def.*, 1111
Product costs
   def., 803
   illus., 804
Product life-cycle management (PLM), 222
Product or service market stakeholders, 4

Product selling prices, setting normal, 1108
Production
   actual, 1017
   compute equivalent units of, 893
   planned level of, 1017
Production bottlenecks
   product pricing under, 1116
   product profitability under, 1114
Production budget
   def., 977
   illus., 978
Production line
   just-in-time, *illus.*, 890
   traditional, *illus.*, 890
Production report
   cost of, 884, 893, *illus.*, 885, 894
   for decision making, using cost of, 888
Profit(s)
   def., 2
   gross, 251, 254
   illusory, 319
   inventory, 319
   net, 18
   target, 932
Profit center
   def., 1060
   reporting, 1062
Profit margin, *def.*, 1065
Profit measurement and accounting systems, 218
Profitability analysis, 755
Profitability, *def.*, 748
Profit-volume chart
   def., 935
   illus., 935
   original and revised, *illus.*, 937
Proofs and security measures, 355
Property, co-ownership of partnership, 527
Property, plant, and equipment, 150, 435, 456
Proprietorships, 526
   characteristics of, *illus.*, 529
   def., 3
   partnerships, and limited liability companies, comparing, 529
Provision for income taxes, 511*fn*
Public accounting, *def.*, 9
Public Company Accounting Oversight Board (PCAOB), 7, 10
Public corporations, 568
Publicly held companies, 348
Purchase allowance, *def.*, 252
Purchase and payment cycle, 212
Purchase order, 214, 308
Purchase return, *def.*, 252
Purchase transactions, 263
Purchases allowance, *def.*, 264
Purchases discounts, 263
   def., 252
Purchases journal
   and postings, *illus.*, 213
   def., 212
   for merchandising business, *illus.*, 274
Purchases return
   and allowances, 264
   def., 264

Q

Qualitative considerations, 1155
Quick assets, *def.*, 501, 750

Company Index ● ● ● ● ● ● ● ● ● ● ● ● ●

Golf Channel, The, 931
Goodyear Tire & Rubber Company, 646
Google Inc., 2, 32, 458, 499, 628, 695, 939, 1017, 1053
Grant Thornton LLP, 554

H

H&R Block, 31, 256
H.J. Heinz Company, 424, 628, 779, 973, 1039
Haliburton Company, 1017
Harris Corporation, 1081
Harris Interactive, 1017
Hasbro, 778–779
HCA Inc., 400
HealthSouth, 6
Heritage Foundation, 1146
Hershey Company, The, 779, 901
Hershey Food Corporation, The, 872
Hewlett-Packard Company (HP), 627, 778, 1057
Hewlett-Packard Development Company, LP (HP), 345, 587, 851
Hilton Hospitality, Inc., 13, 31
Hilton Hotels Corporation, 791–792, 1070, 1085
Home Depot, The, 4, 252, 256, 293, 433, 570, 587, 1056
Howard Schultz & Associates (HS&A), 359
Hyperspace Communications, Inc., 382

I

IBM, 433, 480, 696, 1061, 1155, 1166
IHOP Corp., 1165
Indian Airlines Limited, 929
Infinity Broadcasting Corporation, 931
Intel Corporation, 397, 436, 872, 1016
Internal Revenue Service (IRS), 441, 526, 571, 1021
International Paper Company, 916
Intuit Inc., 204, 238, 712, 952
Ivory, 973

J

Jacobus Pharmaceuticals Company, Inc., 933
JCPenney, 4, 179, 252, 272, 346, 395, 400, 441
JHT Holdings, Inc., 378
Johnson & Johnson, 740, 1017
Jones Soda Co., 692, 726

K

K2 Sports, 1056
Kellogg Company, 432, 570, 902
Keystone Foods LLC, 1019
Kmart, 179
Kohl's Corporation, 727
Korn/Ferry International, 1060
KPMG LLP, 529, 554, 564
Kroger, 49, 254, 293–294, 339, 433, 436

L

L.L. Bean, Inc., 238, 357
Lands' End Inc., 357
La-Z-Boy Incorporated, 394
Levi Strauss & Co., 997

Limited, Inc., The, 179, 424, 1014
Los Angeles Lakers, 936
Lowe's Companies, Inc., 115

M

Macy's, 395
Mahanaim Essentials LLC, 526
Mandalay Resort Group, 417
Manpower Inc., 458
Manugistics, 248
Market Guide, 748
Marriott International, Inc., 3, 436, 458, 791–792, 1098, 1139
Marshalls, 263
Marvel Entertainment, Inc., 104
MasterCard, 259, 260, 396
Mattel, Inc., 381, 587, 778–779
May Department Stores Company, The, 777
McDonald's, 8, 13, 357, 622, 678, 953, 1019, 1123
MCI, 1017
McKinsey & Company, 529
Merck & Co., Inc., 873, 1069, 1155, 1174
Merrill Lynch & Co. Inc., 650, 661
Metro-Goldwyn-Mayer Studios Inc. (MGM), 1164
Microsoft Corporation, 13, 29, 73, 118, 131, 145, 369, 454, 696, 712, 749, 791, 969
Middle Tennessee Lumber Co., Inc., 889
Millennium Chemicals, 1068
Miramax Film Corp., 847
Mohawk Forest Products, 1015
Molson Coors Brewing Company, 758
Monsanto Company, 1161
Moody's Investors Service, 619, 661, 690
Motorola Inc., 712

N

National Audubon Society, 571
National Check Fraud Center, 363
Nature's Sunshine Products, Inc., 586
NBA, 1099
Neiman Marcus Group, Inc., 346
Netflix, 920
NetSuite Inc., 204, 248
NIKE, 3, 1103
Nissan Motor Co. Ltd., 480
Nordstrom Inc., 1060
Norfolk Southern Corporation, 442, 458, 1056
North Face, The, 968
Northrop Grumman Corporation, 637
Northwest Airlines Corporation, 370, 722
Novartis AG, 933

O

OccuLogix, Inc., 391
Office Depot, Inc., 252
Oracle, 204, 248, 587
Orvis Company, Inc., The, 357
Overhill Flowers, Inc., 702
Owens Corning, 1152

P

Pacific Bell, 662
Pacific Gas and Electric Company, 845
Panera Bread, 479, 692, 1152

Parker Hannifin Corp., 1026
PayPal, 627
PepsiCo, Inc., 8, 29, 32, 397, 776
Pixar, 627
Polo Ralph Lauren Corporation, 423
Priceline.com Inc., 222, 625, 1098, 1107, 1139
Pricewaterhouse-Coopers, 201, 432, 433, 529, 564, 647, 740
Procter & Gamble, 31, 51, 433, 511, 611, 754, 770, 873, 891, 1056
PurchasePro, 6

Q

Quaker, 73
Qwest Communications International, Inc., 6

R

R.J. Reynolds Tobacco Company, 570
RadioShack Corporation, 112
RealNetworks, Inc., 1098
Research in Motion Limited, 764
Rite Aid Corp., 480
Ritz-Carlton Hotel, The, 927
Robert Morris Associates, 748
Rogers Corporation, 1051
Ruby Tuesday, Inc., 458

S

Safeway Inc., 339
Sage Software, Inc., 204
Salesforce.com, 248
Samsung, 3
SAP, 204, 248
Saturn Corporation, 322
Sears Holding Corporation, 254, 272, 395, 360
Securities and Exchange Commission (SEC), 349, 740, 1152
Shell Group, 835
Sierra Club, 571
SIRIUS Satellite Radio, 931
S-K-I Limited, 969
Smurfit-Stone Container Corporation, 238
Solectron Corporation, 1123
Sony Corporation of America, 3, 454, 1123
Southern Airways, 55
Southwest Airlines Co., 4, 13, 457, 458, 680
Speedway Motorsports, Inc., 775
Sports Authority, 1056
Sprint Nextel, 954
St. Paul Companies, 446
Standard & Poor's, 619
Starbucks Corporation, 570, 692
Starwood Hotels & Resorts Worldwide, Inc., 458
Steelcase Inc., 994
Stern Stewart & Co., 1068fn, 1096
Sun Microsystems, Inc., 570
SUPERVALU Inc., 49, 326–327

T

Tandy Corporation, 441
Target Corp., 49, 179, 315, 747
Tennessee Valley Authority, 845
3M, 570, 1017
Tiffany & Co., 294
Time Inc., 652
Time Warner, 454, 954